The Subject of Human Rights

Stanford Studies in Human Rights

The Subject of Human Rights

Edited by Danielle Celermajer and Alexandre Lefebvre

Stanford University Press
Stanford, California

Stanford University Press
Stanford, California

Printed in the United States of America on acid-free, archival-quality paper

Library of Congress Cataloging-in-Publication Data

Names: Celermajer, Danielle, editor. | Lefebvre, Alexandre, 1979– editor.
Title: The subject of human rights / edited by Danielle Celermajer and Alexandre Lefebvre.
Other titles: Stanford studies in human rights.
Description: Stanford, California : Stanford University Press, 2020. | Series: Stanford studies in human rights | Includes bibliographical references and index.
Identifiers: LCCN 2020012096 (print) | LCCN 2020012097 (ebook) | ISBN 9781503613195 (cloth) | ISBN 9781503613713 (paperback) | ISBN 9781503613720 (epub)
Subjects: LCSH: Human rights. | Human rights—Philosophy. | Subject (Philosophy)
Classification: LCC JC571 .S8855 2020 (print) | LCC JC571 (ebook) | DDC 323—dc23
LC record available at https://lccn.loc.gov/2020012096
LC ebook record available at https://lccn.loc.gov/2020012097

Typeset by Motto Publishing Services in 10/14 Minion Pro
Cover design by Rob Ehle

Contents

Foreword

MY FIRST REALIZATION that the subject of human rights represented a profound problem for both theory and practice came at an unusual time in an unusual place. I was conducting ethnographic fieldwork in a remote region of the Bolivian *altiplano* during the late 1990s, a period in which international and transnational development was being recast as a form of human rights promotion. This historic shift carried with it a number of important consequences, not the least of which was the fact that actually existing human rights—in all of its discursive, ethical, and social complexity—was taking root in far-flung places, well beyond the boundaries of legal and political institutions, and in relation to coextensive processes of mobilization around particularly vulnerable populations.

It was this wider context that altered my early research. In villages throughout rural Bolivia, local understandings of conflict resolution and social relations were being upended by the infusion of the new idea of "human rights," which was being diffused by an alphabet soup of national, international, and transnational actors as a sort of replacement worldview akin to a new religion, a new and emancipatory way through which people in the region—mostly Quechua and Aymara-speaking subsistence agro-pastoralists—could and should view themselves, their communities, and their futures. Without having planned to do so in advance, I was required to reorient my research on this unstable landscape, on which Bolivian peasants were, I realized later, being taught—through seemingly innumerable capacity-building workshops often organized in dusty, open-air central plazas—to view themselves and their fellow villagers as fundamentally different kinds of subjects, subjects of human rights.

I subsequently followed several of these nascent subjects of human rights over many months and was able to observe the ways in which they grappled—

in subtle and previously theoretically unaccountable ways—with the growing challenge (and social pressure) to make human rights an important new part of the region's legal, political, and social realities. Yet as the 1990s gave way to the 2000s, and the 2000s gave way to later periods of crisis, questioning, and now reappraisal, what was (and remains) clear to me is that the kinds of micropractices of subject-making and subjectification revealed through the diverse project of human rights were never fully confronted, their far-reaching implications never adequately conceptualized, despite a number of tantalizing efforts in the literature.

This is why Danielle Celermajer and Alexandre Lefebvre's edited collection *The Subject of Human Rights* comes as such an immense revelation. At just the moment in which global debates over the future of human rights have become increasingly, and unfortunately, divided between approaches that would jettison the entire framework of human rights on the basis of one structural defect or another, and those that mount a spirited and (on my reading, at least) quixotic defense of black-letter and orthodox human rights as the best hope for global justice, the collective chapters of *The Subject of Human Rights* force open a radically different orientation to the question.

Instead of treating the problems and possibilities of human rights as a legal or political or even sociolegal framework, one whose relation to subjects—individual, collective, relational—is both analytically and practically ancillary, *The Subject of Human Rights* compels something like a decisive reversal. What the volume's chapters convincingly and liberatingly demand is that human rights be formally reimagined and accepted for what they have been, in practice, all along: a powerful, if fraught, means through which subjects-as-social-beings are forged, become agentive, and take their place among existing social, moral, class, and gender assemblages.

By reconceptualizing the grounds of human rights in this way, the chapters in *The Subject of Human Rights* point to a wholly different way of thinking about the future of human rights, one that is keenly attuned to what the editors describe as the "material and discursive conditions of intelligibility" through which the three pillars—the who, how, and what—of human rights subject-making are revealed. The result is a landmark for interdisciplinary human rights studies that is also something arguably more important and potentially transformative: a textual blueprint that carries with it the promise of "redeem[ing] rights in a different mode."

Mark Goodale, Series Editor
Stanford Studies in Human Rights

The Subject of Human Rights

Bringing the Subject of Human Rights into Focus

Danielle Celermajer and Alexandre Lefebvre

THE TERM "HUMAN RIGHTS" conjoins two distinctive concepts—"human" and "rights"—to form what has become a distinctive concept and the basis for a vast set of institutions, practices, and critical debates. Within the now voluminous and multidisciplinary scholarship on human rights, it is the latter of the partner terms, "rights," that has attracted the most systematic attention. Scholars have long asked and argued about where (human) rights come from, what legitimates them, what counts as a right, what makes for a distinctively *human* right, what is their goal or purpose, what institutional forms best protect them, and how they operate in practice.[1]

What about the nature or character of the "human" assumed in human rights theory and practice? Granted, since at least the 1980s, when the Asian values debate was raging and feminist critiques of human rights were gathering steam, the status of the human assumed in human rights has been the subject of reflection and debate.[2] Indeed, as we will explore below, critical scholarship contesting the putative universality and neutrality of the human whose rights have (at least formally) been recognized and protected has, in the past twenty years, arisen from many different quarters. Nevertheless, the "human" in human rights has undoubtedly been the minority partner. The purpose of this volume is to have it step into the limelight, with a specific focus on how the subject of human rights, as a discourse, law, and practice shapes how we understand the human and how humanness is experienced, and to illuminate the political and contested nature of these processes.

To bring the human of human rights into sharper focus, we propose a slight but significant shift. Rather than talk about the human per se, the term that binds this volume together is the subject of human rights. The value of this alternative terminology lies in the multiple meanings of the word "subject," which allow for a multifaceted examination of the nature, limits, and possibilities of the human of human rights. Indeed, this slight shift in language also points to the cogency of expanding the rights traditionally reserved for humans beyond this species boundary. For whereas the term "human" reinscribes a natural unity within (along with a boundary around) a species to whom rights adhere, the term "subject" opens the question of the identity of the rights holder to scrutiny and transformation.

Shifting our focus to the subject of human rights opens up three lines of questioning that organize this book. In this introduction, we will discuss each of them, both to summarize the existing literature and introduce the chapters that follow. To make clear what each line of questioning entails, we commence with a bird's-eye view.

1. Who is the *subject of* human rights? One of the claimed strengths of the human rights approach has been its defense of all persons, irrespective of their ascriptive characteristics. This universal conception of the human person has, according to classical human rights theory, provided human rights with normative purchase against alternative conceptions and political practices based on cultural, gender, racial, religious, ethnic, and other forms of particularism and hierarchy. That said, it is clear that human rights theories and institutions have not historically included all human beings within their conception of the human. The questions that needs to be asked, then, are how is the subject of human rights defined today, and who and what does it include and exclude?

2. Who is *subjected to* human rights? If the first sense of subject concerns those whose rights ought to be protected, the second subject is the one who is the addressee of human rights or, put otherwise, the one whose actions must be subjected to human rights standards. Strictly speaking, in human rights law, the state is the subject of human rights, but this formalism belies the actual operation, which necessarily implicates human subjects who operate within state institutions. In this regard, the "state actor" subjected to the demands of human rights includes a wide variety of subjects: political representatives who make and amend laws; people who act as agents of the state in a range of in-

stitutions such as hospitals, welfare, schools, and social service agencies; and, perhaps most importantly, security sector and law enforcement personnel who are authorized to use violent means to implement state law and policy. Questions about how human rights ought to shape and subject the exercise of state authority provoke contentious debates about the tension between democracy and human rights, security and human rights, and efficiency and human rights.

3. How do human rights *make* subjects? Scholars and practitioners have long recognized that human rights do not simply represent and then afford protection to an already existing subject; in crucial ways, they shape and inform how people see and experience themselves, others, and the wider world. There is, in other words, a formative dimension to human rights discourse and practice, one that, whether intentionally or not, has the potential to establish the very subject it is said to enshrine. How this happens, and what kind of subjects human rights characteristically produce, are central concerns of this volume.

The subject of human rights is, in a sense, the substratum of human rights discourse and practice: it is that "thing" or, better yet, that being to which human rights are attached and owed, that being who is called to recognize and sustain them, and that being who is called into existence by human rights discourses and practices. Naturally, no single volume could hope to settle its meaning or range. That would not be possible, given its plurality. Nor would it be desirable, given its potentiality. Our goal as editors has been to bring the subject of human rights into focus and to systematically lay out the research questions and agenda that this focus suggests. With that in mind, we now take a closer look at each of our three questions.

Who Is the Subject of Human Rights?

Let's begin with an obvious fact: if we take the French and American revolutions as the moment when human rights burst onto the political and constitutional scene, it is abundantly clear that such rights were not—and were not meant to be—universal. The "rights of man" (in France) and "certain unalienable Rights" (in the United States) were, at first, accorded to only a subset of the population, specifically white Christian men, and often only those with some measure of property or formal education.[3] Yet, almost immediately after their having been declared, more and more kinds of people began to claim the right to be and, in some cases, came to be counted as subjects of human rights. Naturally, the ripple effect was small to start with, involving, as it did, variations on white Christian men. But then came a series of hesitant (and always potentially reversible) shifts and expansions—in religion, gender, and color—such that defenders and critics of human rights alike came to recognize that the universality of the human rights idea meant that the boundary of who could be included was always open to contestation. The historian Lynn Hunt ties the process to what she calls the universalizing "inner logic" of human rights:

> The French Revolution, more than any other event, revealed that human rights have an inner logic. As the deputies faced the need to turn their lofty ideals into specific laws, they inadvertently developed a kind of conceivability or thinkability scale. No one knew in advance which groups were going to come up for discussion, when they would come up, or what the resolution of their status would be. But sooner or later, it became clear that granting rights to some groups (Protestants, for example) was more easily imagined than granting them to others (women). The logic of the process determined that as soon as a highly conceivable group came up for discussion (propertied males, Protestants), those in the same kind of category but located lower on the conceivability scale (propertyless males, Jews) would inevitably appear on the horizon.[4]

One important amendment that we would make to Hunt's characterization is that the groups seeking inclusion did not so much "appear on the horizon" as insistently, and often with tremendous opposition and sometimes violence, place themselves there.[5] Nevertheless, it is uncontroversial to observe that over the past 250 years, more and more kinds of people have pressed for inclusion and that, at least formally if not fully substantively, more and more groups of people have been acknowledged as subjects entitled to human rights. Reflecting on this historical trajectory, contemporary thinkers and defenders of human rights find themselves confronted with two pressing questions. First, how do we keep the expansion going? How, in other words, should we conceive of and advocate for human rights, and the subject of human rights, so that the inner logic Hunt describes reaches its ultimate conclusion and remains there? Second, how do we ensure that formal advances deliver the actual enjoyment of such rights to those who were not originally imagined as the subjects of human rights?

Several strands of human rights theory have emerged in response to the first question, each of which configures the subject of human rights in a different way, but all with an eye to securing its universality. Hunt's own position is "sentimentalist." On this account, the universal subject of human rights is one who is liable to suffering and injustice, and the human rights project is advanced by cultivating a widely, indeed global, felt awareness and sympathy for the suffering of even distant others.[6] Beyond the academy, the notion that empathic connection will be the basis for extending rights to those who are currently excluded undergirds a great deal of human rights campaigning, as evidenced by the frequent use of imploring faces looking directly to the camera or of narratives highlighting the hopes, fears, and life projects of people whose humanity has been occluded.[7] Another position is "foundationalist," in that it seeks to identify foundational capacities or interests that all human beings share and have a highest-order interest in protecting. Such a capacity could, for example, be identified in "normative agency" (that is, the capacity to choose and pursue a conception of a worthwhile life), or it could be identified as an interest in "justification" (that is, an expectation that others give us reasons for their actions and beliefs). Either way, the subject of human rights is universal precisely because the capacity or interest in question is said to be universal.[8] Further examples of arguments of this kind could be added, and it would be fascinating to see if and how they could be synthesized.[9] The point we wish to make, however, is simply that several important strands in the philosophy of human rights converge on the claim that the subject of human rights is universal and inclusive of all human beings and proceed, from that basis, to found programs of human rights norm creation, diffusion, and education on it.

That said, many scholars and advocates who observe that in practice, formal advances in universal recognition have often failed to deliver rights to newly included subjects, push back against this universalist story. Skeptical of the promise that when groups formally become subjects of human rights, this will inevitably result in the realization of rights in their lives, the argument is made that what needs to be highlighted and understood are the sources and points of resistance to the translation of universalism from universalism in theory to universalism in practice. Several bodies of critical literature contend that the impediments to realizing the authentic universalism of human rights are not merely the effect of imperfect attempts at this translation. The criticism at work here is that the persistent particularism and exclusionary effects some groups experience arise from the substance or form of human rights themselves. Indeed, the very universalist rhetoric that has provided human rights discourses with a singular legitimacy and purchase may in fact render invisible the exclusions and hierarchies that they inscribe.

As we will detail momentarily, several groups have sought to demonstrate how the logics of human rights exclude them, and in doing so, they point to different assumptions or limitations of the classical understanding of the subject of human rights. They start by calling into question whether the grounds that have justified human rights according to the classical arguments are genuinely universal and suggest that it is at this foundational level that the dynamics of inclusion and exclusion are generated. That is, insofar as foundationalist arguments single out attributes such as autonomy, normative agency, or the capacity for reason as the distinctive qualities that qualify humans to claim human rights, critics point out that these terms encode hierarchies amongst humans and thus implicitly dehumanize certain humans. In particular, those humans who have historically been identified with emotion, the body and the private sphere, and those who are explicitly embedded in relations of dependency—for example, women, people of color, people with disability, and Indigenous peoples—are implicitly, but no less powerfully, seen as less than fully human or, worse, as not human at all and thus not qualified to be subjects of human rights.

Let us consider a series of such arguments. Building on the recognition by second-wave feminists that gender distinctions are embedded in a broader set of dichotomies and hierarchies such as nature vs. culture, emotion vs. reason, body vs. mind, autonomy vs. dependence, and public vs. private,[10] human rights scholars have pointed to the way in which the traditional conception of human rights and the content of human rights laws have failed to encode the distinctive violations experienced by women. The most obvious exclusion concerns sexual violence, which, insofar as it takes place in what is classified as the private sphere, counts, at best, as a crime but not as a human rights violation, which, in the traditional view, must be committed by the state or by agents acting in a public capacity.[11] One sees a related effect in the exclusion of sexual violence from traditional understandings of torture, insofar as such violations, even when committed by security sector officials, have been explained away as private desires, as distinct from being recognized as actions committed on behalf of the state.[12] The point here is that such exclusions are not incidental and will not be remedied solely by adding to the corpus of human rights law (however necessary this may be). The problem is structural. The association of human rights with state or public crimes reinscribes a gendered division of space and forms of life in a manner that systematically disadvantages women.

The feminist critique of human rights universalism is not, however, directed only to the way in which gender intersects with the question of what types of wrongs are recognized as human rights violations. It also addresses the implicit privileging of a certain way of being human that is encoded in the human rights idea and thus indirectly marginalizes women as full subjects of rights. As we observed above, if the ideal type of human rights subject is autonomous and rational, then to the extent that women have been understood as embedded in relations of dependency and care, characterized as more emotional, and associated with the body (their own, as well as those for whom they care), they fall outside this ideal type. The criticism here is twofold. First, the relegation of women to the wrong side of a set of dichotomies marginalizes them as subjects of human rights. Second, to the extent that persons, of whatever sex, actually do occupy these other dimensions of being human, as carers or as emotional beings, they are effectively excluded. The failure of universalism is thus directed not only to people sexed as women but to any human who occupies a social location that is gendered female.

Critical disability scholars have similarly pointed out that privileging autonomy and reason, combined with the common view that people with disability fail to achieve autonomy or lack the full capacity for reason, has structurally excluded them from the category of human rights subjects. One response to such exclusions is to challenge stereotypes of disability, principally by shifting away from a medical model, which locates disablement in the person, to a social model, which locates it at the disjuncture between social arrangements and physical infrastructure, on the one hand, and the distinctive capacities of people with disability, on the other.[13] By shifting the problem away from the pathology or inadequacy of the individual to the failure of social arrangements, people with disability can reclaim their status as humans no less endowed with the capacities that ground claims to human rights. As distinct from what we might call this strategy of equivalence, a more radical response has been to acknowledge that people with disability may indeed be embedded in relations of dependency, and may in some instances have different cognitive capacities, but to refuse the putative incompatibility between these ways of being and full human standing.[14] A related strand of scholarship builds on relational conceptions of autonomy and feminist care ethics to argue that there is something dubious about the mainstream conception of autonomy itself: not only is it unevenly distributed within stratified (and gendered) social geographies, but, more trenchantly, this understanding of autonomy is illusory to the extent that it masks various forms of support that are the conditions of possibility for the functioning of the apparently autonomous individual.[15]

Indigenous and postcolonial critics have similarly pointed to the way in which non-whiteness and indigeneity have been associated with qualities or identities that form the "other" to the subject of human rights—in this case, the barbarian to the civilized subject.[16] Their point is not simply one about the prejudicial and racialized constitution of individual (Indigenous or colonized) subjects but that this asymmetrical distribution of the capacities deemed necessary for a person to be a fit subject of rights was (and largely remains) constitutive of the larger geopolitical projects of imperialism and colonialism. In this regard, the coincidence of the emergence of ideas about universalism and human rights, on the one hand, and projects of imperialism and colonialism, on the other, cannot be dismissed as peripheral to the constitution, meaning and operation of human rights. As Ratna Kapur writes, "[I]nternational law coupled with its humanitarian zeal was structured by the colonial encounter and its distinction between the civilised and uncivilised."[17]

To mention only a single thinker whose ideas are seen as foundational to the development of human rights, critics argue that one cannot disconnect the John Locke associated with the birth of the idea of the rights-bearing individual from the Locke who provided the justification for the dispossession of Indigenous peoples on the basis of their (putative) forms of life.[18] "The project of creating an international order," Jennifer Pitts writes, "has long been commingled with that of European consolidation and informed by European exceptionalism, from Christendom's global project of conversion in medieval and early modern Church doctrine, through eighteenth-century projects for perpetual peace, to contemporary theorizations of the European Union as a democratic model for a post-sovereign world."[19] As imperial and colonial powers encountered others, they encoded them as backward or insufficiently developed along a singular dimension of moral and civilizational progress. Indigenous peoples and people in lands over which Europeans had imperial designs appeared as "unintelligible, irrational, or inferior," requiring management, education, and discipline to bring them into the civilized fold.[20]

This identification of humanity with European civilization has had direct and brutal implications for human rights and the subject of human rights. In particular, it has meant that much of the violence committed against Indigenous peoples—including the forced removal of children from their families and the systematic deprivation of land rights and civil and political rights—far from being recognized as human rights violations and abuses, could be recast as ugly yet necessary stages in a larger project of creating subjects fit for rights.[21] Such constitutive exclusions have not only operated at the level of individual subjects, excluding and justifying abuses against people because of their indigeneity or race. Rather, deeming Indigenous and colonized peoples unfit to be full legal persons and political subjects justified the failure of colonizing powers to recognize their prior status as sovereign over the lands they inhabited. Even when postcolonial states have, at least formally, rejected individual level exclusions—through anti-discrimination laws, for example—the historical refusal to recognize Indigenous peoples as full subjects persists in their ongoing exclusion as sovereign peoples in their own lands and in the contemporary international order.

Finally, in perhaps the most radical of the criticisms leveled at the putative universality of human rights, post-humanists have argued that the very notion of human rights is constituted on the hierarchical exclusion of beings other than humans, principally other animals, but also the environment. The basis for this argument has been made from many philosophical camps. To name only the most prominent, Peter Singer builds on traditional humanist attacks on false universalism that point to the exclusions generated by sexism, racism, and ableism, to insist that the only way to explain the wholesale exclusion of all animals from the category of rights-bearing subjects is by appeal to a pervasive speciesism.[22] If one looks without prejudice at the possession of the actual capacities that are supposed to qualify subjects to claim rights, Singer argues, one can see that some animals possess them, while some humans do not; hence, the inclusion of all humans and exclusion of all animals can only be explained as an act of fiat—the declaration of species preference.

As has been the pattern with contestations concerning other forms of exclusion, in this case also critical scholars have argued that the exclusion of animals as potential rights holders is not accidental and as such, further efforts to expand rights in their current form will provide insufficient remediation of the problem. Rather, the manifest exclusion of animals is the effect of the speciesism at the heart of the definition of human rights and at the heart of the assumed subject of rights. Linking the exclusion in the domain of rights to the larger exclusion effected by the humanist project, Jacques Derrida has argued that the entire history of Western philosophy can be narrated through a focus on the privileging of the human over the animal. Indeed, even seemingly opposed currents of thought are united in their ambition to nominate the distinctive, special, and valuable capacities that only human beings possess in contrast to the rest of the non-human world.[23] Taking up this line of critique, intersectional theorists and ecofeminists draw a line connecting the various dimensions in which putative universalism privileges certain identities or types of subject and marginalizes others, to argue that human rights' constitutive exclusions are structurally connected.[24] In this context, the animalization of women and people of color—and, more recently, of Muslims—well illustrates the way in which apparently disparate exclusions are achieved through a common logic of the subject of human rights.

Part I of this volume is titled "Who Is the Subject of Human Rights?" and is dedicated to these issues. It aims to extend and deepen criticisms of the subject of human rights from the perspective of inclusion and exclusion, but the authors in this section—and, indeed, in this volume—seek to move beyond a critical stance. Their goal is to propose new and positive ways to theorize and imagine the subject of human rights in order to better realize its universality. In this spirit, the volume begins with Jennifer Nedelsky's "The Relational Self As the Subject of Human Rights." Nedelsky is one of the thinkers who first suggested that we might rethink autonomy in a relational mode, and her chapter tackles head-on the concern that, as classically understood, the subject of rights has been conceived in a manner that implicitly privileges certain types of people and excludes or marginalizes others. Specifically, she takes seriously the concern that insofar as their imagined subject is one whose autonomy is understood as grounded in its own being (and as existing independent from relationships), human rights will be constitutively exclusive. Nevertheless, and consistent with the positive aspiration of this volume, Nedelsky does not stop at the point of critique but explores what happens if we rethink rights, in this case, as inherently relational.

Nedelsky suggests that because individual subjects are, in fact, constituted in and through relationships, and because their autonomy depends on the quality of the relationships in which they are embedded, a conception of rights that fails to encode this relational character of autonomy will be not only faulty but will not, in the end, be conducive to the development of autonomy or individual flourishing. Human rights, in other words, do not work to foster autonomy or allow an individual to flourish by protecting the individual, imagined in their glorious aloneness and abstracted from all relations.

Rather, they work by structuring relationships such that individuals can become autonomous and flourish. The implications of this argument are far-reaching, not only for the conception of human rights but for how we come to know their content or substance and for the institutions required to support them. Thus, contra the understanding of rights as fixed stakes in the ground—"trumps," as Ronald Dworkin calls them—Nedelsky argues that to ensure that human rights structure relationships in ways that foster autonomy, we need to acknowledge a certain contingency in the nature of those rights, which always operate within the shifting and contested terrain of values and social change. In concrete terms, this means opening the content of rights up to democratic deliberation and in turn creating institutions that can provide legitimacy for the decisions that are thus reached about rights. In this sense, Nedelsky takes what might seem a damning critique of the subject of rights and redeems rights in a different mode, potentially rendering them more effective and their subject more expansive.

Chapter 2, "The Misbegotten Monad: Anthropology, Human Rights, Belonging," by Mark Goodale, follows on from Nedelsky with a picture-perfect description of the kind of subject she criticizes, one whose autonomy is represented in terms of isolation from others. Playfully borrowing the concept of the monad from the early modern philosopher G. W. Leibniz, Goodale contends that the standard image of the subject of human rights—enshrined not just in academic literature but also in core international documents—consists of entirely separate and independent beings ("monads"), each of whom contains and reflects the entire normative human rights system in their person. And the problem with this, he argues, is not just that it relies on a dubious picture of subjectivity and human rights. Worse, and precisely because this standard "monadic" image is widespread and unreflectively held, it ends up marginalizing alternative conceptions of the subject of human rights that are potentially more accurate, effective, and genuinely global in reach and appeal.

With his criticism of the monadic subject in place, Goodale proceeds to sketch his own positive account of the subject of human rights. Like Nedelsky, he favors a relational approach, one that would see human rights subjectivity as nested in networks of relationship and animated by the value of human (and non-human) solidarity. Specifically, he draws on his discipline of anthropology to put forward three ethnographically based models. The result is a series of decidedly non-monadic subjectivities, in which human rights principles and practices are generated from within overlapping temporal, spatial, and even cosmological networks: with one's own social and political community, past and future generations, and the wider non-human world.

In Chapter 3, "'Are Women Animals?': The Rise and Rise of (Animal) Rights," Joanna Bourke considers arguments that have sought to expand the circle of beings who could be subjects of human rights through the logic of equivalence or sameness—that is, by insisting that these subjects also possess the qualities that have justified the rights of those already recognized as subjects of human rights. In an intriguing comparative reading of "An Earnest Englishwoman" and Catherine MacKinnon, two feminists writing 120 years apart, Bourke examines two arguments that mobilized the relationship between women and animals to press the recognition of women as subjects of rights. In the first case, the rhetorical move was to liken women to non-human animals who, as beneficiaries of certain legal protections, in the author's view, enjoyed greater rights than women. In the late-twentieth-century argument, it was precisely the historical animalizing of women that needed to be rejected, and their likeness to (male) humans that was required for their inclusion as subjects of human rights. Adding to these two cases, Bourke argues that more recent advocacy that seeks to have non-human animals recognized as subjects of rights has largely failed, not least because it relied on this faulty logic of sameness and difference.

For Bourke, achieving actual inclusion of different types of beings, human and animal, requires bypassing a logic that ultimately reinforces ontological solidities: unity or disunity, sameness or difference. Her suggestion is to practice what she calls "negative zoélogy," an approach that constantly reminds us of the incommensurability of different forms of life and of the contingency of our knowledge about other beings. Certainly, on its own, such a negative move cannot provide the grounds to ensure that all beings enjoy decent lives or that they can flourish, nor does it provide guidance as to the content of laws or the shape of institutions that will support the realization of rights. Nevertheless, injected into historical and political struggles, it can serve to stave off what has been a habitual logic that has failed to achieve the full inclusion of the habitually excluded subjects: human and other than human.

In Chapter 4, "Indigenous Peoples As the Subject of Human Rights," Danielle Celermajer describes how the practices and politics of colonialism structurally excluded Indigenous peoples as subjects of human rights and, in turn, how Indigenous peoples have actively engaged the system to transform human rights laws and institutions to overcome this exclusion. In doing so, how-

ever, Celermajer draws out the inherent tension Indigenous peoples face by engaging and seeking to draw benefit from an international institutional order
founded on, and continually reinscribing, their exclusion. To deploy the tools
of this system to remedy their situation, then, Indigenous peoples are forced
to turn to those responsible for the ongoing violation of their rights. That international human rights law occupies this ambivalent place—promise, on
the one hand, and reinscription of a structural exclusion, on the other—has
led to vigorous debates amongst Indigenous peoples about whether it can ever
serve their own ends or whether by becoming subjects of human rights, they
are furthering their own annihilation as distinct peoples.

The second half of the chapter takes up the first-person views of Michael
Dodson, an Australian Aboriginal man who has been at the forefront of advocacy, seeking to ensure that Indigenous peoples are recognized as subjects of
human rights internationally and domestically. In the interview that constitutes this part of the chapter, Dodson contests the more critical view that human rights are inimical to the authentic rights of Indigenous peoples. Rather,
he subscribes to a more dynamic understanding of human rights, one that is
capable not only of accommodating very different groups but is transformed
in the process. Describing what we might call a politics of presence, Dodson
recalls how Indigenous peoples inserted themselves into the treaty-making
processes of the United Nations, processes from which they have habitually
been excluded, raising their voices and concerns and refusing their exclusion
until it became impossible to ignore them. By acting as subjects of rights, by
recognizing themselves as subjects of rights, Indigenous peoples have been
able to demand that recognition from the international human rights system.
Thus, despite a persistent view of Indigenous peoples as not fully human—
not only at the level of individual prejudice but encoded in the institutions of
postcolonial states—Dodson remains sanguine about the potential of the human rights framework to include Indigenous peoples as subjects of rights and
thereby to challenge entrenched patterns of exclusion and dehumanization.

In the final chapter of Part I, "'Escaped': Gendered Precarity and Human
Rights Recognition," Wendy S. Hesford complicates the question of the inclusion or exclusion of certain groups as subjects of human rights by insisting that political subjects are always constituted by particular types of rhetorical narratives (including images) that make them intelligible in certain ways
and not others. Thus, the question of what type of subject certain (groups
of) people are recognized as being is not one that is properly asked in the ab-

stract, because it requires our attending to the "material and discursive conditions of intelligibility" and to the operant "cultural, political, and legal norms that govern" the scene of recognition. This means that the rhetorical devices deployed to claim recognition make a critical contribution to how this recognition occurs, at the same time as their always being shaped by the terrain within which they occur.

Hesford demonstrates the role of constitutive rhetoric in the formation of the subject of rights by considering four contexts in which photographs of Yazidi women have been exhibited, illuminating how each context acts as an interpretive frame that shapes the meaning attributed to these images and, by extension, their subjects. Troublingly, she demonstrates how the presentation of Yazidi women's "gendered precarity" may be oriented less to ensuring the promotion and protection of their rights than it is deployed in the service of particular international security logics and legal objectives. Nevertheless, consistent with postcolonial feminist theory, Hesford insists that however distorting or dominating the rhetorical narratives that frame people as particular types of subjects may be, these are never totalizing. In this case, Yazidi women are also always constituting themselves, thus producing sites of resistance to the dominant interpretive frames.

Who Is Subjected to Human Rights?

Part I took up the broad question of the nature of the subject of rights by reflecting on the rights holder—the person whose identity as a subject of rights affords them a certain status. In Part II, we turn to the question of the institutions and persons on whom those claims are made: those subjected to human rights. Formally, the addressee of human rights is the state. States are parties to international human rights treaties, so it is states that promise to respect, protect, and promote the rights those treaties set out and subject themselves to the scrutiny of oversight bodies. In so doing, states commit themselves not only to respecting human rights in the case of their own actions, but also to ensuring that no party within their jurisdiction, be it a corporate entity or an individual, acts so as to lead to the violation of the rights of any other person. In this specific sense, private individuals are never the ones who violate human rights, even though it might be their actions (for example, acts of discrimination) that the state is obliged to regulate as part of its duty to protect human rights. Formally speaking, then, only the state can violate human rights. In this regard, the state is subjected to rights insofar as it is required to uphold them and to ensure that non-state actors comply with them.

In practice, the picture is far more complicated. After all, it is various individuals or groups of individuals who, operating in their capacities as agents or representatives of the state, are called to act in accordance with the principles of human rights and who should, in principle, be held responsible by the state when they violate these rights. In this regard, the state is subjected to human rights insofar as it is required to develop mechanisms to call to account those who do not uphold these rights when acting under its authority or in its name.

A number of puzzles arise when we try to make sense of who or what is subjected to human rights standards or demands and how this plays out on the ground. The first concerns the fact that the state occupies multiple roles: domestic standard setter, adjudicator, enforcer, and potential violator. Because some of these roles will inevitably be in tension with one another, there is evidently a systemic weakness here. For the state to effectively check or oversee itself will require certain of its branches (say, the judiciary) to retain the capacity and be invested with the power to hold other branches accountable (say, the executive), requiring a robust partition between them. In the case where no branch of the state has sufficient independence and power to oversee other branches and demand remediation, it will be civil society and nongovernment organizations, working in concert with the monitoring mechanisms of the international system, that must take up the critical task of ensuring that states do not simply exempt themselves from accountability to human rights standards.[25] Nevertheless, because the multiple roles the state occupies include that of enforcer, and in this there is no higher sovereign order, the power to subject remains with the state.

A second and related puzzle concerns the character of the rights to which the state ought to be subjected. Although the Universal Declaration of Human Rights includes various social and economic rights—rights elaborated and formalized in the International Covenant on Economic, Social and Cultural Rights (1966)—a number of contemporary scholars have documented and critiqued the relative neglect of economic and social rights in human rights practice.[26] In noting this disparity, their point is that this is not an inadvertent asymmetry but one arising from the liberal foundations of human rights and, in turn, liberalism's symbiotic relationship with market capitalism. So long as human rights approaches rest upon liberalism's deference to "market freedom" and its refusal to challenge the sanctity of private property, the violations of social and economic rights that follow as a matter of course from the radically unequal distribution of capital and its consequences will go unchallenged. The puzzle that arises thus concerns whether human rights can subject the state to demands that will lead to just social and economic outcomes for those disenfranchised by capitalist property relations.

The third puzzle follows from the fact, outlined above, that while formally the state is subjected to the demands of human rights, it is always a particular person, or group(s) of people, acting as representatives or agents of the state, who directly perpetrate violations. This raises difficult questions about responsibility and its attribution. In practice, who or what is to be subjected to the consequences of violating human rights? What does it mean to hold the state responsible, as distinct from holding its representatives or agents responsible? If we recognize that the responsibility for and causality of violations go beyond individual perpetrators, what types of punitive or reformative actions are available to address the structures and institutions that authorize or legitimate human rights violations?[27] Certainly, holding individual perpetrators criminally liable for their acts will be a necessary component of subjecting the state to the demands of human rights, but punishing individual actors, even insofar as this plays a role in the normative constitution of the society and state, is unlikely to have sufficient reach into institutional structures and processes.[28]

A fourth puzzle concerns the status of those who are *subjected to* human rights while also being *subjects of* human rights. This asymmetry is perhaps most evident in the way certain types of violations are referred to as "inhuman treatment." The phrase "cruel, inhuman or degrading treatment or punishment" appears in the title and articles of the United Nations Convention Against Torture and Other Cruel, Inhuman or Degrading Treatment or Punishment (1987), but the idea that certain types of acts are inhuman has a broader purchase, gesturing towards violations that are considered especially grave, such as genocide. In this regard, it seems that certain particularly heinous violations not only undermine the humanity of the one violated but are also indicative of the inhumanity of the perpetrator, perhaps even destroying their humanity.[29] Nevertheless, at least formally, perpetrators still remain subjects of human rights, and it is not permissible to commit human rights violations against them. Even when they act in ways that point to their inhumanity, they remain subjects of human rights.

The authors in Part II of this volume address several puzzles that arise around the question of what it means to be subjected to human rights; how perpetrators—individual and institutional—are, should be, or could be subjected to human rights; and the difficulties, missteps, and failures in so subjecting them. Chapter 6, Danielle Celermajer's "Training Subjects for Human Rights," looks at one of the principal strategies adopted in the human rights world to subject representatives and agents of the state to human rights standards: human rights education and training. Celermajer argues that human rights educational practices, like any strategy that seeks to alter how individuals act (for example, punishing wrongdoing), must hold a theory of the subject they seek to change or effect. Such theories are rarely made explicit, but, she argues, by examining how human rights education is developed and delivered, we can "reverse engineer" to discover the theory of the subject implicitly at work.

In this essay, Celermajer's focus is on human rights education and training for law enforcement and security sector personnel, groups who, because they are authorized by the state to use violent means and because they often hold individuals away from the light of public scrutiny, are at particular risk of committing serious violations such as torture, enforced disappearances, and killing. Through an empirical examination of training material and methods used around the world, Celermajer identifies two assumptions about the nature of those subjected to human rights. The first, which she derives from the overwhelming emphasis in human rights training on developing individuals' *knowledge* about human rights standards, is that, consistent with a foundationalist philosophy of human rights, the subject is assumed to be autonomous, primarily cognitive, rational, and self-determining. The problem is that given what we now know about how individuals' judgements and actions are shaped by their environments, especially where they are embedded in total institutions like the military and police, holding this type of theory of the subject is unlikely to support processes that can effectively reconstitute the potential perpetrator as a subject of and for human rights. Second, insofar as human rights education works both by confronting trainees with the negative consequences of their violating rights (punishment) and by appealing to their capacities to choose a more ethical course of action, it speaks to two types of subject that are not only different but incompatible. In one case, the assumed subject is one who needs to be managed. In the other, the subject is understood as one who, if presented with the full picture, can autonomously choose the good.

In the following chapter, "Who Deserves Inalienable Rights?: The Subjectivity of Violent State Officials and the Implications for Human Rights Protection," Rachel Wahl also takes up the project of using human rights education to shape the subjectivity of potential violators. Picking up on the model of human rights education as a transformative practice, she observes that the vision motivating this approach is one where those who experience human rights education would themselves come to embrace human rights and want to protect them. Realizing this ideal when the people to be transformed operate within institutions where human rights are routinely violated, however, poses a distinctive challenge to the transformative model. The challenge is not simply that it will be difficult, in practice, for human rights learners to challenge the norms and practices of the organizations in which they are operating. It is also that these learners are themselves not empty vessels; they hold antecedent values and beliefs that may well provide an inhospitable environment for the values promoted by human rights.

Drawing on her own extensive field work with police officers enrolled in a human rights masters program in northern India, Wahl finds that despite the fact that they all paid lip service to human rights, when she probed how they actually understood human rights, their interpretations were often diametrically opposed to the understanding intended by their educators. As interpreted by these police officers, human rights might, for example, require torturing perpetrators to protect the innocent or promote justice. Rather than dismiss these findings as evidence that these law enforcement officers simply misunderstood, rejected, or distorted human rights, Wahl argues that the police officers she interviewed in fact refracted the lessons they were being taught through a network of existing concepts, values, and understandings. Thus, contra the general assumption that adopting human rights values involves moving the subject from an unprincipled position (where one acts instrumentally or to maximize personal benefits) to a principled position (where one embraces an ethical precept), Wahl argues that it may in fact be the values or principles already embraced by the subject that impede their being transformed into a subject who fully endorses human rights, as envisaged by human rights education interventions.

In Chapter 8, "Human Rights As Therapy: The Healing Paradigms of Transitional Justice," Ronald Niezen examines how the testimonial and therapeutic format of truth and reconciliation commissions has come to be seen as a way of effecting healing not only for individual victims but also for the community and nation. In this regard, amongst the therapeutic effects assumed to be achieved is the transformation of communities and the nation—in particular, rendering them more fit and able to respect human rights into the future. To use the language of this book, the presumably cathartic testimonies of victims are assumed, through a type of affective and relational transformation, to be technologies for subjecting the society and nation to human rights.

Niezen traces the sources of this therapeutic and testimonial model in religious practice, trauma theory, and the performative catharsis and sympathetic participation of Oprah Winfrey–style shows to demonstrate how public (and, indeed, spectacular) expression of traumatic memory has become normalized as a way of bringing about individual and collective healing. He argues, however, that we have reason to be skeptical of the efficacy of transferring such processes from their original context to the context of individuals and societies dealing with the aftermath of gross and systematic violations of human rights. Through a careful examination of how this process was transposed into the operation of Canada's Truth and Reconciliation Commission (TRC) on Indian Residential Schools, Niezen claims that we have little data to support the hypothesis that either individuals, communities, or the wider nation are "healed" through such processes. Moreover, insofar as these ostensibly therapeutic forums highlight emotional pain, they create a highly individualized narrative of wrongdoing that illuminates the suffering of victims and the implied evil of perpetrators but obscures the institutional and structural dimensions that facilitate and authorize systematic violations. Importantly, the state and its institutions, which ought to be subjected to human rights, do not appear as part of the staged drama.

Niezen's analysis also points to the way in which the therapeutic processes of the truth and reconciliation model shape the subject positions occupied by victims, who are variously coached and assisted to present themselves in a particular way. Similarly, though less explicitly, such processes also shape the subject positions that we are left to imagine are occupied by perpetrators, who, being absent from the process (in the Canadian case, at least), remain abstractions and ideal types. As a consequence, the messiness that characterizes the history of violations, subject positions, and relations is tidied up. Experiences that cannot easily be packaged into narratives of suffering, abuses that cannot be redeemed, as well as perpetrators who are also friends and community members, are all erased in favor of a cast of more easily digestible subjects of human rights.

Part II concludes with Chapter 9, Andrew Rajca's "Cinematic Aesthetics and the Subjects of Human Rights: On Eliane Caffé's *Era o Hotel Cambridge*." As with the previous chapter, Rajca highlights how experiences of human rights abuse can become appropriated by larger politicized discourses in ways that efface the struggles and subjectivity of victims. Rajca's intervention concerns a topic of lively debate in contemporary human rights scholarship and activism: inequality and the relative eclipse of social and economic rights by civil and political rights. More pointedly, his chapter raises the question of what *kind* or *category* of human rights should the state be held accountable for? Should we follow in the footsteps of a preeminent strain of liberal human-itarianism and hold that the state is subject only to claims for civil and polit-ical human rights? Or should we demand a more expansive sense of human rights obligations, such that it is conceivable, just, and necessary that the state also be subject to social and economic human rights claims?

Rajca emphatically pursues the second, more demanding course. To do this, he provides a close reading of a film that blends documentary footage with a fictional story: Eliane Caffé's *Era o Hotel Cambridge* (2016), set in con-temporary Brazil. By following the occupation of an abandoned building in downtown São Paulo by a group of homeless migrants, refugees, and activists, the film grapples with the global financialization of housing. Interpreting this film against the grain of a mainstream aesthetics of human rights—one used with greater or lesser complicity by human rights campaigners alongside neo-liberal institutions—Rajca considers not only how human rights subjects are typically represented in and by art, but also how art can be used to make per-ceptible and sensible novel human rights claims and subjectivities. The film reveals—or, better yet, crafts and creates—a vision of a society where the oc-cupiers of the abandoned building are subjects of economic and social human rights. Far from being helpless victims, they are active political subjects who attempt to hold the state to account to respect their human rights to accessi-ble and affordable housing. At the same time as he investigates what kind of human rights claims the state should be subject to, Rajca demonstrates how human rights ideas, practices, and activism do not simply represent already constituted subjects but have the power to positively and actively call them into existence. This is the third theme of the volume and the topic addressed in Part III.

How Do Human Rights Make Subjects?

In a sense, all of the authors in this volume address the question set out in Part III: how do human rights make subjects? Moreover, they broadly agree that human rights discourses and practices shape and form people in various respects, rather than simply reflecting an antecedently constituted subject. The four chapters that comprise Part III, however, put their own twist on this theme. They ask, how have human rights been knowingly and deliberately used to make subjects, and, crucially, how has this been done for the sake of well-intentioned and perhaps even productive outcomes?

This longer question is so phrased for a reason. In contemporary human rights scholarship, discussion of the formative effects that human rights have on subjects is overwhelmingly critical in nature. The goal—and sensibility, we would add—of this literature is to demonstrate how human rights establish and favor certain kinds of subjectivities that end up consolidating wider social, political, and hegemonic powers.

The sharpest example is the recent literature on human rights and neoliberalism, which takes its cue from Karl Marx's classic early essay "On the Jewish Question" (1844). Nearly two hundred years ago, Marx argued that the French Declaration of the Rights of Man and of the Citizen (1789) enshrined a picture of human nature and selfhood as egoistic and atomic: just the kind of subject and self-understanding, in other words, that a capitalist order requires to thrive.[30] Today, critics have extended this line of argument to our own dispensation of capitalism and examined how human rights norms and institutions work, whether knowingly or inadvertently, to establish and promote a conception of subjectivity and selfhood favored by neoliberalism: an agent, abstracted out from systems of social dependency, who realizes himself or herself through values conducive to market capitalism such as choice, rationality, and individualism. The result, they claim, is that human rights disseminate an image of subjectivity, selfhood, and humanity that mirrors and supports the reigning socioeconomic paradigm of our day and, moreover, impedes other forms of social and political organization.[31]

Postcolonial, feminist, and post-humanist scholars have launched similar criticisms, claiming that the problem with the subject of human rights is not just that it excludes certain kinds of people but, more perniciously, that it encourages all human beings to recognize and cultivate themselves in the image of a subject in a manner that naturalizes and reinforces contingent, unjust, and systemic hierarchies.[32] The influence of Michel Foucault looms large over this literature. Certainly, Foucault was by no means the first to recognize how discourses or regimes of knowledge and truth shape subjects in particular ways—his teachers Louis Althusser and Georges Canguilhem, are crucial figures here—but his critical insight was that this formative process is not one that occurs uniquely through the imposition of constraints; it also occurs through the availability of affordances.[33] In this regard, that human rights appear to empower subjects or open possibilities of life to them is by no means incompatible with the claim that it nevertheless forms them in particular ways. Indeed, that the subject, understood as the site of experience and choice, and subjectification, is formed from the same root is precisely what Foucault makes clear. Building on this insight, critical scholars of various types argue that the subject animated by particular types of desires or aspirations is not only a specific type of subject but one whose very desires have been shaped to replicate and stabilize the order of their own formation.[34]

We—and the authors of this volume—are indebted to these literatures. They are indispensable in problematizing a tendency in human rights law, policy, and advocacy to essentialize the subject of human rights and take a certain conception of the human being as natural, ahistorical, and universal. That said, we believe the critical sensibility they employ is not sufficient to capture the full range and possibility of how human rights shape subjectivity and selfhood. In this regard, we urge a return to the original meaning of the word "critique," understood not as criticizing but as rendering transparent the conditions of possibility for a certain practice or way of being and, correlatively, what certain practices or ways of being make possible. At its best, such critique both sheds light on what might have been obscure and opens different, more expansive possibilities.[35]

We are far from alone in this endeavor. Alongside the critical literature and attempting to build from its lessons is a growing trend in human rights scholarship and practice to affirm the possibility that human rights do indeed have a formative effect on subjectivity and that it can be used for the good, as it were, to advance the inclusive and universal ambitions that the human rights project claims for itself. Several works in recent years have examined the positive and often salutary impact that human rights have had on nearly every human capacity or faculty, whether that be our political imagination, our self-conception as agents, our aesthetic sensibility, our felt awareness of the suffering of others, and even our notion of what it means to be a person.[36] And in the field of practice, the global human rights education movement is itself based on the premise that human rights can modify the hearts and minds of ordinary people and, in the words of several authors in the field, become a fully fledged "way of life."[37] A key challenge of this type of scholarship and practice, therefore, is to push back against orthodox advocates of human rights who see little if any connection between human rights and subject formation (in the sense that human rights would simply represent and reflect an already formed subject), while at the same time resisting the temptation to ally with critics who believe that human rights have a positively deleterious effect on to subject formation.

The chapters in Part III navigate this middle path. In Chapter 10, "Human Rights As Spiritual Exercises," Alexandre Lefebvre highlights an important, recurrent, and yet nearly unacknowledged feature of the human rights tradition. Many of its key thinkers, he claims, represent and recommend human rights as a set of principles and practices for ordinary people to adopt in their own lives as a way of effecting deep personal transformation. Seen in this light, human rights are not exclusively instruments for global justice, they are also tools for individuals to actively and reflectively work on themselves.

At the heart of Lefebvre's chapter is the idea of spiritual exercises. Spiritual exercises are voluntary personal practices intended to cause a transformation of the self. A mainstay of ancient Greek and Roman philosophy as well as Eastern and Western religions, they include such activities as meditation, dialogue, mantras, diary writing, dietary regimes, and much else. To make his claim that human rights have historically operated as spiritual exercises, Lefebvre turns to four key figures in the history of human rights: Mary Wollstonecraft, Alexis de Tocqueville, Henri Bergson, and Charles Malik. Each of them, he claims, represents and recommends human rights in terms of spiritual exercises and, more specifically, as a tool or technique for individuals to work on themselves in light of a whole range of social and psychical problems, including patriarchy, loneliness, hatred, and meaninglessness. In so doing, Lefebvre recovers a conception of human rights based on voluntary self-cultivation that remains available and attractive to us today.

Linde Lindkvist addresses a fascinating phenomenon for human rights and subject formation in Chapter 11, "The Child Subject of Human Rights." Precisely because the subjectivity and capacities of children are obviously in development, Lindkvist's topic contains, *in nuce*, the whole problematic contained in the question "How do human rights make subjects?" For in describing the challenges that the drafters of human rights declarations face, Lindkvist conveys not only the difficulty of trying to capture and codify a subject defined by its "evolving capacities" but also the opportunity they seized to frame a human rights document that could positively contribute to that process of growth and becoming.

Much of Lindkvist's discussion centers on the meaning, implications, and stakes of Article 12 of the United Nations Convention on the Rights of the Child (1989). This Article advances a strongly agentic conception of children, providing for their participation in civil and political proceedings affecting them. The reason it is so significant and has since become a gathering point for wider debate is that Article 12 underscores and promotes the idea that children are individual human subjects and that their rights and interests are irreducible to those of their parents. As such, Lindkvist is able to use Article 12 to explore broader issues of subject formation in human rights. His analysis of the Article serves as a vehicle to examine ideas of subjectivity, selfhood, and personal development of children in human rights law, discourse, and practice. And it is also a privileged site to unpack more general assumptions about what it means to be a responsible rights bearer in both childhood and adulthood.

The next chapter, Jenna Reinbold's "The Secular Subject of Human Rights," addresses the relationship between human rights, religion, secularism, and subjectivity. On the surface, it might seem as though human rights would have little to say about the impact of secularism on subjectivity and self-understanding. After all, a standard narrative of the creation of the Universal Declaration of Human Rights is that its drafters agreed to put aside their religious differences and frame it as a kind of neutral instrument which, while allowing for moral commitment from states and persons all over the world, would remain pragmatically and politely silent on the issue of religion. And, indeed, it is with this narrative that Reinbold begins her chapter, showing how the French philosopher Jacques Maritain, who headed the UNESCO committee in charge of inquiring into the "theoretical problems raised by the elaboration of an International Declaration of the Rights of Man," navigated the problem of religious pluralism. Maritain, she shows, presented human rights as a foundation that could provide apparently opposed religious perspectives with a common denominator. On this standard account, the Universal Declaration would herald later "political" and "public reason" liberalisms in that people are said to retain their prior religious commitments and doctrines yet gain a shared moral and political framework that would serve as a basis for mutual respect and cooperation.

Reinbold does not exactly dispute this role of human rights, but she insists that it has the potential to impact subjectivity much more deeply than the drafters of the Universal Declaration initially recognized. Some people, she agrees, may well retain their religious views and yet affirm a more or less secular human rights framework. Others, however, do not have a separate and distinct set of religious views they can point to, so closely does the secularism of the Declaration match—and eventually inform—their own worldview and ethos. This, she claims, is the "secular subject of human rights"; it is less an alternative to religion, or a light version of it, than a fully fledged religious position itself, though one without transcendence or many trappings of historical religions. Her chapter, then, captures the effect that human rights have on engendering a sensibility and ethos that blur the lines between secularism and religion.

The volume concludes with an interview between Samuel Moyn and Alexandre Lefebvre. A historian and political theorist, Moyn has recast several debates on the historical origins of human rights, the entanglement of human rights and Christianity, and the relationship between human rights and inequality. In this wide-ranging interview, Moyn shows himself to be of two minds with respect to the role and potential that human rights have to shape subjectivity. On the one hand, he strongly affirms the premise that any adequate social and political theory must put the topic of subject formation center stage. As he states, "I have always thought that the horizon for all future social explanation was set in the middle of the twentieth century, when a number of thinkers converged on the premise that any social explanation has to work in and through an account of subject formation, and vice versa."

And yet, on the other hand, he remains skeptical as to whether human rights as an institution and social movement has developed the requisite resources and self-understanding to generate truly effective processes of subject formation. Ranging across the whole of his oeuvre, Moyn describes how human rights comparatively lack the robust practices and narratives of self-formation that we find in historical religions (such as Christianity) and established political movements (such as socialism). His goal is not to close the door on such possibilities for human rights but rather to observe their present limitations and, from that basis, suggest alternative models that human rights theorists, advocates, and organizations might adopt in order to reinforce this vital connection between a social movement and its ability to effectively and enduringly shape the hearts and minds of its subjects. The volume thus concludes not with a self-satisfied survey of the contemporary human rights project but with an extensive and practicable set of suggestions to envisage and engender its subject.

PART I

WHO IS THE SUBJECT OF HUMAN RIGHTS?

CHAPTER 1

The Relational Self As the Subject of Human Rights

Jennifer Nedelsky

Introduction

Today, people throughout the world formulate their claims, concerns, and protests in the language of rights. Institutions such as international criminal courts operate on the basis of claims about universal human rights.[1] Tragedies such as refugees dying as they flee for safety, island countries sinking under rising seas, or state-sponsored massacres are discussed in the language of rights, as are debates over when international intervention is appropriate. Virtually every state that has made a transition to democracy in the past fifty years has created a constitution that outlines protected rights. In Europe, the European Convention on Human Rights recognizes rights; the Treaty on the European Union makes membership conditional on their protection; and the European Court of Human Rights adjudicates claims of state violation.[2] In Africa, fifty-three states have ratified the African Charter on Human and Peoples' Rights, and twenty-five of the thirty-five member states of the Organization of American States have ratified the American Convention on Human Rights.[3]

In short, the prevailing language of justice and entitlement is overwhelmingly that of *rights*. Thus, in my view, the debate over the desirability of rights (as concept and legal institution) has, in practical terms, been decisively won by those who opt for the language of rights. Despite the merits of (ongoing) scholarly objections, the practical issue is not *whether* but *how* the language of rights will be used. The best hope for meeting the concerns of critics and skeptics is to shift the understanding of rights—both what the term means and how rights are best defined and protected by institutions.

The key to a helpful approach to rights is to understand the subject of rights as fundamentally relational. In this chapter I will outline my relational theory of self, autonomy, and law, with a focus on understanding rights in relational terms.[4] I begin with a sketch of my relational framework, then provide more detail about the relational self. I then turn to a relational approach to rights, its response to critiques of rights, and, finally, to a brief discussion of the challenges of institutionalizing rights.

Sketch of a Relational Approach

One way of seeing my approach is that it traces a linear connection from conceptions of self to values (autonomy in particular) to relational approaches to rights and law. Although, as I will explain shortly, this linear connection can be misleading, it can also provide a useful shorthand.

The *self* is relational because human beings become who they are—their identities, their capacities, their desires—through the relationships in which they participate. These include intimate relations with parents and lovers, more distant relationships with teachers and employers, and social structural relations such as gender, economic relations, and forms of governmental power.

When the self is constituted by relations, then the core *values* of human life have to be understood in ways that take account of this centrality of relationship. The role of relationship for autonomy, for example, is clearest in the parent-child context. Everyone can picture how relationships with parents can harm or encourage a child's autonomy. My claim is that constructive relationships are necessary for autonomy to flourish throughout one's life. Teachers can be authoritarian, or they can invite critical thought. Employers can encourage the participation of their employees in structuring the forms and demands of work, or they can focus on discipline and compliance. Governments can set up forms of social assistance that are intrusive and humiliating or systems in which recipients are given the tools and resources to make choices among good options about how to live. Optimal systems could also enhance autonomy by inviting recipients to participate in the formulation and implementation of qualifications for entitlement. All of these relations enhance or undermine people's autonomy. Autonomy cannot, therefore, be understood as independence from others; autonomy is a capacity made possible by constructive relationships.

Since the prevailing Anglo-American conception of *law and rights* rests so heavily on underlying conceptions of self and autonomy, there must be corresponding changes in the understanding of law and rights. Law makes assumptions about the sort of independence and responsibility that characterize mature human beings, and people are entitled to rights such as freedom of expression and association because they need them to be autonomous beings. So if rights are based on a faulty conception of autonomy as independence, they are not likely to do a good job of facilitating the relationships that actually foster autonomy.

The rights the relational self is entitled to will therefore need to be based on relational rather than individualistic conceptions of the self. Both law and rights will then be understood in terms of the relations they structure—and how those relations can foster core values such as autonomy. In sum, a relational self requires relational conceptions of values, which then require appropriate forms of law and rights built around those conceptions.

This sort of linear schema provides a neat summary. But it is also misleading because self, autonomy, and rights and law are each tied to each other—as a set of ideas, beliefs, practices, and institutions. The prevailing liberal conception of the self *is* an autonomous self with rights. And individual(istic) rights are what an autonomous self (or rational agent) is entitled to. Law (in its ideal liberal form) protects equal, autonomous, rights-bearing selves from harm by each other and by the state. There is thus not a linear ordering beginning with self and ending in law. A shift in any of these concepts (and practices) would entail a shift in all of them.

My work in *Law's Relations* aimed to advance such a shift by focusing on each dimension and on their interaction. This transformational project therefore engages the contested concepts of self, autonomy, and rights as intertwined with one another and in conversation with the institutional implications for change. One can begin with rights and the recognition that they are, and have always been, powerful rhetorical and institutional means for structuring the relationships that enable or undermine autonomy and other values. Thus, rights (wherever they are part of the legal and political regime) must be part of efforts to give concrete effect to a relational understanding of autonomy. The idea of the relational self then becomes part of the project of overcoming the limitations inherited from the theoretical and institutional history of rights as well as the recent adaptation to neoliberal ideology and institutions.

In sum, rights need an alternative conceptual framework to do their work well, and new relational concepts need to be given life in the concrete legal forms of rights and law. Theoretical work on a relational self and relational autonomy that does not try to engage rights (because they are cast as hopelessly individualist) misunderstands the social construction of rights and is liable to leave the theory floating in theoretical space while the forces that structure relations go unaddressed. Similarly, efforts to rehabilitate rights without addressing the distorted underpinnings of assumptions about self and autonomy will always be limited.

The Relational Self

All political and legal theorists, and all institutions of law and government, recognize that human beings live together. But a relational approach to human life is something more than the recognition of this fact. In my version of a relational approach (feminists have generated many), the human subjects of law and government are not best thought of as freestanding individuals who need protection from one another. People's interactions with one another matter not simply because their interests may collide. Each individual is in basic ways constituted by networks of relationships of which they are a part—networks that range from intimate ones with parents, friends, and lovers to relations between student and teacher, welfare recipient and caseworker, citizen and state, to being participants in a global economy, migrants in a world of gross economic inequality, or inhabitants of a world shaped by global warming.

What does it mean to be constituted by relationships rather than just living among others? As I suggested earlier, the most familiar example of people being fundamentally shaped by relationship is the idea that children are shaped by their families, and often their parents in particular. Nevertheless, this widespread recognition of the constitutive nature of relationships somehow seems to disappear for people over the age of twenty-one. It is as though once people are "formed," once they emerge as "rational agents," relationships are things they simply have or choose. The idea of adults as autonomous actors seems in tension with, even to contradict, the idea that people continue to be profoundly shaped by relationships. Indeed, I think some find the relational approach off-putting because it seems both infantilizing and feminizing: it treats mature adults as the relationally dependent creatures people see children as, and it grants a kind of importance to relationships typically associated with women.

In fact, however, it is not hard to think of formative adult relationships. Teachers and mentors are common examples. Neighborhood relations may shape the kinds of employment opportunities young adults are able to en-vision and access. Relational norms at a workplace—hierarchy, arbitrary au-thority, cooperation, autonomy, trust, consultation, prejudice—may shape how a person sees the world and how they experience themselves. And all these relations, along with their formative effects, are often affected by larger structures of economic relations such as unemployment levels and the power of employers to fire at will. Many people will see their personal relations with friends and intimate partners as formative. And these relations, in turn, are shaped by wider patterns of relationship such as heterosexual norms, gender norms, and gendered division of caretaking work. Many people can see how these nested relational patterns—from intimate to global—have shaped who they have become. And the relational habit of reflection will reveal that the impact is never unidirectional. At every level, individuals and collectives have the ability to change the norms, legal rights, and political structures that have shaped them.

Human dependence on others, and the collective interdependence that follows, is a central feature of my version of a relational conception of human selves. It is not just when our physical capacities are diminished that people need one another. We are dependent on others for the social world that en-ables us to develop all of our core capacities—for love, for play, for reason, for creativity, for autonomy, among others. We are usually dependent on partic-ular others and always dependent on the webs of relations of which we are a part. And here is my point: our fundamentally social, relational nature—and thus our dependency—cannot be set to the side when we think of any of the core puzzles of law or politics such as justice, mutual obligation, or how to de-fine, implement, and protect rights.

In concluding this section, it is important to be clear about what I do not mean by "relational selves." When I refer to relationships, I mean not just in-timate relationships but mutually interacting relationships that are part of a nested structure from intimate to global. In using the term "relational selves," I do not mean that people are determined by their relationships. (That would, of course, be an odd position for a feminist to take. Feminists have long ob-jected to women being defined by their relationships as wives or mothers.) In my view, relationships are constitutive, yet not determinative. The very con-cept of relational autonomy presupposes that autonomy is possible for re-lational selves; and if that is so, then relationships cannot determine who a person is or what she does or becomes. Otherwise there would be no true autonomy.

Last, I do not presume that relationships are necessarily benign. Part of the point of a relational approach is to understand what kinds of relationships foster—and which undermine—core values such as autonomy, dignity, or security. Legal rights, in turn, are one of the most powerful ways in which relationships are structured—for good and for ill. Let us turn, therefore, to rights.

A Relational Approach to Law and Rights

The core of my claim about a relational approach to law and rights is twofold:

1. Questions of rights (and law more generally) are best *analyzed* in terms of how they structure relations. Doing so can make a difference in how people understand the issues at stake and the kinds of judgment they exercise.
2. What rights and law actually *do*, right now, is structure relations, which in turn promote or undermine core values such as autonomy. This is why a relational approach can and should be (and sometimes is) used in current legal systems. While a relational approach may, in the long run, invite changes in legal systems, it need not await any such change.

Rights structure relations of power, trust, responsibility, and care. It is easy to construct a list of examples of legal rights—from property to tort to fiduciary relationships such as between doctor and patient—to show that in defining and enforcing rights, the law routinely structures and sometimes self-consciously takes account of relationships. What I propose is that this reality of rights structuring relationships should become the central focus of the concept of rights itself and thus of all discussion of what should be treated as rights, how they should be implemented, and how they should be interpreted. It is a matter of bringing to the foreground what has always been the background reality.

All claims of rights involve interpretations and contestation. My position is that people will do a better job of making all the difficult decisions involving rights if they focus on the kinds of relationships that they actually want to foster and how different concepts and institutions will best contribute to that fostering.

This inquiry can be carried on in the following relational terms: (1) One should start by asking how existing laws and rights have helped to construct the problem being addressed. What patterns and structures of relations have shaped it, and how has law helped shape those relations? The next questions are (2) What values are at stake in the problem, and (3) What kinds of relations promote such values? In particular, what kind of shift in existing relations would enhance rather than undermine the values at stake? There may, of course, be more than one value at stake, and they may compete with one another. For example, relations that enhance the freedom and autonomy of a renter may decrease the security and freedom of the landlord. (4) What interpretation or change in the existing law would help restructure the relations in the ways that would promote the values at stake?

As can be seen in my phrasing of the questions above, I make a distinction between rights and values. I treat rights as rhetorical and institutional means for implementing core values, such as security, liberty, autonomy, and equality. I prefer this language to simply defining such core values as rights. Usually when people do this, they mean these values are moral rights. But I am focusing on legal rights, and I want to emphasize that it is a certain kind of choice to describe a value as a legal right and construct institutions for implementing that right. Not all values lend themselves to the language of rights. Harmony, for example, which is an important value for some societies and individuals, does not seem to me to be well captured or implemented through rights.

I also think that debates over how a particular right should be interpreted— for example, freedom of speech with respect to hate speech—should be structured around questions of which interpretation will promote the underlying, possibly competing values. The distinction between rights and values allows such a structuring. The distinction also makes possible a claim that there are universal values, such as dignity and autonomy, but that different cultures choose to foster them in different ways. Some choose the language and institutions of rights; others do not. The distinction between rights and values makes it easier to see when the dispute is about what should be treated as a core value and when it is about the best means of promoting that value.

In some cases, the value at stake will be obvious. In the debate over same-sex marriage, for example, it is clear that the values of equality and dignity are at stake for those arguing in its favor. The values at stake for the opponents are somewhat less clear and take various forms: the stability of society; the stability of an institution (marriage) that long predates our particular legal and political arrangements and that is said to be essential for the well-being of society and its members; the collective norms of sexual morality and the importance of having the state reflect and support them. (Of course, the fact that those collective norms are contested is also key to the debate.)

In technical legal debates over, say, the scope of copyright protection or fiduciary obligations of corporate CEOs, it is sometimes an important contribution to the debate to make clearer what the competing values at stake are. For example, the rules of copyright may have nonobvious implications for access to intellectual resources in developing countries. The obligation of CEOs to maximize profit may interfere with (or be so interpreted as to interfere with) their capacity to take issues of social and environmental responsibility into account in their decision-making.

Once the relevant values are clear, it will be easier to move to the next stage: which interpretation of the legal rights in question will actually foster the values at stake? This question, in turn, will be clarified by asking what kinds of relationships the competing forms of the right will structure and whether those relationships will foster the values at stake. The key here is to recognize that in rights disputes where, say, the value of autonomy is at stake, whatever the outcome, it will affect autonomy. The questions of how an interpretation of a right will structure relations and whether those relations will foster or undermine autonomy will determine whether the right in question is functionally hostile to autonomy or supportive of it.

Let us look at the example of whether a law that precludes same-sex marriage undermines equality. In this case, of course, relations of equality constitute the right at stake. So here the question is, will the very fact of excluding same-sex couples from marriage, a central legal institution, construct relations of inequality? Is it a badge of inferiority that *must* generate relations of inequality? Concretely, one could ask whether it was possible that access to civil partnership,[5] as was the first step in England, would ultimately generate relations of equality and respect just as effectively as access to marriage (and disturb fewer people who were devoted to the historical definition of marriage). In fact, England quietly moved from civil partnership to same-sex marriage after nine years.[6] As this brief example suggests, there is an inevitable element of uncertainty, even speculation, in the claims that a given form of law would promote a certain structure of relations. Sometimes, however, even a short historical perspective can offer evidence. In the case of same-sex relationships, it is striking that within a very short time virtually all Western countries converged on marriage as the appropriate legal form for advancing rights to equality and dignity.

It is important to see that the relational approach is not some sort of collective *alternative* to protecting and enforcing individual rights. It is, rather, a means of doing so. When I say that rights structure relationships, I mean that those relationships make possible the enjoyment of the right. To enjoy one's property rights, for example, requires that most people defer to one's power to exclude others (even if they are cold and homeless). This hierarchy of power relations also structures employment relations: people agree (via contract) to perform labor in order to have property (wages) transferred to them. In a factory, everyone understands the relations of ownership: the people who build the cars do not own them. Their employers do. And everyone understands the power to hire and fire is part of the hierarchy of power relations that flows from the relations of ownership structured by legal rights.

One could also tell a story of the relations of freedom made possible by property and contract law. Indeed, there is a long history of competing narratives about the values fostered by relations structured by property and contract law. (There are particularly clear examples of this in the debates in the early twentieth century in the United States and Canada around minimum wage and maximum hours.[7])

Thus, to engage in debates about what the relations of property should be—how property rights should structure relations (the relations that largely *constitute* the right of property)—is to deliberate about what the rights of property should mean by attending to the concrete manifestation of that meaning. Attending to the relationships that constitute property rights and that are constructed by property law is to deliberate about rights and the value of property to individuals, not some other collective value. This remains the case even if part of the value of property to individuals, such as autonomy, may conflict with another value that is important to individuals, such as equality. (I return later to the ways property rights structure the relations of power and are a central component of a market economy.)

Like all core values, equality may be cast as an individual right, and it can be described in terms of structures of relations between individuals. The fact that one can analyze the debates around both equality and property in terms of the implications for structures of relationship does not mean that a collective value is being substituted for an individual one. One can *also* make the argument that societies as a whole will thrive better with more equal relations among their members. This, then, adds a collective value into the mix. But the fact that a relational analysis may reveal that equality (or freedom of speech) is also a collective value that benefits societies as a whole does not mean that *individual* rights cannot be distinctively recognized and analyzed in relational terms. To say that individual rights (like property) can be given effect only through the relations that give them meaning (as in the examples above) remains an analysis of individual rights. Of course, as in *all* forms of rights debates, sometimes a collective value like national security or economic prosperity will be invoked as an additional concern that must be weighed in deciding how to define and protect individual rights. That addition is in no way peculiar to a relational approach to rights. My claim is that analyzing rights in terms of the relationships they structure (and the ways those relationships enhance or undermine core values) will do a better job of protecting the values that are at the core of individual rights.

In conclusion, I want to note two important puzzles. There are important issues of contingency, uncertainty in prediction, and lack of knowledge that affect the relational analysis I propose. For example, as we saw in the same-sex marriage example, the core question of what relations will foster a particular value cannot be known with certainty. The existence of uncertainty and contestation in interpretation is, however, a feature of all legal systems. There is always some degree of speculation whenever judges or lawmakers try to take into account the impact of a law or legal change. These are not difficulties introduced by the relational approach. They are simply more obvious, and this recognition will make for more open, honest, and democratically accessible legal decisions.

In addition to these questions of uncertainty, there is the even more fundamental question of contestation around values. Elsewhere, I have elaborated a number of examples where the mere identification of a value at stake, like equality, serves to highlight the deep disagreement that exists in all democratic societies about what equality should mean in practice. Such disagreements affect people's judgments about issues such as the meaning of the rights to property, limitations on contract, the powers of corporations, and desirable tax structures. My claim is that identifying the values at stake will rarely determine a unanimous judgment, but a relational analysis will clarify the nature of the disagreement at stake. For example, is it about the meaning of equality—say, the relation between economic equality and the political equality? Or is it a more instrumental disagreement about the best means of increasing economic equality? I think that clarity about the nature of the disagreement will foster better democratic conversations about both core disagreements about the meaning of equality and about tactical policy debates.

In sum, all legal issues, from the most profound to the mundane, are better understood, and thus better deliberated about, if analyzed from a relational perspective.

Critiques of "Rights Talk"

Let me turn to some of the critiques of "rights talk": (1) "rights" are undesirably individualistic, (2) rights obfuscate the real political issues, and (3) rights serve to alienate and to distance people from one another. Here, I will not try to present these critiques in detail but will merely sketch them in order to show how a focus on relationship helps construct a response.

I will begin with the claim that rights talk is excessively individualistic, noting the core of the critique that I find persuasive (and have participated in myself). Implicit in the critique is usually a suggestion that rights are either inherently individualistic or that their historical association with liberal individualism so taints them that they are undesirable tools for political transformation. My argument is that rights are not inherently individualistic, because rights are, in fact, relational in nature. I then hold out the hope that if this relational nature is recognized and becomes a regular tool of analysis in rights debates, the historical taint of individualism can be overcome.

Individualism

Critics of the individualism of rights point to both practice and theory (Lessard 1992; Bakan 1997; Frazer and Lacey 1993). In practice, for example, the failure of American constitutional jurisprudence to adequately recognize systemic disadvantage can be attributed to the excessive focus on individual intent and individual harm. Similarly, the American rejection of hate speech legislation as constitutionally impermissible can be seen as a failure to understand that hate speech can result in both individual and collective harm and silencing (and thus interference with free speech). While Canadian jurisprudence takes a less individualistic stance on these issues, critics also see Charter rights as shaped by the heritage of liberal individualism. For example, the charge that Charter rights express individualistic values is offered as an argument for why they should not apply to the collective decisions of First Nations.

There are good reasons to believe that the contemporary systems of constitutional rights draw on a powerful legacy of liberal political thought in which rights are associated with a highly individualistic conception of humanity. Indeed, the "rights-bearing individual" may be said to be the basic subject of liberal political thought. What is wrong with this individualism, say the critics, is that it fails to account for the ways in which our essential humanity is neither possible nor comprehensible without the network of relationships of which it is a part. Most conventional liberal rights theories do not make relationship central to their understanding of the human subject (Koggel 1998; Gabel 1984). Mediating conflict is the focus, not mutual self-creation and sustenance. The selves to be protected by rights are seen as essentially separate, rather than as creatures whose interests, needs, and capacities are mutually constitutive. Thus, for example, one of the reasons women have always fit so poorly into the framework of liberal theory is that it becomes obviously awkward to think of women's relation to their children as *essentially* one of competing interests to be mediated by rights.

I share these critics' concerns about how the limitations of history and theory may affect the way rights are actually implemented. Nevertheless, as I argued above, I think that rights can be rescued from their long association with individualistic theory and practice. The best understandings of the nature of the human self and the way rights function are on the side of a realignment of the liberal tradition. Human beings are *both* uniquely individual and essentially social creatures. The liberal tradition has been not so much wrong as seriously and dangerously one-sided in its emphasis.

Once rights are conceptualized in terms of the relationships they structure, the problem of individualism is at least radically transformed. At the most basic level, the focus of analysis will shift from an abstraction of individual entitlement to an inquiry into the ways the right will shape relations and into how those relations, in turn, will promote (or undermine) the values at stake.

Finally, the relational form of analysis that flows from a relational conception of rights has another important advantage: it is highly conducive to thinking about human rights in the context of a structural analysis of inequality. The (historically individualistic) discourse of rights is sometimes seen as hindering such structural analyses. But the problem does not lie with rights as such. For example, one very important form of structural analysis that a great deal of rights discourse has failed to address is the threats posed by escalating economic inequality, even in conjunction with a reduction in poverty.[8] In the international context, Samuel Moyn ascribes this failure to a "human rights revolution" that "has at its most ambitious dedicated itself to establishing a normative and actual floor for protection."[9]

A relational approach to rights would recognize the harms of poverty *and* provide a framework for articulating the threats posed by the growing gap between the very rich and everyone else. Under a relational analysis, it is easy to raise the question of whether an increase in inequality at the upper end of the income scale structures human relations in ways that undermine democracy as well as equal access to education, good jobs, and economic security.[10] In this context, a relational rights analysis will immediately see that the "obliteration of the ceiling on inequality" is a problem for the basic right of equality.[11] The fact that international human rights projects have focused (successfully) on "a minimum floor of human protections" does not mean that a shift in focus to thinking about rights in relational terms would be unable to identify the threat to the core value of equality entailed in the growing gap between the very rich and everyone else. To the contrary, relational thinking would help spotlight that threat.

Recognizing the limits of both the history and the current practices of human rights discourse should highlight the importance of a shift to a relational framework for the worldwide language of rights. Rights, as I said in the opening of this chapter, are so fully entrenched in discourses of justice that it is essential to move to a different way of conceptualizing rights so they can transcend these limitations.

Finally, none of this optimism about the intrinsic possibility of transforming understandings of rights should be understood to deny the reality that the language of rights and human rights has been invoked not only to advance values like equality but to justify domination.[12] Relational rights can be used to focus attention on structural inequality, and more broadly, this shift in framing might help to clarify disagreement over the real reason for intervention and whether a justification is persuasive. Invoking a relational framework will not, of course, be a solution for bad faith. Not just the language of rights, but that of democracy as well, has been used to justify violent international intervention. It is wise to be conscious of such practices and not to take the invocation of rights, democracy, or national security as a justification for violence or exclusion. But such awareness is not a reason to abandon the language of rights, especially when the alternative of a relational framework makes rights claims more transparent and thus open to public debate. In addition, the call for democratic participation in the definitions of rights could (as I discuss below, in "Rights As Collective Choices and the Need for a Dia-

logue of Democratic Accountability") challenge the use of rights language by
the powerful.

Obfuscation

Let me now offer some brief suggestions as to how this approach can meet
the diverse body of criticism (often associated with critical legal studies) that
I have lumped into my second category of objection to rights talk as obfuscation. One of the most important parts of this set of critiques is the objection
that when rights are central to political debate, they misdirect political energies because they obscure rather than clarify what is at issue and what people
are really after.[13] As with the objection of individualism, this critique points
to a serious problem. But as I have just argued, those problems are transformed when people understand rights as structuring relationships. A relational analysis will clarify rather than obscure what is actually at stake.

Earlier (see "A Relational Approach to Law and Rights"), I talked about the
ways that property rights are constituted by relationships, such as the willingness of ordinary people to defer to the power of property owners to exclude them. These relations of power are structured by individual rights at the
same time as they shape (and undermine) collective values of equality. We can
now return to the example of property and to the question of the kinds of relations people *want* their systems of rights to promote. If we approach property rights as one of the most important vehicles for structuring relations of
power in our society and as a means of expressing the relations of responsibility we want to encourage, we will start off the debate in a useful way.[14] For example, if we ask whether ownership of a factory should entail some responsibility to those it employs and consider how to balance that responsibility with
the freedom to use one's property as one wishes, then we can intelligently pursue the inevitable process of defining and redefining property. We can ask
what relationships of power, responsibility, trust, and commitment we want
the terms of ownership of productive property to foster, and we can also ask
whether those relationships will foster the autonomy, creativity, or initiative
that we value. By contrast, to say that owners can shut down a plant whenever
and however they want because it is their property is to assert either a tautol-
ogy (property *means* the owner has this power) or a historical claim (property has, in the past, had this meaning). The historical claim does, of course,
have special relevance in law, but it can be only the beginning, not the end of
the inquiry into what property should mean. The focus on relationship will

help to give proper weight and context to the historical claims and to expose the tautological ones. The analytic clarity can then also shape strategies of resistance and mobilization around defining property rights in ways consistent with core values such as equality and dignity.

It is important to add that while a relational approach to rights may overcome the obfuscation of rights discourse, the *political* problem of where to focus one's energies for transformation remains. As long as courts are seen as the primary focus for contesting rights (however understood), there is a serious danger that activists will wrongly direct their energies toward court battles rather than democratic mobilization.[15] My arguments in the final section point toward efforts to democratize rights contestation by undermining the monopoly of judges and lawyers as custodians of rights.

Alienation and Distance

Finally, there is the important critique that rights are alienating and distancing, that they express and create barriers between people. Rights have this distancing effect in part because, as they function in our current discourse, they help us avoid seeing some of the relationships of which we are in fact a part. For example, when we see homeless people on the street, we do not think about the fact that it is in part our regime of property rights that renders them homeless. The dominant conception of rights helps us to feel that we are not only not responsible but not in any way connected to these "others." If, however, we come to focus on the relationships that our rights structure, we will see the connection between our power to exclude and the plight of homeless persons.

Thus, my response to the critique of distancing is that rights conceived as relationship will not foster the same distancing that our current conception does. Relational rights *could*, however, still serve the protective function that thoughtful advocates of rights-based distance, like Patricia Williams, are concerned about.[16] Not only does my vision of rights as relationship have equal respect at its core, but optimal structures of human relations will always provide both choice about entering relationships and space for the choice to withdraw.

In sum, then, a relational approach to rights avoids the core problems that have given rise to the critiques of rights as individualistic, obfuscating, and alienating. There is also an additional advantage that is central to this approach: it is both an important transformation *and* one that is practical within existing legal systems. No radical restructuring of the legal system would be necessary; a move toward habits of relational analysis could begin immediately. Of course, an understanding of the relational nature of rights may encourage changes in legal institutions. My point here is that the use of relational analysis need not wait for such changes. This is because the core of my argument is *not* that rights should begin to structure relationship where previously they have not. My argument is that rights have always structured relationships. Recognizing rights as relational brings to consciousness and thus opens to considered reflection and debate what already exists. My claim is that this recognition and reflection is capable of transforming the legacy of individualism, obfuscation, and alienation in the tradition of liberal rights.

Rights As Collective Choices and the Need for a Dialogue of Democratic Accountability

I have emphasized above that rights always involve interpretation and judgments about what will actually give effect to rights. This is true whether the issue is a dispute over existing rights in a court or a judgment about what should be called a right (a right to a healthy environment, right to health care) or what should be treated as a constitutional right (property is in most Western constitutions, but not in Canada).[17] One of the strengths of a relational approach to rights is that it reveals the underlying contestations and provides guides for thinking them through. But the advantages of this conceptual tool need institutions that provide democratic legitimacy for the inevitable choices about the meaning and implementation of rights.

Let me begin by noting some of the ways in which existing rights discourse serves to obscure the highly contested nature of the meaning of rights. First, in the international context, human rights are often treated as having self-evident content. The focus is on implementation and enforcement. The urge to enforcement is especially strong when people are suffering violence: the language of rights is invoked to inspire moral outrage and the will to intervene, to create a bulwark against government tyranny, or ethnic cleansing, or deeply embedded practices such as intimate partner violence. One can understand why people urgently calling for rights protection do not want to be reminded that part of what underlies the conflict may be competing interpretations of rights.

One can see something similar in constitutional rights discourse, particularly (but not exclusively) in the United States. The notion that there are certain basic rights that no government, no matter how democratic, should be able to violate is a central idea behind the U.S. Constitution and its institution of judicial review. This idea is captured in Ronald Dworkin's famous description of rights as "trumps" that can override legislative judgments about good law and policy. Such ideas hide the difficult problem of who defines rights and how they do it. The relational approach calls for a recognition that the definition and interpretation of rights are collective decisions about the implementation of core values—whether those collective decisions are made by the legislature, bureaucrats, or courts. The question is what forms of decision-making foster widespread democratic deliberation.

Wherever rights are invoked to make powerful moral (as well as legal) calls to action, there is, as I noted above, a resistance to addressing the underlying problem of democratic determination of the content of rights. I take the concern to be this: how can rights simultaneously function as a bulwark against illegitimate force *and* be understood as themselves the product of collective choice? Both constitutional rights and international human rights seem to require being above the fray of politics (and thus democracy) in order to do their job.

Here, it is helpful to notice that constitutional rights change their practical meaning over time. In the United States, neither property nor equality mean today what they did when the Constitution was written in 1787. In addition, under the Trump administration, it is more obvious than ever that there is no consensus on the meaning of basic rights and that the rulings courts issue largely depend on the appointed judges. Similarly, it is increasingly recognized that in the international context there is deep contestation not only over the meaning of property in the context of economic equality but also over claims about gender equality in the context of competing claims of religion and culture. If rights are to serve as constraints on majoritarian outcomes or sovereign power, they must do so in a way that is true to their essentially contested and shifting meaning.

Elsewhere, I have elaborated a model for an institutional "dialogue of democratic accountability," which would provide an alternative to the almost universal use of judicial review to measure legislation against constitutional rights. (I see this as a somewhat crude, if common, form of holding democratic outcomes to a standard of core values.) Here, let me simply raise the issue that leaving these determinations in the hands of judges is questionably consistent with democracy. The issue is not just that judges are unelected and thus not democratically unaccountable. There is a question of whether judicial opinions encourage reflection on the sources of the rights they interpret and on the way such interpretations have changed over time. And there is the broader question of whether judicial review, like any judge-made decision, fosters informed public deliberation on the issues. Of course, sometimes controversial constitutional issues, like same-sex marriage, attract a lot of public attention. But part of the issue is whether judges are, or should be seen to be, uniquely qualified to resolve constitutional disputes. To the extent that they are held out to be so or that formal legal expertise is required to understand the issues, the public capacity for democratic deliberation on core values—and their implementation via rights—is undermined.

Here we connect back to the relational approach to rights. As we have seen, part of the need for democratic legitimacy for rights determination arises from the recognition of the shifting and contested meaning of the rights to which democratic decision-making should be held accountable. This inevitable change and contestation makes more sense when our focus is on the structure of relations that fosters the underlying values. It is not at all surprising that what it takes to foster autonomy, or what is likely to undermine it, in an industrialized corporate economy with an active regulatory-welfare state is quite different from the relationships that would have had those effects in mid-nineteenth-century Canada. These may be different still in twenty-first-century Eastern Europe or South Africa. A focus on relationship automatically turns one's attention to context and makes sense of the commonly held belief that there are some basic human values *and* that how people articulate and foster those values varies significantly over time and place.

In the context of international human rights, this approach suggests that the focus cannot be on implementation alone. Equal attention must be given to the question of who has defined the rights in question. What processes are in place to facilitate (at least periodic) deliberation about the practical meaning of rights? Who has actual access to these processes? Some might say that inviting attention to who gets to define rights will undermine their rhetorical efficacy, their power to command attention and insist upon response. But as virtually everyone who works on human rights knows, the question of definition is already on the table. Its most common form is the allegation that universal human rights are really just the creation of Western/Northern countries and a tool for the imposition of Western/Northern power. One need not reject the possibility of universal human values to recognize the real problem of who participates in the definition of the rights that are supposed to set limits on legitimate sovereign power. If human rights really are to attain universal legitimacy, then the processes by which they are defined must themselves be universally recognized as legitimate. Giving up the allure of rights as trumps that can decisively shut down counterclaims of culture, religion, or democracy is not to give up the hope of workable international processes for holding all nations accountable for rights violations. In the end, only rights that have the legitimacy of a democratically justifiable process behind them will be able to serve that purpose.

Conclusion

In sum, a relational approach to rights can allow the pervasive language of rights to capture and protect the values that different societies find to be central to the flourishing of their people. Such an approach starts from an understanding of the subject of rights as a relational self for whom the realization of all their values is contingent on constructive relationships. The very meaning of the values they hold dear, such as autonomy, needs to be expressed in relational terms—thus dispelling myths of impossible independence. Such understanding of values requires reflection on how to foster the relationships that sustain those values. And in all political systems that use rights, a relational habit of thought will make it clear that those rights are a crucial part of what structures relationships. These relational conceptualizations of self, autonomy (and other values), and rights will enable the language of rights to overcome its historical limitations of individualism, obfuscation, and distancing. Finally, a relational approach should yield a realization that the transformation in concepts must ultimately be accompanied by a transformation in institutional practice. Only then can the conceptual work be given concrete meaning and effect, and only then can a long-cherished language of rights live up to the aspirations of its advocates.

The Misbegotten Monad

Anthropology, Human Rights, Belonging

Mark Goodale

IN AUGUST 2015, I conducted a series of ethnographic interviews with Efrén Choque Capuma, an elected magistrate on Bolivia's Plurinational Constitutional Tribunal (TCP). The TCP was an innovative new legal institution that had been created by Bolivia's 2009 Constitution as part of the wider process of radical transformation that had begun with the unprecedented 2005 election of Evo Morales and the ascendance to power of his Movement for Socialism (MAS) party. The TCP was neither a conventional court of last resort with appellate functions nor a simple "constitutional court" with a responsibility to ensure that government provisions complied with constitutional mandates. Rather, the TCP had been envisioned as an institution that would serve as a sort of juridical incubator in which the normative principles for the new plurinational state would be proposed, debated, refined, and ultimately implemented through legal and political policies.[1]

Among the group of TCP magistrates, a mix of lawyers, social activists, and political functionaries chosen directly by the people, Choque was an extraordinary figure. At the time, he was a fifty-nine-year-old former peasant who had grown up in an isolated corner of Oruro Department and eventually earned his law degree from one of the oldest law faculties in Latin America—that of Sucre's Universidad Mayor, Real y Pontificia de San Francisco Xavier de Chuquisaca, founded in 1624. His office at the TCP was decorated with an astonishing collection of cultural artifacts that expressed his pride in having traveled the path—like the president—from the windswept *altiplano* to the centers of power of what Nancy Postero has called an "indigenous state."[2]

During a more general discussion about the relationship between law and revolutionary change in Bolivia, I asked Choque specifically about the role of human rights. One of the more intriguing developments in the post-2009 period in Bolivia had been the extent to which the country's human rights institutions—most notably the Defensoría del Pueblo, Bolivia's national human rights institution, or NHRI—had been marginalized and even suppressed by the MAS government, despite the fact that the widespread diffusion of human rights discourse had played a significant role in the emergence of and support for Morales as a new type of political leader during the mid-2000s.[3] Choque's response was revealing:

> The fact is that human rights is the law of the elites, like the positive law more generally, as I've been saying. The problem with human rights is that they don't open spaces for generating intercultural justice [or law]. The other problem with human rights and positive law is that they treat indigenous people like objects, not subjects. But we are our own subjects of law and jurisprudence. It's better to build law from the bottom to the top, not from the top to the bottom, as it's always been.

For purposes of the current chapter (and the volume), two aspects of Choque's critique of human rights are salient. First, he points to an alternative epistemology, one in which the conceptual grounding of human rights is built "from the bottom to the top." Second, and even more apropos of the volume's concerns, Choque's critique of human rights centers precisely on the problem of subjectivity, yet in a double sense—who is the subject of human rights, and who gets to decide? For Choque, as with many organic intellectuals, particularly in the Global South at the "capillary ends," human rights promotion expresses itself as a particular form of global power.[4] In this sense, the answers to these questions—who is the subject of human rights, and who gets to decide?—come with practical consequences that can alternately circumscribe or empower people like Choque but which are nevertheless anything but abstract.

My chapter is inspired by Choque's critique of human rights and its dual call to interrogate the limitations of existing conceptions and to work collectively toward alternatives that are grounded in cultural and political context, historical contingency, and the possibility for a thoroughgoing cross-cultural hermeneutics informed by a critical anthropology of human rights.[5] To these ends, I begin the chapter by briefly describing its epistemological orientation in relation to the anthropological study of the practice of human rights. The chapter then turns to the question of human rights subjectivity and explores what I argue is a paradox—both conceptual and phenomenological—at the heart of postwar and post–Cold War human rights projects. To explain this paradox, I draw metaphorically—and somewhat playfully—on the curious category of the "monad" developed by the late-seventeenth-century, early-eighteenth-century polymath intellectual Gottfried Wilhelm Leibniz. As I suggest, the human rights subject at the center of dominant accounts of human rights—the kind that Choque would have us overcome—has, like Leibniz's monad, likewise suffered from the impossibility of encapsulating a closed and totalizing (normative) universe while at the same time reflecting the whole (human rights) system. The chapter then surveys work from the contemporary anthropology of human rights by way of gesturing toward—rather than formally developing—an alternative conception in which human rights subjectivity is no longer seen as centered in rights bearers (individual or collective) but rather in networks of relationships and the specific values that they embody. The chapter concludes with a brief section that provocatively reimagines human rights as a system of rights that does not center on a conception of the subject formulated in the abstract.

Paranormativity and the Practice of Human Rights

Before I examine a problematic paradox at the center of orthodox accounts of human rights—that is, those derived, even indirectly and after many decades, from the founding postwar instruments—something should be said about the epistemological orientation that informs the chapter. First, it is an approach to knowledge about human rights that is anchored in the practice of human rights. So what is meant by "the practice of human rights"?

In the introduction to our volume *The Practice of Human Rights* (2007), Sally Engle Merry and I defined it as "all the many ways in which social actors . . . talk about, advocate for, criticize, study, legally enact, [and] vernacularize . . . the idea of human rights in its different forms."[6] By "social actors," we meant "the different individuals, institutions, states, international agencies . . . without privileging any one type of human rights actor: the peasant intellectual in Bolivia who agitates on behalf of *derechos humanos* is analytically equal to the executive director of Human Rights Watch." And as we argued, this way of understanding the practice of human rights has implications for how the relationship between practice and theory is conceptualized:

> [N]on-elites—peasant intellectuals, village activists, government workers, rural politicians, neighborhood council members—[can act as] important human rights theorists, so that the idea of human rights is perhaps most con-

sequentially [being] shaped and conceptualized outside the centers of elite discourse, even if what can be understood as the organic philosophy of human rights is often mistakenly described as "practice" (i.e., in false opposition to "theory").[7]

Thirteen years on, this is still, with some modifications, how the practice of human rights would be understood from an anthropological perspective. Yet what was not clear at the time was how conventional this approach was when viewed within the longer history of human rights. Recent research on an important process undertaken by UNESCO in 1947 and 1948 that was intended to shape the form and content of what became the Universal Declaration of Human Rights (UDHR) reveals the extent to which leading political figures, intellectuals, theologians, labor activists, and social reformers, among others, argued for a cross-cultural and pluralistic approach to human rights in these early postwar years.[8] This plural vision was promoted as a critical alternative to the official process that was taking place at the heart of the UN system in the United States, a process that the first leaders of UNESCO believed to be overly political, exclusionary, and dominated by powerful national interests.

The second epistemological point is also an ethical one. In the same way as the UNESCO committee attempted to produce a statement of human rights principles that was pluralistic, reflective of global normative diversity, and sensitive to the soft power of international institutions, the approach here is likewise animated by a particular understanding of legitimacy. The argument is that normative assertions that aspire to cross-cultural and historical applicability must be derived from the everyday realities and diversity of what Webb Keane describes as "ethical life."[9] This is not to say that normative propositions and their critical alternatives must be derived empirically from big global data sets on questions about, for example, human rights universality, since this would be based on several false assumptions.[10] But it does militate against the adequacy—as understood anthropologically—of the kind of deductivism that has characterized much of the philosophy and legal theory of human rights, in which "practice" means simply—and only—textual reference to something other than the norm itself (e.g., reference to "the state" or "the law" or "all moral claims").

Finally, the approach to human rights knowledge behind this chapter is committed to the recognition of new forms of solidarity. By "new forms of solidarity," what I intend is an analytical orientation to the practice of human rights that is inspired by debates within anthropology around the relationship between scholar and research "subject." As a response to changes in these relationships, Douglas Holmes and George E. Marcus introduced the concept of "para-ethnography" in recognition of the fact that "our subjects are themselves engaged in intellectual labors that resemble approximately or are entirely indistinguishable from our own methodological practices."[11] This shift in the terms of anthropological research, according to Holmes and Marcus, demands that we treat our subjects as "epistemic partners who are not merely informing our research but who participate in shaping its theoretical agendas and its methodological exigencies."[12] They envision new "collaborative configurations" in which knowledge within domains such as science, engineering, law, finance, and medicine, among others, is produced through decentralized and collaborative exchanges that stand apart from the traditional boundaries that define and privilege authoritative knowledge.

As adapted to the practice of human rights, what might be called a "para-normative" approach would likewise suggest that the task be reimagined as one of developing "collaborative configurations" in which academic theorists, international lawyers, transnational activists, and so on collaborate with the diverse range of social actors for whom the "practice of human rights" is as much strategic as it is analytical and normative. To be clear, this is not, by extension, an argument against orthodox expertise as such; indeed, I think Holmes and Marcus are mistaken in their suggestion that a para-ethnographic approach to knowledge has general application. Conventional expertise plays a critical role in the way knowledge is produced in science and many other technical fields. But knowledge about the what, where, and who of human rights does not seem to me to be of the same type as, for example, knowledge of the properties of irregular geometric surfaces or the structure of DNA or the rate of human-induced climate change. On the contrary, human rights knowledge would appear to be deepened through the kinds of collaborative configurations that, to a certain extent, have been in place all along, as the anthropology of human rights demonstrates.

Of Permanent Living Reflections on a Windowless World

With these epistemological and ethical considerations in mind, let me turn to the problem of human rights subjectivity. What the anthropology of human rights reveals is that the actual diversity of normative practices that take shape in reference to human rights, practices that reflect a certain connotative power, do so against a particular account of the self that is inscribed in fundamental human rights instruments and their political extensions. I will call this a monadic conception of the self, in recognition of the fact that in both its conceptual contours and, more importantly, in the problematic way the human rights subject—as opposed to the subject of human rights—is meant to reflect the whole, it curiously resembles the unit of analysis that formed the basis for Leibniz's solution to the so-called mind-body problem, something that had occupied early modern thinkers such as René Descartes and Baruch Spinoza. The gesture to Leibniz's monadology here is purely metaphorical; I'm obviously not arguing that Leibniz's ontology shaped the conception of subjectivity behind the "human" of mid-twentieth-century human rights. Nevertheless, there is one key resemblance that merits examining, since it suffers from the same conceptual weakness, one that creates a structural tension between what might be thought of as the codified self and the actual self across the historical trajectory and pluralism of human rights practice.

This is the idea that the human rights subject is conceived as a normative-ontological being who embodies the entire normative system, without ontological overlap or necessary interconnection with other like subjects. That is, the monadic conception of human rights assumes both ontological autonomy and omneity. When Article 1 of the UDHR asserts that "all human beings are born free and equal in dignity and rights," it conjures a world of ontologically distinct (human) beings who encapsulate, in themselves, and without reference to others, the entire normative system that (deductively) follows. This monadic image of the human rights subject is not modified at all by what follows in Article 1, which is entirely supplementary and says nothing about the conception of the monadic human rights subject that precedes it—"They [human beings] . . . *should* act toward one another in a spirit of brotherhood." In other words, human rights subjects might or might not act toward one another in a spirit of brotherhood; in either case, the ontological status of the human rights subject remains independent and normatively complete.

Note that this formulation of the human rights subject does not depend on the type or kind of human right in question. With both civil and political, as well as social, economic, and cultural rights, the conception of self remains monadic; what does change is the nature of the intended conditions that follow. Whereas the *should* of civil and political human rights implies simply the absence of violative treatment, the *should* of social, economic, and cultural rights implies assemblages of (largely state) action and investment. Yet even in an imagined community in which networks of state institutions ensure the protection and flourishing of social, economic, and cultural rights, they do so in ways that leave untouched the ontological conception that grounds the individual human rights subject. This is what it means, among other things, to conceive of the human rights subject as a "bearer" of rights.

The essential point for my argument is that the unit at which the rights are believed to repose is imagined as a complete—and completed—normative universe, entire unto itself, without necessary relation to other self-contained normative embodiments. Like Leibniz's monads, human rights subjects are defined as normative beings whose relation to others is purely ancillary. For example, the first and last human being in the world was and will be a human rights bearer, and her normative status as such is not altered in the slightest by the fact that she was and will be the only one of her kind—however briefly. This is the essence of the monadic conception of the human rights subject that, I argue, forms the foundation of orthodox postwar accounts. As Leibniz puts it, in relation to his mysterious monads, "there is nothing which can be moved from one position to another, and it is impossible to conceive of any internal motion, which could be set up, redirected, increased, or diminished inside it. . . . Monads have no windows to let anything in or out by."

Yet the normative autonomy of the human rights subject forms only the first part of what I argue amounts to a paradox at the heart of the postwar human rights project. This paradox comes into full view only when the system as a whole is considered. If the human rights subject is conceived as a closed normative universe, entire unto herself, what is her relation to other human rights subjects? This was the same problem that occupied Leibniz, one that he fudged by proposing that monads came into being programmed with what he called "pre-established harmony." He unconvincingly used this conceit to explain the vague condition of "*interconnectedness*, or this accommodation of all created things to each, and of each to all the rest." Even more, this predisposition to coexist among windowless monads was the reason that, according to Leibniz, each monad was "a permanent living mirror of the universe."

Without having to make a detour into the complexities of early-eighteenth-century metaphysics, I believe that a similar paradoxical weakness affects the status of the human rights subject: despite being normatively sovereign and autopoietically closed, the human rights subject is nevertheless imagined as "endowed" with an intellectual and moral sensibility that predisposes her to a prevailing altruism towards others—that is, to be predisposed to "act toward one another in a spirit of brotherhood." Even more problematically, from this perspective, this unjustified altruism, which is imagined to pass from one human rights subject to the next, is then projected—again, in the UDHR—to culminate not as a "permanent living mirror of the universe" but as the "foundation of freedom, justice and peace in the world."

Since I am an anthropologist and not a political philosopher or an intellectual historian, it is beyond the scope of my interests and capabilities to trace the origins of this monadic conception of the human rights subject. What concerns me here is how this conception of the human rights subject creates an ever-present tension with the subject of human rights—that is, the normative subject(s) that emerges within the practice of human rights. In the next section, I ask what the anthropology of human rights has to say about this tension before considering what it might suggest about an alternative conception of human rights subjectivity, one interwoven into the fabric of actually existing, if highly diverse practices of "ordinary ethics."[13]

The Spirit of the Norm

By the end of the first decade after the Cold War, the discipline of anthropology had developed two distinct orientations to human rights. In the first, anthropologists had created a distinctive disciplinary network of human rights activism that was concerned with the promotion of "emancipatory cultural politics."[14] This network was heavily influenced by developments within the American Anthropological Association (AAA), which had promulgated a formal Declaration on Anthropology and Human Rights in 1999 in order to structure and give philosophical form to these interventions. The basic argument of the 1999 Declaration was that anthropologists had an ethical obligation to use their cultural knowledge and close relations with research interlocutors to advance a putative "human right to culture" as the basis for political and social mobilization by marginalized and vulnerable populations.[15]

In the second orientation, anthropologists had turned to human rights as an emergent domain of legal, political, and ethical practice, often in the course of conducting ethnographic research on other questions around international institutions, truth and reconciliation processes, social movements, and development regimes, among others.[16] The ethnography of human rights thus developed largely serendipitously, at least until the early 2000s, when the study of human rights became well established as a subspecialty within the wider anthropology of law and politics. It is to the ethnography of human rights, therefore, that I turn in order to draw out several lessons for a more general reconsideration of human rights subjectivity. To do so, I briefly survey three case studies: Shannon Speed's ethnography of the place of human rights during the Zapatista rebellion against the Mexican state; Joel Robbins's analysis of meanings of justice in Papua New Guinea; and my own recent study of rights subjectivity within Bolivia's "third revolution."[17]

In her study of the influence of human rights among the indigenous communities of Chiapas, Mexico, in the decade after the Zapatista uprising began in 1994, Speed documents what happened when human rights NGOs and hundreds of foreign activists flooded into Chiapas.[18] These human rights actors were drawn by their support for the claims of indigenous peasants who had suffered decades of persecution and neglect by the ruling Institutional Revolutionary Party, reports of atrocities committed against local activists by military and paramilitary forces, and the figure of the charismatic Zapatista spokesman and ideologist Subcomandante Marcos. As she describes this density of human rights activism in the region, by the late 1990s, "there were ten independent human rights organizations . . . , five national human rights NGOs, and at least nine international ones with a permanent or periodic presence in Chiapas."[19]

As Speed observes, Zapatista community leaders, both men and women, took inspiration from what they learned about human rights to develop a robust local human rights practice that was grounded in what Speed describes as an "organic reformulation."[20] This reformulation was one in which human rights subjectivity was derived from human rights practice; that is, for the Zapatistas, the subject of human rights crystallized only in the course of making claims on behalf of the community. As Speed explains, indigenous activists came to see human rights as a form of political action in defense of local interests against the domination of the Mexican state. According to the Zapatistas, human rights existed only "in their exercise" for productive ends on behalf of the community.[21] At the same time, the Zapatistas rejected the idea that human rights bearing could be equated with personhood, since local conceptions of belonging were shaped by what might be understood as an agentive social ontology, one in which identity was defined through both social inclusion and social action on behalf of the community.

In a second case study, a reflection on alternative conceptions of justice in Papua New Guinea, Robbins analyzes two legal spheres in which local understandings of rights subjectivity clashed—in different ways and to greater or lesser degrees—with those of both the Papuan state and international human rights institutions. The first are "village courts" in West Sepik Province, in which traditional dispute resolution processes take place under the careful watch of a state "district office." The second is the "compo girl" case, which became something of a cause célèbre among international human rights activists when the Papuan Supreme Court invalidated a forced marriage in compensation for a killing on the grounds that local justice practices "must give way to the dictates of . . . modern national laws."[22]

In observing dispute resolution processes in the West Sepik village courts, as well as the national and international debates over the competing normative values at stake in the compo girl case, Robbins derives three elements that fundamentally distinguish Papuan rights subjectivity from that associated with what I have described as the monadic human rights subject. The first is that the individual qua rights-bearing subject does not exist as such, at least traditionally, in Papua New Guinea. Rather, rights and duties, which are tightly bound, inhere in relationships that enmesh people in vast networks of multigenerational kinship relations, ancestor reverence, and marriage. As Robbins puts it, "creating, realizing . . . , and maintaining relationships is the thing Melanesians most value. . . . [Relationships] play a role equivalent to that played by the individual in Western societies (where people are expected to most want to create, realize, and maintain their individual selves)."[23]

Second, Melanesians do draw a distinction between that which is natural or innate to people and that which is not, but in doing so, they construct a very different account of normative subjectivity than the one expressed in orthodox human rights. What is considered innate for Melanesians, according to Robbins, is a person's position in a web of relations to which a person has obligations. In addition, personhood is also understood as the capacity to catalyze these existing relations in the form of new relationships through marriage, dispute resolution, and the care of the elderly so that subjectivity is defined by this dual human essence: a preexisting relationality, present from birth, and the latent potential to transform relationships over the course of a life. Robbins adapts Marilyn Strathern's formulation of this account of normative subjectivity to emphasize its radical non-individualism: "in Melanesia, persons are microcosms of relationships. . . . They are born as images or containers of the relationships that made them."[24]

Finally, Robbins's study of clashing conceptions of rights and normative belonging in Papua New Guinea shows how "rights of relationships" are expected to be nurtured through regular gift exchanges that are structured by reciprocal giving and receiving. Yet what is most important about what might be thought of as "normative reciprocity" is not the things themselves that are exchanged in a way that is meant to leave no one either better or worse off materially (for example, people engage in the daily exchange of food that they can easily produce themselves). Rather, as Marcel Mauss demonstrated in his iconic 1925 study of what he called "forms and functions of exchange in archaic societies," it is the way in which the performance of relationality through gift exchange involves the circulation of the "spirit" of things (called the "hau" in the Maori language).[25] The spirit is the moral and social imperative that is embodied in relationships and moves within a complicated series of exchanges that are never, in a sense, completed: one particular act of exchange both is compelled by what has come before and anticipates those to come.

The final sounding from the anthropology of human rights comes from my own recent study of the place of law within Bolivia's constitutional revolution.[26] As we have already seen, the question of human rights subjectivity is one that occupied the attention of key protagonists in what is known locally as *el proceso de cambio* ("the process of change"). Even more, the emphasis on legal pluralism both in the constitution and in the practice of the Plurinational Constitutional Tribunal (TCP) points to the possibility of many alternative conceptions of normative subjectivity coexisting at the same time. Here, however, I want to highlight yet another aspect of Bolivia's radical experiment in sociolegal alterity: the way in which rights and obligations are embedded in a wider *cosmovisión*, or worldview, in which social life is believed to reflect certain ontological truths about the universe itself. Frank Salomon described this understanding of interconnectedness in Andean cultures as a "unified biological-technological productivity [that] unfolds seamlessly from human-telluric bonds through matrimonial alliance outward to very wide regional alignments and toward cosmological forces."[27]

According to this vision, the normative subject is conceived in terms of nested complementary pairs, beginning with the married couple and radiating out to culminate in a cosmic structure that is itself composed of a complementary division between terrestrial and celestial space. There are two aspects of this broader understanding of rights and obligations—both of which are codified in the 2009 Bolivian Constitution—that bear most directly on a (re)consideration of human rights subjectivity. The first is that the ethical or good or socially valued life is lived in terms of a fundamental—that is, ontological—complementarity. This means that subjectivity itself is understood only through the realization of this multilayered, dyadic interconnectedness. The common phrase in Quechua that expresses this basic interdependence is "*Tukuy ima qhariwarmi*," or "Everything is man-woman" (in the English translation, the absence of the conjunction "and" is the key to this phrase).

The second is the way in which the system of "normative complementarity" (to add to that of "normative reciprocity" above) in Bolivia does not privilege the human subject at all; indeed, human beings as such are merely important actors within a broader holistic ontology that differs radically from the one that Philippe Descola described as "naturalism." This is the ontology (out of four types) that has marked the West since antiquity, in which a rigid distinction is made between "nature" and "culture," a distinction that treats human beings as unique among all other living and non-living things.[28] On the contrary, at the center of Bolivia's "indigenous state" is a conception of being in which a vital life force, which has its source in the Pachamama (very loosely translated as "Mother Earth"), is nourished in perpetuity through an endless series of cosmic cycles marked by millenary renewals called *Pachakuti* (the revolutionary government of Evo Morales identifies itself as a marker of the most recent Pachakuti).

So to return to the question of human rights subjectivity: What do these illustrative case studies from the anthropology of human rights reveal about the possibility for radically non-monadic conceptions of human rights, those that would overcome what I have described as a paradoxical weakness at the heart of the postwar human rights project? Before describing what I see as three main implications, it is important to underscore the fact that alternatives to the orthodox conception of human rights have actually flourished within the practice of human rights, as we have seen. Indeed, it has been the contrasts between human rights theory (often expressed through human rights law) and human rights practice—understood ethnographically—that have provided the basis for imagining what might lie beyond.

Yet rather than thinking of alternatives to dominant conceptions of human rights as a form of opposition or resistance, what interests me here is what it would mean to synthesize elements of these actually living normativities and fold them back into the center within the context of a foundational reformulation. In a sense, the revisionary project I have in mind is similar to the one undertaken by UNESCO in 1947 and 1948, which reminds us that

> human rights comparison and distinction, and not the identification of a common denominator . . . , were at the core of the resulting examination of the po-

tential grounds of an international declaration of human rights. Re-discovering such a differentiated and culturally sensitive philosophical discussion of human rights allows us to hope for reinvigorated debate around pluralistic interpretations in international human rights law after a long interruption.[29]

Thus, in moving beyond the monadic conception of human rights, a conception centered—as I have argued—on a particular and problematic account of human rights subjectivity, three implications drawn from the anthropology of human rights appear most significant.

First, as the study of "organic reformulation" in Mexico during the Zapatista rebellion showed, human rights can be conceived not as an innate characteristic, coextensive with personhood (itself a contested and variable concept), but as a description of a particular form of sociopolitical agency. For the Zapatistas, this meant collective action on behalf of the community against the Mexican state in the name of traditional cultural values. But, though important, the basis on which an agentive account of human rights is constructed seems to me less relevant than the fact that the locus of normativity is displaced from the individual qua rights bearer to what might be thought of as efficacious social and moral practice.

A second piste that points toward a synthetic reformulation of human rights subjectivity is one in which the subject of human rights is conceived in terms of relational interdependence, an alternative that has been fruitfully explored by other scholars.[30] As we saw through the ethnography of law and relational practices in Melanesia, local understandings of "natural rights" run contrary to those that ground orthodox accounts of human rights: instead of the natural rights of individuals versus the social and political constructions that emerge in relation to the "rights of man," Melanesians see individuals as social constructs who emerge and are transfigured in relation to the "rights of relationships." A reformulation of human rights subjectivity that takes account of an inversion of this type would go well beyond even the most expansive versions of socioeconomic rights, since it would require a reconsideration of the meaning and grounds of society itself.

But it is the final implication from the anthropology of human rights that, it seems to me, suggests the most far-reaching challenge to orthodox accounts of human rights subjectivity, a challenge so fundamental that it calls into question the normative category of "human rights" as such. This is an alternative that would require a fundamental repositioning of what the UDHR describes as "all members of the human family," a normative decentering through which the rights, obligations, and interests of human beings—whether as individuals or within collectivities—are subsumed within a broader, indeed universal vision of ontological interdependence.

As the ethnography of Bolivia's revolution by constitution reveals, the country is in the midst of a profound—if contested—experiment in what Arturo Escobar has called "postliberal" subject-making.[31] Although the normative alterity of the process of change in Bolivia is most often associated with the new plurinational legal and political order, it is grounded in a more fundamental reorientation that is meant to reflect an underlying cosmovisión in which collective belonging is understood ecologically. Perhaps the best empirical study of the kind of social formations that emerge in relation to this type of ecological belonging is Eduardo Kohn's 2013 *How Forests Think*, a granular reflection on what it means to conceive of sociality itself "beyond the human."[32] Among other things, a regime of (human) rights based in ecological interconnectedness—which can be seen as the opposite of monadic autonomy—implies a kind of antipodean system in which most of the key elements are reversed or inverted: the parts are the sum of the whole; duties give rise to rights; the (human rights) subject is not a person but persons in relation; and juridical identity is embedded in actions rather than individuals.[33]

Conclusion: Rights Without Humans

To conclude, let me summarize the main arguments of the chapter by way of making several additional points that go beyond the question of human rights subjectivity. First, I argued that orthodox accounts of human rights—that is, those codified in the major postwar instruments and their political expressions —are shaped by a paradox that revolves around a particular conception of human rights subjectivity. Evoking Leibniz's monadology, I described the way in which the conventional human rights–bearing subject is imagined as a closed normative universe. Yet at the same time, echoing a similar weakness at the center of Leibniz's metaphysics, the enclosed and "windowless" human rights–bearing subject is nevertheless imagined to be a mirror of the whole, to which she relates through a mystical "pre-established harmony." I then suggested that this conceptual dilemma played out within the practice of human rights as a kind of ever-present disjuncture with actually existing normativities in relation to which the project of human rights rose and fell in the post–Cold War and beyond.

I then moved to consider these normativities as revealed by several illustrative case studies drawn from the contemporary anthropology of human rights. After surveying what was most pertinent from each study, I synthe-sized these findings as a gesture toward possible, if admittedly radical, re-formulations of human rights (which necessarily implicate its subjects). The broader outlines of such possible—if improbable—recastings pointed toward a normative regime (or, better, regimes) grounded in values and ontologies that differ substantially from those that underlie orthodox accounts.

Yet beyond this recapitulation, two further points must be made: the first regarding the geopolitical and political economic context against which any effort at reformulating human rights must take place, the second regarding the need to move beyond what I have called elsewhere the "myth of universal-ity."[34] It is not a coincidence that much of the anthropological research on the post–Cold War expansion of human rights took place in postcolonial coun-tries that had earlier been the sites of the postwar development project.[35] Hu-man rights promotion, like the massive wave of technology transfers during the Green Revolution, took place within a wider consolidation of political, economic, and military power in which the normative technologies of "glob-alization" (a term used not analytically but historically) were bundled with those of democratic institution building and neoliberal capitalism as part of a global realignment after the end of the Cold War.

At the same time, existing and emerging global powers like the United States, China, and Russia resisted human rights promotion at home while either strategically encouraging it abroad or, like China, actively working against human rights institutions within international bodies.[36] At home, these global powers rejected human rights as a violation of national cultural sovereignty and pursued national and regional policies that involved mani-fest and even gross violations of human rights. Even humanitarian Denmark could not escape from its problematic relationship with human rights advo-cacy. As Julie Mertus has argued, Danes vigorously supported the develop-ment of human rights institutions in the Global South while resisting the ap-plication of a human rights litmus test within national politics.[37] The reason? According to Mertus, many Danes believed that human rights should be pro-moted for countries whose political and legal systems were wracked by cor-ruption, violence, and chronic mismanagement. At the same time, human rights were considered inappropriate for Denmark itself, which had devel-oped over the centuries a particular Danish culture of "extreme egalitarian-ism" and collective sacrifice—embodied in the Danish concept of *Janteloven*, in which the idea of the (monadic) individual rights bearer pursuing her normative self-interest was anathema.[38] It is thus against this problematic background—one that has arguably only become darker for human rights—that the collective effort to rethink human rights subjectivity must stake its claims.

Finally, this chapter suggests that in the struggle to rescue human rights from the trials and tribulations of its "end times," we must reconsider very basic impulses that have generally pushed in the direction of a cosmopolitanism grounded in a "myth of universality." This is the idea that universality was a basic precondition for building a postwar world of "freedom, justice and peace," as the Preamble to the UDHR describes it. By calling this idea a myth, I don't mean to suggest that it is a false story; instead, I conceive of the myth of universality as a key cultural narrative that did particular kinds of work in the postwar period.[39]

Nevertheless, as I have also argued elsewhere, there were hidden dangers to the rising importance—and roughly ten-year post–Cold War hegemony—of this myth. In short, when universal categories like "inherent dignity," "equal and inalienable rights of all members of the human family," and even "all human beings" were put into practice, they quickly withered in the face of often brutal particularities—nationalism, racism, cultural identitarianism, religious fanaticism, and so on.[40]

At the same time, the normative wispiness of human rights universality was no match for the geological depth of global inequality, which continued to grow at the same time as the "age of human rights"—now revealed as a kind of global Potemkin village—was announced with such assuredness and ardor.[41] Thus, there are good reasons to also rethink the meaning and implications of normative universality itself, or, more provocatively, to conceive of "rights"—understood in terms of the full range of anthropological complexity examined in this chapter—without "humans."

CHAPTER 3

"Are Women Animals?"

The Rise and Rise of (Animal) Rights

Joanna Bourke

IN 1999, lawyer and feminist activist Catharine MacKinnon published an essay entitled "Are Women Human?" In it, she cataloged the indignities that women all over the world endure. She sounded exasperated. The twenty-first century was dawning, but women were still set outside the realm of the "fully human." Echoing Richard Rorty, MacKinnon observed that being a woman was "not yet a name for a way of being human."[1] "If women were human," she maintained, "would we have so little voice in public deliberations and in government in the countries where we live?" The Universal Declaration of Human Rights failed to acknowledge "the ways women distinctly are deprived of human rights as a deprivation of humanity." She continued that if "the glorious dream of the Universal Declaration" were to be achieved—that is, if human rights were "to be universal"—then "both the reality it challenges and the standards it sets need to change." When, she asked, "will women be human? When?"[2]

MacKinnon's protest against the masculine design and implementation of "human rights" had been heard before. Earlier that decade, international law scholar Hilary Charlesworth had made a similar plea, and activist Charlotte Bunch encouraged people to ask why "so many degrading life experiences of women" are "not understood as human rights issues."[3]

First-wave feminists had also asked whether women were fully human. More than 120 years before MacKinnon, Charlesworth, and Bunch critiqued the male bias embedded in "human rights," another feminist, signing herself "An Earnest Englishwoman," made a similar argument. In an impassioned letter to the editor of the conservative newspaper *The Times* on April 16, 1872, the Earnest Englishwoman expressed frustration that a parliamentary bill that would allow women to vote in elections had failed. Members of Parliament had refused to concede that legislation that referred to "mankind" applied to both male and female human beings. Parliament had voted to exclude women from the social and political rights assigned to "mankind."

However, the Earnest Englishwoman went well beyond this observation. She also noticed that women were not even fully animal. After all, she fumed, *non-human* animals had more rights under law than women did. She conceded that "whether women are the equals of men has been endlessly debated," adding that for many men it was a "moot point" whether women even possessed souls. But, she pleaded, "can it be too much to ask [for] a definitive acknowledgement that they are at least animals?"

Why was this important? The Earnest Englishwoman had observed that in terms of social entitlements and legal justice, non-human animals were better off than women. The Society for the Prevention of Cruelty to Animals had been founded as early as 1823, and enforceable legislation protecting animals from cruelty had been on the statute books for decades. In court, people who abused non-human animals were treated significantly more harshly than men who attacked women, especially if those women happened to be their wives or daughters. Instead of decreeing that laws referring to "mankind" include female as well as male members of the human species, the Earnest Englishwoman had another idea. Who could object to the suggestion that "whenever the word 'animal' occurs [in legislation] it shall be held to include women?" If women were allowed to become animal in law, then their status and well-being would improve. They would at least be protected from acts of cruelty. The Earnest Englishwoman urged parliamentarians to introduce "at least an equal interdict on wanton barbarity to cat, dog, or woman (even if the latter should happen to be the wife of a barbarian)."[4] Instead of asking, as did MacKinnon, whether women were human, the Earnest Englishwoman titled her plea "Are Women Animals?" In other words, attaining the legal status of animals would be a step toward the humanization of women.

In this chapter, I will compare and contrast the two different approaches to human and non-human animal rights as represented by MacKinnon and the Earnest Englishwoman. Debates about rights have always involved questions of the subject, including hierarchies of sentience, rationality, and autonomy. Human rights have always been less than universal. At various times, slaves, women, religious minorities, and actors (on the grounds that they pretended to be someone else) were set outside of the "rights of man." In the words of Jacques Derrida, paying attention to the full community of sentient beings "poses grave definitional and practical threats to the discourse of humanism," which attributes "authority and autonomy . . . to the man . . . rather than to the woman, and to the woman rather than to the animal."[5] As we shall see, when rights-speak has included non-human animals, it has been similarly concerned with delineating degrees of sameness, thus radically diminishing the worlds of an "infinite number of animal societies."[6] In the end, both MacKinnon and the Earnest Englishwoman remain welded to a discourse of liberal humanism. In contrast, Derrida's more radical vision is better placed to deconstruct the full range of hierarchies and subjections that make us both human and animal.

It is no coincidence that MacKinnon wanted women to be admitted to the fellowship of human rights, while the Earnest Englishwoman quipped that kinship with animals would suffice (at least for the time being). MacKinnon was writing in the middle of the "rise and rise" of human rights. As international legal scholar Kirsten Sellars observes, human rights "have become the *lingua franca* of modern political discourse. . . . Nothing else offered the positive moral appeal of human rights."[7] As was demonstrated during the war in Yugoslavia, human rights seemed to be an unassailable international creed: it was the dominant language of the International Criminal Tribunal for the former Yugoslavia (ICTY). Indeed, only a couple of years after MacKinnon's plea, the rape of women was recognized, for the first time, as a crime against *humanity*, as opposed to a crime against honor or family, by both the Statute of the ICTY and the Statute of the International Criminal Tribunal for Rwanda.

In contrast, the Earnest Englishwoman was immersed in a society dominated by the "rise and rise" of (non-human) animal rights. At the time she was writing, feminists and other social reformers in the United States, Britain, and much of Europe were engaged in furious debates about both the rights of non-human animals to be spared suffering and the rights of women to participate fully in social and political life. Like many feminists at that time, the Earnest Englishwoman recognized the link between the rights of female humans and those of non-human animals of both sexes.

Again, this was not new. For centuries, women had been key to debates about the human/animal divide. Prior to the seventeenth century, animals had been assumed to possess intentionality. They could even be tried in criminal courts for committing crimes. Enlightenment philosopher and natural scientist René Descartes, however, decisively challenged such beliefs, relegating non-human animals to the position of biological machines, driven by instinct rather than cognition. Descartes insisted that animals were mere "automa," or moving machines. For Descartes, animals' screams of pain were simply mechanical responses that functioned as a form of moral edification for *humans*.[8] He effectively sheared apart ideas about the mind from those of the body.

Women were his foremost critics. Most notably, Margaret Cavendish (the Duchess of Newcastle, 1623–1673) corresponded with Descartes, challenging his *Treatise on Animals*. In *Observations upon Experimental Philosophy*, Cavendish refused to accept that non-human animals were machines composed of "dead" atoms. In her words, the "particular parts and actions in an animal body" could be compared with

> workmen employed in the building of a house . . . [who] do all the work and labor to one and the same end, that is, the building of the house. . . . Every one may have some inspection and perception of what his neighbour doth; yet each having his peculiar task and employment, has also its proper and peculiar knowledge how to perform his own work: for, a joiner knows best how to finish and perfect what he has to do; and so does a mason, carpenter, tiler, glazier, stone-cutter, smith, etc.[9]

In other words, Cavendish ascribed agency to every aspect of creation, each part of which animates the whole. Animals, like humans, possess a "peculiar knowledge," not simply a machine-like mechanism. Cavendish was also one of the first to expound a theory of animal rights. She acknowledged that because animals were capable of feeling pain, they should not be treated cruelly.

By the 1790s, the sentience of non-human animals—and, therefore, the responsibility of humans to not deliberately harm them—was increasingly being extrapolated to women. In 1792, Mary Wollstonecraft published *A Vindication of the Rights of Woman*, a protest against men who treated women "as a kind of subordinate beings, and not as a part of the human species."[10] Wollstonecraft insisted that women were entitled to rights on the same grounds as men: that is, social rights would promote morality and virtue, enhance familial ties, and promote the greatest happiness. Wollstonecraft drew on analogies and metaphors based on non-human creatures. She railed against a society that left women "confined . . . in cages like the feathered race" with "nothing to do but to plume themselves, and stalk with mock majesty from perch to perch."[11] "Servitude," she insisted, "not only debases the individual, but its effects seem to be transmitted to posterity."[12] In other words, women had been treated as inferior beings for so many centuries that habits of debasement had become part of their inherited "nature." "Is it surprising," she asked, "that some of them hug their chains, and fawn like the spaniel?"[13] By being denied the rights given to "mankind," women were nothing less than debased animals.

None of these philosophers used the phrase "rights of animals." In the English language, that term was first used in 1796 by political and agricultural writer John Lawrence. In *A Philosophical and Practical Treatise on Horses and on the Moral Duties of Man Towards the Brute Creation*, Lawrence observed that

> It has even been, and still is the invariable custom of the bulk of mankind . . .
> to look upon brutes as mere machines; animated but without souls; endowed
> with feelings, but utterly devoid of rights; and placed without the pale of jus-
> tice. . . . Yet it is easy to prove, by analogies drawn from our own, that they also
> have souls; and [it is] perfectly consistent with reason to infer a graduation of
> intellect, from the spark which animates the most minute mortal exiguity up
> to the sum of infinite intelligence.[14]

He concluded that "life, intelligence, and feeling, necessarily imply rights"— and those were the "rights of animals."[15]

Cambridge don Thomas Young was equally influential. In *An Essay on Humanity to Animals*, published two years after Lawrence's book, Young asserted that the rights of animals were "the same cast of argument as that on which Moralists found the Rights of Mankind." He appealed to scriptural prohibitions against deliberately harming animals as well as the argument that people who were cruel to animals would act with similar brutality toward humans. However, Young's chief reason for giving rights to non-human animals was because they were "endowed with a capacity of perceiving pleasure and pain." As a result, "we must conclude that the Creator wills the happiness of these his creatures."[16]

In other words, for Lawrence and Young, it was *sentience* that gave animals rights not to be treated cruelly. This argument is usually ascribed to utilitarian philosopher Jeremy Bentham. In *An Introduction to the Principles of Morals and Legislation* (1789), Bentham often observes that the important ethical question was not whether a creature could reason or talk but whether they could *suffer*.[17] However, unlike Lawrence and Young, this did not lead Bentham to argue that animals had rights: indeed, he was a fervent opponent of natural rights for humans, let alone animals. As he expressed it in "Anarchical Fallacies; Being an Examination of the Declaration of Rights Issued during the French Revolution" (1843), the men who issued the French Declaration were sowing "seeds of anarchy." Their Declaration was nothing more than "Shallow and reckless vanity! . . . a perpetual vein of nonsense, flowing from a perpetual abuse of words . . . execrable trash . . . nonsense upon stilts." Bentham ridiculed the idea that rights belonged to "all human creatures." Rights for women and children were also nothing more than "smack-smooth equality, which rolls so glibly out of the lips of the rhetorician."[18]

Despite Bentham's own repudiation of rights, his arguments about the importance of "feeling" became central planks in debates about the rights of both animals and women. The Earnest Englishwoman's protest had arisen directly out of her observation that judges gave significantly higher prison sentences for men accused of cruelty to animals or other men than those who tortured or even killed women. Clearly, she reflected, women were not fully "persons" in the eyes of the law.[19] The Earnest Englishwoman asked her readers to remember that it must cause "acute agony" for any "living creature, endowed with nerves and muscles, to be blinded or crushed to death." Being "such a creature, is not woman entitled to a fair amount of that protection accorded by law to other *domestic feræ* subject to man," she reasoned?[20] Women were "living creatures," like other animals: should they not be given the same consideration and protection as other animals?

Other first-wave feminists routinely linked the rights of women, slaves, and animals (that is, sexism, racism, and speciesism); this was, they concluded, the logic of domination.[21] For example, in an article entitled "Cruelty to Animals: Also to Wives and Children," published on August 3, 1867, one author observed that it "would not be amiss to suggest" that the Society for the Prevention of Cruelty to Animals "should extend the sphere of its labors so as to include a few classes of ill-used bipeds." This included children and "poor sewing girls who are swindled out of their hard earnings by soulless employers; broken-spirited wives who are habitually cuffed and kicked by drunken husbands, and the like." She lamented that "nobody interferes to prevent such cruelties as these" and, with only a few exceptions, "they are perpetrated with entire impunity."[22] A woman writing in *The Women's Penny Paper* in 1890 was equally direct. The vivisection of animals was intimately related to the "welfare of women," she observed. The "recognition of women's rights implies the recognition of animals' rights, for both proclaim a higher law than 'Might is right'; both appeal to the human, and not to the brute instincts in man."[23] The *Animals' Guardian*, an important journal dedicated to the rights of animals, frequently made connections between the demands made by feminists and those made on behalf of animals. The editors routinely criticized feminists for being insufficiently sensitive to the jointed fates of women and animals. In 1912, an article in that paper criticized suffragists for being "dressed up in the furs of charming and innocent little creatures, many of which had been obtained at the expense of agony and terror." Surely, the author contended, "in anticipation of the time when women shall get her rights at the hands of man," they should meanwhile ensure that "animals always get their rights at her hands."[24] These were sentiments that the Earnest Englishwoman would have recognized.

These texts have significant blind spots, however. First, it is important to observe that feminist arguments that women should be given rights because they were sentient creatures were not typically used to argue for the rights of *men*. While connections between sentience and rights were commonly made in defense of women's rights, they were rarely appealed to in debates about male suffrage.[25] Much more commonly, widening male suffrage was argued for in terms of a Lockean concept of rights as personal freedom, equality, and autonomy, rather than shared sentience with the non-human animal kingdoms. The contrasting arguments reflected fundamentally different ideas about gender and politics. In other words, human women *were* conceived of as more truly "animal" than human men.

Second, when comparisons are being made to "animals," these commentators were not meaning all non-human animals. As in the 1912 letter to *The Animals' Guardian*, quoted earlier, the concept "animals" referred only to those who were "charming and innocent." They were generally mammals and birds: in other words, domesticated creatures or readily recognizable and attractive ones. As Derrida has pointed out, there are an "infinite number of animal societies,"[26] only some of whom are regarded as truly sentient and therefore deserving of the right not to be harmed. Others could be casually abused, even killed for food.

Third, the *human* animals these feminists were referring to were not all humans: they were also only domesticated and recognizable ones. The 1870

Suffrage Bill that so incensed the Earnest Englishwoman when it was rejected by the parliamentarians was never intended to enfranchise all women, only propertied ones. In other words, most first-wave feminists were not arguing for the rights of women, only for the rights of those who belonged to a particular social class. Thus, the suffragists quoted in an important 1870 tract entitled *Opinions of Women on Women's Suffrage* discriminated between different types of women. In a typical example, suffragist, abolitionist, and poet Dora Greenwell argued that (some) women should be allowed to vote because they were propertied. This raised them above the non-human animal population who "hoard, but can scarcely be said to *own* property." In her words, "the possession of property is, like speech, or like prayer, one of the grand distinctions between rational and merely animal life."[27] According to this view, Christianity (the belief in the efficacy of prayer) as well as the ownership of property constituted the true human. Indeed, the wishes of these feminists came true: in 1918, when the Earnest Englishwoman's longed-for suffrage bill was finally passed in the United Kingdom, it enfranchised only women over the age of thirty years who also owned property.

A final, and related, point is that not all male humans were seen as deserving of rights either. In a speech to the Humanitarian League in the mid-1890s, activist vegetarian Josiah Oldfield began by observing that there was "no essential distinction between pain felt by a human and non-human." Nevertheless, he contended that "men inured to rough life and exposure" and "races like the Red Indians" were not sensitive to pain. In contrast to such men, "some animals are acutely sensitive" to pain and suffer much more than "many a navvy."[28] He believed that these particularly sensitive non-human animals had a far greater right to be protected from cruelty than lower classes of humans.

Indeed, prior to 1918, a large proportion of adult men lacked political rights. Many suffragists argued against certain men becoming enfranchised. They saw no reason why men who were unemployed, working-class, or drunkards should be given rights. They argued that it was a disgrace that "Englishwomen of education, culture and refinement were to wait until ignorant and besotted [that is, intoxicated] men who had been behind the plough for ages were enfranchised."[29] This was what the feminist and social purity campaigner J. Ellice Hopkins meant when she noted that men of the "lower orders" could not claim to be superior to animals. In one of her books, entitled *Is It Natural?* (1885), Hopkins admitted that she was disgusted by the "bestial behavior" of working-class men. She was "extremely annoyed" to hear them begging for "two-pence for a pot of beer. . . . Just like . . . a pig beginning to grunt for his wash the moment you approach his sty!" Indeed, she continued, it was unfair to *pigs* that a man who "gets drunk or sins against his own manhood" is said to be making "a beast of himself." After all, she insisted, a pig did not "go home and knock about his sow."[30] Hopkins's respect for the rights of animals gave her a language with which to express revulsion against certain humans—that is, working men who displayed all the traits that set them apart from both the fully human *and* the animal.

In more recent decades, arguments about the rights of animals have also set some humans in a lower position vis-à-vis rights than certain non-human animals. Peter Singer, the most prominent contemporary utilitarian, contends that the life of a newborn baby possesses less value than that of a pig, a dog, or a chimpanzee. He proposes that "a breathing space of 28 days should be allowed after birth, in which parents and doctors together should have discretion to make life and death decisions about a newborn child."[31] It is a point of view endorsed by philosopher Michael Tooley, who asks "what properties a thing must possess in order to have a serious right to live." His conclusion was that while some "adult animals belonging to species other than *Homo sapiens*" might possess a "serious" right to life, infants lacked the self-consciousness to have a similar right.[32] The severely mentally or physically impaired have also been set outside the fully human.

This assertion that some non-human animals are superior to some humans and should therefore have greater rights has also been argued by Steven M. Wise, the author of *Rattling the Cage: Toward Legal Rights for Animals* (2000) and *Unlocking the Cage: Science and the Case for Animal Rights* (2002) and a vocal legal proponent for the personhood of animals. He points out that some non-human animals function at a higher level than many children. Many are self-conscious, capable of using tools, and able to clearly experience and express emotions. Wise proposes that animals should be categorized in terms of such abilities. Category One animals, such as chimpanzees, bonobos, orangutans, gorillas, and dolphins, possess practical autonomy. They are self-conscious and able to plan ahead, and some may even be capable of learning human languages (such as sign language). Therefore, these animals are "entitled to the basic liberty rights of bodily integrity and bodily liberty." Categories Two and Three, such as cats and dogs, have progressively fewer abilities and fewer rights. By the time Wise reaches Category Four animals, such as insects, he lists those who lack autonomy and are therefore not entitled to rights.[33]

Of all non-human animals, the great apes have typically been thought to possess the highest claim to rights. In 1993, Paola Cavalieri and Singer drafted "A Declaration on Great Apes." The essay proposed that chimpanzees, orangutans, and gorillas be welcomed into the "community of equals," which meant that these animals would be entitled to certain basic rights, including an entitlement to life, the protection of their individual liberty, and the right not to be tortured.[34] The implication that "poor and oppressed" humans might be of "less moral significance" than chimpanzees, orangutans, and gorillas has exasperated many subjugated peoples throughout the world. Cavalieri and Singer did insist that they "have not forgotten that we live in a world in which, for at least three-quarters of the human population, the idea of human rights is no more than rhetoric, and not a reality in everyday life." Nevertheless,

> The denial of the basic rights of particular other species will not . . . assist the world's poor and oppressed to win their just struggles. Nor is it reasonable to ask that the members of these other species should wait until all humans have achieved their rights first. That suggestion itself assumes that beings belonging to other species are of lesser moral significance than human beings.[35]

However, for first-wave feminists such as the Earnest Englishwoman, tying together the rights of women with those of non-human animals (of both sexes) backfired. Those opposed to women's rights routinely justified their position on the grounds that women were closer to animals than they were to men and therefore were not fully human. In 1871, a writer in *The Sporting Times* dismissed feminists as women who spent their time "chattering, like female baboons, on the rights of women, and all that sort of thing."[36] The link between women and animals also backfired for animals. Opposition to animal rights was routinely dismissed on the grounds that animal advocates were sentimental, perhaps even deranged, women. In 1883, for example, physiologist Élie de Cyon taunted readers to "show among the leaders of the [anti-vivisectionist] agitation one young girl, beautiful, and beloved, or one young wife who has found in her home the full satisfaction of her affections!" He believed that animal advocates were "old maids whose tenderness, despised by man, has flung itself in despair at the feet of cats and parrots." They were "old maids" vulnerable to "fantastic charity" of animal welfare.[37] In 1910, socialist surgeon James Peter Warbasse even coined a medical term for such women: they were suffering from a neurological disease called "zoophilic psychosis," which consisted of "an inordinate and exaggerated sympathy for the lower animals often associated with delusions that they are persecuted by man."[38]

So far in this essay, I have been focusing on the Earnest Englishwoman's 1872 question "Are women animals?" She intended the answer to be yes. The year before, Charles Darwin had published *The Descent of Man*, but the Earnest Englishwoman was not reflecting on the evolutionary history of humanity. Instead, she was protesting against the fact that women were not being treated as fully human. At the beginning of the twenty-first century, a similar strategy was used by certain radical American lawyers casting a dispassionate eye over the Endangered Species Act, which had been passed in 1973. They argued that African American men would benefit from being labeled "endangered animals." After all, the homicide rate for African American males is 21 times higher than it is for white females. According to Joseph Lubinski, writing in the *Journal of Law in Society* in 2002, "While characterizing humans as animals traditionally was meant to degrade racial minorities, animal advocates now attempt to use the same analogy for the benefit of those they seek to protect. The hope is that by giving animals human characteristics and relating their experience to that of people, public sympathy can be aroused and their movement bestowed popular legitimacy."[39] There are many problems with conceptions of rights based on issues of similarities to either (other) animals or to "normal," adult male humans. As we have seen, the claims of first-wave feminists such as the Earnest Englishwoman that women experienced pain and suffering, like non-human animals, and therefore should have at least the same protections against being treated cruelly, were not necessarily productive.

Furthermore, arguments based on non-human animals' "sameness" to certain humans leave an infinite number of animal societies without protection. By admitting apes (for example) into a category of "higher species," they leave other animals vulnerable. In the words of legal scholar Taimie L. Bryant, "even if some animals gain entrance to the exalted community of those with moral standing, the result will be simply the entitlement of these animals, through their human representatives, to participate in the oppression of other animal species that have not yet gained entrance to the moral community."[40] More importantly, delineations based on "sameness" are inherently speciesist: they judge non-human animals according to human capacities and values. As Wise explicitly states, rights can be given to animals according to the degree to which "the behaviour of any nonhuman resembles ours."[41] Admitting a few animal species to personhood would simply cement the view that places humans in an exalted category, above all other members of the animal community. As Bryant states, it does not challenge "the presumption that humans are morally entitled to do whatever they please."[42]

This is what concerns many radical philosophers. Donna Haraway, for instance, observes that the "last thing" animals need "is human subject status. . . . The best animals could get out of that approach is the 'right' to be permanently represented, as lesser humans, in human discourse, such as the law — animals would get the right to be permanently 'orientalised.'"[43] Rosi Braidotti also worries about the tendency of animal rights advocates to appeal to liberal ideals that have been shown to be damaging. She makes an argument for moving "beyond anthropocentrism altogether," instead of merely extending liberal humanism "to the formerly exploited others." She also questions the assumption that the "humanization of animals" can simply be imposed on them by humans.[44]

The other question, though, is, are animal rights good for animals? Rights as law are inherently violent, involving categories of exclusion as well as inclusion and always failing to live up to their own impossible claims of justice. Rights "can work for justice or for injustice," observed Simone Weil: they are "a kind of moral noncommitment to the good."[45] They are also inherently anthropocentric – indeed, *andro*centric, reflecting MacKinnon's argument that women are not yet human.

The chief problem with conferring rights to non-human animals according to "sameness," then, is a fundamental one for post-humanists: it merely shores up a specific notion of "the human." This is exactly the point that Derrida makes in his critique of Cavalieri and Singer's "A Declaration on Great Apes." He argued that it is "a fault or a weakness" to extend to animals a "certain concept of the juridical, that of human rights." The proponents of "A Declaration on Great Apes" seek to reaffirm the particular "concept of the human subject, of post-Cartesian human subjectivity," that is "at the foundation of the concept of human rights." Such a position is "naïve." Derrida goes on to clarify his position by pointing out that

> To confer or to recognize rights for "animals" is a surreptitious or implicit way
> of confirming a certain interpretation of the human subject, which itself will
> have been the very lever of the worst violence carried out against nonhuman

living beings. . . . Consequently, to want absolutely to grant, not to animals but to a certain category of animals, rights equivalent to human rights would be a disastrous contradiction. It would reproduce the philosophical and juridical machine thanks to which the exploitation of animal material for food, work, experimentation, etc., has been practiced (and tyrannically so, that is, through an abuse of power).[46]

Granting rights to a certain category of animals will simply reinforce the human/animal distinction: it will solidify a particular conception of what it means to be human. In fact, it reifies the distinction between animals and humans. Furthermore, since the project can implicitly *exclude* certain humans from rights—the neurologically impaired, for instance—it (in Derrida's words) "amounts to reintroducing, in effect, a properly racial and 'geneticist' hierarchy."[47] This is the strongest reason for being wary of animal rights: it is modern humanist politics for a world that has already gone post-human.

We might also ask whether "human rights" are, in fact, good for humans. There is no question that oppressed peoples throughout the world have used the language of "rights" in their struggles against oppression. The "rise and rise" of rights speech has meant that it is one of the few languages that is heard and respected in international forums.

There is also little question that it has failed to live up to its promise.[48] Oppressive regimes have flourished; "human rights" are one of the justifications for wars declared by Western nations. As we have already seen, it shores up a notion of who is fully human, which is used in destructive ways to classify some humans as "beyond the pale."

One response would be to retain the rhetoric of rights and merely ensure that it is used for "the good." In the present political context, this may be the most practical response.

However, we might also think seriously of alternative responses to the oppression of non-human animals and human oppressed groups. This requires a focus on radical alterity. This is the position I maintain in *What It Means to Be Human*, where I suggest that we need to acknowledge the unknowability of all beings, including human ones. Standing naked in front of his cat, Derrida acknowledged that "it [*sic*] can look at me. It has a point of view regarding me. The point of view of the absolute other."[49] But the great philosopher might also stand naked in front of other "unsubstitutable singular" beings: human animals.[50]

This position appeals to "negative zoölogy" (pronounced "zow-*ee*-low-gee"). The term takes its inspiration from "negative theology," albeit with God resolutely excised. From the late fifth century onwards, so-called "negative theologians" puzzled over how mere humans could speak about God, since "He" was a transcendent being beyond all human knowledge, language, and mystical intuition. They concluded that speaking about God requires some form of affirmation, which must then be denied, only to then deny the denial, and so on.

An identical form of "incommensurability" faces us when we attempt to understand all forms of life. Negative zoölogy insists that violence is done by assertions of ontological solidities: unity or disunity, sameness or difference. Bluntly, it undermines assumptions of superiority/inferiority inevitably popping up when making comparisons with other worlds ("different *compared to what/whom*?").[51] In other words, it injects instability and indeterminacy into our discussions and serves as a (much needed) reminder that we are not masters of the universe and that all our knowledges are contingent. As I argue in *What It Means to Be Human*, there is nothing otherworldly or redemptive in negative zoölogy (unlike negative theology). It insists on a radical alterity that is not liberating in itself, only within the milieu of specific political and historical struggles. Negative zoölogy insists on affirming the relevance of what is *not like "us"* for the present. It allows us to think *with* different worlds by reminding us of the beauty of motion, of affirmation and denial and further affirmation.

I began this essay with two feminists asking whether women were animals (Earnest Englishwoman) or whether they were human (Catharine MacKinnon). For the Earnest Englishwoman, women's animality gave them rights that they were excluded from by not being part of "mankind"; for MacKinnon, women's humanity granted them rights above those of animals. Both feminists were committed to questions of sameness, whether to non-human animals or to male humans. The Earnest Englishwoman, for instance, fantasized about becoming animal. Rather than forging an alliance with her oppressors (men as the only fully human creatures and therefore the only ones capable of "giving" women the vote), she defiantly proclaimed solidarity with fellow sufferers (animals). In doing so, however, she left the pecking order intact. She reconciled herself (admittedly, in satire) to the fact that women *are* animals, with all the subordination that such a position entails. MacKinnon equally adheres to a problematic ethic, dependent on a notion of a liberal humanist subject who believes in the liberationist rhetoric of "rights." Her argument is welded to the idea of autonomous human and non-human animal subjects that is at the heart of our patriarchal, capitalist society. Both feminists render themselves incapable of posing a radical challenge to either the subjective experiences of women or animals. They effectively adhere to a speciesist image of the world. As Emily Clark reminds us,

> Feminism and in particular feminist animal scholarship needs to incorporate a more sustained critique of the human and humanism. It is not sufficient to add a concern for animals to a concern for humans, or to justify work on animals by showing how such work bears on humans. Failing to question feminism's own humanism reinforces speciesism and rehearses a well-worn political strategy in which disenfranchised others are allotted some small stake in a constitutively oppressive, hierarchical system, rather than challenging the system itself.[52]

Face-to-face with the fundamental fluidity in definitions of human/animal, it is important to move beyond comparisons based on similarities and dissimilarities, injecting instability and indeterminacy into our discussions. This is essentially a relational argument, consistent with dialogical theory. As literary scholar Josephine Donovan explained, in discussing the construction of the human, it is necessary to "understand and comprehend what is not identified and recognized in these constructions"—that is, to "attempt to reach out emotionally as well as intellectually to what is different from oneself rather than reshaping (in the case of animals) that difference to conform to one's own human-based preconceptions."[53] Situated within material and ideological worlds, we are then encouraged to tell better stories and affirm our partial knowledges, while always knowing that there is more—much more—to come.

CHAPTER 4

Indigenous Peoples As the Subject of Human Rights

Danielle Celermajer and Michael Dodson

Introduction

The apparently singular category of Indigenous peoples refers to diverse peoples whose ongoing presence in, and connection with, a particular territory predated the imposition of colonial and other forms of imposed rule that became the basis of the contemporary sovereign state recognized in the international order.[1] Despite the diversity in the circumstances and identity of those involved, the processes of invasion, colonization, and the imposition of foreign sovereign rule have consistently situated Indigenous peoples as particular types of degraded subjects—to be eliminated, constrained, or managed by more or less explicitly brutal means.

Tracing this positioning of Indigenous peoples in the imaginary and then institutional infrastructure of settler colonial states, Mohawk scholar Audra Simpson tracks the permutations of "subject peoples," "children," "dependant wards who required protection from white unscrupulousness on the frontier," and, later, concomitant with the rise of the welfare state, "clients who need to be administered and managed."[2] Focusing in on the principal regulatory regime in Canada, the Canadian Indian Act, she argues that its "structuring presupposition is that Indians reside somewhere between ward, citizen, and people presumed to be savage who must have their savagery recognized first, in order to be governed."[3] Here, she echoes Dakota scholar Philip Deloria's depiction of the regime regulating Indigenous lives as the institutionalization of a colonial dream aspiring to "fixity, control, visibility, productivity, and, most importantly, docility."[4]

One of the motivations for the establishment of an international human rights regime was to put in place a higher set of principles and laws that would constrain the abuses that states had been empowered to commit against peoples within their jurisdiction. So at face value, human rights would seem to afford the promise to Indigenous peoples of a passage beyond this range of degraded subject positions. The fundamental claim of the modern human rights regime is that the subject of human rights is the human person, unqualified by any particular status: "all members of the human family"; "all human beings." Once Indigenous peoples were recognized as the bearers of such universal rights, their subject position should then (if implemented) move to that of persons who are both guaranteed a range of non-negotiable claims on and against states and who stand on an equal footing with all other persons, with the traditional grounds used to justify differentiation and discrimination barred from consideration.

As has been the case with a number of groups however, formal inclusion in the de jure category of the universal subject of rights did not result in the de facto realization of equality or rights. In this regard, Indigenous peoples have mobilized in a range of forums—domestic and international, in the media, through legal avenues and social movements—to bring evidence to demonstrate that the commitments set forth in human rights treaties had not been applied in the context of their lives.[5] These claims have formed the basis for a demand for an honest reckoning of the historical and contemporary truth of their exclusion as full subjects of human rights and the development of the types of far-reaching reforms that would ensure authentic inclusion.[6]

Certainly, it would be a grave mistake to conflate the colonial subject position into which Indigenous peoples have been cast with their self-understandings, sustained through community relations and lifeways that persisted in the face of colonization.[7] The vast disparity between the promise of their inclusion and the realities of persistent exclusion, combined with the felt disparity between the position afforded to them in settler colonial societies and their own sense of collective or individual selves, has catalyzed vigorous advocacy for the realization of the unfulfilled promise. In the most immediate context, this took the form of multidimensional activism pushing for enforcement of the state's human rights obligations vis-à-vis Indigenous peoples. Indigenous peoples have, however, been acutely aware that the shortfall was not just a matter of poor implementation; it was also the result of a structural exclusion of Indigenous peoples from the human rights regime itself.

Admittedly, no human rights treaty made this exclusion explicit. Nevertheless, the silence on Indigeneity as an explicitly protected category, the absence of a treaty specifically setting out the rights of Indigenous peoples, and the exclusion of Indigenous peoples from the institutional apparatus of the international regime, effectively amounted to the same outcome: "excepting Indigenous peoples." For Indigenous peoples, this exclusion was poignantly performed in the structural realities of the United Nations, where the only parties fully authorized to represent their claims or interests were the very nation-states that systematically abused their rights and had a persistent interest in constraining international efforts to afford them distinctive recognition. Being required to speak under the banner of officially recognized nongovernmental organizations—the sole available category for non-state parties in a regime whose members are exclusively recognized sovereign states—only underlined the injustice of the international political system that reinscribed their political invisibility.

In light of this institutional political geography, Indigenous peoples have long sought to establish for themselves a distinctive political status within the international human rights regime. Doing so would not simply be instrumental to inscribing their claims in law; it could also provide the means to become authorized architects of human rights. Thus, when the Working Group on Indigenous Populations, comprising five non-Indigenous experts, was established in 1982, Indigenous peoples from all over the world began to turn up in Geneva every July by the hundreds. They came to give voice to their grievances and, more importantly, to press for the establishment of international legal and institutional reforms that would de facto ensure their inclusion as subjects of international human rights.[8] Their efforts have, at least from a formal point of view, met with some success, principally in the form of the promulgation of a distinctive treaty, the Declaration on the Rights of Indigenous Peoples, adopted in 2007.[9] They have also succeeded in achieving some modest institutional reforms of the United Nations system, through the appointment of a special rapporteur on Indigenous peoples and the establishment of the United Nations Permanent Forum on Indigenous Issues (UNPFII) and the Expert Mechanism on the Rights of Indigenous Peoples (EMRIP), a subsidiary body of the Human Rights Council. More ambitious institutional proposals, like being accorded seats alongside nation-states at the General Assembly and in other forums, remain unrealized.

Still, in their aspiration to be subjects of justice, Indigenous peoples have not experienced the human rights regime as a straightforward ally, and not only because of the strength of its ideological, political, economic, and cultural forces and investments in their continued exclusion. Several other factors complicate the picture.

First, as the nomenclature adopted in this struggle (Indigenous *peoples*, as distinct from *people*) indicates, what is at stake is not simply the inclusion of the many individual Indigenous people as the subjects of human rights. It is also a struggle about the recognition of Indigenous *peoples* as politically empowered collectives with the types of rights that the nation-states within which they now live generally claim as their unique preserve. The struggle is not only to be a subject of human rights but also to establish what counts as such a subject. This is most evident in the long fight concerning whether a treaty setting out the rights of Indigenous peoples would include the right to self-determination and whether the language of people (i.e., individuals) or peoples (sovereign collectives with self-determination rights) would be included.[10]

A second and related complication concerns whether human rights, as currently conceived, make assumptions about the nature of their subject (the individual human being) that are themselves inimical to Indigenous peoples' flourishing. At the most basic level, the critique is that human rights abstract individuals from the collective to which they belong, thereby giving ontological priority to the autonomous individual in a manner that belies Indigenous ontologies.[11] Beyond this, the challenge to traditional understandings of the subject of rights concerns how humans are embedded in the "natural" world more broadly.[12] Thus, for example, when Indigenous peoples have insisted on the importance of recognizing their rights concerning land and "environment," the ontology in which the human rights framework is traditionally grounded would necessarily conceive of the relationship within the logic of property. As Dodson explains in the interview below, questions of rights to "country," as Indigenous peoples in Australia say, are wrongly conceived in terms of property relations and imply more interwoven relationships with the subject.

A third and related complication arises from the claim that human-rights-based approaches conceive of and institutionalize justice in a way that, as Jennifer Hendry and Melissa Tatum argue, is not just one amongst a number of different others but "is foreign to most traditional Indigenous communities and cultures, many (if not most) of whom have a notably less individualistic conceptualization of societal interactions."[13] Noting Indigenous peoples' "more collaborative approach to resolving conflict," they go so far as to claim that the conflictual structure of such conceptions and institutions of justice are "anathema to some Indigenous groups."[14] Understood thus, human rights potentially distort the type of relational subject positions that Indigenous societies have fostered and value, recasting Indigenous peoples as subjects of justice only to the extent that they forsake their own understandings and practices of justice.

The fourth and most damning complication takes a similar structure to Third World Approaches to International Law (TWAL), which have analyzed how the development of international law (including human rights) was, despite its apparently liberational thrust, embedded in imperial and colonial projects. As such, it is structurally disadvantageous to "third world" and Indigenous peoples, who, located as they have been on the "wrong side" of the civilized/barbarian divide, were cast as "objects" and not subjects of international law.[15] The objection here, then, is that insofar as human rights are rooted in the tradition and logic that was the source of Indigenous peoples' being cast as barbarian, uncivilized subjects outside the law, this logic and tradition, no matter how expanded or reformed, cannot be the source of the solution.

In this vein, a number of Indigenous scholars have cast serious doubt as to whether there is, in fact, a real break between colonization and assimilation, on the one hand, and the contemporary regimes of recognition and rights that are supposed to counter them, on the other. As Taiaiake Alfred and Jeff Corntassel argue, "[T]o a large extent, institutional approaches to making meaningful change in the lives of Indigenous people have not led to what we understand as decolonization and regeneration; rather they have further embedded Indigenous people in the colonial institutions they set out to challenge."[16] Transformation, they insist, requires a radically different approach, one that breaks with the colonial system of which human rights remain a part. A similar concern applies to the political economic logics at work, particularly given the centrality of land to Indigenous peoples' claims. Thus, a number of scholars argue that processes apparently designed to provide settlements of Aboriginal land claims have in fact been instrumental in incorporating indigenous claims within capitalist property regimes.[17]

Evidently, there exists a wide spectrum of Indigenous peoples' positions on the advantages and disadvantages of advancing a human-rights-based agenda and whether it is one to which Indigenous peoples ought to aspire. In what follows, Professor Michael Dodson discusses these complexities. For over thirty years, Dodson has been at the forefront, both in Australia and at the international level, of the efforts to formally encode and then, in practice, recognize the human rights of Indigenous people.

Danielle Celermajer (DC): Mick, can you tell me about the first time that you encountered the idea of human rights?

Michael Dodson (MD): I'd always had this sense of what was just and what wasn't, or what was fair and what was unfair. And I think that an understanding of fairness is at the heart of what human rights are about.

I grew up Aboriginal. There was very little respect in Australia—this is in the 1950s and early 1960s. There was still a view, and it still persists to some extent today, that we are a lesser race of people. Not that the term "race" is that useful these days. We are considered inferior, and there was no respect or willingness to afford us dignity as fellow humans.

You could see that even when I was a boy. There is always this sense that we were treated differently. My mother had an exemption card, because all Aboriginal people were treated like children.[18] I grew up in the Northern Territory, and I was born there, even though my people come from Western Australia, in the Kimberley. My mum had this card which exempted her from being regarded as an Aboriginal person. So the government could actually determine that a black person was a white person by some gazette or a regulation.

So that puzzled me when I was young. But really getting into human rights didn't come until I was at university. My first year of university, I was in the draft to be conscripted to go to Vietnam. I was pretty naïve about that, but the prospect of going to war against people I had no truck with really focused my mind. The Vietnamese had done nothing to me, and I'd increasingly got radicalized at that first year at Monash University, which was a hotbed of protest against Vietnam. My thinking was pretty crude at the time, but it came back to my sense of "Why are we fighting these guys? What threat do they pose to us?" Save this theory that somehow communism is going to cascade down through Southeast Asia and take over Australia, some sort of domino theory.

I didn't find out till years and years later, when doing a research project documenting Aboriginal peoples' military service, that Aboriginal men who were called up could actually be exempted from being conscripted under the National Service Act. Strangely, every Aboriginal soldier who was a Vietnam vet had known about that, and none of them wanted to claim the exemption. They all went. They all thought that if they went over and fought for their country, things would be better when they came home. They weren't, of course. A lot of men didn't go home; they stayed in the cities because they weren't going back to the mission or the government settlement to be ordered around by some young white bureaucrat regulating and controlling their lives. After they'd served—some of them got wounded, a lot of them died, a lot of their mates died—to come home to some petty bureaucrat telling you where you could work, who you could marry, where you could travel, it's absurd. So they didn't go home. They stayed in the city, which took a lot of the leadership out of those places.

I didn't get fully involved in human rights until I went out to practice as a lawyer, and then it must have been ten years after I left university that I started to get involved in the United Nations, getting really interested in human rights, reading about it. It grew from there.

I had to get very serious about human rights in relation to the first Royal Commission into Aboriginal Deaths in Custody.[19] That focused my attention on the human rights aspects of how prisoners are treated, what ought to be done to prevent, or at least minimize, the occurrence of deaths in custody. And then I became the Aboriginal and Torres Strait Islander Social Justice Commissioner. By that time, I'd had a long experience internationally being involved in human rights worldwide for Indigenous peoples, but with the Commissioner's job, it became 24/7.[20]

DC: Today, human rights is the lingua franca when we talk about justice or equality, but that wasn't always the case. You were one of the early people who started using human rights language in Australia in relation to indigenous issues. How did people, both Aboriginal and non-Aboriginal people, respond to using a human rights framework?

MD: The governing elites think that it's an insult to talk about Australia's infringements of human rights, because "We are not like those other countries that are really bad." Generally speaking, people think Australia has a good record on human rights, which, on close examination, is not true if you look at the record of Aboriginal and Torres Strait Islander people over the past 230 years. There has been a genocide in this country.

People don't fully understand what genocide is, either. The governing elites were shocked when we made a finding in the *Bringing Them Home* report that the forcible removal of children from their families and communities is a form of genocide.[21] It really shocked the political conservatives: "How dare they accuse us. We are decent people." Their level of decency extends to people who either agree with them or who are white. Because they have never treated us decently, and they still don't. Our human rights are still violated every day.

We are the only group of people who can't get relief for racial discrimination under the Commonwealth Racial Discrimination Act (RDA). The Parliament has specifically banned us from getting the redress that every other citizen in this country can under the RDA and the Race Convention, a treaty we have signed and vowed to honor. Not for black fellows, though. We don't get that protection.

Part of it's in the most fundamental things to our society, our culture, our language, our values, our worldview, our religious and spiritual traditions, the land. We cannot litigate for actual racial discrimination against us with respect to our lands because we are banned from doing that.

DC: What is the history here?

MD: After the High Court's decision in *Mabo* in 1992, where it was recognized for the first time in Australian law that Indigenous peoples' original rights to their land had not been dissolved when the British Crown declared sovereignty over this country, the federal government then wanted to move to create legislation and an administrative regime to control how the recognition of that title would work. We essentially had a gun pointed at our heads, saying, "If you don't agree not to make claims over the land that was taken in the past, we are not going to pass the Native Title Act." I hesitate to call it that, but it's a form of blackmail.

The worry was, I think, that if you allow Aboriginal people to exercise their rights and to say, "These past transactions were racially discriminatory, because they happened without any reference to us and to our native title," then there would be zillions of dollars of compensation payable. I'm talking here about all of the cases where the Crown alienated Indigenous peoples from their lands, creating, say, leasehold or other forms of title, and then that land was bought and sold, resulting in Indigenous peoples' never being able to make a claim, even after *Mabo*. So to avoid that, we were, in effect, forced to say, up until the decision in *Mabo*, no one knew about our rights, so it would be unfair to prosecute them for illegal transactions on the land. We understood that, because it wasn't the individuals who bought land under the Commonwealth's regime who were at fault; they didn't know about the existence of native title. They acted in good faith. And we were prepared to accept that.

And we had the date of the enactment of the legislation as the cut-off date. And to stop people who didn't agree with that, the government put in a provision to prevent people from suing for such transactions as breaches of the Racial Discrimination Act.

Then, when (conservative Prime Minister) John Howard came into power in 1996, he extended that date without any agreement from us to the later date when a new piece of law, the Native Title Amendment Act, was passed. So instead of it being 1991, it became 1997. So anything before that was forgiven.

Then there was another case- the Hindmarsh Island case also disallowed the application of the RDA. Aboriginal women sought protection of a sacred site from the construction of a bridge, but the federal government went ahead and legislated to authorize the bridge. It's a complicated case, but for the purposes of this discussion, the relevant issue concerned how the High Court interpreted the provision of the Australian Constitution that authorizes Parliament to make laws with respect to "the people of any race for whom it is deemed necessary to make special laws." Originally, that provision included the words "other than the aboriginal race in any state," but in 1967 Australians voted in a referendum to remove these words. When they took that vote, in response to a campaign about equality for Aboriginal people, Australians certainly believed they were authorizing the Commonwealth to pass legislation that benefited Aboriginal people. But the High Court did not agree. So we are left with a situation where, effectively, the Commonwealth is authorized by the Constitution to legislate in ways that may be detrimental to Aboriginal people in particular. Not only does the Constitution not ban discriminatory legislation, it authorizes it!

And then, most recently, the Northern Territory intervention did the same thing: denied us the right to redress for acts of racial discrimination. In the name of protecting Aboriginal children, the government passed a raft of laws incompatible with the Racial Discrimination Act, and obviously so, because they deprived Aboriginal people of the same rights as all other Australians. But the government did not see that as a reason not to pass those laws or take those measures—it simply suspended the pesky parts of the RDA.

We as a country are prepared to do that against some of our citizens, and our constitution allows us to do that. The application of human rights law in these instances can be ignored by the Parliament.

DC: When you started to use the language of human rights when you were talking with Aboriginal people, how did they respond? Do you think that the language or frame of human rights is one that "fits" for Indigenous peoples?

MD: Most people know what human rights are. They have a feeling and understanding of what they are, but they don't talk about it like human rights lawyers talk about it. When you talk to Aboriginal people about self-determination, they don't use that language, although it's increasingly being used. For example, when an Indigenous person says they want their community to make the decisions about those things that most impact their daily lives, they are using the language of self-determination. Indigenous people talk about human rights all the time, just not in the same way that lawyers and advocates for human rights do!

Back in the 1980s, when I worked with the Land Council in the Northern Territory around land rights, people were saying, "We want to make our own decisions about what happens in our lives." That wasn't "We want to exercise our right to self-determination," but they knew what they were talking about. We should be allowed to have our culture and our language protected. We should be allowed to have our religious and spiritual traditions honored. We should have our fundamental freedoms sanctioned and protected. And we should be making decisions about what affects our lives the most. That should be our decision, not some government or bureaucrat or somebody else. We as a group should be allowed to make those decisions.

Your humanity comes with this right to be treated with dignity and respect, and that has not been the case for Indigenous peoples, by and large. Not just in this country, but around the world.

Then there is the level of exposure Aboriginal people have had to police over generations. In the face of this, people say, "This is discrimination. We just get targeted all of the time." Most Australians use the language of fairness, and fairness is fundamentally about human rights, in my view. Human rights are inherent. We have them because we are humans.

In some cultures, everybody has rights, not just the humans, but the animals and the flora. The rest of them, they are our relatives; there is our mother. The trees and the plants help sustain us. We are all part of one being, and we have ways of protecting each other.

When we talk about country, we don't talk about it in the same way a non-Indigenous person might. Country is much more to us. Country for us is centrally about identity. Our lands and seas underpin who we are, where we come from, who our ancestors are. What it means to be from that place, from that country. How others see and view us. How others identify us. How we feel about each other. How we feel about our families and ourselves. Country is fundamentally about our survival as peoples.

To understand us, you have to understand our law, our culture, and our relationship to the physical and spiritual world. Everything about Aboriginal society is inextricably interwoven with and connected to the land. You have to understand this and our place in that land and the places of that land. Our cultural beliefs and our reason for existence is the land.[22]

DC: The type of understanding of what it is to be a person that you are describing here seems to be one that is quite different from the conception of the person encoded in human rights. There, what is valued is the individual, and human rights are very much about supporting the dignity of individuals understood in a pretty decontextualized way. For example, land in the human rights framework would be understood only in terms of property relations. Some Indigenous scholars have argued that human rights, because they are grounded in Western values, cannot support Indigenous worldviews and aspirations. What are your thoughts on the compatibility of human rights as a framework with the understanding you just articulated?

MD: I don't see why they can't be compatible. The Declaration on the Rights of Indigenous Peoples is drawn from all sorts of human rights standards and instruments. Native Title, Indigenous Title is an accepted title. You have to exercise your rights to land in conjunction with others in the group. You have rights and responsibilities in relation to that, and you have religious and spiritual regulations in relation to where you fit in the kinship system of your own mob and your status in the law and custom of your own people. So not only does it recognize rights to country, but it allows for and recognizes collective rights. It does not individualize land as property. So, in my opinion, human rights are not incompatible with Indigenous understandings of country.

DC: Do you think that taking human rights as an approach to address the problems Indigenous peoples have faced has made a difference to their lives?

MD: I think it gives pause to governments and that things have improved in some quarters. I think it has benefited us in trying to persuade government to not be as excessive as they could be. Politicians in Australia, particularly conservative politicians, get very irritated when you talk about human rights, which is sad. I think they are sad people. It is by not talking about it that you let people get away with clear breaches of human rights, because you have a view of yourself as being a good international citizen who will not be called out for any of this stuff.

We have a false impression of ourselves as a country. We are a pretty good international citizen, but we could be better.

Where the greatest human rights problems occur with us is firstly with criminal law and with the racially discriminatory constitution that we have. The international norm prohibits discrimination based on race absolutely; it is what is known in International Human Rights law as a peremptory norm or *jus cogens*, or "compelling law." Australia signed a treaty as a member state of the United Nations to prohibit racial discrimination. We also agreed to the principle of *pacta sunt servanda*, meaning "Agreements must be kept." We don't do that with our constitution or our law.

And we have a criminal justice system that profoundly and disproportionately impacts on our people. We are 3 percent of the population, and we make up 25 percent of the prison population, and amongst females it's much higher—over 50 percent. In some jurisdictions, we are 80-percent-plus of young kids in detention. It's not because we are inherently bad people or criminal or antisocial. There has got to be some other explanation for that. And I think it's the breach of human rights that's the explanation. There is something fundamentally wrong in the criminal justice system that disproportionately impacts on us. And I think that's really the coalface of the violation of Indigenous rights in this country. It's the way the criminal justice system treats our people. And when I say the system, I mean the entire system—the police, the welfare system, the political decisions that are made, public policy positions. All of these things compound the problem. And we have spent millions of dollars with Royal Commissions and inquiries. We have mountains of material; we could fill a couple of suburban libraries with all of the reports, the assessments, the evaluations, the inquiries, the papers, the plethora of things we have done to try to confront these problems. But we get nowhere. I think we get nowhere because there is too much of an attitude of "Well, my human rights are OK, I couldn't care less about anyone else's. We are a good country; we look after our people. You can't do much for the natives; they just don't get it."

DC: Which goes back to what you said about your mum and a basic assumption. . . .

MD: I think the problem is this: that the political assumptions and processes perceive us as Aborigines. This goes back to the notion of the savage. This was before the *Odyssey* and the *Iliad*. Homer just puts it more concisely. "The problem with you Aborigines is that you are Aboriginal." And that is a breach of human rights, denying who we are, that we somehow have to be assimilated and behave like white fellas, and if you don't, we are going to keep locking you up, and that is going to solve the problem. It's not going to solve any problem. It's getting close to half a million dollars a year to keep one juvenile in detention, and a female, it's about $310K, and for a male, it's approximately $240K. You could put the whole prison up in the Hilton for that.

DC: In the academy, you see the claim that the human rights framework represents a very individualist way of making sense of the world. That human rights starts with the idea of the sovereign individual who has rights, and some people say that this is inconsistent with Aboriginal ontologies, with the way Aboriginal people understand what it is to be a human being. What do you think of that view?

MD: I don't put much store in it. As individuals, we have fundamental freedoms and rights. But we all live in a collective of some type or other. Humans tend to live in societies, whether that society is Indigenous or non-Indigenous. You don't exercise human rights in a vacuum. You exercise them in relation to other people that you live in a society with. And you agree to that society; there is some social contract. That is a collective thing; it's not an individual thing. But you as an individual come to it, and as a collective, you agree on it.

The right to self-determination is a collective right; the right to language is a collective right. It'd be meaningless if it was an individual right. Language, how can it be individual? You share it with someone else who speaks that language; it's collective. We as Aboriginal people have a right to our languages. Any peoples have a right to their language. We live in a so-called democracy, and we, as a collective, elect people to represent us and to have a license to exercise power over us. There is so much of what we do in societies that is not individual, that is collective.

DC: All societies.

MD: Yes. Aboriginal people talk about collective and individual rights. Maybe there is more emphasis on the collective. Most of our forms of title are communal. I think colonization in Australia has had a negative impact on our thinking; some of our people are into demarcating collective land or trying to do that. The use of the land and its resources has been a communal right.

You have a right to life. That is an individual right, and it's the most fundamental: life. But why do we have laws against genocide? That's a collective right. We have a right not to be subjected to genocide as a group.

Some people think of it a bit differently. Within collectives, there are individual rights. It's not so clear-cut as if you could say, "With Indigenous people everything is collective; with non-Indigenous people everything is individualized." I don't think it is that clear-cut.

DC: You said that one of the effects of colonization has been to break down a sense of collective ownership (for some people). Do you think that the human rights framework, traditionally, gives enough recognition to the collective dimension of rights?

MD: Well, if you look at the Declaration on the Rights of Indigenous Peoples. . . .

DC: No, I want to look before that. The Declaration represents how Indigenous peoples have changed human rights law.

MD: I don't think we have changed human rights. What we have changed is the extent of recognition of human rights to extend to the Indigenous domain.

I think international human rights law was always capable of recognizing Indigenous peoples' particular take on human rights. The beauty of human rights is that it is able to accommodate Indigenous thinking about human rights and able to encapsulate it into an instrument that represents what Indigenous peoples were saying for twenty-one years. This is how we view our human rights.

The Declaration on the Rights of Indigenous Peoples isn't just about collective rights; there are a lot of individual protections expressed in that instrument.

DC: So you are saying that human rights as a body of principles is sufficiently flexible to accommodate Indigenous perspectives.

MD: Indeed. It took a long time, twenty-one years, but it might even be longer than that. It's probably 500 years from the era of discovery.

In 1948, they thought they'd captured it all, the worst of the atrocities—Nazism—and we needed to stop that from happening. Although we haven't stopped genocide. It's been happening since. But it was always going to develop. It was never going to be locked in 1948, and so many international instruments evolved from the UDHR. It was always going to accommodate that. We needed special protection for children, so we got a treaty on the human rights of children. We needed special protection for women, and so we got the Convention on the Elimination of All Forms of Discrimination Against Women (CEDAW). We have the International Labor Organization (ILO) for workers. More recently, we have created protections for the environment. We had standards for economic and social rights. We had standards for political and civil rights. And we now have standards for the specific protection of the rights of Indigenous peoples.

And a majority of the articles in the Declaration on the Rights of Indigenous Peoples (DRIP) are borrowed from other existing instruments, but they are put in an Indigenous context and an Indigenous framework about human rights, which tends to be a more collective view of the rights of the society rather than the individuals. But the instrument protecting Indigenous peoples' rights very much protects individual as well as collective rights.

DC: How do you think that Indigenous peoples' coming into the UN has pushed human rights principles? You talked before about the importance of land, for example, so what has changed?

MD: We spent many years talking to the international human rights system through the Working Group on Indigenous Populations. Now we have the Expert Mechanism on the Rights of Indigenous Peoples and the Permanent Forum on Indigenous Issues. We are constantly talking to people who set these standards. Annually there is a conversation taking place, and in between those sessions we have special rapporteurs traveling around the world, keeping a watch on what is happening. Sometimes we are powerless to prevent abuses, but sometimes we do. It is not a very powerful system, but we have been unable to come up with a better system, unless we are prepared to go and kill each other through war, and that is not a solution to human rights. It can bring pressure to bear to try to persuade nation-states to do the right thing.

DC: There were no Indigenous peoples who were part of building the human rights system in 1948. It was relatively late that Indigenous peoples pushed their way into the UN, the mid-1970s and into the 1980s.

MD: That is not entirely true. Chief Deskaheh, from the USA, went to the League of Nations with others in the 1920s. And you had Ratana, the Maori spiritualist, the Maori chief, who went around about the same time. You even had an Australian agitating with the British about the treatment of Aboriginal people in this country, the lone protester in the 1920s. . . . So there was a presence.

DC: What I meant was that in 1948, Indigenous peoples were not allowed to sit around the table. So how have Indigenous peoples changed human rights?

MD: It is in the vision of the people who are responsible for these things. Indigenous peoples are there in your face.

The greatest thing that the drafting of the Declaration did was to raise awareness and to educate governments about Indigenous peoples. And I think governments pause now, with some notable and tragic exceptions, but generally speaking, governments are now well acquainted with Indigenous peoples and their rights because Indigenous peoples have spent forty or fifty years educating them, sitting around the table. We still sit at the back and government delegates sit at the front at the UN, but we are there, and our voices are being heard. At the big quorums we get Indigenous speakers. We have a special rapporteur on the fundamental freedoms and human rights of Indigenous peoples who speaks to all of the UN bodies and reports to the Human Rights Council, so there is a presence there now. We have the Permanent Forum, we have the Expert Mechanism, and there are occasional reports about Indigenous peoples' situations that get reported to the system.

Now, the UN, as you know, is not a giant universal policeman that enforces the standards, but it does give pause and makes people think "We might be in trouble with the UN."

DC: You have always said that the right to self-determination is the foundation of all human rights. Self-determination is a very political right; it is not an individual right. . . .

MD: Well, it's about determining your own political status and your socioeconomic development. I like to express it in the way that Indigenous peoples express it. Two things often get repeated to me. One is "We want to make the decisions about the things that are happening in our lives. Those things that affect us the most, we want to make those decisions." And the second is "It's our problem. Why don't they let us solve it? Why don't they help us solve it, instead of coming in and telling us how to solve it?" That is an expression of self-determination, in my book, saying, "It's our problem. We are the best ones to fix it. You help us to fix it, but do it our way." And the second part of it is "We'd like to have a say about what is happening in our lives. We want to make the decisions that affect our lives on a day-to-day basis. Therein is a fundamental call for self-determination, in my view. That is what they are saying: "Get out of our lives. If you want to help us, help us on our terms."

DC: That says to me that the assertion that Indigenous peoples are making is very much a collective and political one. It really speaks to who has the right to govern.

MD: I agree self-determination is a different dimension of human rights. It is bound up with the question of sovereignty and treaty in an Australian context.

DC: Why do you think that Indigenous peoples' right to self-determination is so difficult for states to respect?

MD: Because they muddy the waters deliberately, and for political reasons, they say it means a separate state. That is not what we are talking about at all. It won't be too long before you are going to have a self-governing Torres Strait Islands. So that is coming; it's going to happen. And these self-governing entities are going to break out across the country, eventually. And they don't need to be territorially based.

It works now. I don't live in Broome, but I get to vote for who represents me in my traditional lands in Broome. I get a say in any major issue that affects our native title in Broome. I don't live there, but I still have rights in the decision-making process, to be involved in the decision-making process. My tribe affords that to me because they think that's my right as a member of that tribe, what the First Nations call the Yawuru people. It's not a difficult thing for us.

DC: So do you think that the reason that the state is so loath to recognize self-determination is because they see it as potentially a claim on statehood or sovereignty?

MD: They think they might have to give up some power. I think that is at the heart of it.

DC: Won't they?

MD: They will have to give up some power, obviously. But it's not going to affect the sovereignty of the nation.

In the last years, we have been doing a lot of work on developing proposals for reforming the system of Australian government so that Indigenous peoples were afforded proper recognition. That resulted in part in the Uluru Statement and the call for a voice to Parliament.[23] A voice to the Parliament is not going to threaten Australian democracy or Australian sovereignty. If you look around to the experience in other countries—Sami Parliaments in Scandinavia, the Assembly of First Nations in Canada, the National Congress of American Indians, the Maori Waitangi Treaty Council—it is clear that their arrangements to talk to their parliaments haven't threatened their sovereignty. We just need to have the conversation.

Now, what did the ruling classes do here when the Uluru Statement came out? They shut down the discussion. "Oh no, we can't do that. It's a third chamber of Parliament!" How narrow-minded and insular, bigoted, and ignorant that response is. Beggars belief, and in lots of respects, it's just simple mean, nasty racism. You can't possibly accommodate the people who have been here for over 60,000 years in the governance of the country. "We are going to make decisions for them. They are not going to be allowed to make decisions about the things that affect their lives the most. We are going to make those decisions for them." Therein lies the problem. There is the inability to recognize what we are saying when we talk about self-determination.

DC: What is your assessment of the Uluru Statement from the Heart?

MD: I don't have a problem with a voice to Parliament, but I think it has an element of the mendicant to it and it concedes too much of our sovereignty to the British Crown. It also paints us as being totally powerless. That's not the case. "Look at us poor buggers; we've got no power. Give us some power." It's almost *Oliver Twist*.

DC: How would you like to see it framed?

MD: We haven't conceded sovereignty. There has never been an agreement about our sovereignty. Here is an opportunity for us to redress that in a fair and honorable way. Let's start doing that. Let's work out a way for how the First Nations people of this country fit into the governance of the country. What do we need to do to make that happen?

DC: Would that be a treaty or treaties?

MD: It could be a treaty. It could be a constitutional change. It could be regional agreements. It could be a range of things. But at least let's get to the table and talk about it. You've shut the door: "No, it can't happen." That has been your response. We are trying to reignite that discussion.

Indigenous peoples in Australia are in active conversations with the Indigenous peoples from other parts of the world, talking about some of the types of institutional arrangements I mentioned earlier. We want to learn from them. And we are not telling the Australian government that we have to go down the path of the Sami Parliament or down the path of the Assembly of First Nations or whatever. We are asking them to consider how, in light of the experience of other peoples and nations and in our context, we should move forward.

DC: When you say that Aboriginal people have never conceded sovereignty, what does that mean to you?

MD: Again, it comes back to self-determination. It's the right to make decisions that most affect your daily life. You should be making those decisions, not some outsider. Your group should be making those decisions.

Where is the treaty? Even under the international law of the time, there had to be some agreement. We have never said, "Oh, yes, you can come in and invade our country and take over the land and kill us all and lock the survivors up, take our kids away, destroy our culture, destroy our language, rip the heart out of our land, destroy our sacred sites, denigrate our worldview," etc., etc.

If we were a decent people, we would do something about that. We have a constitution that allows racial discrimination. Why aren't we in an uproar about that? And it's been allowing racial discrimination since federation. It's been happening for 117 years.

DC: Do you see the situation of Aboriginal people in Australia as representative of the place of other Indigenous peoples?

MD: Colonialism isn't very imaginative or inventive. It screws over people wherever it goes, in the same fashion. There is not a hierarchy of good and bad colonizers. They are all bad, and they are driven by conquest and domination to acquire new dominions, on whatever false grounds they create. The doctrine of discovery is sometimes called the doctrine of "Christian discovery" because Christians thought they had a God-given right to dispossess natives and convert them to Christianity. It's why you got the papal edict that allowed Columbus to supposedly discover the Americas.

DC: Do you think a human rights framework is capable of taking on those primal crimes?

MD: Not alone. The key support for human rights is domestic acceptance and international action and the exercise of power favorable to human rights. Things aren't as bad as they used to be, but they could be better. Kids don't work in the coal mine any more. Women are allowed to vote. We have made progress, but we could do better. That is what moderate people would say. There is no point in being a zealot with respect to human rights. Much human rights protection depends on persuading people to exercise that power in a way that is favorable to human rights.

DC: Yes, but if part of the problem lies with the legitimacy of contemporary forms of sovereignty, then are nation-states that have, in many cases, stolen other peoples' sovereignties going to "implement" human rights to correct that wrong? Is the problem beyond human rights?

MD: It is not a black-and-white thing. There are lots of very good states, and in fact, the majority of sovereign states are not colonizing countries, so you can't discount the United Nations as being based on the theft of Indigenous peoples' land.

The existing international human rights standards certainly have a role to play in setting Indigenous peoples' rights, including rights to land.

I don't think that human rights are stuck. The Declaration on the Rights of Indigenous Peoples (DRIP) can't be discounted—it is a qualifier on all other rights. It says you have to consider the rights of Indigenous peoples. All the rights articulated in the DRIP are exiting rights put in a context.

DC: You have been working in human rights for forty-odd years. It sounds like you still really believe in human rights as a framework for justice.

MD: Yes, and there has been increasing discussion around this country about treaties or agreements and how we should frame them, what they should contain. My response has been, the template for developing the provisions in a treaty ought to be the United Nations Declaration on the Rights of Indigenous Peoples. Let's work through that as the treaty foundation, the framework document for negotiating a treaty, because everything is there. We spent two-plus decades working that out. And we have had centuries of on-the-job experience with human rights. That is where I would start. I would start with that as my fundamental framework document.

CHAPTER 5

"Escaped"

Gendered Precarity and Human Rights Recognition

Wendy S. Hesford

A PHOTOGRAPH OF three young Yazidi women veiled and dressed in traditional white Yazidi wedding attire appeared in National Geographic Society's
online journal *Proof* in November 2015. The image was excerpted from a larger
project by Kurdish photojournalist Seivan Salim entitled "Escaped," which
features the individual portraits and testimonies of fifteen Yazidi women between the ages of eighteen and thirty who were held captive by the Islamic
State (ISIS/Da'esh) for four to ten months.[1] The Yazidi are a distinct ethno-
religious minority who maintain Indigenous pre-Islamic and pre-Zoroastrian
practices.[2] They are neither Muslim nor Christian, though their faith has elements of both Christianity and Islam. ISIS has targeted the Yazidi minority
in northern Iraq because they see them as infidels. ISIS leadership emphasizes
a narrow interpretation of the Quran and other religious rulings to justify
the enslavement of Yazidi women and girls—a reading that moderate Muslim
scholars condemn. In an attempt to expand their "caliphate," ISIS overtook
the northern Iraqi city of Sinjar—the homeland of the Yazidi—on August 3,
2014. ISIS killed thousands of Yazidi men and boys and older women and abducted thousands of younger Yazidi women and girls, many of whom were
taken into Syria to be sold in markets as sex slaves. According to a recent UN
report, of those abducted, 971 Yazidi women and girls have been freed and
1,882 remain enslaved in Iraq and Syria.[3]

The women that Salim interviewed and photographed were living in a refugee camp at an undisclosed location. Traditional Yazidi wedding attire does
not require women to wear a veil, but during this shoot the women were covered to ensure their anonymity and safety. Salim describes her decision to

photograph the women in traditional wedding dress as follows: "Traditionally and religiously, the right to have sex is only after marriage. This right was stolen by ISIS. I wanted to say that they are still chaste and pure in heart."[4] The portraits are linked to survivors' testimonies, which focus on the women's sexual violation and psychological abuse at the hands of ISIS. "Many or most of the victims were married before," Salim indicates, "so they did not lose virginity by rape, but they have been assaulted and soiled by the fanatics. The idea of dressing them in wedding gowns has a deeper meaning than cultural recognition. I did not dress them to make the men happy, but rather to make a statement, and that is: No matter what the evil men have done to them, they remain standing."[5] "Each of their stories was tragic," Salim continues. "Their suffering was so great. I felt it was my duty to show it, as a Kurdish woman and a photojournalist who can connect with them in their own language. The world must know what is happening to the girls still in captivity." Salim's intent is "to heighten awareness of the still-missing thousands of Yazidi women, men, and children and to stir the world to demand the disposition of those missing and to bring the perpetrators of this atrocity to justice."

"Escaped" is a powerful testimonial project that has brought increased international attention to the ongoing crisis of trauma and violence that ISIS has inflicted on Yazidi women. In this chapter, I focus on how four different rhetorical contexts frame the Yazidi women's images and testimonies. To focus on the framing contexts is not to undermine the photojournalist's intention or to depreciate the courage of the women interviewed or of the photographer herself, who faced material risks in collecting the images and testimonies. Rather, my goal is to consider how context shapes interpretation. Thus, central to my project is the following question: in what rhetorical contexts, under what conditions of visibility, and in support of what political or cultural investments are Yazidi women seen and heard? To better understand the discourses of gendered terrorism and their mobilization, this chapter calls for the rhetorical analysis of how different contexts constitute Yazidi women and girls as human rights subjects. Constitutive rhetoric emphasizes how ideologies create political subjects through a "process of identification in rhetorical narratives [and images] that 'always already' presume the constitution of subjects."[6] Constitutive rhetoric also focuses on how subjects affirm or contest their subject position(s). A constitutive rhetorical approach to human rights representation, including visual representations, therefore, turns our attention to the material and discursive conditions of intelligibility and cultural, political, and legal norms that govern the recognition (or lack thereof) of human rights subjects.[7]

Within the international imaginary, women's human rights are often linked to the spectacle of gendered precarity—namely, images and narratives of sexual violation, which construe the female body as a site of moral, cultural, and political crisis. Drawing on Judith Butler's influential work on precarity, I use the term "gendered precarity" to refer to "politically induced condition[s] in which certain populations . . . become differentially exposed to injury, violence, and death."[8] Precarity is linked to gender norms, and, as Butler suggests, power operates through gender norms.[9] International and national security discourses often mobilize gendered norms in linking women's rights to sexual subjection, and this proclivity limits public understanding of gendered precarity by failing to recognize the relation between conflict-based sexual violence and geopolitical, economic, and environmental conditions of precariousness. Attention to the conditions of intelligibility and constitutive processes of human rights recognition, as the various contextualizations of "Escaped" exemplify, reveals how gendered precarity is intimately tied to how violent conflict, war, and terrorism are understood.[10]

Transnational and postcolonial feminist critics have drawn attention to how the visualization of sexual violence against women and girls functions as a site of power and exploitation in cultural and juridical contexts and to the limited capability of rights-based arguments to address the complexity and diversity of women's struggles around the world.[11] Rejecting the universalizing tendencies of human rights and essentialist notions of gender, many transnational and postcolonial feminist scholars nevertheless continue to draw on human rights' political force. This chapter builds on these critical traditions in its focus on the constitutive discourses and contexts that shape the recognition of Yazidi women's human rights. Yazidi women's stories may stand on their own as testimonies to the atrocities of Islamic terrorists, but these stories are also caught between international debates about women's victimization and agency, and between global and local political agendas.

My focus on the relational positioning of Yazidi women as human rights subjects in varying rhetorical contexts troubles binary configurations of agency and power that might read "Escaped" as an uncritical capitulation to Yazidi hetero-patriarchal structures and would thereby erase Yazidi women's active political participation and assertion of rights. In contrast to the binary (victim/agent) construal of human rights subjects, I turn to critical theorists

who focus on precarity and precariousness as the basis for understanding political intersubjectivity[12] and the relational constitution of human rights subjects[13] and feminist security scholars who mobilize the concept of vulnerability as it "relates to the unjust distribution of resources and voice/agency."[14]
Precarity as an analytical tool presents a challenge to the sovereign rights-
bearing subject of the liberal legal tradition and notions of agency as an individual attribute or possession, recalibrates the human rights subject as relational, and calls for greater attention to how rights discourses mediate the
imperatives of state and local power.

In this chapter, I analyze how four different rhetorical contexts frame Salim's "Escaped," namely *National Geographic Magazine*, the UN "Rape in
Conflict" exhibition, the UN Report on Conflict-Related Sexual Violence, and
the "Map of Displacement" project. The testimonies and portraits of the Yazidi women take on particular meanings within each of these contexts, which
function as interpretive frames. *National Geographic Magazine*'s framing of
"Escaped" links the recognition of the Yazidi women as human rights subjects
to the U.S. military-humanitarian intervention in the region. The UN's prosecutorial gaze at gendered precarity highlights legal recognition and international resolutions on conflict-based sexual violence. Through its focus on
stories about familial resilience and cultural belonging, the "Map of Displacement" shifts attention away from security logics and the legal objectives that
gendered precarity is expected to perform in the international arena and toward a relational understanding of the material conditions of precariousness
and consequences of the forced displacement of nearly three million Iraqis.
My analysis of these four contextual mediations of "Escaped" illustrates the
transnational-looking practices and disciplining discourses that frame the international recognition of Yazidi women as human rights subjects and the
mediation of their stories. Understanding the rhetorical constitution of Yazidi
women as human rights subjects whose political subjectivity is linked to gendered precarity is just as important a project as documenting human rights
violations, because how subjects are framed sets the parameters for political
engagement and action.

National Geographic Magazine Unveiled

How and to what effect does *National Geographic*'s prioritization of U.S.
military-humanitarian intervention and history of pictorial orientalism fore-

close opportunities for alternative or fuller understandings of Yazidi women's human rights and political subjectivity? In what ways does *National Geographic*'s history of representing women in the Middle East as objects of curiosity resurface in its framing of Yazidi women's images and stories? How are we, as scholars who wish to depart from orientalist and habitual uncritical readings, to understand our implication in this historical optic?

The magazine leads with a story about the U.S.-backed Kurdish forced removal of ISIS from Sinjar in mid-November 2015—one of several U.S.-backed offensives to intervene to rescue Yazidi stranded on the mount after ISIS overtook Sinjar on August 3, 2014. In an attempt to flee from ISIS, many Yazidi headed up Mount Sinjar, where hundreds perished because of high temperatures and lack of food, water, and medical care.[15] In highlighting the U.S. role in the offensive, the *National Geographic* article minimizes the instrumental role of other forces in the liberation of Sinjar, including the Kurdish Peshmerga, as well as the fact that U.S. support for the Peshmerga came late because the U.S. administration feared that in arming the Kurds they might inadvertently promote the ethnic group's legitimate quest for independence.[16] While "Escaped" does not employ the rhetoric of rescue, *National Geographic*'s accompanying text exhibits the persistence of rescue narratives that saturate Western media portrayals of violations of women's human rights in the Middle East. Similarly, depictions of Yazidi women as victims without agency or as victims of cultural traditions mask Yazidi women's struggles and resistance and fail to consider the "role that Westerners already play—whether in their everyday practices, their governments' actions, or their economic strength—in perpetuating global inequalities that exacerbate (and sometimes cause) the sufferings of women elsewhere."[17]

National Geographic Magazine's visual field is haunted by gendered orientalism and its fantasies of Middle Eastern women as distant and exotic others.[18] The veil has long been configured in Western discourse as a symbol of Middle Eastern women's cultural imprisonment—a configuration that the United States has readily drawn on in its nationalist discourse of military intervention against ISIS.[19] Our scholarly implication in this orientalist optic and its mechanisms of erasure requires that we understand the spectacle's potential ambiguities, including, in this instance, how Yazidi women seize the process of recognition and put pressure on Yazidi cultural expectations. Individual *National Geographic* readers will inevitably engage "Escaped" differently; however, readers who recall the journal's legacy of pictorial orientalism and its moral typologies might rely on these historical frames in their engagement with Yazidi women's images and testimonies.

Conservative Christian news coverage of the Yazidi crisis in the United States draws on similar moral typologies in its fusing of the freedom-slavery binary with other dualisms, including the configuration of Christianity as civil versus Islam as uncivil. Western conservative news reports on the crisis repeatedly position the Yazidi metonymically as a stand-in for Christians and for arguments that call for increased attention to the persecution of Christians worldwide.[20] Such representations also often traffic in cultural pathologies about Islam and gender-based violence.[21] In contrast, the UN "Rape in Conflict" exhibit highlights international resolutions and legal means of accountability. Yet, as I argue below, the UN's contextualization of "Escaped," while providing important historical context, risks reproducing the spectacle of gendered vulnerability, which links Yazidi women's political subjectivity and legal recognition to sexual subjection and thereby prioritizes gender over other relations of power and difference.

Gendering Security: The UN "Rape in Conflict" Exhibit

In contrast to *National Geographic Magazine*'s affirmation of American exceptionality and moral security, the UN "Rape in Conflict" exhibit aligns the Yazidi women's portraits and testimonies with the aspirations of liberal internationalism and UN resolutions on conflict-based sexual violence, specifically international criminal and human rights law on rape warfare. In the 1990s, there were formative debates over conflict-based sexual violence among transnational activists, international women's rights networks, and legal feminist elites. The UN's response to rape warfare in the former Yugoslavia propelled sexual violence against women in conflict zones to a prominent international position and prompted an important shift in the conceptualization of rape from what was then viewed as essentially a private violation of individual victims to a systemic feature of war that mandated a global response.[22] In 1998, rape as a crime of war formally entered the international legal lexicon, as did calls for the prosecution of perpetrators at the International Criminal Court (ICC). The ICC, established in 1998 by the Rome Statute of the International Criminal Court, declared rape, when committed as part of a widespread or systematic attack directed against any civilian population, a crime against humanity (Article 7) and a war crime (Article 22), along with sexual slavery, forced prostitution, forced pregnancy, forced sterilization, and other forms of sexual violence. These legal developments were vital in bringing conflict-based sexual violence to the foreground of international politics. Yet, in becoming the "starkest example of the sexual vulnerability of all women,"[23] genocidal rape law also recalibrated the universalism of liberal internationalism in linking women's political subjectivity to sexual subjection.

"Rape in Conflict" was on display in the visitor's lobby of the UN headquarters in New York from January 30, 2017, to February 28, 2017. The exhibit situated Yazidi women's rape testimonies among those of male and female rape survivors from countries including Nigeria, Iraq, and the Democratic Republic of Congo (DRC). One featured testimony was that of a male rape survivor from Uganda, where, the exhibit notes, male rape survivors often risk police arrest because of anti-gay laws. The exhibit included a panel about the Minova rape trial and the failure of the operational military court to hold senior DRC officers accountable for their role in the 2012 mass rapes of more than 1,000 women, children, and men. "Rape in Conflict" also featured six photographic panels with the testimonies of young Nigerian women abducted by Boko Haram and subjected to forced marriage and rape. Although the exhibit included individual survivors' testimonies, the overarching framework and visualization prioritized the logics of security that underwrite international civil society's two main approaches to conflict-based gender violence: *gendering security*, which "inserts women into a chain of protection" and *securitizing gender*, which focuses on "rape and sexual violence in the context of war regulations."[24] "Rape in Conflict" securitized gender in its focus on rape as genocide and gendered security in positioning Yazidi women as subjects of the UN prosecutorial gaze. Indeed, the convergence of these two approaches drives the UN's recognition of Yazidi women's political subjectivity and their status as human rights subjects.

The UN Independent International Commission of Inquiry on the Syrian Arab Republic also found that ISIS's actions amounted to genocide and crimes against humanity, as did the United States' in June 2016.[25] Yazda, a Yazidi women's rights organization, has likewise brought international awareness to the Yazidi genocide. Holding ISIS accountable for genocide will be an uphill battle, however, not only because of the complexity of fighting in northern Iraq and Syria and the challenges of international law but because of the veto power of the five permanent members of the UN Security Council, namely China and Russia, who vetoed a UN draft resolution (May 2014) calling for the crisis in Syria to be brought to the ICC. The reason this matters is that because Syria is not a party to the Rome Statute, the ICC can exercise jurisdiction only over crimes committed in its territory where there is a referral from the Security Council. In addition to these challenges, transnational and postcolonial feminist security scholars point to the limitations of the UN Resolutions on Women, Peace, and Security, such as UNSCR 1325 (2000) and Resolution 2122 (2013). These, they argue, do not sufficiently address the causes of conflict or "confront the structural roots of gender inequalities, including entrenched understandings of patriarchy, masculinity, and militarized power."[26] In prioritizing gender over other relations of power, the UN Resolutions on Women, Peace, and Security risk re-creating essentialist gendered and racialized boundaries that legitimize "white masculinist protection" and fail to account for how gender is constitutive of race, sexuality, class, and other relations of power.[27]

The international focus on gendered vulnerability and, specifically, sexual slavery as a form of terrorism, recalls the liberal feminist lexicon of sexual slavery derived from early anti-violence platforms that universalized women's victimization and tied their political subjectivity and human rights to bodily vulnerability. The UN "Rape in Conflict" exhibit heightened the visibility of women's vulnerability to rape and sexual slavery and thus echoed the UN Security Council platform in its call for greater attention to survivor-centered justice, though the discourse of the Council is more heavily steeped in securitization logics. While international anti-trafficking legislation may have shifted in the past decade from national security to a victim-centered approach, in its ongoing attachment to the UN Convention Against Transnational Organized Crime, anti-trafficking legislation continues to prioritize "state security over the individual well-being of trafficked persons."[28]

Similar attachments to state security and their entanglement with victim-centered objectives frame the UN "Rape in Conflict" exhibit, the April 2017 UN Report of the Secretary-General on Conflict-Related Sexual Violence, and the March 15, 2017, UN Security Council meeting, the latter two of which I discuss in the following section. Like *National Geographic Magazine*, the United Nations' contextualization of "Escaped" demonstrates how Yazidi women's human rights are entangled with visual forms of recognition and narrative curation. To some degree, the UN Report on Conflict-Related Sexual Violence, like the "Rape in Conflict" exhibit, foregrounds women's bodily vulnerability as the problem and aligns women's rights with this vulnerability.[29] The report, however, notably addresses infringements on women's rights via counterterrorism measures, such as detaining those released from captivity and needing to challenge norms that perpetuate victim blaming.[30] Below, I elaborate on the importance of understanding how representations of Yazidi women's gendered precarity are contingent on the discursive and material frames and forms of recognition through which it is addressed.

United Nations Report on Conflict-Related Sexual Violence

One of Salim's fifteen portraits from "Escaped" also appears on the cover of the 2017 UN Report on Conflict-Related Sexual Violence, submitted by the Office of the Special Representative of the Secretary-General on Sexual Violence in Conflict. In contrast to the "Rape in Conflict" exhibit, the report excises Yazidi women's testimonies. It indicates that the cover photograph is "part of a set of photographs of Iraqi Yazidi survivors of ISIL captivity" and refers to the UN "Rape in Conflict" exhibit. Although the report does not provide particularities about the woman depicted on the cover, the image retains evidentiary value as a pictorial reference to the "use of sexual violence as a tactic of terrorism" that the report highlights.

The report focuses on nineteen countries, including Iraq and the Syrian Arab Republic, and non-ISIS actors, including seven designated terrorist groups. The section on Iraq specifically mentions the rise of the Islamic State in 2014, brutal attacks by ISIS against civilians, and sexual violence primarily against women and girls from ethnic and religious minority groups. Both one-page country reports acknowledge the legal and cultural challenges to ensure the acceptance of survivors and their children, particularly children born to rape survivors, and call for legislative action to address these challenges as well as for intra- and intercommunity engagement and reconciliation. Both country reports address the plight of Yazidi women and girls who have been trafficked from Iraq into Syria. The report also briefly mentions "mass migration [and] the attendant risk of trafficking in persons for the purpose of sexual violence/exploitation" and how criminal-terrorist networks use "the bodies of women and girls as a form of currency in the political economy of war."[31]

The UN Office of the Special Representative of the Secretary-General on Sexual Violence in Conflict is one of the few intergovernmental entities that focuses on conflict-based sexual violence. But the institution also operates within a structure that far too often fails to address fundamental global interdependencies, culpabilities across and within nations, and the multidirectionality of power, including the multidirectionality of the power of culture. Like *National Geographic Magazine*, the UN exhibit and report render only certain stories and bodies and not others legible. "Only when 'embody[ing] the universal principles of peace and security,'" as Giddings notes in another context, "are women allowed to speak as representatives of other women."[32] The UN's focus on women's vulnerability, feminist security scholars argue, is shortsighted because "Women's vulnerability is . . . a problem that is continuous and persistent. Violence in war zones and peace zones are connected."[33] Feminist security scholars have therefore moved toward more relational modes of analysis. Greater attention to precarious interdependences and relations of power that constitute Yazidi women and girls' vulnerability would yield not only different analyses but also potentially different international, national, and regional responses and solutions. As Nicola Pratt argues, it is not "culture" alone that creates the conditions for gender-based violence but a range of factors, including failing political economies, the undermining of state institutions, the inflow of small arms, and backlash against foreign interventions, in which UN member states may be implicated.[34]

In her briefing to the UN Security Council on June 2, 2016, Zainab Hawa Bangura, the UN Secretary General's Special Representative on Sexual Violence in Conflict, highlighted the significance of conceptual frameworks in addressing violence against women in conflict zones, explicitly mentioning Yazidi women and girls. Bangura said, "The war of conquest of extremist groups is being fought on and fought over the bodies of women and girls." She continued, "It is the revival of the slave trades in our own life and times. Extremists know that to populate a territory and control a population, you must first control the bodies of women." Bangura described the terrorists' abduction of and sexual violence against Yazidi women and girls as a "revival of the slave trade," and she appealed to the Yazidi and international community to turn away from the cultural framing of sexual slavery. "Sexual violence is not cultural but criminal," she said. "When we think of terrorism," she asserted, "we tend to think of hijacking, hostage taking, explosions, and property destruction. But we cannot deplore the public face of terrorism while ignoring the violence that terrorists inflict on women and girls in private, behind closed doors."

In a similar move, Yazidi spiritual leader Baba Sheikh Khurto Hajji Ismail appealed on two occasions (September 6, 2014, and February 6, 2015) to

Yazidi families to welcome women and girls who had been held as sex slaves back into the community. Traditional marriage norms forbid Yazidi women from marrying or having sexual relations outside their community or caste. He said, "These survivors remain pure Yazidis, and no one may injure their Yazidi faith because they were subjected to a matter outside their control. We therefore call on everyone to cooperate with and support these victims so that they may again live their normal lives and integrate into society."[35] The edict followed meetings with longtime Yazidi activists, such as Khider Domle, who told the spiritual leader, "We need the religious councils to help these women who returned back."[36] The iteration of the doctrinal change importantly diminished the shaming of victims, and, as Bangura reports, once the women heard they would be welcomed back, the number of escapees increased and suicide rates declined.

Bangura's call to the international community to shift from framing sexual violence and terrorism as cultural pathologies and the spiritual leader's appeal may counter stereotypes about gender violence in the Middle East and represent a rupture of traditional Yazidi attitudes about sexual purity and marriage. Nevertheless, we also have to consider that by allowing for a process of reclamation, these appeals may in the end reify rather than fundamentally challenge normative cultural codes. Consider the explanation of another Yazidi spiritual leader, Baba Chawish, for the doctrinal change: "Iraqi's Yazidis are already an extreme minority in the country. Losing thousands of Yazidi women and their children would be unsustainable. Now we've said that the door is open for everyone who has been raped, they can still be purified and baptized . . . as if nothing happened to them."[37] To point to how male Yazidi spiritual leaders serve as cultural brokers responding to the vulnerability of the entire Yazidi community is not to suggest that Yazidi cultural traditions are the cause of women's vulnerability to Islamic terrorism.[38] Islamic fundamentalism, not Yazidi cultural traditions, is ISIS's primary inspiration for these atrocities. Moreover, many of the women were married before; their husbands were slaughtered by ISIS. Therefore, the women's concerns transcend the concept of purity. For example, there remain unresolved issues such as the status of children born to those who were raped.[39]

A 2015 UNHRC (UN Refugee Agency) report, "Yazidi Women Welcomed Back to the Faith," characterizes the religious edict as follows: "Religious leaders break with tradition, letting women and girls rejoin the Yazidi community after surviving abductions, forced conversion, and rape." As one survivor put it, "For us, tradition is the most important thing." She continued: "I don't know how else to say it. I was just so happy, because I had been hurt. . . . I wanted to be clean again." Reporter Susannah George indicates that the young woman was very thankful for the new religious interpretation that enabled her to reunite with her family and writes that she had been "baptized back into the faith—a rite that would have been impossible just a few months ago." While Leila (survivor above, pseudonym) notes that although the "community support and religious ceremony have helped, it hasn't erased her ordeal completely. 'I don't feel back to normal. I don't think I'll ever be normal again.'"

Leila's testimony points to the need to understand precariousness as embodied and relational, namely as linked to relations of power and the forms of recognition that such relations render legible. Moreover, the religious ceremony and "baptism back into the faith," one might argue, recode the criminal violation as a cultural violation and, in so doing, reveal the fundamental interdependence of legal and cultural formations of women's rights. While highlighting cultural discrimination and stigma is important, the cultural legitimacy thesis counters Bangura's proposition and as such points to a slippage in the UN stance on conflict-based sexual violence between the cultural and criminal framework, which overgeneralizes the patriarchy as the root of the problem. In this regard, the UN turns international public attention away from the host of economic, political, and military processes in which other UN member states may be implicated and that empower the distinct and local forms of hetero-patriarchal gender ideologies that facilitate violence against women.[40] These critical tensions are essential to understanding the international response to Islamic terrorism and the plight of the Yazidi people.

In contrast to the UN exhibit and report, the embedding of "Escaped" within the context of the "Map of Displacement" project shifts from an international security framework toward an understanding of the precarity of women's rights in relation to mass displacement, dispossession, structural vulnerabilities, environmental hazards, and familial and community resilience.

The "Map of Displacement" Project: Community Building and Resilience

The "Map of Displacement" is a collaborative project by Kurdish Iraqi photographers of the Metrography photo agency and international journalists. According to its curators, Stefano Carini and Dario Bosio, the goal of the project is to counter the media industry's impulse to sensationalize violence. Bosio states,

> International readers need to understand the magnitude of this crisis. In Europe, there are 900,000 refugees and rising escaping the Middle East. This influx looks like a really big deal to these countries, and so you get these propagandist speeches saying it's an invasion, that there's no money, that all Muslims are bad, and so on. Well, Kurdistan had an existing population of about 5 million people, and that's now increased by a third—all displaced people. The magnitude of the problem here is ten times bigger. This project will help international audiences frame the situation, tackle the issues with the right attitudes, and avoid lazy generalizations.

Situated as part of a larger story about the internal displacement of millions of Iraqis, Salim's portraits and the Yazidi women's testimonies serve as evidence of Islamic terrorism but also take on an additional rhetorical function: "to tell a more human story." Iraq currently contains the largest internally displaced populations in the world. Due to ISIS control of territory in western and northern Iraq, more than 3 million people have been driven from their homes since January 2014. The "Map of Displacement" is organized according to the six largest displacement events in the Kurdistan Region of Iraq. "Escaped" is one of four features that appear under the "Sinjar massacre" designation. The other three stories are the "Grand Baghdad Hotel," which follows displaced Yazidi families sheltering in old hotels; "The Exemplary School of Sitak," which is about a Muslim man who started a school with help from a British NGO; and "Oil and Blood," which focuses on a family that escaped to the Kurdistan region and found refuge in an oil refinery. The Sinjar massacre stories are preceded in the time line by stories about the fall of Fallujah (January 4, 2014), which led to the displacement of 380,000 Iraqis; the fall of Mosul to ISIS (June 9, 2014), when more than half a million fled; and Nineveh's ethnic cleansing (August 7, 2014), when ISIS took the largest Christian city in the Nineveh Plains, causing more than 100,000 to flee to the Kurdistan Region. The other three displacements are the battle between July 2014 and April 2015, when the Iraqi army and Shia militias battled ISIS in Diyala, Mosul, and Tikrit, from which tens of thousands fled; the Iraqi military and U.S., British, and Iranian coalition offensive forces to retake Tikrit on March 2, 2015, after which 30,000 people were displaced; and the fall of Ramadi (May 14, 2015), which displaced 180,000 and brought the total number of displaced people in Anbar Province to 450,000.

According to the "Map of Displacement" website, the Islamic State is the primary perpetrator of these violent displacements, though Saddam Hussein's regime, which perpetuated ethno-religious conflicts, Al Qaeda, and anti-government forces, is also implicated.[41] United States coalition airstrikes, which assisted Kurdish fighters in pushing back ISIS in August 2014, appear throughout the featured stories. However, the "Map of Displacement" does not establish a causal link between the U.S. and coalition forces' illegal invasion and occupation of Iraq in 2003 and the present violence, though international security scholars have linked these events.[42] The "Map of Displacement" characterizes the Sunni militants' massacre as a "genocidal campaign" that killed "tens of thousands of people and kidnapped over 5,000 women who they later sold into sexual slavery." Like the UN "Rape in Conflict" exhibit, sexual slavery and genocide are the primary frames for understanding the plight of Yazidi women and girls.

Though the project does not explicitly deploy the language of human rights, it presents the displaced as citizens "caught in the crossfire" and as "true victims of this intractable conflict" and Iraq's war against ISIS. "Through intimate narratives of these people who have been violently forced to flee, the 'Map of Displacement' illustrates the magnitude and poignancy of this under-reported crisis." The "Map of Displacement" includes stories of individual and familial resilience, tolerance, and community building. There are several stories about families rebuilding their lives; about men discussing politics and socializing over tea or drinks; about two families, one Christian and the other Sunni, living under the same roof; and about a thirteen-year-old boy who fled violence and now works as a butcher in a remote Kurdish village. Here, we understand how violence fractures families and how the men and boys who are displaced navigate new territories and relationships.

The absence of such stories about Yazidi women, however, replicates the stasis of Yazidi women as victims. One sees this, for example, in the representation of Syhan, a Yazidi woman whose story has been translated into a third-person narrative of her movement from Turkey to northern Iraq as evidence of forced mobility and displacement. Syhan does not have any agency whatsoever in this narration, other than posing for the camera. The narrative that appears within the exhibit reads as follows: "Syhan fell pregnant during her captivity and escaped when she was in her eighth month. She stayed in Turkey for two months until the baby was born. She came back to northern Iraq but wasn't able to bring the baby with her from Turkey. She doesn't know where he is." Her story is told in the passive voice, as if there is no perpetrator, as if neither she nor the perpetrator was an agent. Although Syhan is absent as the narrator of her own story, we also need to question our desire for first-person narratives, and acknowledge the potential that such desires minimize the need for more people to tell these stories, so as not to place the burden of representation solely on victims. The "Map of Displacement" introduces the possibility of understanding how displacement makes women more vulnerable as targets for abduction, but in contrast to its depiction of Iraqi men and boys, the project is silent on the aftermath of abducted women's escape.

Although the "Map of Displacement" also does not explicitly address the link between gendered vulnerability and violent displacements, it does afford greater attention to the history of conflict in the region and precarious material conditions and interdependences. Take, for example, 'Oil and Blood,' the featured story in the 'Sinjar massacre' section depicting a family who escaped to the Kurdistan region of northern Iraq and found refuge in an oil refinery. The family made a substantial profit running the small refinery, but their time there was accompanied by serious health risks as a result of exposure to carbon monoxide and benzene. The story also addresses the intricate transnational oil economies of Iraqi Kurdistan, namely after 2003 Iraq's autonomous Kurdistan region experienced "unprecedented oil exploration." Gulf Keystone discovered the reserve but soon sold out to larger companies, such as ExxonMobil, Chevron, and Total. Not only are the environmental consequences of violence significant; they are also linked to health-care crises. The International Organization for Migration reports far-reaching humanitarian needs as nearly 2 million displaced Iraqis return home, including shortages of food and clean drinking water and lack of electricity and heat.[43]

The "Map of Displacement" frames displacement not only as a security problem but also as a condition of economic dispossession and environmental devastation. The exhibit as a whole does not make the sexual subjection of Yazidi women the sole condition for the recognition of their rights. In this regard, it paves the way for an analytical and contextual shift toward a relational understanding of Yazidi human rights and political subjectivity. The UN and U.S. declaration of ISIS's atrocities against the Yazidi as genocide is highly significant, but the designation problematically positions some nations as the couriers of rights and others as recipients and thereby truncates the assessment of how national and foreign policies, not to mention multinational companies' acquisition of natural resources, contribute to the present crisis. More broadly, some UN representatives have argued that neoliberal capitalism and imperialism, not terrorism, are the primary facilitators of forced migration and displacement. At a March 15, 2017, UN Security Council meeting, for example, representative Sacha Sergio Llorenti Soliz, of Bolivia, claimed the "neoliberal system had led to mass migration, but war and conflict arising from efforts to effect regime change had exacerbated the problem."[44] At the same meeting, Iranian representative Gholamali Khoshroo indicated that "occupation, war, political instability, terrorism, genocide, ethnic cleansing, and foreign aggression created conditions that forced millions to become displaced . . . and vulnerable to human trafficking."[45] Like the "Map of Displacement," these UN representatives point to the political economies of mass migration and violent conflict.

These four contextual mediations of "Escaped" foreground how geopolitical discourses and global and local systems of power set the parameters for the recognition (or lack thereof) of Yazidi women's political subjectivity and how the gendering of international security, human rights, and cultural legitimacy intersect in various rhetorical contexts to position Yazidi women as human rights subjects. Yet, as Jessica Auchter reminds us, "the subjects we talk about are constantly being constructed and are [also] constructing themselves."[46] Our duty as scholars studying representations of sexual violence against women in the context of war and terrorism, therefore, is to not only engage in critical reflexivity when representing victims' experiences but also expose the politically precarious position of women's human rights in domestic U.S. and international political contexts and media, as well as to acknowledge the partiality of all interpretive acts and the contingencies that shape our own engagements.

PART II

WHO IS SUBJECT TO HUMAN RIGHTS?

CHAPTER 6

Training Subjects for Human Rights

Danielle Celermajer

FROM A FORMAL POINT OF VIEW, the addressee of human rights is the state, and as such, appropriately fashioned law and policy would be the means for ensuring respect for human rights. At the same time, however, states' actions, laws, and policies are shaped and implemented by people acting separately and in concert. The task of bringing about changes to the state is thus necessarily mediated though changing people. As I will argue in this chapter, such a picture of humans steering and implementing law and policy is complicated by the fact that those people are themselves already embedded in and continually shaped by existing institutional and cultural contexts, and these may be hostile to human rights. This implies that change ought not to be thought of as a linear process—where we would seek to change persons so that they will then change institutions, or vice versa—but in more interactive or co-constitutive terms. Nevertheless, the business of bringing about changes to state laws and policies (and their implementation) so as to better align them with human rights standards will always involve human actors and their first-person perspectives on normative issues.

For analytic purposes, we can imagine a map of the relationship between individuals and states' human rights laws and policies including, on one side, individuals' input, or how they shape and influence the state, and on the other, the state's output, or how its laws and policies are implemented or interpreted by individuals. On the input side, in democratic states at least, individuals occupy the role of citizens, who can bring pressure to bear to influence the state in relation to its respect for human rights: minimally at the ballot box, and more fulsomely through civil society activism. Where people are themselves victims of violations, they may assume, or be encouraged to assume, an active role in demanding or advocating for their rights to be respected. On the output side, in their capacity as agents of the state, different classes of people, such as judicial officers or security sector and law enforcement officials, constitute the "face" of state law and policy, and it is through their choices and actions that human rights are, in practice, either realized or violated.

It thus makes sense that one of the principal approaches that human rights organizations have adopted to translate the ideals laid out in international instruments into practical respect for human rights has involved seeking to influence human subjects in these various capacities. On the input side, human rights campaigns adopt rhetorical and affective strategies to try to heighten the public's sense of responsibility for the plight of victims—even distant ones—and thence take action.[1] On the output side, the most prominent means of exercising influence over state agents, particularly those at risk of violating human rights, has been through the promulgation of criminal sanctions, intended to alter individuals' incentive structures by attaching highly undesirable consequences to their violating human rights. The promulgation of formal legal sanctions is also grounded in the understanding that beyond this direct role, laws play an expressive or constitutive role in establishing the officially sanctioned normative environment within which subjects are formed and act.[2]

Beyond the threat of punishment, a more formative approach to ensuring that the people who implement state law and policy are the types of subjects who will respect human rights is human rights education and training.[3] The explicit objective of such educational interventions is to produce subjects who are informed about human rights, who hold values consistent with them, and who will act in conformity with their standards. Human rights education can, in this sense, be understood as the technology adopted for producing the subjects of and for human rights.

If this is the case, human rights education must, even if only implicitly, contain a theory about the nature of that subject. Any strategy or technique directed toward changing how or whom the subject is, or what she values and believes, necessarily entails a theory about the nature of the subject. Criminal law, for example, may be thought to work on the basis of a theory that the subject is the type of being whose choices and actions are determined (at least in part) by a desire to avoid punishment; this subject is one who is moved by a utilitarian calculus. If one understands criminal law in expressive or constitutive terms, the subject is imagined differently, as one whose individual normative orientation is given by their normative environment. Insofar as the field of human rights adopts criminal law as one of its principal mechanisms, it could be said to assume these different models of the subject.

Human rights education, by contrast, operates according to a different logic and so will assume a different theory of the subject. Tracking how human rights education sets out to achieve its objective of forming subjects who will act in conformity with human rights can provide us with a distinct window into how this human rights strategy understands its subject. In other words, by examining the methods of contemporary human rights education we can discern—or, if you like, reverse engineer—the theory of the subject that underpins and informs it. In this chapter, I reflect on the question of how the subject of human rights is imagined in human rights education and then consider the implications of such assumed models for the efficacy of the approach.

The field of human rights education has become vast and is developed, supported, funded, and undertaken by a large number and variety of organizations adopting a broad range of approaches and operating in very different contexts. Moreover, consistent with the different roles that people play vis à vis human rights, human rights education is directed at very different types of audiences, and it would be presumptive to assume that the same theory is (or ought to be) at work when the subject in question is the citizen or bystander (who might be indifferent or concerned), the victim (who might be cowed or politicized), or the state agent (who might be a perpetrator or whistle-blower). For the purposes of this chapter, then, I focus on human rights education as it has been developed for, and is delivered to, law enforcement officials, specifically police. Because law enforcement officials are invested by the state with the means of violence, and in light of their asymmetrical relationship with ordinary citizens, they have a singular capacity to commit serious human rights violations, and this remains true even when their actions are formally regulated by law.[4] As such, and given the feared default—that is, a subject inimical to human rights—law enforcement officials constitute a useful group for thinking through how the process of positively creating a (respectful) subject of human rights has been imagined.

An examination of how human rights education of law enforcement officials is undertaken turns out to be quite revealing. Based on an analysis of dominant educational approaches, I make two arguments. The first draws on the observation that although formal lip service is given to the importance of attitudes and values, the overwhelming emphasis is on developing individuals' knowledge about human rights standards. Providing such knowledge not only forms the most substantive portion of the content of educational interventions; it is also assumed to be the means for effecting attitudinal as well as behavioral change. In this regard, the subject of human rights is understood in primarily cognitive terms, as one who makes rational, calculated decisions about what they ought to do, based on what they know to be the case. Moreover, the assumed subject is one whose actions are a correlate of their knowledge, beliefs, and values. This picture of the subject as autonomous and primarily cognitive is, I would argue, consistent with the foundational philosophy of human rights, grounded as it is in an understanding of the human being whose dignity lies in their status as an individual, rational, and intentional agent. Given, however, what we now understand about the extent to which it is the situation and system, and not one's individual disposition, that shapes the actions of law enforcement officials, this picture of the subject may ill serve us when it comes to reconstituting the potential perpetrator as a subject of and for human rights.[5]

My second argument concerns what I see as a certain degree of ambivalence in the field of human rights education about how subjects make judgments about right and wrong. This argument builds on the observation that education programs oscillate between two different conceptions of normative principles and judgements. The first understands principles as operating according to a consequentialist logic: there, subjects are confronted with the costs and benefits associated with violating or respecting human rights. The second understands principles in more deontological terms: subjects are invited to embrace human rights as an ethically superior form of life. When educational interventions operate with the first logic, they treat the subject as one who acts so as to maximize their individual benefit and minimize costs. For this subject, the self-determination described above occurs through a process of *calculating* the most efficient and effective means to achieve ends that are assumed to be given or natural—maximizing well-being and minimizing pain. By contrast, when human rights education operates according to the second logic, it treats the subject as a free and reasoning being capable of embracing a form of life on the basis of an independent ethical judgment that is not simply the outcome of a utilitarian calculus designed to produce an assumed end. These are, I suggest, two quite different types of subjects: one we are resigned to managing and one to which we might aspire.

To substantiate these arguments, this chapter begins with some background on the development of human rights education and its principal conceptual components, focusing, then, on the key characteristics of the prevalent approaches to human rights education for law enforcement officials. By way of contrast, I consider how education for normative change is approached in the field of public health, highlighting its significant attention to the contexts within which individuals form values and take actions. I then return to how the dominant educational approach assumed in the field of human rights conceives of the "subject to be transformed" and reflect on how implicit assumptions about the subject may impede the transformation they seek.

Human Rights Education and Training for Law Enforcement Officials

Already in its Preamble, the Universal Declaration of Human Rights (UDHR) of 1948 proclaimed "that every individual and every organ of society, keeping this Declaration constantly in mind, shall strive by teaching and education to promote respect for these rights and freedoms." This proclamation is reiterated in Article 26(2), which explicitly charges education with the role of promoting "understanding, tolerance and friendship among all nations, racial or religious groups," and, more generally, furthering the "activities of the United Nations for the maintenance of peace." Many of the core human rights instruments that flowed from the UDHR similarly and explicitly require that states party provide members of relevant groups with human rights education to promote the specific rights recognized in the treaty. Most applicable to our subject, Article 10 of the Convention Against Torture and Other Cruel, Inhuman or Degrading Treatment or Punishment (CAT) explicitly requires that states party ensure that law enforcement personnel receive education regarding the prohibition against torture. Correlatively, it is standard practice for those organs of the UN that have jurisdiction to oversee the implementation of norms against torture, such as the Special Rapporteur on Torture and the Committee Against Torture, to seek information about and report on the extent to which this is happening. Where this is not the case, or where the educational programs are found to be inadequate, they generally call for the state in question to fulfill its obligations and provide or improve its educational programs.[6]

The UDHR's initial and general embrace of the role of education in realizing human rights was reaffirmed by the 1993 Vienna Declaration and Programme of Action (Section 1, para. 33), which in turn underpinned the proclamation of the United Nations Decade for Human Rights Education

(1995–2004).[7] This initial time-limited decade was followed by an open-ended second phase, the World Programme for Human Rights Education (2005–present).[8] On December 19, 2011, the General Assembly adopted the Declaration on Human Rights Education and Training, which reaffirms "that education and training is essential for the promotion of universal respect for and observance of all human rights" (Article 1.2); sets out some of the main target groups for human rights education (Article 3.2), explicitly including law enforcement personnel (Articles 7.4 and 11); and clarifies that the term "human rights education" refers to education "about" human rights, "through" human rights, and "for" human rights (Article 2).[9] That is, its content ought to inform people about human rights, its methodologies ought to be consistent with the principles of human rights, and it ought to effectively produce better practical respect for human rights.

Parallel with these formal standard-setting activities, the past two decades have seen the rapid proliferation of specialist nongovernmental organizations, or specialist units within mainstream human rights organizations, focusing on the development and delivery of human rights education and training resources and advocating their rollout across a range of sectors.[10] While there is a range of approaches to human rights education adopted by these various organizations and programs, they are generally oriented by the tripartite approach that the UN World Programme for Human Rights Education articulated: to bring about behavioral change by effecting changes in knowledge, skills, and attitudes.[11]

Turning to human rights education specifically for law enforcement personnel, it remains unclear precisely what proportion of police across the world receive human rights education and training, or exactly what type of training they receive, but we can glean from the reports provided to the committee that oversees the CAT, which periodically examines the actions of all states party in implementing the treaty, that at least some type of human rights education for police occurs in much of the world. Such education is either delivered as part of standard induction and training or as part of ongoing professional programs, either in-house by specialist (or at least designated) training personnel, or, in many cases, by external specialist experts or organizations. To resource such efforts, a number of international organizations and international human rights nongovernmental organizations, such as the UN Office of the High Commissioner for Human Rights, the International Commission of the Red Cross (ICRC), the Council of Europe, the Organization for

Security and Cooperation in Europe (OSCE), the Commonwealth Secretariat, and Amnesty International, have developed a significant body of educational material that is frequently used in such training and education.

All that said, obtaining accurate knowledge about exactly what occurs during such programs, and thus being in a position to critically analyze them, is no easy task.[12] While it is possible to access many of the written training resources that are officially used, if the actual training is unobserved it remains unclear how those resources are deployed and what types of pedagogic approaches are in fact employed. This data gap becomes particularly problematic when we are trying to understand *how* an intervention operates. Here, for example, we are interested in how trainings seek to bring about value or attitudinal change and in assessing the pedagogic approaches that, in practice, may depart significantly from those set out in formal guidelines. Indeed, even if we have empirical data on training methods gathered by asking police training institutions or police departments detailed questions about how they go about doing human rights education, we are reliant on the (very shaky) assumption that self-reporting accurately reflects practice.

To find out more about what actually happens during human rights training for security sector personnel, and as part of a larger project on the prevention of torture in the police and military, I led a team to conduct empirical research on the substance and methods adopted in human rights trainings delivered across the world.[13] In response to a questionnaire we sent out to police and military in countries across the world, and in interviews with trainers, we were informed on a number of occasions that experiential and varied pedagogic approaches were adopted, but upon further probing, or when we had the opportunity to observe trainings, it transpired that virtually the sole educational approach taken was lecture-style delivery of information about human rights. Evaluations carried out on the impact of human rights trainings are also problematically thin, often providing little more than sparse data on the number of participants, their rating of the training, and the results of basic tests of knowledge acquired.

Nevertheless, the comprehensive analysis we conducted of the educational materials that have been developed internationally and that circulate through the field, combined with direct empirical research of and with law enforcement organizations and trainers, does provide useful information about the type of training that is undertaken and the dominant approaches. Despite some variation in practices—and, no doubt, occasionally truly innovative pedagogy—there exists significant uniformity in educational content and approach. The standard approach can be captured by reference to four main pillars: making the case to participants of the importance of human rights; setting out the relevant laws and penalties; linking human rights standards with particular operational aspects of policing; and seeking to change participants' values.[14] I discuss each briefly below.

Virtually all educational programs commence by introducing the key principles of human rights, such as universality, indivisibility, and inalienability, and setting out some of the fundamental aspects of the human rights idea, such as the equal dignity of all persons and non-discrimination. This introductory material sometimes includes a history of the development of human rights, at times oddly referencing aspects of that history remote from the lives or educational backgrounds of participants.[15]

Next, the training lays out the case for why participants ought to recognize the importance of human rights in their professional capacities. We might regard this component of the educational process as the invitation or enrollment of subjects into the educational process: "Why should you care, and why should this matter to you?"

This appeal generally takes one of two forms, often in combination. The first is deontological and purely ethical. Here, participants are presented with the foundational premise of human rights: that all humans have a fundamental and unassailable dignity. Once we recognize the validity of this premise, it follows that as ethical beings, we are under a duty to respect the various obligations that flow from this recognition. Thus presented, human rights are ends in themselves, and subjects are called upon to recognize them insofar as they are themselves free and ethical human beings, capable of reason, amongst other equally free, ethical, and reasoning human beings.

The other approach is instrumental; here, respect for human rights is presented as the means to ensure the achievement of certain independently valued ends, which need not in themselves be ethical. In the case of human rights education for police, human rights are presented as conducive to achieving the types of ends that police already embrace in their professional capacity, such as efficiently and effectively ensuring that criminals are apprehended and appropriately punished. Respecting human rights is thus framed as the best way to get their job done (for example, by obtaining admissible evidence that will lead to a conviction), and, correlatively, the failure to respect human rights could well impede their work, either because it may result in police themselves coming under sanction or suffering reputational damage that undermines their ability to effectively work with the public or other institutions. More immediately, in this kind of instrumental reasoning, respecting human rights is connected with beneficial outcomes for the individual (promotion or esteem) and the avoidance of undesirable outcomes (being punished or not getting promoted).

Returning to the components of most human rights training curricula, the next and most substantial component of education and training programs comprises information or factual material about human rights norms, laws, and institutions. Programs generally set out the core international human rights treaties, with a particular emphasis on those dealing with the relevant rights (such as those pertaining to respect for persons and bodily integrity). Information may also be presented on related instruments directly relevant to policing practice, such as the UN Code of Conduct for Law Enforcement Officials, or on relevant regional treaties, national constitutions, domestic human rights and antidiscrimination laws, and more local organization-specific codes of conduct. Material frequently includes information about the various mechanisms for enforcement. Notable here is the considerable emphasis placed on informing personnel about the formal punishments that they might (hypothetically) face for violating human rights, despite the rarity of formal sanctions actually being implemented. Communicating the presence of laws that ought to regulate and constrain behavior—and, contrariwise, the threat of punishment for violations—constitutes perhaps the principal tool in the arsenal of human rights education.

The third pillar involves explicitly linking formal human rights standards with operational dimensions of policing. The development of this component represents an innovation in training approaches in response to earlier criticisms that that training was overly abstract and removed from the practical concerns of police personnel.[16] What this actually looks like, though, is generally a list of standards attached to particular policing duties. A series of modules consider key aspects of policing practice such as arrest, detention, the use of force, and investigation, accompanied by citations or paraphrasing of the relevant human rights standards.[17] Whether providing informational links between standards and areas of practice effectively satisfies the original criticism is questionable, assuming, as it seems to, that if people know the rules that apply to particular areas of practice, they can and will (if appropriately motivated) apply them. When I spoke with experienced trainers, they indicated that addressing concerns about practicality requires intensive and experiential pedagogic methods, such as realistic case studies or role plays. Our research indicated, however, that the conditions required to support this type of pedagogy (small class sizes, trainers who have both pedagogic skills and detailed, site-specific operational knowledge) are extremely rare, and as such, this ideal is rarely operationalized. For the most part, the approach remains abstract, cognitive, and didactic.

The fourth pillar addresses the second dimension of the human rights education approach: changing values and attitudes, with a view to participants' embracing values conducive to their respecting human rights. What interests me here is how human rights education programs typically go about trying to bring about such attitudinal and value change. When one looks at the contents and methods of trainings, what one finds is that the achievement of this quite distinctive dimension of change is, for the most part, assumed to be affected by telling people that human rights are important, setting out the reasons why they should care about them, and providing them with information about the content of human rights standards. An excerpt from the United Nations training manual, advising trainers on how to approach this problem, illustrates the pattern:

> Address attitudes as well as knowledge (what is important, why it is important for the audience and how they can use that knowledge for their betterment). Having exposed the audience to the relevant standards and practice, you must explain how and why present attitudes and behavior must change. Emphasize why it is important for, and in the interest of, the target audience to respect the standards and follow the practice.[18]

Changes in values and attitudes are, in other words, assumed to occur as a by-product of changes in knowledge. The problem is that it is now well established that, while necessary, knowledge is by no means sufficient for bringing about attitudinal change.[19] As William O'Neill points out in his analysis of UN human rights training for police, "[M]ost police officers in most places know already that they are not supposed to beat or torture people, extract bribes or become involved in trafficking of any kind—drugs or people. And most people know that the police should not do these things. Training and increased knowledge of rights alone will not change behavior or prevent human rights violations by the police."[20] Indeed, in those cases where telling people which values they ought to hold does have some impact, this tends to be an effect of the authority of the speaker and the dynamics of compliance amongst peers, rather than the result of people simply receiving the semantic content of the message.[21] That this is the case is even more concerning when we recognize that training units and trainers generally enjoy a fairly low status in law enforcement organizations, with human rights training often seen as a box-ticking exercise that carries little organizational weight. Nevertheless, trainers' admonishing participants to change their attitudes remains a prevalent approach.

Recognizing the limits of cognitive-based knowledge, some training resources encourage trainers to use potentially more productive approaches to changing values and attitudes—such as presenting participants with difficult ethical cases and asking them to work through them[22] or bringing participants into controlled and mediated contact with members of those groups toward whom they are likely to hold discriminatory or stereotypical attitudes.[23] Again, however, the gap between the ideals that emerge from the theories that underpin these strategies and what occurs, or is able to occur, in actual (and generally highly constrained) practice is vast. Even when such approaches draw on fairly robust theories, considerable expertise is required to operationalize them and specifically to manage the way participants respond to ethical dilemmas or what occurs when hostile groups are brought together. For example, observations of trainings in Sri Lanka evidenced the real danger that when ethically difficult cases are raised, trainers may simply affirm the attitudes that participants express and that are inimical to respect for human rights, particularly if those trainers belong to the same institution or are not skilled in dealing with ethical conflict. While manuals may recommend the discussion of difficult cases, none of the training resources we examined provided robust guidance for trainers about what to do when participants express views that are highly inimical to human rights.[24] With respect to bringing police together with groups toward whom they are hostile, one highly experienced trainer I interviewed described her team's attempt to do this with police in the Philippines and the unintended consequence that it provided police with more "evidence" that human rights advocates were simply interested in protecting "communists."[25]

Coming back to the dominant approach to attitudinal change, as O'Neill's comments above evidence, I am by no means the first person to observe the flawed assumption that improving knowledge could be sufficient to effect attitudinal and behavioral changes. Nor am I the first to point to the implicit assumption that a lack of knowledge is causally related to personnel's committing human rights violations. Nevertheless, and in contrast to cognate fields where it is now well understood that successfully changing attitudes requires strategies that target the context within which attitudes are formed, the cognitive and individualist emphasis remains virtually ubiquitous in the human rights field.

To further bring this flaw into relief, we might briefly look at some developments in how attitudinal change is understood and approached in public health, a field similarly concerned with the values and attitudes that underpin pathological behaviors, such as sexual and gender-based violence. Admittedly, there are important differences between the two, most notably that in the human rights case, the individuals in question are operating in their official and institutional capacity, whereas in the case of the behaviors that public health targets, people are generally operating in a private and individual capacity. Nevertheless, insofar as both seek to shift how people understand themselves and their values, there are important commonalities. Indeed, if anything, the effect of the institutional context on individual attitudes and values is likely to be stronger in the case of law enforcement officials. This being the case, one would expect interventions taking place in this context to place a greater emphasis on attending to the "atrocity producing situation."[26] However, precisely the opposite is the case.

While it is beyond the scope of this chapter to discuss the theories underpinning public health interventions or to survey the types of educational practices they have developed, a few observations point toward those components that are most important for our purposes. First, many contemporary public health interventions take as their starting point the understanding that an individual's attitudes and values are constituted through, and sustained by, their social context and within relationships that matter to them. A person's attitudes and values are largely responsive not only to what others around them appear to believe and value but, importantly, to what the person assumes these others expect of them.[27] In this regard, it is important to distinguish between a person's "espoused theory of action," which is how they believe or report that they would (hypothetically) act in a given situation, and their "theory-in-use," which governs how they actually act when the situation arises.[28] Effective educational interventions need to target change in terms of the latter.

According to the Fishbein-Ajzen theory of motivation, a prominent theory of behavioral change, a person's attitude (in use, not espoused) to performing a certain act is influenced by their beliefs about the consequences of performing the action, as well as by their evaluation of those consequences. Such beliefs and evaluations are in turn shaped by others' beliefs and evaluations. More specifically, a person's evaluation of what others whom they consider significant believe should be done determines their motivation to act in a particular way. They will thus look to those significant others, sometimes known as referents, to orient their own beliefs and thence work out what they ought to do. In summary, what others believe and value, as mediated by how important those others are to the person in question, will shape what the person in question believes and values. None of this is to say that individuals are just pawns in collective dynamics nor that they are incapable of resistance or divergence, but a significant body of research on the dynamics of conformity, much of it, importantly, in institutional settings, indicates that contravening collectively held norms represents the exception.[29]

The lesson that follows for human rights education is that attitudinal and value change cannot be achieved simply by targeting people at the level of that particular individual, because their attitudes and values are shaped by the beliefs and attitudes of significant others or by salient social norms and are always contextual. Recognizing this complex interaction between individual attitudes and values, group attitudes and values, and social norms has led public health practitioners to insist that effective value and attitudinal transformation requires interventions at multiple levels and, most importantly, at the level of social networks and the community environment.[30] In practice, this has been the basis for educational programs that address the attitudes, values, and behaviors of the people to whom target individuals look for guidance (their referents), as well as interventions that encourage positive bystander behaviors.[31] In other words, the educational approach taken in many contemporary public health settings approaches the subject to be changed as a subject who is formed and reformed in context and who recognizes that the context, not the abstracted subject, needs to be the principal target of educational efforts.

The Imagined Subject of Human Rights or (to Be Educated) for Human Rights

The analysis of the four dominant pillars of human rights education for police now places us in a position where we can deduce the dominant understanding of "the subject to be educated." In this final section, I turn to how we might characterize this imagined subject of human rights education.

The first conclusion we can draw about the assumed subject of human rights is derived from an analysis of the first pillar of educational programs, which seeks to enroll the subject into human rights and convince them that adopting a human-rights-based approach to their work is worthwhile. As noted above, this invitation tends to take two forms, one deontological and the other instrumental. When the first is adopted, the subject is invited to recognize that living in a manner that affords paramount value to respect for human rights is ethically superior, irrespective of the apparent outcomes that refusing to violate rights might produce, either from the point of view of one's own interests, or even according to the results of a broader (collective) utilitarian calculus. Indeed, characterized in its purest Kantian form, accession to the moral imperative precisely involves the renunciation of the interests that would arise from satisfying appetites, passions, or desires and cannot be evaluated according to the ends of the action.[32] The tensions between acting so as to fulfill what might be identified as interests or benefits, or acting so as to produce desirable consequences, on the one hand, and acting according to the moral law (in this case posited as human rights), on the other, is clearly evident in the insistence that certain rights, such as the right to be free from torture (or, as it is more usually expressed, the prohibition on torture), are non-derogable. That is, the prohibition on torture holds as an absolute commitment irrespective consequentialist arguments that would seek to justify the overall benefit of its deployment.[33] Understood thus, putting to people the proposition that they ought to observe human rights for fear of punishment and desire for reward or benefit not only introduces irrelevancies, it positively contaminates the process whereby properly moral agents would decide to live according to principles of human rights. It is to treat them as subjects who make moral decisions based on instrumental calculations that are, in turn, based on appetitive (and thus nonethical) ends.

It is, however, precisely this proscribed instrumental approach that is adopted when personnel are enticed to respect human rights by being confronted with the pros and cons of doing so: punishment to follow violation, benefit to follow respect. Compliance cast within this modality is brought about through a manipulation of the desires or passions that we might, in Kantian or Spinozist terms, think of as determining how human beings act insofar as they are natural or amoral beings. "Man" in his natural identity (as understood here) desires to maximize pleasure and minimize pain. Thus, when educational processes seek to shape subjects by aligning the desirable attitudes or behaviors with "natural" dispositions or affects, they assume that the subject before them is this "natural" creature of passions and desires. Such educational processes are then adopting the same structure as Spinoza recommended for the civil law. Laws, on this model, will be most effective where they associate the desirable behaviors with pleasure and the undesirable ones with pain.[34]

One way of characterizing the difference between these approaches is by distinguishing the type of ethical reasoning process that each adopts: Should I act on the basis of absolute principles that I pursue independent all other (instrumental) considerations, or should I act so as to produce certain outcomes that I already deem to be good, because they bring me (consequentialist) benefits? Given that what interests us here, though, is the type of subject that one imagines one is addressing in each case, I would draw the distinction slightly differently. There are a few ways we might do this. Following Kant, the distinction might be drawn along the boundary between reason, on the one hand, and appetite or passion, on the other. This does not seem quite right either, in part because if one looks at how human rights educational processes actually work, recognition of the humanity or dignity of others is often induced through processes of empathy or bringing people to feel and sense the humanity of others who might otherwise be excluded from one's existing circle of concern.[35] Alternatively, one could distinguish between a subject motivated to maximize their own benefit and one motivated by more pro-social or other-directed objectives. Again, this seems to be not quite right in the case of human rights education, especially as one of the justifications that security sector personnel offer for not abiding by human rights standards is a commitment to state security, which is very close to saying the well-being and security of majorities.[36]

Thus, following the argument above, I think a better way to draw the distinction is through one that Kant and Spinoza, for all of their differences, both use: between humans when they are active, and humans when they are passive.[37] To act in a way that conforms with the desires that one already has, insofar as these are our natural or automatic modes of operating, is to be passive. This is true even if we seem to be making a decision that involves reasoning about the types of means that one needs to adopt to best achieve the (naturally desired) end. An example of such passivity would be deciding to conform with human rights standards because doing so will attract praise and possibly career advancements—outcomes that fulfill the person's natural or automatic desires for pleasure or happiness. Reasoning in this case is purely instrumental. By contrast, both Kant and Spinoza envisage the possibility of the *active* use of reason. For Kant, this entails acting according to the moral will; for Spinoza, it involves acting on the basis of active concepts, based on adequate ideas that allow us to come to understand and thus actively embrace "the right way of living."[38] An example of this type of active use of reason would be where a decision is made to respect human rights because one understands, through a process of reasoning, that doing so promotes the most peaceful and just society for everyone.

Why does this matter in terms of the type of subject assumed in human rights education? I would suggest that it matters a great deal, because these two types of subjects operate according to very different logics and will be convinced by very different types of arguments. Moreover, to the extent that we speak to the subject as one who needs to be enticed by benefits and frightened by threats, we metaphorically chase away the first type of subject. If I treat my addressee as part of a mechanical process, as a type of object who can be made to move in a certain direction by manipulating the attractions and repulsions, I can hardly then hail them as an active, ethical subject. The two types of subjects would seem to be mutually exclusive, and either of the two types of discourse appropriate only to one or the other. Perhaps, though, in practice, it is not so unusual to "have a bet both ways" and to see which one "sticks." Indeed, as Spinoza argued in his *Political Treatise*, we might look toward the possibility that people would act insofar as they have adequate ideas and so aspire to "the right way of living." Prudence, however, counsels that when it comes to the public affairs of the state, we would do best to establish processes based on a realistic assessment of how people are.

The second conclusion, which takes us in quite a different direction, is based on the overwhelming emphasis in human rights education and training on knowledge transmission. As discussed above, increased knowledge about human rights, both about what they entail and how they are enshrined in law, is assumed to be the path toward bringing about multidimensional changes in the subject, including altering their values and actions. To be clear, the problem is that the theory of change at work is not simply that if we provide more information about human rights, the subject will know more about human rights; rather, it is the assumption that if they know more, they will have different values and will behave differently. Knowledge is, in other words, sovereign. Moreover, it is the individual's own knowledge that matters and that is thought to determine their values and actions. The types of educational approaches taken in the field of public health, by contrast, recognize that values, attitudes, and behaviors are shaped in more complicated ways involving social context and collective dynamics and that motivations are shaped by affectively colored evaluations.

Undoubtedly, we would all like to think of ourselves as the type of self-determining subjects whose knowledge about the world steers our beliefs and actions. The problem is that we now have extensive evidence that this is not the case and, in particular, that it is not the case for precisely the types of behaviors at issue here. Indeed, consistent with the theories that underpin the public health approaches, study after study of institutional violence provides support for the hypothesis that it is situations and not dispositions that are the principal determinant of whether people commit violent acts or not.[39] Compliance with peers, obedience to authority, responding to incentive structures, working within the institutional opportunities and constraints all prove more important, in most cases, than the individual's knowledge about what the right thing to do is. By implication, their acquiring more and more knowledge about what they ought to do may have a minimal impact on what they do or on their attitudes in use.

The implications of these findings are that the subject of or for human rights ought to be conceived as a subject in context and not, as assumed in dominant educational models, the sovereign knowing and deciding subject. If human rights education is to effectively change how subjects make sense of the world, what they value, and most importantly what they *do*, it needs to first problematize the theory of the subject it presupposes and, second, design its theory of change around a more accurate theory of the subject. Moreover, and linking this with the first conclusion, this would be true for either the active or the passive subject. If, in other words, the objective is to produce the subject of and for human rights, the best approach would be to establish the social and situational world within which such a subject is most likely to form. This is because even the active subject—that is, the subject who brings to bear principles on their own actions—always does so in the context of the world in which they are embedded, and never as an abstract agent. Taken to the extreme, this raises the question of whether it makes sense to think of the subject of human rights as a subject at all or whether the language of the subject unavoidably leads us to imagine a subject who, as Spinoza wrote, lives only in our dreams "of the poets' golden age or of a fairy tale."[40]

CHAPTER 7

Who Deserves Inalienable Rights?

The Subjectivity of Violent State Officials and the Implications for Human Rights Protection

Rachel Wahl

REGARDLESS OF THE APATHY or even antipathy that may lurk in their hearts and minds, it would be enough for many human rights activists if state officials would simply *comply* with human rights standards. Hence, many activists are willing to risk alienating violent state officials through "naming and shaming" campaigns and lawsuits in the hope that this will motivate them to refrain from violence. Yet these tactics raise two concerns. First, they might generate backlash from resentful police and other targets of shaming. Second and relatedly, without buy-in to rights principles, state agents might comply minimally, paying lip service to international norms only to avoid recrimination.

Recognizing these dangers, the human rights movement has long held another aim: to create a "culture of human rights" that alters not just what people do but who they are.[1] In other words, there is an effort to create not simply human rights compliers but human rights subjects. These would be people—police, lawmakers, and local governance councils, as well as teachers, children, and parents—who believe in the validity of human rights and aspire to protect them. They would become human rights "subjects," as their subjectivity would be shaped by rights values and depend upon those values: they would understand their own moral identities in the terms of human rights. With this aim in mind, human rights education (HRE) that focuses only on laws is routinely critiqued for neglecting students' hearts, minds, and circumstances.[2] Indeed, the best HRE programs are often understood as those that are not only informative but transformative.

Here we have, then, two distinct approaches of the human rights movement. One is oriented toward creating and enforcing laws as well as pressing for accountability when law falls short. The second has more comprehensive aspirations, whereby such measures would be unnecessary due to the embrace of human rights by governments and the public at large. While the legal system and protest are typically the tools of the former, education is often the means of the latter.

For the most part, however, HRE scholars and practitioners do not wish to see their work as akin to what the Brazilian educator and activist Paulo Freire has called the "banking" approach to education, wherein an expert teacher fills students with knowledge.[3] On the contrary, HRE researchers and educators emphasize that such education should be not only *about* and *for* human rights but also that rights should be realized *through* the educational process.[4] Teachers should encourage students to develop and articulate their own ideas. Scholars write of the importance of "critical" HRE, which draws on Freirean methods, wherein students are encouraged to identify what they see as the most pressing social problems and generate their own solutions.[5]

But what happens when the students are the people who violate human rights? It is one thing to encourage the independent thought of a person whose rights have been taken away or even to bolster the self-expression of students who may be comfortably removed from these struggles. But it is quite another to inspire such confidence in a person who opposes the rights framework and, through his actions, undermines it. It is perhaps no surprise, then, that education and training for people who are in a position to violate rights tends to emphasize compliance over empowerment.[6]

The trouble is that Freirean critiques of the limitations of the "banking" method still apply. Lectures on rights may do little to spread them. State officials interpret rights concepts in their own terms, which are shaped by their ideals, constraints, interests, and concerns. Thus, when human rights norms disseminate to state officials, they may change dramatically as these actors not only reinterpret them but also actively renegotiate their meaning.

This resistance to being reshaped by human rights education was revealed during my conversations with law enforcement officers in India, whose beliefs, aspirations, and actions human rights educators hoped to reconfigure. During twelve months in the North Indian states of Uttar Pradesh, Punjab, Delhi, and Haryana, I conducted sixty interviews with thirty-three law enforcement officers who were participating in a two-year human rights course. Many of these officers enrolled because they hoped the course would lead to promotions or postretirement opportunities. As law enforcers who were listening to human rights ideas but were not yet convinced of their validity, they were ideal interlocutors for understanding what happens in attempts to re-shape subjectivities in the image of human rights. At their homes during din-ner, in cafés over tea, or on the phone when they were too busy or far away to meet me, I asked questions about how they understand what is good and right to be and do, as well as what frustrates those aspirations.

In the first interview with each officer, for example, I asked them to tell me about the challenges they face in their work, examples of times in which they have felt successful and times when they have been frustrated, and their views of how an ideal officer should act. I also gauged their responses to sources be-yond the human rights course, such as by asking them about local media cam-paigns that accuse the police of violating rights. In the second interview with each officer, I asked for their thoughts on the report of a regional human rights organization accusing particular police officers of torture. I asked them to ex-plain the report: what does he (i.e., the police officer I was interviewing) think the police officer did in that case and why, and why is the NGO criticizing this officer? I then provided them with quotes from their human rights textbooks, asking what the quotes meant and soliciting judgments on their validity.

I focused our conversations on an especially pressing need: to change what these police believe, and hence what they do, about their use of violence. In our exchanges, police affirmed the value and logic of human rights—but they interpreted rights in ways that support violence such as torture. Officers then drew from these interpretations to negotiate aspects of the human rights framework that condemn such violence. In this process, they adopted the lan-guage of rights and used it to make rights-based arguments for violations.

Officers' responses are not simply the thoughtless, automatic reaction of "state agents" defending state interests. For instance, these officers grappled with the suggestion that torture is always wrong through reference to their sense that justice is defined by harming the appropriate people for what they see as good reasons. This sense of justice has been strongly shaped by the po-litical pressures of officers' work and their interests within it. Yet they are still individuals who draw from this sense to question and judge the new norms being introduced to them. So while officers' ideas have been formed through their political and professional contexts, they remain people within these contexts who respond to the world through an already-operational interpre-tive framework.

Many theorists recognize that both instrumental motivations and princi-pled beliefs contribute to compliance with new norms.[7] Different schools of thought emphasize these factors to greater or lesser extents. Neoliberal and neorealist scholars typically privilege instrumental motivations that have little to do with the content of the norm.[8] Scholars in the "social constructivist" tradition, however, give more weight to the content of the norm for whether and how it will be taken up. For many constructivists, it matters whether the new norm matches domestic norms and values.[9]

But social constructivist scholars typically focus only on the beliefs that motivate people to *endorse* human rights.[10] Scholarship on why state actors *violate* human rights often implicitly assumes immoral or amoral motivations. Explanations for violations typically emphasize the absence of principled actors, such as the absence of domestic and transnational activist networks or the lack of constraining institutions such as an independent judiciary.[11] This lack of attention to violators' beliefs among theorists who emphasize the importance of these commitments suggests an assumption that human rights norms do not contend with alternative principled beliefs or that these beliefs are unimportant for norm diffusion. Yet to understand how state actors respond to new norms, it is crucial to examine how they explain their current behavior and the beliefs they draw from to support it. In other words, it is important to understand their subjectivity not merely for its potential alignment with rights values but as it exists beyond and in response to those values.

Subjects, Human Rights and Otherwise

The human rights movement emphasizes the prevention of suffering as a core principle.[12] Theorists allege that the avoidance of bodily harm, in particular, is among the most universal values and that as a result, norms related to bodily harm will diffuse most successfully.[13] This is why the Convention Against Torture has such widespread endorsement, according to some scholars, even though it limits the state's use of force and hence could be seen by the state as jeopardizing security.[14]

But the police I spoke with believe that what matters is bodily harm to whom and for what reason, rather than the prevention of bodily harm per se. In contrast to the universal conception of the human embodied in the human rights movement, officers believe that there are different types of people who deserve and require different treatment, represented by distinctions such as between "hardened" and "regular" criminals. As such, they draw from a conception of justice based on each person getting what they "deserve" rather than on the equal protection of inalienable rights to be free from harm.

Officers express this understanding of justice consistently throughout the interviews, defending certain types of torture as ethical. This is striking, considering that officers have no incentive to admit support for torture and do have an incentive to deny such support. They are not personally being accused of torture, so they could easily distance themselves from the practice by condemning it. This would be in their interest, since they are pursuing a degree in human rights and hope to advance professionally by aligning themselves with the human rights movement. In addition, they demonstrate that they know torture violates human rights standards as they are defined by human rights organizations. That they still endorse it as legitimate in certain circumstances suggests that they genuinely believe torture is a defensible practice. Furthermore, it is not that officers simply defend all police action. They condemn corruption and do not admit to it, in spite of the fact that widespread corruption in the police force is commonly acknowledged in India.[15] That they defend and admit to torture but not to corruption further suggests their commitment to the belief that torture is justifiable.

To be sure, factors beyond officers' conceptions of justice contribute to torture. No person's sense of the world is formed without influence from the conditions in which they live and work. Police are no exception: both their conception of what is just and their sense of how they must compromise their sense of justice are shaped by their context. Police perceive their supervisors, politicians, and the general public as expecting them to use torture to close cases, through extracting confessions or information that may be contrived or true, or to "settle" a case without formally registering it. Reports from civil society groups also support officers' perceptions of these expectations, though human rights advocates emphasize the self-interest of the police in this equation: police may receive bribes to torture (or to abstain from it) and may also benefit from a relationship in which they carry out politicians' wishes. In addition to these problems within the political and legal system, government and civil society reports also point to material reasons for torture, such as a lack of resources and training available to the police and the often grueling conditions under which police work.[16]

Most reports on police torture focus on these political, legal, and material flaws as reasons for torture. Rarely is it recognized that officers also believe that torture is both necessary and right. Yet the police I interviewed believe that even if these constraints did not exist, they would still use torture in certain cases.

These conceptions of justice help officers justify torture even in cases that violate their own beliefs. Police differentiate between torture they believe is legitimate (i.e., that which serves the "common good" by upholding justice or security) and that which they believe is illegitimate (i.e., that which promotes their own interests or the interests of politicians). Their conceptions of justice rest largely on the distinction between these two, based as they are on the premise that each person should get what he or she deserves, which would not occur in a case where the police are motivated by a bribe or external pressure.

My interviews suggest, however, that any particular act of torture is likely motivated both by officers' conviction that it is the right thing to do, because of their perception that it serves a larger good, *and* by his or her self-interest as well as pressure from supervisors, the public, and politicians. Once again, these officers are neither operating purely from their ideals nor their self-interest alone. This makes the spread of human rights all the more complex: rights norms diffuse into settings in which people are responding not only from thick and competing conceptions of justice but where they are already attempting to navigate between their own conceptions of justice and self-interest, pressure, and constraint. Human rights introduce an expectation that is neither the good nor the necessary and must compete with both.

For example, a police officer may receive a bribe from someone who suspects a particular person of wrongdoing, his supervisor may expect the case to be quickly resolved, *and* he may believe that it is his responsibility to so settle it. Their beliefs about justice offer them a way to align themselves with a legitimate moral identity without following human rights norms, particularly as this conception of justice is resonant with that of a broader public. While many scholars suggest that state officials often comply with human rights norms in order to identify as legitimate and ethical actors,[17] these officers can claim moral legitimacy while admitting and defending human rights violations.

At the same time, although they claim moral legitimacy in their defense of torture, officers still wish to be seen as proponents of human rights. Below, I discuss how officers then reconcile their support for torture with their professed identity as protectors of human rights.

Officers' Response to Attempts at Norm Diffusion

In spite of their opposition to core human rights laws and principles, the law enforcement officers I spoke with do not reject the idea of human rights. On the contrary, they draw on human rights concepts and language to explain their beliefs and behavior. And in fact, they use human rights concepts and language to defend torture.

These officers are motivated to align themselves with the human rights framework for reasons that social constructivist scholars might predict. Human rights discourse carries official normative weight and may be attached to professional rewards. Officers chose to enroll in the human rights course because they believe that a degree in human rights will assist their professional advancement. In addition, many officers wish to identify as moral actors and participate in activities that serve a greater good.

Officers reconcile these conflicting interests and desires by negotiating with the human rights framework and adapting it to support their current beliefs and practices. They do this by drawing from aspects of the framework that are coherent with what they believe and do. They then use these aspects to undermine the legitimacy of human rights principles that conflict with their beliefs and actions. They also interpret the general meaning of human rights in ways that support what they believe about torture and their practices regarding it. In these ways, they are able to maintain an identity as rights protectors while still defending the use of torture.

Below, I describe how officers interpret and negotiate the human rights framework. When officers *interpret* human rights, they express their beliefs about what "human rights" means. When they *negotiate* human rights, they explicitly express judgments on what should or should not be considered a human rights violation and which aspects of human rights they endorse. These processes are linked, as they draw from their interpretations to explain and defend their negotiations.

I first describe one way that officers interpret human rights as based in the breakable social contract of classical liberalism, rather than in *inalienable* rights. Next, I examine how they draw from this interpretation to negotiate human rights by narrowing who deserves protection and arguing that rights are inherently in conflict. In so doing, they assert their own subjective understandings against the efforts of human rights educators to reshape that subjectivity.

Interpretation: Classical Liberalism and the Social Contract

Officers often invoke a classical liberal understanding of rights to justify violations such as torture.[18] This model of a just society provides officers with a means of reconciling their own sense of justice with a rights framework. Classical liberal theorists often viewed rights as based in a social contract: each person upholds the laws of the state and respects the rights of others so that they may be protected from the intrusions of others or of the state itself. In this view, it is rational to restrict one's own natural freedom if the state ensures that in exchange, other citizens follow the same code.[19]

Officers echo this conception of society when they argue that only those who abide by the rules of the state deserve the protection of the state. This reasoning draws from and extends the idea of the social contract: classical liberal theorists typically considered some rights inalienable, but officers view all rights as conditional upon the social contract. They argue that security is necessary for the realization of all rights and hence stress that all rights must be conditional upon each person's willingness to respect the laws of the state.

This interpretation of liberalism aligns well with officers' conception of justice: A view of rights as conditional upon the respect of others' rights is consistent with the belief that what each person deserves is dependent on their actions. Hence, rather than rejecting "human rights" in favor of their conception of justice, officers express their conception of justice through those aspects of the rights framework that are most consistent with it. They then use such aspects of the rights framework to undermine tenets that conflict with their views, such as the inalienability and universality of certain rights.

This accomplishes a reshaping of the human rights framework more so than of officers' subjectivity. Police are able to refer to a conception of justice that reconciles their sense that protection should be conditional upon behavior with a language of rights. In this way, they protect their self-understanding as legitimate legal actors who use violence. The attempt to reshape their subjectivity fails because officers instead reshape the meaning of rights. By contesting the kind of human that human rights should protect, they defend their own actions and sense of justice without rejecting this framework outright.

The words of an army officer serving in Kashmir exemplify this. Human rights advocates accuse the security forces in Kashmir of frequently arresting and torturing political activists. When I ask whether he is concerned about arresting innocent people or using too much force, he replies, "There are concerns about human rights values, but it is give and take," and adds, "only if you abide by the law will you have it." This officer does not explicitly reject human rights laws in favor of a competing value; instead, he reframes the issue as one in which those who abide by the law deserve it and those who do not lose its protection. Hence, he articulates his disregard for the law as a principle of the law itself.

To some extent, the contemporary human rights movement also abides by this maxim. Human rights workers as well as domestic legal institutions endorse the premise that people convicted of crimes should lose some rights. Officers draw from this shared premise but extend it. In this way, they draw from a tenet of human rights and the law to reframe both.

Officers extend the conditionality of rights in two ways. First, they suggest that those who violate mutual security should lose all rather than only some rights. In this way, they use a tenet of liberalism to negate a human rights tenet. Officers reject the human rights regime's insistence that some basic rights must be inalienable in favor of the tenet that those who violate rights must be controlled. Second, officers extend the category of *who* should lose rights. For example, the international human rights regime would not consider being "against the nation" as criminal in itself, depending on to what extent and how a person acts on this sentiment. Freedom of expression, even of antinational sentiments, is a key civil and political right. Officers, however, often include people who express anti-national sentiments in the category of people who must lose even the right to life. An army officer serving in Kashmir argues, "One of the basic human rights is the right to live, but the right to live is given only when you are living according to the rules and in harmony with society. If you are against peace and security, if you are against the nation, then you lose that right." With these words, the officer draws from and extends a tenet that can be derived from classical liberalism: if society rests on the social contract, then each person must live "according to the rules" in order to benefit from the rules. The officer is able to draw from a rights-based framework to justify a violation of it.

Officers also invoke social contract theory when they make a related argument. They point out that liberty is dependent on security. They argue that if they do not violate the rights of those whom they believe violate others' rights, security will be compromised. If security is compromised, the innocent will lose their liberty. In order to defend the liberty of innocents, therefore, human rights require that they (that is, the police officers) violate the rights of some people. In this way, officers reframe "human rights" and "liberty" so that they are synonymous with and defined by security. For example, one officer asserts:

In all situations we have tried to our last to maintain human rights, but in some situations we use the minimum required force. Because to maintain law and order is primary. If the authority fails to maintain law and order, then there will be great violations of human rights by anti-social elements, by miscreants, by terrorists. So it is necessary to maintain law and order in the nation and in the world. To maintain law and order, sometimes the human rights of some people will be affected.

The officer justifies violating some people's rights in order to prevent greater violation of human rights. This suggests that rather than "universal" protection of rights being possible, he sees the rights of different people as in tension with each other. As such, he is able to justify violations of the rights of some people with the need to protect others. Similarly, when I ask an air force officer how he interprets the meaning of human rights, he asserts:

When I say "human rights," from whatever I have studied—I am in my first year at [the human rights course] only—or from my experience is, people must get basic needs. That includes security. In J & K [Jammu and Kashmir], security of normal people is jeopardized. Who should you blame, militants or the armed forces? This is the difference of opinion. We are trying to bring peace, while terrorists are the ones violating human rights.

Here, we can see the officer reverses assumptions about who is upholding and who is violating rights. The human rights community routinely and sharply criticizes the armed forces' actions in Kashmir. Here, the officer does more than justify violence in Kashmir through the need for security. He makes a rights-based argument for the violence: security is a basic right, so the armed forces are protecting basic rights by violating the rights of those who threaten security. This draws from but reverses the widespread criticisms of violence in Kashmir made by the international and domestic human rights regime, which typically posits the armed forces as violating the rights of Kashmiris.

Similarly, a high-ranking prison official who had justified torture earlier in the interview interprets liberty as defined by and based on security. I read him a quote by Woodrow Wilson from the human rights textbook used by his course, which is "The history of liberty is the history of resistance, it is the history of the limitations of government power." When he asks for clarification on the quote, I ask him, "To be free, is it necessary to limit government? How should we balance security and freedom?" He responds by asserting, "Free-

dom is our birthright. Liberty is part of freedom, and security comes after liberty. To maintain freedom and liberty, security is necessary." This officer first
endorses the priority of liberty, wholly agreeing with liberalism in theory. He
then moves to base liberty in security. This allows the officer to support "human rights" while still justifying violations of key rights. The officer goes so
far as to say that liberty comes before security but, paradoxically, can exist
only with security.

Other officers do not link security explicitly to liberty and rights but still
draw from it to justify rights violations. Similar to the other arguments they
make, they take a basic tenet of law and extend it. For example, one police officer, who conducts human rights trainings within his department, argues:

> If someone says bad things about America, can you tolerate it? . . . No, no, if
> someone says bad things about America, there is nationalism. There is a feel-
> ing. If someone says bad things about America, you cannot tolerate that. Peo-
> ple make conspiracies to break up the country. When police try to stop these
> things, some innocent people may die. To provide the security is the job of the
> police.

In this excerpt, the officer draws from a widely shared assumption: those who
conspire to break up the country must be stopped. However, he extends it
to cover a far wider range of actions, to include people who merely say bad
things about the country. He also extends the consequences considered acceptable, asserting that it is acceptable for innocent people to die to prevent
such actions.

Another officer also draws from the need to uphold security as a rationale
for his actions and extends this to include that which the human rights community would not consider an offense. He explains:

> We in [town name] have very rare instances of human rights violations. I am
> proud to say I have not ever violated human rights. But whatever we do, we do
> to maintain peace and tranquility for the safety of the law-abiding people. We
> try to safeguard the value of human beings, but whenever a criminal retali-
> ates, then we have no option other than to use force. That, too, is within the
> ambit of the law. If you come across people who are using filthy language in
> open society, in front of ladies, what should the police do?

His basic framework is shared with the human rights community and the rule
of law: he advises that one should use force only to "maintain peace and tran-

quility for the safety of the law-abiding people." But his interpretation extends that which is considered a violation of such tranquility to include "filthy language in front of ladies." A human rights advocate would see police violence against a person who has used filthy language as a clear violation of human rights and the rule of law. This officer sees it as in keeping with rights and the rule of law, as he has extended what is considered a violation of these.

Negotiation: Narrowing Who Deserves Rights

When officers *interpret* human rights, they articulate the meanings they attach to rights concepts. When they *negotiate* human rights, they express judgments that explicitly argue against more standard interpretations of human rights. Officers draw from the above interpretation of human rights as based in a social contract in order to negotiate who deserves them. Starting from the premise that the state must limit the rights of those who violate the rights of others, they argue that certain categories of people should be excluded from rights. This includes "hardened" criminals or "terrorists" or, in some cases, anyone suspected of committing any crime. One officer summarizes this viewpoint in his assertion "Human rights should be for the innocent."

This negotiation creates the normative and rational premise for officers to support "human rights" but still rely on categories of people (e.g., hardened criminals) who stand outside the community of such deserving humans. In this way, officers once again redefine the subject who should be included within human rights, contesting the "human" who is deserving of such regard. When they negotiate the rights framework using this rationale, they not only resist the attempt to reshape their own subjectivity (such as by drawing on a framework that legitimizes their actions), they also actively attempt to reshape the rights framework by directly critiquing it.

Interviews abound with examples of this negotiation, in which officers endorse the concept of human rights yet continue to narrow the kind of person who is deserving of these rights. A high-ranking Indian Police Service officer exclaims, "How can you say someone who is not observing the human rights of others has human rights?" He then concludes that in cases where officers are accused of violating the rights of civilians, judges should generally favor the officers. He asserts, "So in flagrant violations, yes, but in borderline cases it should be interpreted in the favor of security officers. I deeply feel that way." Another police officer argues, "Human rights should come to the rescue of the innocent person. Criminals are taking advantage of human rights." Similarly, a mid-ranking police officer reasons, "Human rights is necessary, but there should be . . . criminals should not be able to take advantage. Nowadays criminals are very smart." Another officer asserts:

> Society is constituted by the people. Everyone has a responsibility to behave as he wants to be treated. One man is respecting human rights, and another is not. If someone is trying to commit a wrong, then it is not possible. Treat them as they require. Tit for tat. If someone doesn't understand in the simple way, then they must be taught.

In this way, officers use their understanding of rights as contingent on rule-following rather than the contemporary human rights movement's understanding of certain rights as inalienable. They adapt this to their conception of justice, in which criminal suspects do not deserve the same treatment as others. And hence they can support "human rights" as well as endorse practices that violate human rights.

Officers use this line of reasoning to negate human rights arguments to the contrary. For instance, I ask the above paramilitary officer whether he thinks that "people who are suspected of wrongdoing should have any rights." He replies:

> Now that I am enrolled in [the human rights course], I know they should have the right to life. But I consider that their life is not more important than the hundreds of people they kill. . . . People who commit crime knowingly, they are out of society. He [who] loves to kill, it is not possible to put them in normal civilization.

Another police officer negotiates human rights similarly. He argues, "It is necessary to physically torture the hardcore criminals" and laments that "human rights says not to do it." His comments do not reflect ignorance of legal and ethical reasoning. He demonstrates that he understands the legal protections and basic ethical premise of human rights, noting with regret that "the law also protects criminals" and stating, "It has been told in human rights that we cannot undermine the self-respect of anyone, even if that person is a criminal. Man is not an animal. We cannot harm anybody." I ask him what he thinks of this, and he continues:

> I agree with it that people are born in an independent manner and have their self-respect, but those who are hardcore criminals, those who have murdered people, they should not get human rights protection.

When I ask him why this is so, he asserts:

> The hardcore criminals themselves violate the human rights of other people. Someone who violates the human rights of other people, why should his human rights be protected?

This is a typical example of how officers use the concepts and language of human rights to undermine and argue against core rights norms such as the Convention Against Torture. He rejects the key premise of human rights as inalienable, but he does so by drawing on a rights-based argument. He is in this way able to negotiate the human rights framework so that he can support it while still defending violations such as torture.

Some officers explicitly argue that the human rights system should change to accommodate these divisions. One high-ranking Indian Police Service officer advises that human rights should apply "when the criminals are not terrorists, when the criminals are not serious." Like other officers, he then makes the case for differentially applied rights, asserting:

> Criminals have to be classified. When the criminals are very serious, then the police may resort to extrajudicial killings, violence, but this is rare. Ninety-nine percent of cases, police must adhere to the law, keeping human rights and civil liberties. If we act in this way, and there is some profiling and classifying and making extrajudicial killings permissible and keeping human rights for others, then the system can work.

By narrowing who deserves human rights, this officer is able to identify as a supporter of human rights while still defending extrajudicial killings.

Officers often respond directly to the human rights course material by affirming the aspects of it that align with their narrowed conception of who deserves basic rights. As I did with most officers in the second interview, I ask a low-ranking police officer for his opinion on quotes from the human rights textbook. I ask him for his view of the assertion (made by Thomas Jefferson) that "the God who gave us life gave us liberty at the same time." He replies, "This is right. Human beings can think. They have conscience. Wherever he goes, they will respect each other and cooperate with each other. Such people have the right to live freely." This officer seems to entirely endorse the textbook's view until the qualifier at the end, where he adds that "such people" deserve to live freely. Here, he uses the human rights course material to make a subtle argument for his conception of justice, which he had earlier articulated, in which it is right to detain and torture suspects. Only such people who abide by certain standards have rights, in his view. Hence, he supports human rights but narrows who deserves them.

In sum, officers use human rights concepts and language to undermine the legitimacy of the human rights they are most often accused of violating. This negotiation, wherein some but not all people deserve human rights, allows them to support "human rights" in theory without seriously undermining their beliefs and practices to the contrary. In this way, officers reframe human rights in accordance with their conceptions of justice.

Subjectivities That Matter

Officers' negotiations undermine a key way that human rights norms spread. Social constructivist theorists argue that state actors adopt human rights norms in part because they wish to maintain the identity of a liberal state. In fact, scholars typically define "norm" as that which constitutes or regulates appropriate behavior for actors with a particular identity.[20] If actors wish to adopt an identity, they are more likely to accept the norms that regulate or constitute it.[21]

These officers are prime examples of people who are motivated to align their identity with human rights. They have enrolled voluntarily in a Human Rights course. Hoping to advance professionally by representing themselves as qualified in this area, they have good reason to at least articulate human rights beliefs, even if they do not follow them. But these officers do not even pretend to endorse human rights activists' views in order to take on a liberal identity. Instead, they reframe human rights so that they align with their extant beliefs and practices. They argue that they are better representatives of human rights than the activists who criticize them. Hence, they can take on a rights-friendly identity without undermining, even in speech, their support for torture.

Theorists of human rights norm diffusion might point out that their arguments about identity and norm diffusion are applicable to state leaders on the international stage, not individual domestic state actors such as law enforcement officers. If so, this suggests a problematic gap between the interests of international actors who endorse norms and the domestic actors who must uphold them. This gap may help explain why pervasive violations of human rights continue long after a state has endorsed a norm.

Extant theoretical work has suggested that state endorsement is important regardless of the beliefs and interests of domestic state actors. This is because once a state signs an international treaty, domestic human rights groups can use it as leverage against errant domestic state actors. Rigorous research supports this claim.[22]

The above findings reveal what may be one obstacle to this process. When domestic state actors can identify themselves as rights defenders while still violating rights, it may be more difficult for human rights activists to mobilize support. This is particularly likely to be the case where strong alternative conceptions of justice exist in the domestic sphere that compete with human rights. And it is further likely to be the case where common perceptions of the local environment lead domestic state actors and members of the public to believe that human rights norms are not appropriate or possible to uphold.

In India, my interviews with public officials and police reform experts suggest that it is not only law enforcement officers who hold the views elaborated above. Domestic public officials who are responsible for holding law enforcement officers accountable also express concerns about sacrificing security for the sake of human rights, and they sometimes articulate doubts about whether it is always possible or good to maintain the rights of suspected criminals. In addition, human rights advocates who work on police reform lament that the general public often shares the law enforcement community's views on policing and rights. Furthermore, police in India have few direct incentives to portray themselves as rights-respecting. Public officials are rarely punished for violations such as torture and are sometimes professionally rewarded for them.[23] These findings suggest that just because state actors wish to present themselves as maintaining a particular kind of liberal identity on the international stage, it does not follow that domestic state actors prioritize presenting themselves this way.

This does not mean that the process by which local state actors make choices never mirrors that of high-level state representatives. Previous research suggests that state leaders are more likely to violate international norms when they view the transgression as a way to protect another value or norm.[24] A similar process may be at work among local-level domestic state actors in regard to torture. Interviews suggest that police, their supervisors, and the public view this violence as a necessary means of upholding security and justice and that the existence of these competing values makes the self-interest involved in such violence more forgivable in the view of those who commit it.

In theory, officers' sense of justice does not support every form of torture. Officers differentiate between torture they see as legitimate, by which they mean torture that promotes security and justice, and torture they see as illegitimate, by which they mean torture that results from personal or political interest, a lack of training, and external pressure. Interviews suggest, however, that any single act of torture may be motivated by *all* of these factors combined: police believe they must use torture due to external pressure; they have a material interest in doing so in the form of bribes or professional rewards; they are not equipped or motivated to solve cases nonviolently; *and* they believe that torture is necessary to uphold security and justice. The existence of this last reason may make the other motivations more palatable to officers and to the public.

Conclusion

Both human rights professionals and scholars of norm diffusion often assume that while members of transnational advocacy networks act on principled beliefs, state actors who violate rights are motivated primarily by self-interest. Even though many social constructivist researchers acknowledge the importance of whether and how a norm "matches" local norms and values, there has been little in-depth research on what these competing norms and values might be.[25] This can give the impression that human rights norms diffuse into a normative vacuum, in which all they replace is self-interest. My research suggests that local state actors' beliefs about the legitimacy and necessity of torture inform how they respond to attempts to disseminate human rights norms.

Because local police interpret and contest human rights according to their own sense of what is just and possible, international norms do not remain the same as they travel but are negotiated by the actors who use them. In the case of state actors who are responsible for norm implementation, this can involve using the language and logic of the norm in ways that subvert its core principles. The law enforcement officers in this study are motivated to engage with the human rights framework and wish to associate themselves with it for professional and personal reasons. Yet they hold strong beliefs and interests that conflict with human rights. They reconcile this by using the language and logic of human rights to justify violations. This suggests a way in which state actors negotiate international norms without suffering the potential costs of explicitly rejecting them.

Furthermore, officers' comments in interviews are a reminder that they do not act alone. As state actors, they exist within a web of expectations, commands, rewards, and punishments that typically center—at best—on the goals of the state and—at worst (in cases of corruption)—on the private goals of individuals. Although some decisions officers make are likely within their control, their role as "frontline" representatives of the government at times poses inherent difficulties for their role as defenders of human rights against the government. This is especially the case when characteristics of the national context exacerbate this tension, such as when elected officials have significant influence over police officers' careers, as is the case in India. Hence, officers' resistance to norm diffusion is in their interest (as state actors and as individuals), and it is also in accordance with their beliefs. The combination of these instrumental and principled motivations makes a particularly difficult case for the spread of human rights.

Efforts to spread human rights norms must then contend not only with the flawed political and legal systems of which human rights professionals are well aware but also with the beliefs and conceptions of justice that make such systems acceptable to state actors and, at times, to some members of the domestic public. Yet so often, human rights education for police and other officials relies on the provision of information without attending to either their circumstances or their ideals.

Recognizing the importance of engaging the realities in which police operate and also of generating their buy-in, a number of important initiatives have taken innovative approaches. For example, in one experimental project on the prevention of torture, an intervention was designed for police in Sri Lanka and Nepal premised on both of these concerns.[26] Officers were invited to share the challenges and constraints that make them more likely to use torture, and reformers helped them to assess how they could respond to these circumstances nonviolently. Importantly, this program recognized the objective conditions and subjective experience of the officers, such as by examining together the power politicians have over police and how police experience this control. They then grappled with how they might navigate this circumstance without using torture.

This is a promising direction for human rights education. For officers who wish they could protect human rights, it has great potential. More difficult, though, are the many police who believe that violence is justified. For while global human rights norms may dominate international ethical discourse, the subjectivities of those meant to uphold these norms is far harder to transform. This is not simply a failure of any intervention, as there may not be a perfect "fix" for such subjective difference. If activists relent in their efforts to change officers' hearts and minds, focusing on extrinsic motivations to respect human rights through shaming campaigns, they may succeed in achieving minimal compliance—which is no small accomplishment. If instead they help officers to navigate the constraints that lead to torture, they may provide crucial tools to officers who already wish to change. Perhaps the two of these together will produce promising results: shaming campaigns may provide the motivation, while context-sensitive partnerships offer officers the means to change. Neither, however, fully achieves that far more elusive aim: to create human rights subjects.

CHAPTER 8

Human Rights As Therapy

The Healing Paradigms of Transitional Justice

Ronald Niezen

Victim-centrism and Healing Narratives

Without fanfare or controversy, with no headlines or speeches to draw attention to it, a new way of thinking about mass crime has gone global. It used to be, not so long ago, that victims didn't really matter. Prosecutions for crimes large and small almost always proceeded on behalf of the state. During the past three decades or so, however, public testimony by the victims of violence has gained prominence and become *the* pathway to justice, healing, and commemoration, in which human rights have increasingly taken on therapeutic virtues. Human rights have been key to this transformation, providing the framework for evaluating who counts as a traumatized victim and which forms of violence and rights violations require the attention of transitional processes.

If victims did come to matter, this occurred first in what Felman and Laub describe as the testimony from witnesses of events that transcended the individual, from those who could provide "bits and pieces of a memory that has been overwhelmed by occurrences that have not settled into understanding or remembrance . . . events in excess of our frames of reference."[1] Then human rights venues placed emphasis on another form of significance. Not only were claims pursued and recognized through the testimonial practice of those who were victims of abuse, those victims themselves were assumed to heal, if not flourish, through the cathartic effects of giving testimony. Human rights have thus become a paradigm for healing under circumstances in which efforts to secure recognition of the historical reality of mass violence combine with efforts to overcome its traumatic consequences for survivors. Programs to hear testimony from and assist those who are experiencing trauma in the aftermath of political violence, terrorism, and forced displacement have expanded rapidly over the past several decades and are now standard components of humanitarian relief efforts and post-conflict aid programs.[2] Consistent with this conception of intervention, Diana Million points to an "internationally recognized economy of justice," in which "the victims of traumatic events suffer recurrent wounding if their memory/pain is not discharged."[3] Through their public unburdening, the injuries to their individual and collective psyches are, so it is widely assumed, overcome, and the psyches are restored to health.

As part of this process, victims became the main participants in truth and reconciliation commissions (TRCs), especially when, as in South Africa's commission in the early 1990s, their narratives were seen as central to goals of constructing a new national history/memory and creating a testimonial foundation for national reconciliation. Following the influential South African model, the advent of human rights as therapy is especially apparent in TRCs oriented toward affirming and eliciting the experiences of survivors and recording them for posterity. These commissions are now widely assumed to promote healing and reconciliation between individuals and communities, locally and at the level of the nation, with their therapeutic effects seen as having intrapersonal and intrapsychic implications for conflict resolution through identity transformation.[4] Martha Minow has similarly noted the prevalence of the rhetoric of trauma and the healing power of testimony that undergird many TRCs. "Like therapy for individual survivors of trauma," she writes, "the TRC is supposed to overcome repression and a sense of powerlessness for the entire society as well as for individuals."[5] A key ingredient of the therapeutic ideas behind victim-centric forms of truth commission is a theory of catharsis connected to public testimony, the idea that expressing strong, repressed emotions or "saying the unsayable" will produce relief for individuals together with a sympathetic form of collective unburdening and, ultimately, healing for the nation.

Not all truth and reconciliation commissions among the forty or so that have taken place, starting in the late 1970s, have taken on a victim-centric therapeutic role. If anything, the early models of transitional justice in the aftermath of regimes identified as having perpetrated mass violence were linked to parallel structures with prosecutorial powers and oriented, at least in part, toward establishing the criminal responsibility of those who set policy, gave orders, and carried out genocide or crimes against humanity. For example, the commission that was established in 2001 in the wake of the political violence that took place in East Timor between 1974 and 1999—violence that led to the death of up to 200,000 East Timorese—had as part of its mandate the "duty to inquire into and make findings as to which persons, authorities, institutions and organisations were involved in the violations, and whether they were the result of a deliberate plan or policy."[6] The inquiry was supported by a Serious Crimes Unit, with prosecutorial authority that reached into the highest echelons of the Indonesian government.

If the victim-centered "therapeutic" truth commissions were not conceived within the logic and structures of achieving goals of criminal justice, then what produced this move to a therapeutic paradigm of victim narrations as healing? This question becomes more complex in light of the difficulty of "bearing witness." The public testimonies of trauma and healing that have influenced the discourse of truth commissions certainly do not always correspond with the natural inclinations of victims who are struggling with memories of pain and loss. There exists a vast gulf between the occurrence of trauma and the capacity of victims to publicly narrate their experience of it. Psychologists and anthropologists working in a variety of contexts find that suppression of emotion and self-expression is a predictable outcome of the harrowing circumstances of state-sanctioned violence.[7] Rosalind Shaw, for example, observed that in Sierra Leone's truth commission there were contrasting and contested approaches to memory and that for many survivors, healing and reconciliation were seen to depend on forgetting rather than truth telling.[8] Wendy Coxshall, in her study of Peru's truth commission, established in 2001 in an effort to come to terms with the political violence that occurred in the 1980s and 1990s under the regime of Alberto Fujimori, noted the same kind of reticence to publicly give voice to suffering. The Andean villagers asked to participate were indifferent to the commission and had difficulty narrating their experience of *la violenza*. Instead, silence, particularly women's silence, was a protective substitute for self-revelation. Coxshall concludes from this difficulty, "Concealing personal pain by refusing to speak and share this knowledge is a means of both self-protection and preserving one's personal integrity."[9] This leaves us with the questions concerning the sources of this shift toward public narrations of pain and the consequences it might have for survivors and the wider goals of reconciliation that underpin programs of transitional justice.

This chapter explores the juxtaposition of the prevalent notion of the therapeutic nature of survivor narratives with the inherent difficulties of publicly narrating deeply painful experiences. The assumption that survivor stories, told in conditions of affirmation and acceptance, are a sufficient foundation of healing and reconciliation—at the individual and the collective (including national) levels—has gone largely unexamined. We are also faced with the challenge of better understanding the intellectual history of the ideas behind human rights as therapy, which goes well beyond the readily recognizable church-sponsored models of testimony. In the next section I outline some of the sources of the shift from prosecutorial to therapeutic goals in human rights and the popular receptiveness to the narration of traumatic memory as a source of personal catharsis and sympathetic healing. I then situate the confluence of these ideas in Canada's Truth and Reconciliation Commission on Indian Residential Schools, which serves as my main reference point for assessing the ideas and practices of human rights as therapy.

Sources

Much as we might like to think that there are deep, impenetrable structures of collective thought and emotion that find expression in victim narratives, there are in fact particular persons and institutions that have demonstrated the capacity to shift the popular assumptions and behaviors that lie behind the sense of injustice and the ways that suffering (through the violation of justice) is expressed. The certainties that people absorb without awareness or reflection from their milieu are not inescapable and are not at all fixed or immobile but are "continually transformed, enriched by scientific notions and philosophical opinions that have entered into custom," often under the influence of key intellectual reformers.[10] This kind of shift in the collective psyche is evident in the pivotal moments of the emergence of truth commissions as sources of healing. In illustrating this point, I present brief sketches of five influential events or institutions: the Nuremberg trials, the Eichmann trial, the rise of church-sponsored initiatives, the popularization of trauma theory, and (yes, seriously) the *Oprah Winfrey Show*. This is not to say that human rights as therapy does not have other important sources of influence, merely that the combined intellectual and institutional history of the transformations of public consciousness that gave prominence to therapeutic approaches to mass crime can be sketched through these examples.

The Nuremberg Trials

The starting point for my account of the emergence of therapeutic models of transitional justice is the Nuremberg trials, which placed almost exclusive emphasis on the documentary evidence of Nazi crimes (of which there was an abundance, due to the German penchant for fastidious record keeping) and that explicitly steered clear of survivor narratives. Some of the Nazi defendants in Nuremberg did give powerful testimony, such as SS officer Otto Ohlendorf, who impassively testified that his troops in southern Russia had rounded up and killed some 90,000 Jews, and Walther Funk, the former president of the Reichsbank, who was presented with, and compelled to recognize, incontrovertible evidence that he was aware of bank deposits originating from jewels and gold teeth taken from prisoners of the concentration camps.[11] During this kind of testimony, however, the survivors themselves, along with their experiences, were kept in the background, and emotion emerged out of a mental exercise of filling in the blanks of bloodless, fact-oriented narratives from which the horror had been abstracted. Nuremberg can thus serve as a reference point or baseline for the victim-centrism and testimony-as-therapy that would later emerge as important qualities of the truth and reconciliation phenomenon.

The Eichmann Trial

The 1961 trial of Nazi war criminal Adolf Eichmann was dramatically different from Nuremberg in the central place it gave to victims and in the public nature of the proceedings—it was the first high-profile trial to be broadcast to a mass audience.[12] Sonali Chakravarti argues that the Eichmann trial was a watershed moment in the way that victim narratives were employed in the combined pursuit of justice and public awareness in the aftermath of mass crime. The chief prosecutor, Gideon Hausner, made the oral testimony of victims central to the case against Eichmann. Amplifying the impact of this testimony, the American firm Capital Cities Broadcasting Corporation (better known as ABC) obtained the exclusive rights to broadcast the proceedings, giving greater immediacy to the event than its global newspaper coverage.[13] In a marked departure from the evidence presented in the Nuremberg trials,

Chakravarti argues, this was "the first case of a trial in the aftermath of war to consider the emotions of victims as central to the practice of justice," which "laid the foundation for a new, still unrealized type of transitional justice that has the potential to address the psychological needs of a society after war."[14] It is precisely this new type of mediatized transitional justice that eventually took the further step of offering victim narrations as sources of healing.

Christianity, Churches, and Ecclesiastics

Church involvement in promoting confessional forms of survivor testimony is clearly part of the background to the therapeutic turn in human rights. In this shift, churches have played institutional roles as sponsors of testimonial practices in a variety of testimonial initiatives while at the same time providing a source of the logic of confession as a method of healing. South Africa's TRC offered a particularly influential model—seen by many as a watershed in the history of truth commissions—in which many perpetrators were offered amnesty on condition of truth telling and in which the focus of the hearings was on the testimony of the victims of apartheid. The ideas that truth is healing and that the trauma inflicted on the victims of apartheid would be overcome by public testimony were promoted most prominently by Anglican Archbishop Desmond Tutu, who argued that "[t]he purpose of finding out the truth is not in order for people to be prosecuted. It is so that we can use the truth as part of the process of healing our nation."[15] In its orientation toward this goal, South Africa's truth commission offered a therapeutic model of truth telling, which, Giuliana Lund notes, "elevated testimony to a new height, promoting the belief that public depositions would not only help to establish the truth of past events but would also afford healing to witnesses."[16]

Church influence on the way that transitional justice initiatives offer healing has sometimes involved the construction of templates, in which preferred story arcs and forms of testimony are presented and in which there is even a selection of those who can speak for all victims in accordance with the values of the faith. When talks were taking place in Havana between FARC rebels and the government of Colombia in 2016, for example, the Catholic Church, under Archbishop Luis Augusto Castro Quiroga, took an active role in selecting witnesses from among some 8 million victims of Colombia's civil war and accompanying them in groups of 12 to the talks in Havana. Archbishop Castro told the Catholic News Service that the victims "went with their hearts filled with bitterness, yet they were able to express all that they had lived and felt, and they asked for an explanation of what happened in their situation. At the same time, each victim had the possibility to hear 11 other victims and to realise that they weren't the only ones in the world who suffered."[17] The templates of witnessing begin quite simply with the selection of those given the opportunity to narrate their experience, which no doubt also involves bringing out the preferred messages of forgiveness, healing, and reconciliation that they have to offer.

Trauma Theory

The development of the theory of trauma, and conjointly of post-traumatic stress disorder (PTSD), provided a key idiom for the pathology that is the source of the therapeutic benefits of human rights intervention. The genealogies of the concept of trauma consistently emphasize its constructed origins, as a counter-narrative to accounts of the scientific "discovery" of objectively perceptible forms of mental illness. Among the most forceful of these accounts, Allan Young's study of post-traumatic stress disorder, *The Harmony of Illusions*, argues that the classification of PTSD "is the product or achievement of psychiatric discourse, rather than its discovery."[18] For Young, "traumatic memory is a man-made object. It originates in the scientific and clinical discourses of the nineteenth century; before that time, there is unhappiness, despair, and disturbing recollections, but no traumatic memory, in the sense that we know it today."[19] Taking a historical approach to the same argument, Didier Fassin and Richard Rechtman in *The Empire of Trauma* illustrate some of the ways that trauma, as a socially constructed phenomenon, has undergone a dramatic transformation in the past century, from a tool to understanding the battle neurosis, or "shell shock," of soldiers on the front lines of World War I (with the morally offensive goal of returning them to battle), to eventually achieving mainstream status in psychiatric discourse and therapeutic practice as an accepted, if not dominant, idiom of distress.[20]

To the concepts of trauma and PTSD, it is necessary to add the ideas concerning the victim or the individual subject who bears the scars and struggles to heal from the catastrophic experiences of mass violence. The first reference point for this personalization of trauma was the Holocaust. Henry Krystal's 1968 edited volume *Massive Psychic Trauma* introduced the concept of "survivor syndrome" to describe the mental health consequences of the death camps of the Holocaust. Giving greater specificity to this concept, Bruno Bettelheim's essays in *Surviving* introduced the idea of survivor guilt as a significant element of a syndrome that arises out of the survivor's strong will to stay alive while others perish, manifesting itself in self-blame that is morally ungrounded yet obsessive, destructive, and formative in the survivor's personality. From this starting point in the study of post-Holocaust trauma, the concept of the survivor was applied more broadly, eventually adopted in a unified theory to refer to those who had in some way been victimized by almost any kind of mass traumatic event, such as combat (particularly the Vietnam War), genocide, natural disaster, or childhood sexual abuse.[21]

As concepts of psychiatry (including its psychological and psychoanalytic variants) that have taken hold as much from social agitation as from clinical practice, trauma and PTSD have become central to the story of human rights as therapeutic practice. From the point at which these concepts were widely circulated, the testimonial practices of human rights added another ingredient—or, better, another context—to the concepts drawn from psychiatry. The witness and subject of mass violence, the traumatized survivor, must narrativize their experience of horror in the public sphere, supposedly for therapeutic ends, but in ways meant at the same time to expose their listeners to the painful realities of mass violence. The public nature of such witnessing, as I now discuss, is a practice with its own intellectual and institutional genealogy.

The Oprah Winfrey Show

Finally, the advent of the daytime talk show, with the suffering-as-spectacle models of Phil Donahue, Dr. Phil, and Oprah Winfrey reaching unprecedented mass audiences, was another source of the testimonial practices and therapeutic ideas now widely adopted in collective claims making. Of course, the place of popular media in transforming widely shared notions of public and private selves is a much wider phenomenon than talk shows, but this genre of programming epitomizes the growing acceptance of the idea of personal exposure—including exposure of personal vulnerability—to anonymous consumers of entertainment and information as a pathway to healing. Winfrey contributed more influentially than any other individual to the popular acceptance of suffering as a source of the self, including in truth commissions, by cultivating the television talk show as a venue for therapy, oriented toward moving people beyond their pain and into healing, in which ordinary people present and perform their problems to mass audiences and receive advice from "experts."[22]

One of the qualities emphasized in Oprah's version of the daytime talk show is its affirmation and universalization of suffering, drawing from the model of group therapy and applying it to a mass audience. Irvin Yalom and Molyn Leszcz, in a study of the methods of group therapy, refer to this kind of affirmation as "universality": patients often come to a life-transforming realization that their social isolation and the accompanying sense that their experiences are aberrant are unfounded, and that others—potentially many others besides those in the group—share those same experiences and feelings.[23] They refer to this as a "'welcome to the human race' experience." This is the very kind of experience that Oprah cultivated in her show by emphasizing and repeating the message of the universality of suffering, cultivating her role as therapist (supported by qualified experts), and, as Marshall and Pienaar put it, "invoking discourses of therapy, confession and catharsis which construct a public space where guests bare their souls and seek to transform their lives."[24] At the same time, through the guidance of the talk show host, audiences are ideally also learning how to ask therapeutically oriented questions about themselves and about those in their lives who are suffering.

Another important ingredient that explains the show's public reach has been its marshaling of public opinion in defense of the views it promotes. Online discussion of the conflicts and pathologies aired on the show are carefully vetted, producing templates for the expression of ideas and attitudes that are publicly presented. Opinions that are inconsistent with the agenda of the show are excluded. Viewers themselves perform some of this vetting work, with outlying views or attitudes marked as anomalous and shut down by those who set themselves the task of reinforcing the accepted narratives.[25] The astonishing success of the *Oprah Winfrey Show* can be attributed in part to its mediatization of public mantras of suffering and the idea of the cathartic effects and healing—for both the narrator and their audience—that follow from public presentation of the suffering self.

Broad as its influence was, this model was picked up by truth commissions and public inquiries, which adopted its main assumptions in the context of the aftermath of mass atrocities. The new institutional response to the past crimes of the state included suffering as a central feature of public spectacle and the display of personal pain to mass audiences as a source of catharsis and healing. By putting suffering individuals on display to a mass audience, the public became accustomed to the experience of sympathetic participation in the pain of others with the wider goal of alleviating suffering. The expression

of traumatic memory through the spectacle and performance of public narrative has become part of the naturalized, widely shared assumed knowledge
that made it possible for the ideas of catharsis and personal transformation to
find a prominent place in the discourse and procedures of human rights and
transitional justice.

Survivor-centrism in Canada's TRC

Nowhere is the human-rights-oriented expression of suffering as a source of
individual and public catharsis more visible than in Canada's Truth and Reconciliation Commission (TRC) on Indian Residential Schools, which began
hearings in 2010 and held its last meeting and submitted its final report in
2015.[26] This TRC was explicitly designed to be an affirmative process for Survivors (spelled with a capital S in the Commission's documents) who sought
to avoid public confrontations with possibly unrepentant priests. In this
TRC, the concept of the residential school survivor was embodied and enacted, with only passive or publicly invisible opposition from "the accused,"
the government, and the churches. The mandate of the Commission, laid
out in "Schedule N" of the Settlement Agreement, is the formal source of its
"victim-centrism." Under the terms of the Indian Residential Schools Settlement Agreement (IRSSA), the TRC was prevented from holding formal hearings, acting as a public inquiry, or conducting any kind of legal process. It
lacked subpoena powers and had no other mechanism to compel attendance
or participation in any of its events or activities. What is more, it was prevented from identifying any person in any of its activities or reports without
the consent of that individual. In other words, it could not "name names" of
perpetrators who had not yet been formally identified and prosecuted.

The strictly voluntary nature of testimony to a commission that had no judicial powers was not, as might readily be imagined, imposed by the government and the churches in efforts to limit the criminal liability and public exposure of "naming names" in the Commission's hearings. These features of
the Commission were actively solicited by the representatives of the survivors
in the negotiations leading up to the settlement agreement.[27] The Commission was purposefully defanged from the outset, with the goals of healing emphasized over the discomforts of facing, hearing, and confronting the words
of those who fit within (or were consigned to) the category of perpetrators.

The approach taken by Canada's TRC to the connection between the narration of pain and healing followed a thread that connected it with the self-

revelation of Christian confessionals, along with the self-revelation and catharsis of group therapy and the public spectacle of daytime television. Victim-centric truth commissions, like confessionals and psychotherapy, are not just about the telling of painful experiences; they promote conceptions of the healing that is expected to take place by the act of listening to them. What makes them different from the relationship between those who confess and those who give absolution, or (in the language of psychoanalysis) between analysand and analyst, is in the public and performative narration of suffering and reinforcement of corresponding conceptions of illness and redemption.

Arguably more than in any other truth commission, the organizers of Canada's TRC saw one of their principal goals being to create public awareness of the crimes of the state and to generate sympathy toward those who had been subjected to them. In the aftermath of apartheid or civil war, there would have been little call for raising awareness of the collective harms that had been endured during previous regimes. This aspect of the Commission's work was therefore similar to the lobbying activities of justice-oriented NGOs that seek to bring public attention to their chosen causes. As the Commission took up its mandate, the elaboration and dissemination of concepts of cultural genocide, survivor experiences, historical trauma, and healing occurred—or so many in the TRC believed—in a context of public apathy and ignorance. Healing was conceived in close connection with the publicity goals of the Commission. In their public statements, the commissioners emphasized the catharsis expected to occur when survivors "shared their truth," which would at the same time contribute to "healing the nation," as an accumulated mass of testimony raised awareness of the troubling history and consequences of residential schools.

TRCs that lack judicial authority tend to be oriented more exclusively toward the affirmation of victim experience and the shaping of testimony through a preferred kind of narrative.[28] In Canada's TRC, the cultivation of preferred narratives took place in outreach to survivors who might have been reluctant to "share their stories" before a large audience. One such narrative, which emphasized the healing that can take place by giving voice to painful memories, was expressed by the Commission in nearly every opportunity it had to present survivors with information about the value of giving a statement. A preparatory film, *Sharing Your Truth*, first screened at the Atlantic National Event, for example, stated this goal explicitly: "We . . . aim to make the process of giving a statement to the TRC as much of a healing experience as possible. We are here to listen, and we care deeply about your experiences."[29] The head commissioner, Murray Sinclair, frequently repeated the Commission's promise of healing, such as in his opening speech to the Saskatoon National Event: "It has contributed significantly to the healing of these individuals who have come forward. And it has contributed significantly to the healing of relationships between these individuals and their families and communities."[30] Darlene Auger, the TRC Regional Liaison for Alberta, gave the idea some practical specificity in a preparatory workshop for survivors:

> It is healing when you begin to talk about it because it becomes real, and you put it out in front of you, and you can look at it. You separate yourself, you begin to separate yourself from it. You are not your pain. You are a beautiful, wonderful spirit, beautiful, wonderful human being that has had a really bad experience perhaps, a really painful experience. But it is not what you are all about. And so to talk about it, to share it, and even more, to record it, to create a permanent record of it, so that the future generations can hear it, can see you, that's even more profound.[31]

The affirmation of survivor experience went further than the oblique persuasion of reluctant witnesses to appear before the microphone. In the Sharing Circle, in which a microphone (referred to as a "talking stick") was passed clockwise from speaker to speaker, those in the circle or in the audience who emotionally broke down in the midst of the at-times harrowing, sorrowful testimony were offered the consoling effects of burning sage, fanned by eagle feathers, and water blessed in a morning ceremony by women from the Three Fires Midewiwin Lodge, an Anishinaabe medicine society. Blankets placed in the center of the circle were used to collect tear-soaked tissues, which, the moderators explained, would later be burned in a sacred fire, returned in gratitude to the Creator.[32] These practices were promoted by the Commission as a way of bringing attention to the value of the traditional knowledge and practices that were the target of assimilation through residential education, in part by emphasizing the ways that knowledge keepers and elders "restored harmony to families and communities" and served as a "foundation of Indigenous law."[33] At the same time, these practices, and the selective focus on victim experience of which they are a part, were founded on an unquestioned assumption that giving voice to the experiences of survivors in these supportive contexts has individual and collective therapeutic effects (a question that I discuss further below).

Victim-centrism was also actively cultivated through testimonial practice. Before giving the floor to those who had registered on the speaker's list, for example, each National Event also offered model testimonies by guest speakers, survivors who were accustomed to telling their stories, who provided examples for others to follow, which similarly conveyed preferred messages, usually with a certain balance of suffering, hope, and redemption. These model testimonies were presented in an environment that was unfamiliar to the participants, in which the expectations of them were unknown or unclear. The experienced witnesses were there to provide encouragement, to make it safe to narrate painful memories before an audience of strangers. Of course, not every survivor followed the model that was offered. Some were silent at the microphone, mute with grief, unable to speak. Others went off topic, preferring to talk about injustices that had no apparent connection with the schools. But the templates were there as points of reference, acting to encourage narratives that touched on long-buried memories and to give them voice.

Encouraged to come forward to tell their stories, survivors offered memories that vividly and emotively depicted their experience with the schools. One volume of the TRC's report, *The Survivors Speak*, offers a compendium of survivor narratives drawn from testimony offered to the Commissioner's Sharing Circle, most built around themes of suffering and loss, such as "Forced Departure," "Separating Siblings," "Fear, Loneliness, and Emotional Neglect," "Despair," "Regimentation," "Discipline," and "Abuse." Some of the selected narrations resonated with the history of the Holocaust, as in Shirley Leon's account of the transport used to bring students to the school in Kamloops, British Columbia: "[I remember] seeing the cattle trucks come onto the reserve and scoop up the kids to go, and seeing my cousins cry, and then, and they were put on these trucks and hauled off and we didn't know where, and my grandmother and mother hiding us under the bed."[34]

Pierrette Benjamin's statement, drawn from memories of her experience in residential school at La Tuque, combined the themes of language loss and brutal regimes of discipline:

> They put a big chunk [of soap], and they put it in my mouth, and the principal, she put it in my mouth, and she said, "Eat it, eat it," and . . . she put her hand in front of my mouth, so I was chewing and chewing, and I had to swallow it, so I swallowed it, and then I had to open my mouth to show that I had swallowed it. And at the end, I understood, and she told me, "That's a dirty language, that's the devil that speaks in your mouth, so we had to wash it because

it's dirty." So every day I spent at the residential school, I was treated badly. I was almost slaughtered.[35]

Although the Commission report is built around a variety of themes, including lip service to "warm memories" and "improvements," the overwhelming majority of survivor statements that I heard in the seven National Events, even more than the themes of the Commission's reports, emphasized physical abuse and sexual sadism. The statement by Richard Hall is one example among many. He recalls the regime of sexual abuse established by Arthur Plint, a dormitory supervisor at the school in Alberni, British Columbia, who was later convicted and sentenced to a lengthy jail term for the abuses he committed.

> And there's times when that, the bullies, I called them goons, I called them. They chased me, get me, and bring me to that pedophile so he could molest me, have his way with me. And you would live in constant fear . . . I went home for the summer. I went home a different person, back to Bella Coola for the summer. I was twelve years old. At twelve years old I began drinking alcohol to forget."[36]

The obverse side of this tendency toward narrations of sexual abuse and its aftermath took the form of narratives that were excluded, as in the reluctance of students who did *not* have deeply traumatic experiences and thus did not appear before the microphone. This reluctance came out, for example, in an interview conducted by my research assistant Marie-Pierre Gadoua with a former student, away from the microphones and cameras of the Commission: "I almost feel guilty because, I mean, I had it rough in residential school. . . . Sister N wasn't the nicest person in the world. I didn't starve, though. I had clothes. I had a warm bed. I wasn't abused physically, you know, or sexually abused. . . . But my story, compared to our elders . . . it almost seems insignificant, if I could say that."[37] Those who had little to say about the horrors of the schools were also unable to contribute to the themes of healing and reconciliation. The two were closely conjoined, with healing as the counterpoint to the emphasis on trauma and triggering. To heal and be restored, one must first be in a condition of injury and suffering. Without this condition, there is little need to narrate a "healing journey."

This brings us to what was arguably the most consistent and possibly the most necessary theme in the survivor testimony that I heard in the Commission's National Events: a concluding account of healing and redemption. This could take a variety of forms, including rediscovery of aboriginal spiritual traditions, activism in the promotion of indigenous rights, finding truth in Christianity (a faith seen by many survivors as being distorted and sinned against by those operating the school), achieving sobriety in a twelve-step program, or simply finding solace in family life. Concluding the statement in this way was as important for the audience as it was for the survivor at the microphone. Listeners were made uncomfortable by raw, unreserved accounts of personal pain, which left both them and the narrator with a sense of inescapable immersion in despair and helplessness. It was, above all, a salve to the audience and public, listening to affect-laden stories of broken, violated childhood. The account of redemption was usually slipped in at the end, presented almost in passing. Yet it was probably the only quality of TRC testimony that could at some level be considered fundamentally necessary. It put a cap on the narration of pain, diminished its intensity and, by extension, the audience's responsibility for emotional engagement. The lack of it stood out, particularly if the survivor at the microphone concentrated on traumatic events—with tears, trembling hands, and quavering voices—and stood to return to their seats while still drowning in grief.

Consequences

The most immediate question that arises out of the emphasis on catharsis and healing in victim-oriented truth commissions is their possible contribution to the personal healing of those who appear before the microphone. Are these commissions in fact therapeutic for individuals, as they so frequently proclaim? While this question has not been a subject of rigorous inquiry, anecdotal evidence encourages doubt. As Lund points out, "some witnesses and health-care professionals have criticized the process for causing psychological harm by forcing victims to relive their experiences, by failing to provide therapeutic services, and by delaying reparations."[38] Leys, approaching this problem from another angle, points to a misunderstood and overlooked approach to healing from trauma, which "often depended on getting the patient not to remember but to *forget* the traumatic origin" of their psychic pain.[39] There is, at the very least, no consensus on the therapeutic benefits of human rights testimony and good reason for skepticism toward it.

In a meeting with representatives of the Cree Board of Health and Social Services of James Bay in the aftermath of the Commission's community hearings and the Montreal National Event, I heard firsthand the overwhelming demands placed on community-based mental health workers by the "re-traumatization" effect of the hearings. Mental health workers were understandably skeptical about the healing claims of the Commission in the context of demands placed on their services following the hearings. And as reported by a mental health worker, the same kind of re-traumatization took place in the aftermath of hearings in Inuvik:

> [The TRC] re-traumatized us . . . there was nobody there to say, "Well, what can I do to help you now? Do you want to go for counseling?" They tell us there are facilities across Canada where our survivors can go and get after-care. I know of people who have applied for after-care who are still waiting. Long lines. People who have waited so long they've gone right back into drinking.[40]

This common experience reveals that, if anything, there occurs what might be referred to as a "hurricane effect" in the aftermath of commission hearings, a sudden escalation of the collective velocity and force of traumatic memory that follow from public telling and listening to traumatic memories to the point that healing services are overwhelmed.

More consequentially for the purposes of truth commissions is the impact of the therapeutic model on the wider, political goals of healing and reconciliation, which are situated in the space between individual testimony and the widely proclaimed goals of "healing the nation." Here, too, we have good reason for doubt. Mpho (Desmond) Tutu, in recent reflections on the legacy of South Africa's Truth and Reconciliation Commission, points to the emotional impact of the testimony that he helped to put into place, especially to the fact that the victims "made us—the commissioners, their fellow South Africans, and the global community—listen, cry, and feel with them." But he also points to the Commission's unmet wider goals when he goes on to observe that the "victims' suffering did not necessarily stop when the commission's work ended."[41] The meaning and purpose of healing and reconciliation for Tutu was the construction of a just South African society outside the adversarial system of litigation—which, in the context of contemporary South Africa, is thus far an unachieved goal—rather than the catharsis that is commonly assumed to follow from the public exposure of pain.

A similar disjuncture between the emotional impact of survivor statements and the incompletion of justice can be seen in Canada's truth commission. Commissioner Marie Wilson retrospectively noted a recurrent theme in the survivor statements of Canada's TRC, which she discussed under the heading "Lack of Perceived Justice," and cites a statement given by one survivor as an illustration: "They make me remember things I've spent my whole life trying to forget . . . and they still don't believe me . . . If the Apologies from the Government and the churches were so sincere, where are the Government and the churches now? Who is in the room?"[42] The absence of those who represented the institutional responsibility for the crimes of the state in the activities of the Commission was in itself a source of a sense of injustice and incompletion.

Victim-centric truth commissions promote the possibilities for healing in the absence of knowledge of the wider effect of emotion-laden testimony on public understanding of the survivor experience. Does it lead to the kind of popular sympathy that results in activist engagement and support, or does it create a stereotype of weakness and vulnerability, without political appeal? More likely, does it encourage a combination of both in various constituencies, with those who fail to be persuaded by the survivors' political claims tending to associate testimony with the harmful stigmas of victimization and mental illness?

This question makes clear that the influence of the therapeutic model of transitional justice goes well beyond the mental health of those who occupy the category of survivor-narrator. There are also, and perhaps most importantly, implications for our understanding of perpetrators and their acts—and, by extension, of the history and origins of mass crime—that follow from testimony-as-therapy. These implications begin with the fairly straightforward concern expressed by Kevin Avruch, to the effect that reconciliation processes that do not demand the participation of the perpetrator will always be partial.[43] Beyond this, the idea of human rights as therapeutic now has such influence that perpetrators are not only morally excluded from the power of "truth telling"—they are created by it. The category of "perpetrator" follows from the construction of an "ideal"; they are abstract (perceived as inhuman), represent the overall harm, and, once labeled, are excluded from "truth telling" because their identification as perpetrators denies their legitimate speech.[44] As the focus of attention because of the inhumanity of their actions, listeners deny perpetrators any humanity, as well as any recognition as having a legitimate story. Abstraction is essential for the reification of their essential qualities. The simplified and distorted ideas about perpetrators, in turn, mask the origins of mass crimes and make it more difficult to see and intervene in the early conditions of their occurrence.

Therapeutically oriented truth commissions avoid proximity to perpetrators not so much to avoid the discomforts of their humanization but more with a view to protecting the mental health of survivors. To the extent possible, survivors are sheltered from the traumatic, "triggering" consequences of the encounter with perpetrators and, above all, from the shock of confrontation with their explanations or denial of their participation in mass crime. There are, of course, post-violence contexts in which victims live next to former offenders in daily life, but Canada's TRC was among those oriented toward protecting survivors from such encounters. This kind of insulation is the corollary of victim affirmation and an inherent aspect of victim-centric truth commissions.

By insulating participants from the realities of perpetrators and their sources of power, victim-centric truth commissions at the same time reduce to one dimension the most important capacity of human rights: the ability to expose painful truths. A critical approach to the kinds of truth that are the foundation of human rights sometimes takes us to uncomfortable places where we might be forced to confront facts that lead us to reconsider our beliefs and even our basic loyalties. This holds true both for representatives of states that commit abuses and for those who represent the victims of those abuses. Taken together, for example, the motives and actions of the priests, brothers, and nuns who ran the residential schools in Canada do not constitute an "ideal perpetrator" but commonly blur the boundaries with the sincerity and good intentions behind their (usually) unwitting contribution to mass suffering. Child soldiers in Uganda, Sierra Leone, and elsewhere similarly break down the assumptions and ideals about victims. Blind spots of this kind do not arise naturally but develop through repeated, institutionally sanctioned testimonial preferences and selectivities. The discursive management of survivor statements might tell us a great deal about their experience of suffering, but it leaves out of view the institutional and policy-driven sources of that suffering and the people who acted on them, sometimes out of the belief that they were doing good.

The reification of victims and perpetrators is not limited to truth commissions but appears as a more general feature of human rights discourses with a central component of claims-making and persuasion. As Danielle Celermajer points out with reference to the prevention of torture, the social imaginary of human rights privileges the agency of autonomous individuals, such that unique sites of responsibility are emphasized in preference to the structural conditions of violence.[45] "Telling and retelling the story of torture in terms of evil perpetrators and innocent victims" she notes, "reinforces a causal explanation based on individual-level factors and occludes other ways of understanding the etiology of torture."[46] Applying this argument to the discourses of organizations like Amnesty International, Human Rights Watch, or Survival International similarly reveals that victims are commonly idealized and stereotyped, stressing their innocence and vulnerability, while, in a conjoined way, perpetrators are made remote from ordinary life, portrayed as an abstract force or one-dimensionally, like comic book villains.

Truth commissions are among the main purveyors of this tendency in human rights. By limiting our view to those in pain, victim-centrism creates distorted understandings of history and narrows our vision of the perpetration of harm. And in the absence of prosecutorial authority, it ironically does those in pain a disservice, taking their stories and failing to give them an empowering sense of justice in return. Lacking both therapeutic and judicial efficacy, the model of therapy on offer in survivor-centric TRCs and related institutions is ultimately demeaning to victims, first by constructing templates of discourse and emotional expression that identifies them, almost inescapably, as victims. In their efforts to uncover and disseminate truth, these commissions tend to reduce perpetrators and victims to one-dimensional figures, making it more difficult to understand the violence suffered, the ideas that underpinned it, and the ways that institutional abuse might be there, latent or manifest, in other forms, in the present.

No amount of affirmative discourse and packaging can make up for judicial weakness, which shifts the goals of reconciliatory change away from those who abused their power and onto survivors, their families, and their communities. In this sense, the therapeutic approach to human rights remedy heals neither individuals nor the nation but merely offers a temporary distraction, a spectacle of suffering, with little reflection on what that spectacle produces and what it leaves unchanged and unexamined.

CHAPTER 9

Cinematic Aesthetics and the Subjects of Human Rights

On Eliane Caffé's Era o Hotel Cambridge

Andrew C. Rajca

A COMMON APPROACH to the visual aesthetics of human rights centers upon beautifully shot images of children, women, racial and ethnic minorities, or abject subjects of war, trafficking, or poverty who are presented as innocent victims of an atrocity perpetrated by some evil entity. Spectators, primarily coming from an educated and economically secure background, are discursively disconnected from the cause of this suffering and also aesthetically interpellated by artists, photographers, or filmmakers to act politically to correct a given injustice. This type of "political" aesthetic engagement with human rights is commonly produced through a discourse of liberal humanitarianism, focusing on civil or political rights to the exclusion of economic and social rights in ways that ultimately depoliticize the subjects of human rights as "helpless victims" who need to be saved—absolving both the artist and the spectators from their role in maintaining the very economic, political, and social structures that produce human suffering. The relationship between the portrayal of human rights subjects in a work of art and its reception by viewers has been critically interrogated by much recent work on politics and aesthetics in the fields of cultural studies and critical theory, seen in important contributions by Jacques Rancière, Nelly Richard, Wendy S. Hesford, Susana Draper, and Fernando J. Rosenberg, among others.[1] In tune with the approaches of these scholars, my research has focused on Latin American film, photography, audiovisual installations, and literary works that problematize idealized notions of humanitarianism and trace new forms of agency for the subjects of human rights via the relationship among politics, aesthetics, and spectatorship.[2] In particular, I am interested in cultural production that disrupts what Hesford has called the "spectacular rhetoric" of humanitarianism by attempting to reframe human rights discourse and spectatorial practices as forms of resistance to neoliberalism and not as its ideological accomplices.

In this chapter on the aesthetics of human rights I focus on a recent example of Brazilian cinema that offers a disruptive and productive engagement with human rights discourse through the contradictory relationships among aesthetics, politics, and spectatorship: Brazilian director Eliane Caffé's 2016 film *Era o Hotel Cambridge* ("*It Was the Hotel Cambridge*"). The movie is a fictional story of the occupation of an abandoned building in downtown São Paulo by a group of homeless Brazilian migrants, immigrant refugees, and activists—filmed on location at the site of an actual occupied property and with many of the real-life occupiers playing the characters. The first section of the essay offers a brief overview of my approach to examining the visual aesthetics of human rights, focusing in particular on concepts developed by Rancière that offer a useful framework to examine the relationship between film form and spectatorship. Next, in dialogue with academic work in urban cultural studies by Brazilian scholars Raquel Rolnik and Vera Pallamin, whose contributions are often absent from global academic debates due to the fact that they are written in Portuguese, I explain the context of the occupations of abandoned buildings in São Paulo that serve as the backdrop for *Era o Hotel Cambridge*. In the final section of the essay, I engage in a detailed analysis of the cinematic form and content of Caffé's film, teasing out the ways that the director inscribes the tenuous relationship between directorial intent and spectatorial practices in the production of meaning in a work of "political" art. I contend that the film offers an innovative example of how cinematic aesthetics can portray subjects fighting for economic and social rights in ways that resist both neoliberalism and the rhetoric of liberal humanitarianism that has come to dominate global human rights discourse today.

Aesthetics, Spectatorship, and Human Rights

In order to think critically about aesthetic engagement with human rights, it is necessary to examine the form of a given photograph, film, or art installation and the ways in which an artist or filmmaker constructs the relationship between the image and the viewer in order to produce meaning. In this analysis, we must be careful not to idealize the political effects of artistic creation on spectators, not to assume that political art will automatically equate aesthetic presentation with political action. My thinking in this area has largely been influenced by Rancière, who has problematized both mimetic notions of the relationship between art and politics (i.e., that an artist uses a cultural medium to portray an injustice or social problem, through which the spectator is made aware of and moved by this representation and then acts to correct the injustice), as well as notions of political art that seeks to eliminate mediation by melding art and everyday life (e.g., the idea that producing art itself constitutes a political act or that artists can fill the inherent gaps of representation between aesthetics and politics through material artistic interventions into the built environment or community).[3] While so-called critical or political art often erroneously presents "a straightforward relationship between political aims and artistic means . . . to create awareness of political situations leading to political mobilization,"[4] Rancière reminds us that there "is no straightforward road from the fact of looking at a spectacle to the fact of understanding the state of the world; no direct road from intellectual awareness to political action."[5]

As those of us working in the realm of cultural studies and human rights have seen, aesthetic portrayals of suffering, victimized subjects, and testimonial truth telling in the manner that I noted above do not guarantee that spectators will act to correct a given injustice nor that the intended effect of the filmmaker or artist reflects the desires of the human subjects at the center of the representation. The experiences of subjects of human rights abuses are often appropriated within a larger discourse or presented as a prop to attack political opponents or support the goals of an organization, party, or business in ways that vacate the political subjectivity of the victims. In other words, works of visual culture that depict poverty, police abuse, state-sanctioned violence and torture, racism, sexism, and other violations of human rights—even those presented in a documentary, testimonial, or archival mode—need to be considered as "sites of material and ideological struggle over meaning."[6] We need to tease out the complex and contradictory relationships among aesthetics, politics, and spectatorship when examining the portrayal of issues related to human rights in works of visual culture. This means taking into account the specific context of a given situation or cultural work; the goals and political agency of the human subjects at the center of the human rights issue being represented; the ways that directors, photographers, and artists frame these experiences; and the multitude of meanings that can be produced for spectators through what Nelly Richard describes as "the operations of signs and the techniques of representation that mediate between the artistic and the social."[7] While I maintain an optimistic outlook on the *potential* political effects of art in the struggle for material improvements to the lives of marginalized subjects, we must also have a critical approach to the analysis of the relationship between art and politics, one that does not automatically assume the political effects of art on spectators but instead takes into account the contradictory tensions of these themes in a given cultural work.

Rancière's exploration of the relationship among aesthetics, politics, and spectatorship in *The Emancipated Spectator* offers an ideal theoretical framework to engage in a close analysis of a film such as *Era o Hotel Cambridge*. Rancière conceives of an aesthetic experience as "a multiplication of connections and disconnections that reframe the relation between bodies, the world they live in and the way in which they are 'equipped' to handle it. It is a multiplicity of folds and gaps in the fabric of common experience that change the cartography of the perceptible, the thinkable, the feasible."[8] Here, Rancière offers a way of considering the relationship between a film and a spectator that moves beyond the forms of political or critical art that assume a direct cause-and-effect relationship between the content of a film and action by a spectator. He instead highlights the multiple possible "connections and disconnections" in the relationship between a given aesthetic work and its reception by viewers, between the spectatorial bodies and the bodies of human rights subjects presented on-screen. In place of forms of political art that fill in the gaps between aesthetic representation and political action by offering prepackaged meanings to spectators, Rancière conceives of the space between artistic representation and reception by a spectator as the site of political aesthetics, the "folds and gaps in the fabric of common experience" that make visible new ways of seeing the world. It is precisely here, in the complex and contradictory tensions between aesthetic production and reception, where a multitude of interpretations come in contact with one another and open up new ways for a spectator to perceive a given issue in the active production of meaning.

One concept that Rancière develops to think about the relationship among politics, aesthetics, and spectatorship is that of *pensive images*, which he conceives as "regimes of expression that intersect, creating unique combinations of exchange, fusion and distance ... forms of pensiveness of the image that refute the opposition between ... the operative character of art and the immediacy of the image."[9] In other words, a pensive image is an image—or a relationship between different images—that forces spectators to hesitate, contemplate, and actively produce meaning from a film, a photograph, an audiovisual in-

stallation, or any other example of visual culture. It is this relationship between images that goes beyond the two common forms of "political" art critiqued above—i.e., the presumption that showing injustice automatically
generates understanding and action by the spectator or that eliminating representation could collapse the difference between art and life—by placing *both*
forms in tension and highlighting the contradictory relationship between directorial intent and spectatorial reception, articulated through the form and
content of a given film. A pensive image doesn't produce meaning directly for
the viewer; rather, it provides a site where the "emancipated spectator" must
actively produce meaning within the uncertain relationship between politics
and aesthetics. As I demonstrate below, we can consider *Era o Hotel Cambridge* as a series of pensive images that don't call spectators to action but
rather call attention to the complex and contradictory relationships among
cinematic aesthetics, political subjectivity, and spectatorship in the portrayal
of human rights issues. Yet, prior to engaging in a close examination of these
processes in the film, I would first like to provide a little context on the growing occupation movement in São Paulo.

Occupy Movements in São Paulo

Since 1997, multiple organizations composed of homeless, poor, migrant, and
refugee populations living in São Paulo—along with their activist and artist
allies—have occupied dozens of abandoned properties in the center of the city
in order to draw attention to the lack of adequate and affordable housing in
the central neighborhoods, where most working-class jobs are located. While
the most visible organization is the *Movimento de Trabalhadores Sem Teto*
(or the Homeless Workers' Movement, MTST), led by Guilherme Boulos, the
2018 presidential candidate for the *Partido Socialismo e Liberdade* (the Socialism and Freedom Party, PSOL), there are dozens of organizations that have
occupied abandoned buildings over the past twenty years—justifying their
actions by citing the guarantee to housing in the Chapter II Social Rights section of the 1988 Brazilian Constitution and a 2001 provision in the Federal
City Statutes Law (10.257) that states that urban properties must serve a "social
function." The active appeal to the right to affordable housing within the constitution and the statute of requiring a social function for urban properties as
tools to combat real estate speculation makes São Paulo an important site to
examine acts of political subjectivation by those attempting to exercise the social rights afforded by law but denied as a result of the public/private partnership between capital and the municipal government in São Paulo.

The occupation of abandoned buildings in São Paulo by those who can no longer afford the rents in its central neighborhoods illustrates a localized experience of the effects of neoliberal capitalism, particularly what Brazilian urbanist Raquel Rolnik has identified as the global "financialization of housing"[10] and the "transmutation of housing into a financial asset."[11] In line with the work of geographer David Harvey, Rolnik notes that these processes have led government policies to abandon the practice of considering housing and public access to the city as social rights, instead transforming them into a "mechanism for the extraction of rent, financial profit, and the accumulation of wealth"[12] that has resulted in the "creation of an urban poor with no place to go, new processes of subjectivation structured through the logic of debt, and significantly increased segregation in cities."[13] The trajectory of turning housing into a speculative investment, as opposed to a social guarantee, has displaced poor and working-class communities from the center of São Paulo since the 1980s, contributing to the physical segregation of housing for low-income workers, who are forced to live in peripheral communities where rents are cheaper but which require them to commute to work on the bus for hours every day. Here we can observe a correlation between the global economic turn to housing as a "market" and the violation of laws that guarantee housing for citizens in local contexts. Taken together, they can be considered parallel paths of neoliberal thought and practices that are not seen as violations of human rights due to processes of eliminating economic and social rights from dominant strands of human rights discourse since the 1970s.[14]

Yet Rolnik also highlights the active resistance to these processes through what she calls the *guerra dos lugares* ("war of places"), such as in the occupation of abandoned buildings where the "city, colonized by finance capital, explodes in insurgencies, conflicts, and violence . . . the war of places . . . that simultaneously questions these policies and points toward other possible urban worlds."[15] This active questioning and material resistance to real estate speculation, predicated upon the partnership between private capital and government policies and practices, offers an ideal space for us to reconsider what it means to be a subject of human rights. The occupiers of abandoned buildings in São Paulo are the subjects of economic and social human rights that have been placed under erasure by the dominant discourse of liberal humanitarianism since the 1970s. These occupiers are not helpless victims without rights who need to be saved but active political subjects inserting a claim for the accessible and affordable housing guaranteed by law to residents of São Paulo that has been denied to them as a result of neoliberal economic and political practices. As Brazilian urbanist Vera Pallamin has argued, drawing from Rancière's notion of dissensus, "the movements for housing and the occupations that have been occurring in São Paulo since 1997 are clearly of a dissensual nature, and, in this sense, are fundamental agents of the political in this city."[16] Pallamin emphasizes the importance of the occupiers as active political subjects of human rights who create a space of visibility both in their material occupation of abandoned buildings in the center of the city and by inserting themselves within dominant social discourse that does not consider poor people, migrants, immigrants, or refugees as equal speaking subjects in the community: "Abandoned people and closed buildings are transformed . . . into political subjects and litigious places. Initially anonymous, without a home, they come to control their own mode of political subjectivation."[17]

Both Rolnik and Pallamin note the relationship between art and politics involved in these acts of resistance, how they disrupt the "accepted" practices of human rights subjects to insert new forms of political and artistic representation in the city. For Rolnik, the "'occupations'—of streets, squares, and buildings—have been multiplying in Brazilian cities through the interventions of both cultural collectives and homeless movements, often in strategic alliances."[18] She points out that while artists often insert themselves within the urban fabric to materially intervene upon the built environment through innovative aesthetic representations, social movements such as those occupying abandoned buildings challenge traditional notions of what constitutes the political by inserting new forms of self-representation into the city.[19] This relationship between art and the city of São Paulo is a main focus of Pallamin's work, as seen in her excellent analysis of the occupation at the Prestes Maia building between 2002 and 2007 by the *Movimento Sem-Teto do Centro* (the Downtown Homeless Movement, or MSTC), which included the collaboration of art collectives to formulate "symbolic strategies geared towards amplifying the visibility of this movement in the media, particularly in its most critical moments associated with the judicial order to vacate and the police presence."[20] Importantly, Pallamin also notes that as a participant in the symbolic production of urban space, "urban art—understood within the layout of social relations, and not reduced to an aestheticized dimension—echoes the contradictions, conflicts, and power relations that constitute this space."[21] This leads her to trace the inherent tensions in the relationship between aesthetics and politics recognized by the art collectives themselves, who, despite the political goal of supporting the occupations by marginalized subjects of economic and social rights, noted a series of contradictions in the relationship between artists and occupiers made visible by questions of class.[22]

In discussing the aesthetics of human rights, it is crucial to incorporate a close analysis of the complex interactions between artistic intent and spectatorial interpretation of a given work of cultural production. The examination of artistic forms and modes of addressing spectators is an essential component of the study of cinema in the humanities, one that tends to be ignored by social sciences, which often narrowly concentrate on the sociological, political, or documentary aspects of a given film without examining how meanings are produced and circulated through discourse. To this end, I now turn to Caffé's *Era o Hotel Cambridge* to examine its use of cinematic structures in the depiction of subjects of human rights in the occupations in São Paulo, along with the complex, contradictory interaction between visual representations of these political acts and their reception by spectators.

Aesthetic Occupations of Human Rights in *Era o Hotel Cambridge*

Era o Hotel Cambridge portrays a battle within the "guerra dos lugares" described by Raquel Rolnik: between the "financialization" of housing and public urban spaces by global capitalism in partnership with city, state, and federal governments, and resistance to these processes through the occupation of an abandoned building in the center of São Paulo. Based on a fictional script, with the initial intention of exploring the experiences of immigrant refugees in São Paulo, the movie was filmed within the real occupation of the Hotel Cambridge in the center of the city by the MSTC, in conjunction with the *Frente de Luta por Moradia* ("the Struggle for Housing Front," FLM)—and many real-life occupiers play fictional characters in the film. The Hotel Cambridge was built in 1951, and until the late 1970s the hotel and the jazz/bossa nova bar on the ground floor was considered one of the "most chic venues in downtown São Paulo."[23] During the 1980s and early 1990s the space ceased to function as a hotel and became vacant, along with much of the old downtown areas of São Paulo, as the financial and cultural center of the city gradually moved toward the Avenida Paulista and Marginal Pinheiros districts. By 2000, this left approximately 40,000 vacant, livable dwellings in the city center as registered by the municipality, while urbanist Jeroen Stevens estimates that "at least one-third of the centre's architecture was probably abandoned"[24] once unregistered apartments, vacant hotels, and government buildings are taken into account. Throughout the 2000s the former bar at the Cambridge hosted underground dance parties, while social movements lobbied the city to transform the building into affordable public housing. The municipal government finally purchased the former hotel in 2011, but it did nothing with the property for over a year, and in November 2012 approximately 200 families connected with the MSTC occupied the building. After successfully defending themselves for days from initial attempts of forced removal by military police, the "*Ocupação Cambridge* developed into one of the movement's most cherished bulwarks in the city"[25] and is currently undergoing government-funded renovations to be transformed into social housing called the *Residência Cambridge*.

Incorporating documentary footage into a fictional film, and using both professional and non-professional actors, *Era o Hotel Cambridge* constitutes a symbolic and material intervention into São Paulo's housing crisis, which has been exacerbated by government-abetted real estate speculation. Much of the film includes beautiful, documentary-style shots of everyday life in the occupation: brief glimpses of the residents and their activities, rooms, conversations, and relationships, as well as multiple images of the architecture of the building itself. The seemingly local meaning about this specific building/experience in São Paulo, Brazil, transforms into a wider exploration of the global effects of capitalism, racism, and citizenship. The occupiers include both Brazilians, largely migrants from the Northeast, and international immigrant refugees, such as those escaping violence in Palestine and fleeing the Congo's violent extraction of "blood minerals" for corporate and government profit. At first blush, the film seems to be an example of the sort of political art critiqued by Rancière, where "activist artists draw the conclusion that no mediation is required; that the work can be the direct presentation of another form of community in which artists are directly fashioning new social bonds."[26] Both director Caffé and her sister Carla Caffé, a professor of architecture and design at São Paulo's *Escola da Cidade* and the film's artistic director, have emphasized the material contributions made to the occupying community by Carla's students, who, for example, constructed a computer lab and lounge for the film that residents were able to put to practical use post-production.[27]

However, while *Era o Hotel Cambridge* is unabashedly intended as a political film in support of the FLM and the occupation movements in São Paulo, it does more than attempt to meld art and everyday life or show an injustice in the hope that spectators will act. Instead, the film *occupies* the tensions among aesthetics, politics, and spectatorship in the portrayal of human rights sub-jectivity by incorporating the contradictory interactions of these themes into the very cinematic structures that compose the work. These contradictions are "inscribed in a different politics of art . . . in which the form is not split off from the construction of a social relation or from the realization of a capacity that belongs to everyone."[28] Caffé traces the contradictory relationships be-tween artistic intent and spectatorial communities within the form and con-tent of the film, in which three levels of cinematic narrative are placed into productive tension with one another. At one level is the fictional story, focused on the experiences of immigrant refugees in Brazil, which was then expanded to include depictions of the everyday lives of the occupiers of the building. A second component is the incorporation of documentary images shot with dif-ferent camera formats and image textures into the larger fictional film, thus opening up a multiplicity of meanings related to the original footage. Some examples include the real occupation of another abandoned building carried out by the real-life occupiers of the hotel; scenes from documentary films by other directors inserted into the fictional narrative; and independent media footage of military police forcibly removing residents of a different occupied building that was inserted as the fictionalized *despejo* (eviction) of the occupi-ers of the Cambridge at the end of the film. Finally, two characters (Apolo and Uta) produce a fictional blog about the occupation, complete with video inter-views, images, and texts about the residents, as well as performance art pieces seeking to create public support for the occupation via aesthetic means. It is the tension among these different cinematic elements that allows Caffé's film to move beyond both the mimetic tradition and the idealized erasure of me-diation between art and politics to produce the series of *pensive images* that I discussed earlier.

A primary way that Caffé creates pensive images of human rights subjects in the film is by playing with the relationship between fictional and documen-tary representation of the occupiers and by having real-life residents of the Cambridge play roles in the fictional film. A good example of this is the char-acter Hassan, a refugee from Palestine, played by actual Palestinian refugee and occupier Isam Ahmad Issa. Through the role of Hassan, Caffé attempts to connect the occupation of Palestine with the occupation of the building in São Paulo, equating violations of the human rights of Palestinians in Gaza with the active struggle for social rights to housing in Brazil. In an early scene, the occupiers are informed at an *assembléia* (community meeting) that there is a court-ordered eviction for the building, which they democratically decide to resist by staying in their homes. The meeting is shot in such a way that spectators aren't quite sure if this is documentary footage or part of the fictional film augmented by shots revealing multiple cameras filming the meeting. There is then a cut to a small group discussing the decision to fight, with Apolo (played by professional actor José Dumont) attempting to convince a doubtful colleague of the plan by telling him to listen to Hassan, who knows more about occupations than anyone. Hassan replies, "Now we are occupiers of a place, while I was kicked out of my homeland by occupiers who, at one time, were victims. This does not give them the right to be criminals." Here, Caffé portrays Hassan as inverting his previous experience with an occupation by becoming an active political subject in Brazil, and the overt critique of the killing of Palestinians and the destruction of their homes by the Israeli army is repeated multiple times in the film. Yet the uncertainty about whether this is a scripted fictional conversation or testimonial truth telling causes spectators to hesitate to interpret this and other scenes in the film, resulting in the creation of pensive images that call attention to the tensions between artistic creation and political activism.

This can be observed in other moments involving Hassan in the film, where the camera changes from the sharply contrasted tones that run through the main visual narrative to grainy, documentary shots of Hassan in a refugee camp and a Skype conversation with his sister. The latter scene, which is actually a conversation with Issa's real-life cousin in Gaza, offers an excellent example of the interaction between different types of media within the film to produce a pensive image in the Rancièrean sense, "neither the raw record of a social fact nor the composition of an aesthete engaged in art for art's sake . . . It marks the contamination of two arts, two ways of 'making us see.'"[29] As Hassan speaks to his sister in Arabic (with Portuguese subtitles), she moves her laptop to the window, and spectators are provided with documentary footage of the complete destruction of the building next to her apartment by the Israeli military. While the viewers watch these images, Hassan's sister informs him (and us) about the death of one of her children, the bombing of a UN school in their town, the realities of eighty people living in one room, and other details about the violence of everyday life experienced by the Palestinian residents of Gaza. This "fictionalized testimony" serves to reveal Hassan's sister/Issa's cousin as someone whose human rights have been violated, while simultaneously fleshing out the background of Hassan's character in the fictional narrative. The scene is framed through a series of cuts and *rac-*

cord shots that alternately place spectators in Hassan's viewing position of the Skype conversation and close-up shots of Hassan taken from an angle next to the computer. This creates a positionality for the viewers that is simultaneously within and outside the conversation, creating a sense that we are experiencing what Hassan is feeling both from his perspective and as witnesses, both in the cinematic realm and the real effects of violence for Palestinians living in Gaza.

At the end of the conversation there is a jump cut to a close-up shot of Hassan sitting in front of a window in another part of the Cambridge, drinking coffee, smoking, and staring at the ground as if he is reflecting on the conversation with his sister. A voiceover of Hassan reciting a testimonial poem in Arabic about the lack of a true homeland for Palestinians is then overlaid on the scene, while the image cuts to full-screen documentary shots of everyday life in a refugee camp, with Hassan at the center of both these images and the quick cuts back to him sitting in reflection. The sequence ends with a shot of Hassan in the hotel as his voiceover concludes with the hope that his journey ends in Brazil; he lifts his head and stares directly at the camera. The "documentary" images spliced within Hassan's reflections are shot in a different format than the majority of the film, evoking the idea that these are meant to represent Hassan's memories of life in Gaza. This clip was in fact taken from the 2009 documentary *A chave da casa* ("*The Key to the House*"), directed by Brazilians Paschoal Samora and Stela Grisotti, about a group of Palestinians—including Isam Ahmad Issa—living in the Al-Rweshed refugee camp on the border of Jordan and Iraq who later migrate to Brazil. In this way, in *Era o Hotel Cambridge*, Caffé incorporates documentary images of Issa's real-life experiences in the camp into the cinematic construction of reflections on life in Gaza for Palestinians through a fictional character played by Issa himself.

The intricate interplay of documentary images and cinematic scripts echoes the complexity of the aesthetic representation of Hassan as a subject of human rights, as an actor and as Isam Ahmad Issa, in Palestine and in São Paulo. This reflects the constant tension between reality and fiction throughout the entire film, which causes viewers to hesitate in drawing conclusions or meanings, as testimonial "truth telling" and cinematic fiction bleed into one another in a series of pensive images. We are not sure what the direct political message is, how we are supposed to react to the "testimonial" accounts of the daily violence experienced by Palestinians in Gaza and refugees in São Paulo. Spectators are simultaneously presented with conflicting discourses of human rights subjectivity. On the one hand, Palestinians are presented as victims of military violence (Hassan's sister) and iterant migrant refugees with little control of their lives (Hassan), both articulated through the rhetoric of liberal humanitarianism. Yet this discourse is placed into tension with the portrayal of Hassan and the other occupiers of the Cambridge as active political subjects fighting for economic and social human rights, and both representations of human rights subjects are further complicated by the confusion between fictional characters and the real-life experiences of the actors playing the characters. These scenes reveal the complexity of human rights aesthetics, making visible the contradictory relationship between a political film and its reception by spectators, as well as the processes of producing meaning related to specific discourses of human rights—which are inscribed directly in the cinematic form and content of *Era o Hotel Cambridge*.

The fictionalized role of Dona Carmen, played by real-life FLM leader Carmen da Silva Ferreira, is another important vehicle through which Caffé explores the inherent conflicts and contradictions among aesthetics, politics, and spectatorship in the visual representation of human rights. Carmen is central to all aspects of the film, organizing meetings and ensuring that residents participate in and follow the strict rules of the occupation; standing up to military police when they attempt to enter the hotel prior to the court-ordered date of evacuation; and leading a real-life occupation of another building, which Caffé filmed after completing most of the shooting and then incorporated into the fictional narrative of *Era o Hotel Cambridge*. While the changes in camera formats and image tones in different scenes with Carmen are not as explicit as with Hassan, there are some subtle aesthetic cues that lend themselves to creating a space of indetermination between fiction and reality, pensive images that force spectators to pause and contemplate the meanings produced by the character Dona Carmen in relation to the real-life Carmen Silva.

One such example are the interviews of Carmen speaking directly to the camera about the purposes of the occupation, the goals of the FLM, and the incorporation of refugees into the movement, which are visually framed for spectators as clips on a computer screen. These interviews appear during an earlier scene in the computer lab, where Ngandu, a refugee occupier from the Congo, is speaking with his brother via Skype on one computer, while Uta, an occupier from Brazil, works on the computer next to him, editing interview footage for the fictional blog. As the brothers have a heated conversation in French about Ngandu's reluctance to recognize his recently born son and to

bring him and the mother to Brazil, there is a cut and sound bridge to Uta editing footage of an interview with Carmen about the occupation as Ngandu's
argument with his brother continues in the background. The sonic and visual
connection is reiterated in the content of the interview, as Carmen is explicitly talking about the experience of immigrant refugees seeking out the occupations as soon as they arrive to São Paulo because they need a place to live.
There is then a cut back to a medium shot of Uta from behind, placing both
her and the computer into the frame for spectators, as she edits the footage in
order to splice in interviews with the immigrant refugees to echo this comment by Carmen.

These interviews with immigrants are meant to evoke compassion and
solidarity from spectators—those of both *Era o Hotel Cambridge* and the fictional blog within the film—by portraying the refugees as innocent, victimized subjects escaping the evils of their homelands to seek a new life in Brazil. For example, Uta edits an interview with another immigrant, Kazongo,
from Congo, who describes the sociopolitical violence caused by the mining
of "blood minerals" used in smartphones and computers and explains that he
had to leave Congo because he had no other options. The shots of Uta doing
editing and montage work for a film and website about the occupation allow
Caffé to highlight the constructedness of any cinematic representation of human rights, be it categorized as documentary or fiction. The directors and editors of a given film select which scenes to use, what to cut, and how the visual
frames will be placed together in order to portray the victims of human rights
violations in a particular manner, often eliding the faults that people may
have in their personal lives. In this scene, however, the personal problems of
refugees are being simultaneously articulated in the background via Ngandu's
Skype argument with his brother, and these moments of conflict experienced
by all human beings appear in other parts of the film, showing arguments between family members and residents. By incorporating these elements into
the very narrative structure of the film, Caffé captures the messy realities of
occupations that are generally excluded from the promotional material of organizations like the FLM or the MTST—and the fictional blog within the film.
This de-idealizes the occupiers as innocent subjects of human rights activism
while at the same time portraying them as active participants in the struggle
for economic and social rights in the form of adequate housing.

The complex negotiations of the visual rhetoric of human rights are highlighted in another scene led by Carmen, with a group of occupiers preparing to go see the judge to request that the eviction decision be reversed. As

the group gathers around her, Carmen says, "We're going to have to take a lot of kids with us, take the mothers who have kids, so that we can show that only families live here." At the very moment she makes this comment, the camera moves suddenly to capture a shot of a mother carrying a child down the stairs before returning to focusing on Carmen and the group. This fleeting and seemingly spontaneous image of the mother and child reinforces for spectators the truth that, indeed, many of the occupiers are "responsible" mothers taking care of their children who deserve to have their human rights protected. This visually mimics the performative discourse of human rights that Carmen and the group practice as the scene continues, acting as mothers who only want to protect their children in order to garner sympathy from the female judge who ordered their removal from the hotel. As Fernando Rosenberg notes, "children are a privileged subject of rights . . . easily unaccounted for, available and therefore also vulnerable"[30] within adult-centered discourse, leading to what Hesford has described as "the symbolic repertoires and hierarchical scenes of suffering that dominate representations of children in transnational human rights discourse."[31] This use of women and children as the visible subjects of human rights occurs in other parts of the film, where they appear as the moral face of the occupation to critics on the outside—such as the time Carmen tells a military policeman to let a mother and child through to their house, or the inclusion of numerous images of children on the blog being produced by Apolo and Uta. There is an interesting tension here, as the women who occupy the hotel play strong leadership roles in asserting their right to adequate housing as a human right, while at the same time Carmen and other female leaders in the occupation employ the figures of women and children as the ideal subjects of liberal humanitarianism as a tactic for success in their political struggle for economic and social rights.

There is one more scene involving Carmen that alters the camera tone—through an out-of-focus image from what appears to be a hidden location next to her desk—which causes spectators to hesitate, unsure whether this is Dona Carmen the character or Carmen da Silva Ferreira speaking as the real-life leader of the occupation. The scene starts with documentary-style shots of families and organizers of the FLM arriving at the hotel, getting ready to participate in a public march in support of the movement's call for adequate and affordable downtown housing. There is then a cut to Carmen interviewing a potential resident at the Cambridge, shot from the side and looking up toward the conversation, offering viewers a voyeuristic perspective. When the man begins to describe his short-lived experience at another building on "Ouvidor Street that is occupied by . . . ," Carmen accompanies him in completing the sentence, "by artists next to the São Francisco area," while nodding. This provokes a comment by Carmen about the artists in this occupation: "The artists don't want anything there, they just want to immerse themselves in their culture, smoke their weed, do their own thing . . . They're the present-day hippies, without commitment. They want to disseminate a, a freedom. The moment they get tired, each one goes back to their house." This critique by the leader of the FLM—both in real life and in the fictional narrative—highlights the fact that artists in the occupation are often highly educated members of the middle class who can easily return to their comfortable lives whenever they want, echoing the self-critique made by artists in the Prestes Maia occupation that Pallamin examines in her work. In *Era o Hotel Cambridge*, we could view this as a self-referential critique of the film's director and the primarily middle-class, educated spectatorship of the movie: that despite our expressed solidarity with the occupiers, we ultimately can return to our good lives at any time. The inclusion of these comments and the approach of Eliane and Carla Caffé in making the film serve as a self-referential recognition of their privileged position in representing the occupation, which guides their decisions in the production of the film. For example, they sought to leave a material contribution to the site after the completion of the film; they continue to support the activities of the Residência Cambridge; and, perhaps most importantly, they incorporated the occupiers themselves as actors and writers for the film—as aesthetic political subjects of human rights engaging in self-representation, not merely aestheticized political objects portrayed by the director.

The relationship between aesthetics and politics in the representation of the occupation is most clearly explored via the incorporation of the fictional blog as a narrative thread in *Era o Hotel Cambridge*. While I have already alluded to some elements related to the production of the blog, I would like to discuss a few specific scenes here that illustrate the tensions among aesthetics, politics, and spectatorship related to the subjects of human rights. In one scene, Apolo leads a group of residents in preparing a performative art piece to include on the blog, exclaiming that they are "ARTivists" and that he wants to experiment with *quadros vivos* (live paintings): "A live painting has to have the force and the synthesis of an idea in the form of a poem." As Hassan then offers a poetic, testimonial "live painting" on displacement and the experience of refugees in Arabic, spectators observe Uta filming the scene, with

Apolo positioning her to better capture the footage for inclusion on the blog. The aesthetic components involved in the visual articulation of the subjects of human rights are further accentuated later in the scene, when Apolo explains how he will play with light and shadows to shoot the "testimony" of Kazongo—the refugee who fled violence related to the extraction of "blood minerals" used to produce cell phones in the Congo. This moment is presented in a lighthearted manner, with Apolo comically wheeling Kazongo around in a chair and placing him in the center of the circle of participants to physically show his vision for the shot, highlighting the cell phone that, ironically, Kazongo must now use to maintain contact with his family via Skype. In this scene, Caffé calls attention to the fact that both Uta and Apolo, like the director herself, are framing the experiences of the occupiers in order to create a specific narrative about the residents as active political subjects of human rights, showing them in a positive light in order to justify their actions and to gain the support of the general population viewing the blog.

However, echoing Rancière's warning that there is no guaranteed relationship between cause and effect in political art, that showing an injustice will not automatically translate into action by spectators, we later see Apolo reading the comments on the images and videos published on the blog. The comments echo the typical right-wing critiques of occupations couched in the rhetoric of private property and anti-immigrant sentiments such as "A bunch of bums, trespassers on private property!" and "Get out foreigners from third world countries, poor immigrants with no skills only slow us down!" These comments in fact reflect a dominant view of human rights as "privileges for bandits"[32] for a large portion of the Brazilian population, criminalizing poverty and the active struggle for economic and social justice through the racially tinged rhetoric of "law and order" and neoliberalism that is repeated by Jair Bolsonaro, the right-wing ideologue who is now president of Brazil. The comments are contrasted on the computer screen with beautifully shot portraits of the residents, with blurbs explaining their backgrounds and their reasons for occupying the building. In these images, which include a number of children, each occupier holds an object of their choosing that represents their lives—and spectators have already seen how these images were made in earlier scenes. Here, again, Caffé incorporates a recognition of the contradictory relationships between artistic intent and its reception by spectators into the very structure of *Era o Hotel Cambridge*. Despite Apolo's goal of building support for the occupation via an aesthetic intervention, there is no guarantee that spectators will be moved to act politically, and many observers in fact respond with a critique of the occupation articulated through racist language.

The film ends with a series of still-frame shots of real occupied buildings in São Paulo, offering a visual articulation of an urban community to come, accompanied by an upbeat, drum-driven musical soundtrack. The sequence is meant to end the film on a hopeful note, in contrast with the previous scene, which depicts the violent eviction of the community of occupiers by the military police. In the middle of this sequence of images there is a pause in the soundtrack, which Caffé visually matches with a longer duration shot of one of the occupied buildings, the Wilton Paes de Almeida, in the center of São Paulo. This building caught fire and collapsed on May 1, 2018, leaving at least seven occupiers dead, dozens missing, and hundreds without shelter. The paused shot of the Almeida building, in a film that was completed in 2013 and released publicly in 2016, prophetically creates another pensive image that conjoins multiple modes of representation—fictional, documentary, photography, news, and social media—and suspends a final meaning for spectators in the present. Today, the still-frame image of the Almeida in the film enters into dialogue with the flood of photos and comments on the collapse of the building that proliferated through the news and social media in the following months. Like the response to Apolo's fictional blog and *Era o Hotel Cambridge* itself, the reactions to the images of the collapsed Almeida building have ranged from solidarity with the displaced migrant and refugee occupiers to the use of racist and xenophobic language to argue that the "criminals" got what they deserved and that the remaining occupiers should be imprisoned or killed. As I have argued throughout the second part of this essay, *Era o Hotel Cambridge* recognizes the tenuous relationship between the intent of a director or photographer and the political response of spectators. What makes Caffé's approach unique and effective as a work of political art is that she does not produce a singular meaning about the occupations for spectators; she instead inscribes multiple, contradictory interpretations in the representational gap between politics and aesthetics within the very form and content of the film. Caffé presents a series of pensive images that force spectators to explore the complexities and contradictions of different cinematic modes of representing human rights subjects in the struggle for economic and social rights by marginalized populations in São Paulo.

Conclusion

In this essay I have attempted to show how a detailed analysis of the aesthetics of human rights employed by a particular film director in a specific social context can serve to problematize idealized notions of the relationship between art and political action—the belief that showing an injustice will lead spectators to act in order to correct a violation of human rights. Although images depicting the effects of human rights violations can evoke shock, horror, and other visceral reactions in viewers, this alone does not lead to political action to correct a given injustice. It does not guarantee that spectators will draw similar meanings as those intended by the photographer, director, or artist, nor that the injustice portrayed will even be considered as a violation of human rights. In the evaluation of artistic representations of human rights issues, one must examine the contradictory and ever-changing relationships among the aesthetics, politics, and spectatorship of a given work. This is particularly important for directors and artists who are attempting to reinsert issues of economic and social justice into human rights discourse, issues that have largely been elided from a global humanitarianism focused on abject victims of war and state violence that tends to dominate human rights discourse today.

Era o Hotel Cambridge makes visible the complexities and contradictions of the aesthetics of human rights, while presenting the occupiers—many of whom are also victims of state violence and the focus of global humanitarian relief—as active political subjects struggling for the social rights to adequate and affordable housing guaranteed to them by law. Through the incorporation of documentary images into a fictional film, the use of real-life occupiers to play fictional roles, the direct critique of neoliberal economic and political practices, and the self-critical recognition of both her privileged position and the impossibility of controlling the spectators' interpretations of the film, Caffé offers a prime example of how artists can trace the complex processes involved in the aesthetic representation of human rights issues while still making an aesthetic-political intervention into a localized site of the global discourse of human rights. Caffé is one of a number of Latin American directors, artists, writers, and activists currently engaging in similar innovative aesthetic work that seeks to reinsert economic, social, and environmental justice into humanitarian interpretations of human rights, interventions that deserve more visibility in academic debates on these issues.

PART III

HOW DO HUMAN RIGHTS MAKE SUBJECTS?

CHAPTER 10

Human Rights As Spiritual Exercises

Alexandre Lefebvre

OVER THE PAST TWENTY YEARS, human rights organizations have called with increasing frequency for human rights to be taught and promoted "as a way of life." The United Nations, to name only the most prominent institution, first made use of this idea in the announcement of its Decade for Human Rights Education (1995–2004), which depicted human rights education and training as a "comprehensive lifelong process."[1] Since then it has been repeated many times over. By the General Assembly, which states that "human rights learning should contribute to the fulfilment of the Universal Declaration of Human Rights as a way of life for people everywhere."[2] By the United Nations Development Programme, which defines human rights culture as "a way of life based on human rights, where respect for the fundamental dignity of each individual is recognized as essential to the functioning and advancement of society."[3] By UNESCO in its human rights education programs.[4] And by the *UN Chronicle*, which devoted a feature to "Human Rights as a Way of Life."[5]

Why has this phrase become prominent? From one perspective, the answer seems obvious. To speak of human rights "as a way of life" draws attention to the fact that in order to be effective, human rights must become integrated into the day-to-day lives of ordinary people. If human rights orient people in this manner, the hope is that its principles and institutions will not seem remote from everyday existence. In this chapter, however, I propose to examine the idea of human rights "as a way of life" not from the perspective of the agencies and organizations advancing it but from the perspective of the individual end user, as it were. My question is, how can ordinary people—and

I will need, of course, to specify who exactly I am talking about—take up human rights as a way of life? And, just as importantly, why would they want to?

Guiding my investigation is the concept of spiritual exercises. This term was developed by the classicist Pierre Hadot (1922–2010) to describe the ancient Greek and Roman conception of philosophy. In his account, ancient philosophy does not consist of a body of abstract doctrines or theories but is, instead, a personal commitment to a certain mode of being: what he calls "philosophy as a way of life."[6] Spiritual exercises are simply the techniques and practices by which an individual becomes "a philosopher"—that is, someone who loves and pursues wisdom—and strives to bring about a comprehensive change in his or her way of living. Such exercises, we will see, can take on many different forms, including physical (for example, dietary regimes), discursive (for example, dialogue with a teacher), and intuitive (for example, mediation and contemplation). Yet, despite all this diversity, the underlying goal remains the same: to help practitioners to become other and better than they currently are.

In this chapter I propose that throughout their history, human rights have been seen in a similar light. To make my case I advance interpretations of several well-known authors, such as Mary Wollstonecraft, Alexis de Tocqueville, and Charles Malik. All of them, I claim, argue that human rights provide principles and practices for individuals to undertake deep personal transformation. By highlighting this strand of the history of human rights, we will see that the contemporary interest in imparting human rights as a way of life is by no means new. Many great and beloved authors describe human rights in terms of spiritual exercises for people to adopt and apply to themselves.

Three Assumptions About Human Rights

What is gained by viewing human rights in terms of spiritual exercises? One benefit is practical: as I suggest at the end of my chapter, human rights education and advocacy stands to gain an additional tool to embed human rights in the self-understanding of its audience members (and, ideally, in their ambitions for personal and spiritual growth as well). I will begin, however, with a theoretical contribution. Conceiving of human rights as spiritual exercises allows us to take a step back from and cast into relief certain key assumptions made today about human rights. The issue is not, as I will emphasize, that these assumptions are problematic per se but that they are so taken for granted as to orient human rights theory and practice without our noticing it.

An advantage, then, of showing how human rights can operate as spiritual exercises is to provide an alternative point of departure for reflection on human rights in general and to expand our sense of what they can be used for.

Allow me to present these dominant assumptions one by one. They concern the purpose, object, and mode of human rights. Start with what is widely assumed to be the fundamental purpose of human rights: to protect human beings. Any number of texts or documents could be cited as evidence, but consider the opening sentence of James Nickel's entry on "Human Rights" for the *Stanford Encyclopedia of Philosophy*: "Human Rights are norms that help to protect all people everywhere from severe political, legal, and social abuses."[7] From this point of view, the addressee of human rights is the state, and the purpose of the wider human rights project is to protect all human beings by ensuring appropriately fashioned national law and policy, as well as making certain that states are adequately monitored and compliant. Thus, when we picture the institutional world of human rights—with all of its covenants and conventions, myriad tribunals, and multitude of nongovernmental organizations—it seems safe to conclude that its mission is to safeguard human beings by protecting their dignity, security, autonomy, or whichever basic feature of human life that happens to be in jeopardy.

The second assumption we make about human rights has to do with, for lack of a better word, their object: other vulnerable people. Today, human rights have become the standard-bearer for global justice. For people from privileged and rich countries, and especially from the North Atlantic region, where human rights have so powerfully shaped and channeled the moral and political imagination, the cause of human rights is championed as a way to help other and less fortunate people. For proof, we need look no further than to the banner on Amnesty International's website: "We are campaigning for a world where human rights are enjoyed by all."[8] A stand-alone statement of this kind makes sense only insofar as its readers already appreciate that human rights norms, discourses, practices, and campaigns fight for the welfare of disadvantaged, vulnerable, and precarious people all over the world.

The third assumption concerns the mode of human rights: relational and intersubjective. Here, I do not mean to refer to any particular author or approach to human rights that makes relationality its centerpiece (such as, for example, several chapters in this volume). I am trying, rather, to signal something more basic: rights and human rights, by their very nature, are seen to regulate relationships *between* people. The following observation, by Duncan

Ivison, gets the message across nicely: "Rights are fundamentally relational in character. . . . To claim a right, for example, is by definition to affect the interests and actions of others. . . . More generally, the activities involved in the practice of rights—claiming, waiving, negotiating, accepting, recognizing, justifying, and so on—are all activities that go on between persons."[9] As Ivison's list of "things we can do with rights" shows—whether claiming, waiving, or any of the other actions—the assumption that rights regulate relationships between different people informs the grammar of how we think and speak of them. Given this grammar, it is difficult to imagine what rights (and human rights) would do besides that.

Here, then, is a trio of assumptions standardly made about human rights: the purpose is to protect; the object is other vulnerable people; and the mode is relational. As I said a moment ago, my goal is not to raise objections or doubts about any of these assumptions. Nor do I wish to deny that, taken together, they are foundational for human rights theory and practice. My point, rather, is that if we consider human rights along the lines of spiritual exercises, then a very different picture and set of premises come to light. Naturally, I will need to define the idea of spiritual exercises more precisely and also explain how human rights have and can plausibly work in that manner. At the outset, however, I would like to state the contrast in bright and bold colors: between, on the one hand, human rights as spiritual exercises and, on the other hand, the standard conception of human rights as protections for vulnerable others. For the sake of symmetry, I present three departures from the assumptions about the purpose, object, and mode of human rights as set out above.

First, as spiritual exercises, the purpose of human rights is personal transformation. My main claim in this chapter is that time and again in the history of human rights, celebrated authors and touchstone documents represent human rights as tools and techniques that can be deployed for people to work upon and transform themselves. As such, the emphasis of these accounts is on the self-cultivation rather than on the protection of human beings.

Second, as spiritual exercises, the object of human rights is the self and the cultivation of the self. This characterization, as I will argue in the following pages, is not be confused with the claim that, understood as spiritual exercises, human rights are intended to produce selfish, individualistic, or inward-looking subjects. On the contrary, spiritual exercises are very often required to help shift attention away from ourselves—from our own cares, needs, and worries—and toward other people and wider horizons. Moreover, as I will propose in my conclusion, human rights as spiritual exercises have the potential to foster a critical ethos of resistance, insofar as the work of self-transformation sets individuals at odds with dominant forms of power operating in their own milieu. Nevertheless, it is essential to the concept of spiritual exercises, and hence to human rights considered as spiritual exercises, that their object is the self and the amelioration of the self. Such self-care is not instrumental or merely preparatory labor to better care for and attend to other people.

Third, as spiritual exercises, the mode of human rights is not relational. Or, better put, the mode of relation is first and foremost intrasubjective rather than intersubjective. From this point of view, human rights work to redress the relation we have to ourselves, all the way down to the level of our desires, ideals, pursuits, perceptions, and self-understanding. Certainly, this has consequences as to how we relate to other people, but once again, what continues to be primary is how human rights are used to inform and shape the self.

I began this section by claiming that one advantage of representing human rights in terms of spiritual exercises is to cast into relief deeply ingrained assumptions we tend to make about human rights. These assumptions, in other words, are revealed *as* assumptions, rather than as givens and necessities, once we are presented with an alternative package of what human rights can be. At this point, however, a skeptic might well object that I am, in effect, discussing apples and oranges. Human rights, they would say, are spiritual exercises only metaphorically speaking, and the real core business remains the protection of vulnerable people. Worse, seeing human rights as spiritual exercises threatens to distract from that mission, inasmuch as it misrepresents what is fundamentally a justice-seeking and other-regarding discourse and turns it into, let's say, just another opportunity for self-help (or, frankly, self-obsession). I admit this is a powerful objection. Answering it requires us to observe how eminent authors not only treat human rights as spiritual exercises but also emphasize the complementarity of their vision with the goal of protecting vulnerable others. But to do any of that, I must first more fully introduce the idea of spiritual exercises in and of itself.

Spiritual Exercises

To make our way, let us return to the classicist I introduced at the beginning of the chapter: Pierre Hadot. He, more than anyone, has raised the concept and history of spiritual exercises to wider historical, philosophical, and even popular attention.[10] Hadot had a long and successful career, writing on (and translating) an impressive array of ancient and modern thinkers, including Plato, Marcus Aurelius, Plotinus, Goethe, and Wittgenstein. Still, for all this diversity, at the root of his work we find a simple organizing intuition. Ancient and modern philosophy, he believes, are different in kind, and to understand one on the model of the other—in particular, to think that the ancients practiced philosophy in the same way as we tend to nowadays—is a profound mistake. Consider the opening lines from his late work, *What Is Ancient Philosophy?*

> In this book, I intend to show that a profound difference exists between the representations which the ancients made of *philosophia* and the representation which is usually made of philosophy today—at least in the case of the image of it which is presented to students, because of the exigencies of university teaching. They get the impression that all the philosophers they study strove in turn to invent, each in an original way, a new construction, systematic and abstract, intended somehow or other to explain the universe, or at the least, if we are talking about contemporary philosophers, that they tried to elaborate a new discourse of language. These theories—which one could call "general philosophy"—give rise, in almost all systems, to doctrines or criticisms of morality which, as it were, draw the consequences, both for individuals and for society, of the general principles of the system, and thus invite people to carry out a specific choice of life and adopt a certain mode of behaviour. The problem of knowing whether this choice of life will be efficacious is utterly secondary and accessory; it doesn't enter into the perspective of philosophical discourse.
>
> I think that such a representation is mistaken if it is applied to the philosophy of antiquity.[11]

The basic idea is this: Modern philosophy, with its roots in Scholasticism, but really receiving its decisive turn with Descartes, is primarily conceived of and practiced as a theoretical enterprise. And if it gives rise to certain practical propositions and stances—whether that be in morality or politics or art— these derive from prior abstract and systematic theories. Thus, for example, Kant's Second and Third *Critiques* (on morality and aesthetics, respectively) follow the First (on knowledge). Or, to continue with the case of German idealism, Hegel's *Elements of the Philosophy of Right* (on political philosophy) is a late work that applies the metaphysics he developed earlier in *The Phenome-*

nology of Spirit and *Science of Logic*. Ancient philosophy proceeds entirely differently. Certainly, its theoretical doctrines rival the complexity and subtlety of its modern successor. But from its own point of view, at least, it correctly puts the horse before the cart: the choice of a way of life stands at the beginning, not the end, of philosophical activity. Philosophy, in other words, originates in a commitment to living and seeing the world in a particular way, and theoretical discourse (that is, the abstract and theoretical doctrines we moderns tend to equate philosophy with) is undertaken to reinforce and refine this initial commitment.

Where do spiritual exercises fit in? These are techniques and practices whereby an individual becomes a philosopher—in the sense of a devotee of wisdom and living wisely—and brings about a comprehensive change in their way of living. Defined by Hadot as "voluntary personal practices intended to cause a transformation of the self," spiritual exercises are designed to lead people away not exactly from everyday life but away from a poor, unhappy, and unreflexive relation to it.[12] Here is the key passage:

> In all [ancient] philosophical schools, the goal pursued in spiritual exercises is self-realization and improvement. All schools agree that man, before his philosophical conversion, is in a state of unhappy disquiet. Consumed by worries, torn by passions, he does not live a genuine life, nor is he truly himself. All schools also agree that man can be delivered from this state. He can accede to genuine life, improve himself, transform himself, and attain a state of perfection. It is precisely for this that spiritual exercises are intended. Their goal is a kind of self-formation, or *paideia*, which is to teach us to live, not in conformity with human prejudices and social conventions—for social life is itself a product of the passions—but in conformity with the nature of man, which is none other than reason.[13]

Let's be concrete: what kind of exercises are we talking about? It varies from school to school, but suppose you wake up one fine morning as a Stoic, circa late second century. Your first exercise of the day would be a premeditation, in which you mentally rehearse potential difficulties of the hours to come so as to bear them when they happen. Marcus Aurelius, emperor that he was, braced himself daily with these words: "Today I will be meeting with interference, ingratitude, insolence, disloyalty, ill-will, and selfishness—all of them due to the offenders' ignorance of what is good or evil."[14] In the same vein, you could add a negative visualization, in which you imagine you lose everything that you love and hold dear, so as to contemplate impermanence.[15] After these solitary exercises, you might later meet and dialogue with a friend or teacher, which for Stoics were occasions for spiritual activity.[16] Maybe the conversation dwells on physics and your place in a rationally ordered cosmos; or maybe discussion steers toward ethics and the need for coherence in your wider pattern of actions; either way, you acknowledge your place within a larger whole and remember the need to harmonize with it.[17] Finally, to finish the day and prepare for the next, before bed you examine your conscience to observe where your thoughts and deeds fell short of a philosophical ideal and then reflect on how to become worthier of the events both "good" and "bad" (and appreciating the fundamental revision Stoicism performs on these terms) that have befallen and will befall you.

I could go on to list additional examples of spiritual exercises in antiquity. There are hundreds to choose from.[18] But allow me to cut to the chase and identify a spiritual exercise in the field of human rights. The reader might wonder whether I'll need to go digging into obscure texts and documents. But no, not at all. In fact, all I have to do is cite the best-known section of the best-known document from the history of human rights: the Preamble to The Universal Declaration of Human Rights (1948). A spiritual exercise is hidden in plain sight:

> THE GENERAL ASSEMBLY proclaims THIS UNIVERSAL DECLARATION OF HUMAN RIGHTS as a common standard of achievement for all peoples and all nations, *to the end that every individual and every organ of society, keeping this Declaration constantly in mind*, shall strive by teaching and education to promote respect for these rights and freedoms and by progressive measures, national and international, to secure their universal and effective recognition and observance, both among the peoples of Member States themselves and among the peoples of territories under their jurisdiction.[19]

To identify the spiritual exercise here, it helps to take a small step back from the Preamble and look to the title of the document. As historians have observed, the Universal Declaration of Human Rights was not always called "the Universal Declaration of Human Rights." When its drafting process began, in 1946, there were various working titles: "the International Declaration of Human Rights," "the International Bill of Human Rights," and simply, "the Bill of Human Rights." Beginning in late 1947, however, and then consistently in 1948, it acquired its official name. The reason for the change was to emphasize that human rights were held to address individuals as well as states and institutions. "The new title," Mary Ann Glendon explains, "had been in casual use for some time, but [René] Cassin, who proposed the official change, rightly considered the name to be of the utmost significance. The title 'Universal,' he later wrote, meant that the Declaration was morally binding on everyone, not only on the governments that voted for its adoption. The Universal Declaration, in other words, was not an 'international' or 'intergovernmental' document; it was addressed to all humanity and founded on a unified conception of the human being."[20]

Turning to the Preamble, we see that it reaffirms what the title of the Declaration had only implied: human rights are, indeed, universal and addressed to "every individual" (as well as to "every organ of society"). Moreover, and here is the crucial point, individual human beings—that is, *every* individual human being—are not only the addressee of the Declaration; more precisely, the Declaration calls on every individual human being to carry out a personal transformation of him or herself, with the Declaration itself serving as the inspiration for and instrument of this transformation. That is what the phrase "keeping this Declaration constantly in mind" is all about. One way to interpret this clause is that it urges everyone to take up the Declaration as a mantra—that is, as a set of principles and articles to be frequently repeated. But, and to return to Hadot and ancient philosophy, a more apt term is available: *hupomnēmata*, notebooks in which individuals wrote for themselves and collected key dogmas and rules of life so that these would always be at hand.[21] Marcus's *Meditations* is a classic of the genre, but more widely speaking, it is a staple of ancient spiritual exercises: philosophers (a term that, again, refers to lovers and pursuers of wisdom and living wisely) furnish themselves with short, striking maxims for living, such that the right principle would always be close by. With time and practice, this task would acquire the status of a habit. As the great Stoic Epictetus states, "You must not separate yourself from these general principles; don't sleep, eat, drink, or converse with other men without them."[22]

With the clause "keeping this Declaration constantly in mind," I am not suggesting that the drafters thought to themselves, "Aha! Here is a fine place for a veiled reference to Epictetus and the ancient tradition!" My claim is that with this clause, the drafters conceived that the Declaration could operate in an analogous way: as a transformative document that explicitly announces its aim to steep each and every human being in the articles it enumerates. This clause, to put the point directly, transforms the entire Declaration into a spiritual exercise: it seeks to persuade and inspire "every individual and every organ of society" to take up the document for him or herself and to repeat each of its articles until these become integral to their own worldview and conduct. In this vein, the "declaring" at issue in this document goes beyond the publication of a list of human rights norms and urges individuals to declare themselves in and through those very norms. And so when P. C. Chang, the Chinese member of the drafting subcommittee, states that the Declaration should aim to "build up better human beings . . . [and] to promote the best in man,"[23] or when Hernán Santa Cruz of Chile states, "[the Declaration] should not just be a Bill but rather a true spiritual guide for humanity,"[24] it is clear that they are not voicing general aspirations for how the document might be taken up. They are laying down a mission statement, the spirit of which was built into— operationalized, if you like—the text of the Declaration itself.

In the following sections, I demonstrate that this clause from the Declaration is not a one-off example of spiritual exercises in human rights. At key junctures in the history of human rights—such as the French Revolution, the American Revolution, the League of Nations and interwar crisis, and, of course, the drafting of the Declaration—we find renowned authors depicting and recommending human rights as spiritual exercises. In multiplying these examples, I aim to convince readers that, yes, this is an underappreciated but still significant phenomenon in the history of human rights.

Human Rights As Spiritual Exercises

Allow me to introduce the idea of human rights as a spiritual exercise by way of a contrast with recent human rights scholarship. Today there is a rich array of work on how human rights affect subjectivity and the sense we have of ourselves, others, and our wider (social and political, but also natural) world. To name a few prominent examples, in *The Last Utopia* and *Not Enough* (2010, 2018), Samuel Moyn examines how human rights shape contemporary social and political imaginations; in *Inventing Human Rights* (2008) and *Human Rights in Camera* (2011), Lynn Hunt and Sharon Sliwinski investigate how human rights depend on and deepen a felt and aesthetic vulnerability to the suffering of distant others; and in *The Sacredness of the Person* (2013) and *Seeing the Myth in Human Rights* (2016), Hans Joas and Jenna Reinbold trace how human rights inform the sense that we have of ourselves as dignified and even sacred beings.

As valuable as this work is, none of it directly captures my phenomenon. By likening human rights to spiritual exercises, my goal is to designate something quite specific: how individuals can consciously and intentionally use human rights to work upon and transform themselves. There is, in a word, a prominent voluntarist and volitional element. It is not only, as per the works listed above, that human rights inform, in a wide and diffuse sense, a background culture—or social imaginary, in Charles Taylor's sense, or episteme, in Michel Foucault's sense[25]—in which we act and make sense of our lives. On top of that, there is in the history of human rights a tradition of authors who recommend to people in their own milieu—that is, to people who share their social, cultural, and political world—that they self-reflexively and voluntarily adopt human rights as tools to transform and improve themselves.

In what follows I present three extended examples as to how human rights have been advanced as spiritual exercises.[26] As will become immediately apparent, there is no single perspective on the matter. No two authors completely agree as to how human rights should be utilized to work on the self or, just as importantly, why it is rewarding to do so. That said, if we agree to step back from the particulars of their accounts, the prominence and recurrence of this conception and usage of human rights is striking. What is more, we will also observe another convergence: all of the accounts of human rights as spiritual exercises I present are critical in nature. By that I mean that each author sees the work of personal transformation undertaken through human rights as directed against a dominant form of power that operates in their own milieu. Thus, while human rights as spiritual exercises are dedicated to self-transformation and self-cultivation, we will see that this transformation characteristically takes the form of personal resistance—that is, resistance in one's own person and self-conception—to wider social, cultural, and political forces.

Spiritual Exercise #1: Mary Wollstonecraft and Seeing Oneself As the Subject of Human Rights

Mary Wollstonecraft is, to my knowledge, the first author to have represented human rights as spiritual exercises. To see why she did so, we need to bring the problem she confronts into view. Taking her masterpiece, *A Vindication of the Rights of Woman* (1792), as our guide, it is twofold. On the one hand, there is the problem of injustice: women of her time suffer from the inequality of male social, political, and conjugal power. With respect to this problem,

Wollstonecraft appeals to the language of human rights in its conventional sense—that is, as protections for women to contest patriarchal power—by laying claim to an equal status as enfranchised, free, and independent agents. On the other hand, there is the problem of unhappiness. Here the issue is less that women are repressed by men but rather that girls and women are educated into and eventually adopt the virtues and values of their patriarchal world, with disastrous consequences. Trained as pleasing and amusing mates, and actively cultivating such enfeebling virtues as delicacy, littleness, sensitivity, and bashfulness, women, Wollstonecraft argues, actively dehumanize themselves—"brutalize" themselves, to cite her deadly literalism—and become less than fully human.[27] Her criticism is not just that this self-image is demeaning and disempowering but that it inevitably leads to dissatisfaction, bitterness, and rage at the world and oneself.[28] Women who live by these lights are gripped by "emotions which rather embitter than sweeten the cup of life," to the degree that they become unable to enjoy such basic goods as friendship, work, and parenthood or to tolerate such facts of life as solitude and aging.[29]

What is the solution? Human rights as spiritual exercises. As is to be expected, the French Declaration of the Rights of Man and of the Citizen (1789) looms large in *Rights of Woman* and is a repeated point of reference. Yet Wollstonecraft scarcely devotes any attention to analyzing its specific articles. She focuses instead on its underlying subject, a subject of human rights represented in terms of freedom, equality, and fraternity. And here is what she does with it: throughout *Rights of Woman*, Wollstonecraft exhorts women to adopt human rights as a perspective on themselves—that is, to view themselves *as* the universal, free, and equal subject of the Declaration of the Rights of Man. She does so with respect to equality, by imploring women to regard and cultivate themselves as human rather than female beings—"to obtain," in her words, "a character as a human being, regardless of the distinction of sex."[30] She does so with respect to freedom, by urging women to develop "sovereignty" and "self-government" over their own selves and desires.[31] And she does so with respect to fraternity, which she renames "friendship" and explicitly designates as a "natural right" by appealing to women to recognize that friendship, rather than passion, must be the basis for love and marriage.[32]

Obviously, just because women start reflecting on themselves as the subject of human rights does not magically make it come true. A lifetime of enculturation into the values of patriarchy does not so easily disappear. What such reflection provides, however, is an indispensable foothold for women to orient future work on the self and to gain critical distance from a culture that enfeebles them and devastates their chances for happiness and spiritual fulfillment. That is why, in Wollstonecraft's treatment, human rights—or, more specifically, the subject of human rights—is represented as a spiritual exercise: the subject of human rights serves as the standpoint of an ideal self, one that can be recalled at any moment to inspire and guide personal development.

Spiritual Exercise #2: Alexis de Tocqueville and the Practice of Political Rights

Writing about a contemporary revolution on the other side of the Atlantic, but working forty years after Wollstonecraft and seemingly without the awareness of her efforts, Alexis de Tocqueville also developed a conception of human rights as spiritual exercise. The problems he responds to are, of course, altogether different. Broadly speaking, in *Democracy in America* (1835–1840) Tocqueville is worried about two things. First, the social and political dangers of democracy and its tendency to slide into despotisms of various kinds.[33] Second, and more significantly for us, the spiritual dangers of democracy and its tendency to create or inflame desires and outlooks in its subjects that leave them anxious, isolated, and dissatisfied.[34] Foremost among these outlooks is "individualism," a term Tocqueville coins to describe the tendency in democracy for subjects to disengage from collective obligations and retreat to private life and personal interest. His criticism of this stance is instructive. Unsurprisingly, he attacks it as socially and politically shortsighted. But individualism for Tocqueville is also self-defeating at a personal level: with nothing to anchor their attention and desires beyond narrow self-interest, democrats become susceptible to loneliness, mediocrity, restiveness (*inquiétude*), and distraction (*divertissement*).[35]

This is where human rights step in, in the form of universal rights to political participation.[36] On Tocqueville's account, the practice of such rights serves to counteract not only the sociopolitical ills of democracy but the spiritual ones as well. Look at how he describes the effects of civil and political rights on the psyche—or better, on *l'esprit*—of individual American citizens:

> The free institutions that the inhabitants of the United States possess and the political rights of which they make so much use recall to each citizen constantly and in a thousand ways that he lives in society. At every moment they bring his mind [*son esprit*] back toward the idea that the duty as well as the interest of men is to render themselves useful to those like them; and as he does not see any particular reason to hate them, since he is never either their slave

or their master, his heart readily leans to the side of benevolence. One is occupied with the general interest at first by necessity and then by choice; what was calculation becomes instinct; and by dint of working for the good of one's fellow citizen, one finally picks up the habit and taste of serving them.[37]

In this passage, Tocqueville effectively recreates Blaise Pascal's famous spiritual exercise from the *Pensées*: we do not pray to God because we believe in Him; we believe in Him because we pray to God. "Follow the way by which [believers] began," he advises. "They acted as if they believed, took holy water, had masses said, etc. This will make you believe naturally and mechanically."[38] Tocqueville's argument is the same. Individuals in democracy, he admits, are not inclined to political participation and the collective administration of public affairs. But if they follow the example set by American citizens and try it, and if they agree even reluctantly to put their political rights to use and join in, they will find themselves drawn away "from the midst of their individual interests" and "from the sight of themselves."[39] Therein lies the spiritual exercise: social and political benefits aside, Tocqueville urges democrats to realize that there is real personal felicity to be had in the practice of political rights. By getting individuals out of their own heads, out of obsessive regard for the private interests, the exercise of political rights allows democrats to resist—and to resist in their very tastes and desires—individualism and to recognize it as the impoverished outlook it is. Hence the reason why in *Democracy in America* Tocqueville has recourse to the language of spiritual change, even of conversion, to describe the personally transformative potential of political rights in democracy. "I do not say that it is an easy thing to teach all men to make use of political rights," he states. "I say only that when that can be done, the resulting effects are great."[40]

Spiritual Exercise #3: Charles Malik and Reaffirming Our Humanity

The third example of human rights as spiritual exercises brings us back to where we started: the Universal Declaration of Human Rights. Two of its main drafters envisaged human rights along the lines of spiritual exercises: Eleanor Roosevelt and Charles Malik. In this short space I will not be able to treat Roosevelt.[41] Turning to Malik, however, we can shed light on the clause of the Declaration I drew attention to earlier: namely, the exhortation in the Preamble to "[keep] this Declaration constantly in mind." The historian Johannes Morsink has shown that this clause was part of the French submission written by René Cassin, and it hearkens back to the French Declaration of 1789.[42] Nevertheless, and regardless of who actually penned it, Malik very much makes it his own and puts it at the center of his vision of the Declaration as a spiritual guide for the modern age. Consider this passage from "The Challenge of Human Rights," paying special attention to the litany of r-verbs—to remind, to reaffirm, to remember—that Malik uses to describe the main objective of the Declaration:

> Under [the] external social and material pressure [of modernity], man is about to be completely lost. What is needed therefore is to reaffirm for him his essential humanity. He needs to be reminded that he is born free and equal in dignity and rights with his fellow men. He needs to know that he is endowed by nature with reason and conscience. He must know that he cannot be held in slavery or servitude, that he cannot be subjected to arbitrary arrest, and that he is presumed innocent until proven guilty. He must remember that his person is inviolable, that he has the natural right to freedom of thought, conscience, religion, and expression, and so on down the list of proclaimed rights. This reaffirmation, if only he heeds it, might still save him from being dehumanized. Society and the state under modern conditions can take perfect care of themselves: they have advocates and sponsors on every side: their rights are in good hands. It is man, the real, existing, anxious, laughing, free and dying man, who is in danger of becoming extinct. It is man who is the unprotected orphan, the neglected ward, and the forgotten treasure. Therefore, it is good that the Declaration has not lost sight of its main objective: to proclaim man's irreducible humanity to the end that he may yet recover his creative sense of dignity and re-establish his faith in himself.[43]

In these lines, Malik positions the Declaration against two different problems and has it speak to two different audiences. The first is the standard problem and addressee of human rights: the repression of vulnerable individuals by the state. Here, the value of the Declaration is to inform subjects susceptible to abuse by their own governments of their rights and to assert their inviolability. In this respect, Malik powerfully articulates the standard conception of human rights I sketched at the beginning of the chapter: the protection of vulnerable others.

The second problem and addressee, however, is altogether different: to remind individuals, and especially those living in modern and liberal democracies where rights are not under attack by states, of their stature as dignified human beings. This takes a word of explanation. In his writings and speeches on human rights, Malik is not only concerned with vulnerable people and abusive states. His dominant theme is the spiritual decline of the Western world and a lament that people living in it are so attracted to its materialism, secularism, and collectivism as to forget their true nature.[44] As he states in a meeting to his fellow drafters, "[I] believe every effort must be made to check this rise of the lower, the subhuman, the merely instrumental, and therefore to enshrining man in his proper place, especially in the formulation of the Bill of Human Rights."[45] Hence the purpose of the r-verbs ("remind," "reaffirm," "remember") in the passage above: to write a Declaration of human rights that would remind its audience—which is to say, each and every individual—of his or her humanity and, more pointedly for Malik, of his or her nature as authentic moral and intellectual beings. Vulnerable people may need a reminder of their human status for important reasons—for example, to draw attention to injustice, to reaffirm for themselves that what they suffer is intolerable, and to redouble their courage and resistance. But there is a whole other public Malik is writing for as well: people who, although safe and sound in liberal democracies, have genuinely forgotten—or, more pointedly, have willingly forfeited—their own higher nature. Seen in this light, Malik is explicit that the objective of the Declaration is the personal and performative realization of our humanity and human standing. And that is precisely the interpretation he gives to the clause in the Declaration about needing to keep it "constantly in mind." A spiritual exercise with a spiritual vocation, its role is to help the wayward individual "recover his [or her] creative sense of dignity and re-establish his [or her] faith in him [or her]self." To recall a term we used earlier, for Malik the Declaration is a veritable *hupomnēmata* for individuals to fortify themselves against our day and age.

Conclusion

Just now I presented three extended examples of how human rights can operate as spiritual exercises. Stepping back from their specific features, what can we say about them as a group and, more than that, about human rights as spiritual exercises more generally?

First, human rights as spiritual exercises can be critical. By this I mean that each author I have discussed positions human rights as spiritual exercises against a dominant form of power in his or her own milieu. Thus, human rights as spiritual exercises are set against patriarchy (Wollstonecraft), individualism (Tocqueville), and collectivism (Malik). And the specific nature of this criticism is worth emphasizing. Each of the spiritual exercises we have covered is designed to help individuals overcome a dominant power *that they themselves are attracted to.* Allow me to run though the list again: the tragedy of patriarchy is that women seek their self-image in it (Wollstonecraft); the danger of individualism is that it is the most natural stance for democrats to adopt (Tocqueville); and the problem with collectivism is that modern subjects are seduced by it (Malik). My point is that human rights as spiritual exercises have the potential not merely to stir up resistance against hegemonic powers but to target the support such powers have in the desires of subjects themselves. As Michel Foucault once remarked, "there is no first or final point of resistance to political power other than in the relationship one has to oneself."[46] Human rights as spiritual exercises actualize that insight by disenchanting subjects with the very forces that threaten their individual and collective wellness.

Second, human rights as spiritual exercises can complement the standard conception of human rights as protections against vulnerable others. At the beginning of the chapter I set out a bright set of contrasts between two visions of human rights, with regard to purpose (protection vs. personal transformation), object (other people vs. oneself), and mode (intrasubjective vs. intersubjective). I do not wish to soften these lines, as they draw attention to the richness and polyvalence of the concept of human rights. That said, in all three examples human rights as spiritual exercises reinforce the standard conception. How? By constituting a subject potentially better able to carry it out. Take Tocqueville, for example. As with all our authors, he insists that subjects transform themselves with human rights for their own sake. Individualism, after all, is spiritually deadening. But the effect of such transformation is to establish a subject able and willing to take an interest in things beyond his or her personal advantage. There is no guarantee that this interest will be channeled into human rights (intense nationalism, for example, is another path it might take). Nevertheless, a crucial obstacle in the direction of human rights—namely, individualism—has been removed. And the same goes for all the authors surveyed. Personal transformation accomplished by way of human rights, while an end in itself, establishes a subject who may well be inclined to concern him or herself with the protection of vulnerable others.

Third, spiritual exercises build motivation into human rights. I began this chapter by drawing attention to the recent trend in human rights education to depict human rights "as a way of life." I also said that from the perspective of human rights organizations, it makes perfect sense to advocate for human rights in this manner: the viability of the wider human rights project is strengthened if human rights come to guide ordinary people in everyday life. Still, the question remains: why should ordinary people take up human rights as a way of life? There are, of course, many potential answers, and the best work in the field of human rights education makes a concerted effort to address that question head-on and propose compelling motivations.[47] But seeing human rights as spiritual exercises opens up one promising line of response. For if we were to ask any of the authors I discussed why people should take up human rights as a way of life, a very direct response would follow: "Because," they would say, "living according to human rights will directly help you deal with *this* problem." The *this*, as we know, shifts from author to author, and it is up to us to determine which problems and solutions are most pertinent for our times. Yet the *this* is not what is important here. What is, rather, is the fact that when we take all of these authors together—and, naturally, we are free to add others as well—we become aware of a facet of human rights that could become a powerful resource to support a wider human rights culture.

CHAPTER 11

The Child Subject of Human Rights

Linde Lindkvist

ON NOVEMBER 20, 1989, the United Nations General Assembly promulgated the UN Convention on the Rights of the Child (UNCRC). The enactment of this treaty is now widely regarded as a milestone in the progressive development of international human rights law after 1945 and as one of the starting points of an integrated post–Cold War human rights discourse, centered on the idea that different categories of rights—civil, political, social, economic and cultural—belong to an indivisible whole.[1] The jury is still out on whether the Convention has improved the status and well-being of children and young people globally.[2] However, the fact that it has so far been ratified by 196 states (more than any other treaty in the field) provides some indication of its present-day status as the central normative frame for efforts to conceptualize and promote the human rights of children. Some even claim that the Convention has been too successful, at least in so far as it has short-circuited more independent and critical reflection on children's rights as a moral and political concept.[3]

To be sure, the drafting of the Convention was not the first attempt at codifying children's rights in an international setting. In 1924, the League of Nations adopted the Geneva Declaration of the Rights of the Child, a document which generated widespread interest at the time and which some scholars later identified as the first international declaration in the field of human rights.[4] Three decades later, this text inspired the making of the similarly nonbinding and aspirational—but much less publicized—UN Declaration of the Rights of the Child (1959).[5] Clauses on children's rights also appeared in the Universal Declaration of Human Rights (1948) and the UN's core human rights covenants of 1966, not to mention the rather elaborate framework on the protection of children in international labor law and international law on situations of armed conflict.[6]

Instruments prior to the UNCRC often invoked a terminology of rights, at least in their titles. But they did not envision children as active, rights-bearing subjects. Their general objective was to spell out standards that would help to protect vulnerable and innocent children against suffering caused by adult exploitation and neglect or, more broadly, by the direct and structural violence of war, unregulated labor, and poverty. In the child rights declarations of 1924 and 1959, such protections were coupled with calls for humanitarian action, either in the form of transnational philanthropy or institutionalized development assistance. The core message, stated in both of these texts, was that "mankind owes to the child the best that it has to give." Children were thus imagined as recipients of care and protection, not as individual subjects capable of claiming rights.

When placed against the backdrop of these earlier international instruments on children's rights, the UNCRC appears revolutionary. This is not only because it was cast as a binding treaty (thus transforming children's rights into a subfield of international human rights law). The Convention also inaugurated a new idea of "the child" as a rights-bearing subject. Although the Convention resembled the 1924 and 1959 declarations in that it foregrounded the idea of child protection, it also contained clauses presenting children as individual subjects of "evolving capacities" who are entitled to a broad range of human rights and fundamental freedoms. The Convention is frequently said to have recognized children as full human beings with significant moral agency, as opposed to merely vulnerable objects of protection, or pre-rational "human becomings."[7] Or, as leading child rights scholar John Wall puts it, the UNCRC involved "new means for children's social freedom, voice, and participation, on the assumption that children should bring their own full moral capabilities into society."[8]

This paper retraces developments that paved the way for this refiguring of the child in the drafting of the UNCRC. At the same time, it demonstrates how the rise of a more agentic understanding of children's rights was mitigated in a number of ways, not least through interpretations reducing children's civil and political rights to rights of participation. More broadly, this paper reveals how the process of articulating children's human rights involved numerous struggles over how to handle assumed understandings of the human subject as inherently autonomous and capable, understandings which remain implicit in much of mainstream human rights discourse.[9]

The focal point of my analysis is the making and early reception of the Convention's best-known expression of children's so-called participation rights, Article 12, which covers both freedom of expression and the right to be heard in judicial and administrative proceedings.

> 1) States Parties shall assure to the child who is capable of forming his or her own views the right to express those views freely in all matters affecting the child, the views of the child being given due weight in accordance with the age and maturity of the child.
>
> 2) For this purpose, the child shall in particular be provided the opportunity to be heard in any judicial and administrative proceedings affecting the child, either directly, or through a representative or an appropriate body, in a manner consistent with the procedural rules of national law.[10]

What is interesting about Article 12 is not only its content but the way it quickly evolved into something more than just an item on the list of children's human rights. In the early 1990s, child rights activists and scholars began to use Article 12 to underscore that children were indeed individual human subjects whose rights and interests were irreducible to those of their parents.[11] In 1991, the then–newly established UN Committee on the Rights of the Child (the treaty responsible for overseeing state compliance with the UNCRC) further bolstered Article 12's status by singling it out as one of the Convention's core principles, suggesting that a child's freedom of expression and right to be heard should be taken into account in the implementation of all other children's rights.[12]

Efforts to play up the significance of Article 12 for the wider international framework of children's rights generated a voluminous literature exploring the article's practical implications. As a result, the past three decades have seen an endless stream of publications by scholars of law, political science, psychology, anthropology, and education aimed at clarifying the meaning of children's participation rights and what it means to work for their realization. That said, critical children's rights scholars have also begun to question on a more philosophical level the merits of viewing children's civil and political rights through the lens of participation.[13] Some claim that projects aimed at improving the involvement of children always run the risk of becoming tyrannical, especially since they are often accompanied by expectations of involvement and tend to privilege "rationality and autonomy" instead of "emotions and relationality."[14] Yet the still-dominant focus on implementation has led scholars to overlook some of the more fascinating conceptual and ideological issues at the heart of debates on children's civil and political rights. As a result, the topic of how children's rights and, more specifically, children's rights of participation, have often been tied to specific ideas of the subjectivity, selfhood, and personal development of children remains virtually unexplored.

In the first part of this chapter, I return to the drafting of the UNCRC with the aim of discerning some of the factors that paved the way for the inclusion of children's agency rights in general and the rights of Article 12 in particular. My contention is that this move was more informed by international human rights politics in the 1980s than any idea of the child as a subject of human rights. Nevertheless, once the drafters had agreed to include civil and political rights in the treaty, they were confronted with questions of what kinds of human subject such rights presupposed and also what kinds of adults such rights would encourage children to become. In the second part, I turn to the early commentary on Article 12 and the efforts to associate children's civil and political rights with the concept of participation. Here, I show how much of the ensuing work to conceptualize and promote the civil and political rights of children has also involved more or less elaborate ideas of what it is to be and become a responsible rights bearer.

The Making of Article 12 of the UN Convention on the Rights of the Child

November 20, 1989, was a historic day: the UN General Assembly enacted the first binding international treaty on the rights of the child. During the preceding week, state delegates had taken turns pledging their commitment to the rights and principles laid out in the Convention and expressing gratitude to the designated Working Group under the UN Commission on Human Rights. But for the final session, the delegates were accompanied by children from the United Nations International School, in New York. In his brief concluding remarks, UN Secretary General Javier Pérez de Cuéllar turned to the children and said, "These are *your* rights. Humanity owes its best to each and every one of you. You are our hope for the future."[15]

Save for the children in the room, the scripted ceremony resembled earlier enactments of international human rights instruments. The event not only served the purpose of adopting the actual text, it also functioned as a symbolic closure to the many uncertainties and disagreements that had accompanied the negotiations. For even if many practitioners and commentators at the time claimed that questions of child welfare and children's rights belonged to a sphere beyond politics, the process of codifying such rights turned out to be protracted and marred with political contestation.[16] It took more than ten years to reach the final outcome, and until the mid-1980s it remained uncertain whether there would be any Convention at all.

To be sure, the drafters themselves were astonished by how difficult it was to reach international agreement on even the most fundamental rights of children. When the Polish government submitted the first draft in 1978, it felt confident that the text—which duplicated the content of the nonbinding 1959 UN Declaration of the Rights of the Child—would be finalized before the end of 1979, which at that point had been proclaimed the International Year of the Child.[17] But to the dismay of the Polish UN delegation, the initiative sparked virtually no interest. Some waved it off as nothing more than a "propaganda ploy," a Communist attempt to slow down the Western-led process of crafting a UN Convention Against Torture (CAT) and to draw attention away from other activities planned for the upcoming Year of the Child.[18] Several state delegates also voiced substantial concerns about the draft's content, pointing to the fact that it did not cover the full list of already recognized universal human rights in the UN covenants of the 1960s, which had recently entered into force.[19]

The most tangible result of the Polish initiative was the creation of an open-ended working group tasked with drawing up the Convention. But for the first few years, negotiations were slow. Then, around 1984 and 1985, interest in a child rights treaty suddenly surged. This shift of fortune is difficult to explain, but clearly, it was aided by the finalization of the CAT, in 1984, intensified cooperation among nongovernmental organizations,[20] and UNICEF's embrace, albeit reluctant, of rights talk in the same period. At this point, critics of the project realized that they were "fighting a lost battle."[21]

Still, the burst in international support was not accompanied by greater agreement on the conceptual meaning of children's rights. In this respect, the negotiations on the UNCRC were no different from those of other human rights instruments. In her brilliantly multifaceted account of the drafting, Anna Holzscheiter shows how the UNCRC emerged not as a robust and coherent structure but as a patchwork of different, oftentimes conflicting conceptions of both rights and childhood. Some parts of the text echoed a well-established humanitarian discourse, which imagined children as inherently innocent, passive, and vulnerable objects of care and protection. To some degree, this discourse was inherited from the child rights declarations of 1924 and 1959, but it acquired new life in the drafting of the UNCRC, including in debates on female genital mutilation, human trafficking, and child soldiers. In these instances, the drafters rarely spoke of the "rights of children as individual human rights," Holzscheiter notes. Instead, they appealed to notions of children as victims of adult exploitation.[22]

Other parts of the Convention reflected a paternalistic discourse, resting on a view of the child as a fundamentally irrational being in constant need of adult assistance and direction. This perspective was an essential source for the Convention's frequent references to the family as the "natural environment" for the child's "growth and well-being" and to the rights and responsibilities of parents and legal guardians. Some of the more heated exchanges in the drafting process concerned the triangular relation between the child, his or her parents, and the state, including the question of who has the primary right to determine what counts as being in the child's "best interest."[23]

Holzscheiter sees Article 12 as one of the clearest expressions of a third and more agentic discourse of children's rights, presenting children as individual subjects of "evolving capacities." Advocates of this view, most of whom were state representatives from Northern Europe and North America, stressed that children were full human beings and therefore entitled to the same human rights as adults. The caveat was that children had to reach a certain level of understanding and maturity before they would be able to make effective use of their rights and before their views were given due weight. This idea was also reflected in the Convention's Article 5, which specified that it was the right and duty of parents or guardians "to provide, in a manner consistent with the evolving capacities of the child, appropriate direction and guidance in the exercise by the child of the rights recognized in the present Convention."[24] In short, in order to make use of the rights they allegedly already had, children had to first reach a certain level of competence.

Still, Article 12 and related clauses represented a novel way of imagining the child in international settings. The question I want to grapple with here is where the ideas for this article came from. Some scholars have pointed to the legacy of "child rights pioneers" like the Polish-Jewish pediatrician and Holocaust victim Janusz Korczak, who already in the 1920s had advocated an idea of children's rights focused on respect for the views of the individual child.[25] 1978 was the national Year of Korczak in Poland, and some have used this fact to suggest a link between his thinking and the Polish government's work to codify children's rights at the international level.[26] Others have pointed to developments in the 1970s, when established ideas of childhood came under attack in many Western countries.[27] The short-lived child liberationist movement, spearheaded by American civil and women's rights activists like John Holt and Shulamith Firestone, depicted the very idea of childhood as a modern myth and drew parallels between the subjugation of young people and other forms of discrimination, including discrimination based on race and sex.[28] And while many of their proposals—including voting rights and sexual liberation—were too radical to be taken seriously, as one commentator argues, they still "served to heighten public sensitivity to the fact that children are people too."[29]

As far as I can tell, none of these intellectual advances were significant points of reference in the drafting. The inclusion of children's civil and political rights had more to do with contingencies related to international human rights politics than they did with any philosophy of the child as a subject of rights. Arguably the most important factor here was the drafters' early decision to set the end point of childhood at eighteen years. This was itself a departure from the child rights declarations of 1924 and 1959, which listed children's rights but provided no definition of childhood. Linking childhood to age and setting the age limit as high as eighteen effectively opened up the possibility of including rights that had not appeared in earlier instruments. One reason why it was imperative to include civil and political rights, a delegate of United States argued, was "because the 'child,' as defined in the draft Convention, included adolescents who had often acquired the skills needed to participate fully and effectively in society."[30]

Another factor that drove the inclusion of children's agency rights was that the UNCRC emerged as part of a rapidly expanding corpus of international human rights treaties. By the late 1970s, international lawyers, UN experts, and state representatives argued that treaty-making processes should involve mechanisms for "quality control" to ensure that the new instruments did not exclude or weaken already recognized human rights.[31] Such concerns were already voiced in response to the first draft of the child rights convention, which did not mention due process rights or fundamental freedoms. Some Northern European states delegates argued that the Convention should "be brought into line with other existing international agreements" simply because it otherwise might suggest a general weakening of the international protection of human rights.[32]

Responding to such criticism, the Polish UN delegation tabled a second draft in 1979, this time including the prototype for Article 12. Like the final version, it applied only to the "child who is capable of forming his [or her] own views." But at this stage, it did not cover the right to be heard and applied only to "matters concerning [the child's] own person," including "marriage, choice of occupation, medical treatment, education and recreation."[33] In 1981, the United States proposed an alternative wording, highlighting that the right to freedom of expression must be exercised "non-violently" and adding "religion, political and social beliefs, matters of conscience, cultural and artistic matters" to the list of issues over which the child should have a say. The United States also proposed a separate text intended for the article on the best interest of the child, providing that the child "that has reached the age of reason" should be given the opportunity "to be heard as an independent party" in judicial and administrative proceedings.[34] As the negotiations progressed, these different proposals—on the freedom of expression and the procedural right to be heard—were bundled together into what is now Article 12.[35]

The U.S. interest in these aspects of children's rights can partially be seen as emanating from contemporary developments in U.S. case law, which suggested that children were entitled to equal constitutional protection of due process rights, such as the right to cross-examine witnesses and the right to remain silent.[36] However, it is also important to bear in mind the Cold War context in which these negotiations unfolded. The American draft amendments were, as Cynthia Price Cohen argues, "inspired more by the desire to irritate the Soviet Union than from any grand philosophy regarding children's rights." From the outset, U.S. delegates tagged the child rights convention as an "Eastern bloc treaty," which the U.S. government had no intention of ratifying.[37] The American proposals were thus perfectly in line with the Reagan administration's view of human rights as a useful vehicle for anticommunist rhetoric, at least to the extent that it was possible to draw a bright line between authentic civil and political rights and secondary (if not false and injurious) economic and social rights.[38]

The United States found support among a group of Northern European states, especially from the Nordic countries (Denmark, Finland, Norway, and

Sweden). They, too, advanced agency-centered language in various parts of the Convention text, including in the negotiations on freedom of religion, where, controversially, they claimed that the child should have a right to "adopt a religion or whatsoever belief of his choice."[39] Toward the end of the decade, Finland led the work of finalizing the structure of Article 12, which, unlike earlier drafts, recognized that the child had a right to speak and be heard, not only in matters of personal concern but "in all matters affecting the child."[40] The Nordic delegates couched their arguments mainly in terms of safeguarding the integrity of human rights law. But as the Norwegian representative Per Miljeteig-Olsen claimed, they were also intent on making the UNCRC reflect the change in attitude toward children that had taken place in their countries during the 1960s and 1970s and, above all, the basic understanding of the child as an "independent individual" whose right should be "exercised by the child, not only by representatives from the adult world."[41]

To be clear, there was no uniform understanding of childhood or of children's rights that underpinned the child rights convention. Different interpretations—humanitarian, paternalistic, and agential—coexisted in the discussions, were fueled by political and strategic concerns, and fed into different parts of the final outcome. At various points, these three discourses on children's rights intersected with a fourth, centered on the idea of childhood as a time of preparation for adult life and an understanding of children's rights as a means of both personal development and social and political transformation. The drafters frequently returned to an understanding of children as tomorrow's citizens, "valuable investments" and "the hope for our future."[42]

This was familiar language in international discourse on the rights of children. In the beginning of the twentieth century, such future-oriented visions had been central to "child rights pioneers" like Ellen Key and Eglantyne Jebb.[43] The Geneva Declaration of 1924 even specified that "the child should be brought up in the consciousness that its talents must be devoted to the service of its fellow men."[44] Jebb, the Declaration's principal architect and the leader of the British Save the Children Fund, spoke of the purpose of the early child rights movement in religious, utilitarian, and pacifist terms. Arguing in the context of the post–World War I famine in Russia and Eastern Europe, she claimed that meeting children's basic needs would produce a kind of moral and religious revival in future generations, which in turn would help to prevent future wars. The idea was not simply that basic rights of subsistence and protection would help children evolve into virtuous and responsible citizens. The work for children's rights was also presented as a road toward the improvement of mankind.[45]

Sixty years later, when the UNCRC was being negotiated, this future-oriented way of thinking about the purpose of children's rights was much more subdued. Still, it occasionally resurfaced, both in discussions on the project's general purpose and in painstaking deliberations on individual articles. The most vivid example is an intervention by a Soviet representative during general discussions in the Commission on Human Rights in 1987. Alluding to a passage in the French writer and aviator Antoine de Saint-Exupéry's 1939 memoir *Wind, Sand and Stars*, he exclaimed that "[if] every dead child might have been another assassinated Mozart, it must be acknowledged that the situation of child victims of war was a particularly shameful phenomenon."[46]

In the final text of the UNCRC, we see reflections of the so-called investment motive in the Preamble and, perhaps even more clearly, in Article 29, which is concerned with the purposes of education. The Article contains an extensive list of different (and possibly conflicting) goods that schooling should help to stimulate, including "respect for human rights and fundamental freedoms, and for the principles enshrined in the Charter of the United Nations"; "respect for the child's parents, his or her own cultural identity, language and values, for the national values of the country in which the child is living, the country from which he or she may originate, and for civilizations different from his or her own"; as well as "respect for the natural environment." Finally, the child's education is meant to prepare him or her for a "responsible life in a free society."[47]

What is less frequently acknowledged by child rights scholars is that this consequentialist interpretation also fed into the drafters' debate on children's civil and political rights, including the structure and purpose of Article 12. When it was brought up for discussion in 1981, Denmark suggested an alternative wording: "as the child gets older, the parents or the guardian should give him more and more responsibility for personal matters with the aim of preparing the child for the life of a grown-up."[48] This formulation conveyed the idea that there was a dynamic relationship between maturity and freedom. It was not only that the child needed to enter "the age of reason"—to quote the U.S. amendment—in order to legitimately exercise the rights of Article 12. Performing the acts covered by these rights was also seen as conducive for the child's development toward becoming a more autonomous and responsible adult.

Although the Danish amendment did not make it through the final cut, it foreshadowed a way of thinking about the child's civil and political rights that would become dominant after the UNCRC had been finalized. The child's fundamental freedoms and due process rights were not just human rights of intrinsic value; they were also a means for stimulating personal and, to some degree, social transformation. It was through the piecemeal exercise of rights that the child would evolve into a mature human rights subject. Or, as one early commentator of the Convention argued, "participation is the process with autonomy as the goal."[49]

Transformative Participation: What Article 12 Came to Mean

Leaving the complexities of the drafting process aside, in this section I turn to the early reception of Article 12 among child rights experts and practitioners. Specifically, I am concerned with the way children's civil and political rights were equated with rights of participation and what implications this had for the child subject of human rights. On the one hand, this move helped to foreground children's agency in the work of international agencies and nongovernmental child rights organization. On the other hand, the discourse of participation involved a particular understanding of the child as a subject who would be transformed into a reasonable citizen through harmonious cooperation with adults. This view of children's rights may have strong merits—especially since it draws on an understanding of children as dependent on supportive relationships.[50] Yet, in this context, invoking the concept of participation also served to underscore the idea that children's civil and political rights were not a license for protest, dissent, or full self-direction and autonomy. Instead, their purpose was to involve children in judicial, administrative procedures and other forms of decision-making, often with the expectation that such involvement would be transformative, both for the individual subjects and for the wider community.[51]

Shortly after the UNCRC was adopted, scholars and practitioners began the process of making its content intelligible for a wider audience and exploring the treaty's practical implications. In 1991, the then–newly established UN Committee on the Rights of the Child suggested that the Convention's fifty-four articles rested on four general principles: nondiscrimination (Article 2), the best interest of the child (Article 3), survival and development (Article 6), as well as "respect for the views of the child" (Article 12).[52] In international development circles, and especially within UNICEF, one instead began to talk of the Convention's message in terms of "the three P's": provision, protection, and participation.[53]

The civil and political rights enumerated in Articles 12 through 17 were consequently re-described as rights of "participation"—a term that had been gaining currency in international development policy since the 1970s, partly due to a stronger focus on human rights and, consequently, on the agency of local actors in the construction of international programs.[54] While the three P's were originally intended as little more than a heuristic device, they turned out to have an immense impact on the way the Convention has been interpreted and put to use. In 2009, the UN Committee on the Rights of the Child conceded that Article 12 has come to be equated with the concept of participation, "although this term itself does not appear in the text."[55]

These two developments—Article 12's elevation to one of the Convention's core principles and its association with the language of participation—helped to inspire a stream of handbooks, guidelines, and scholarly literature on how to make sense of and realize children's rights of participation. As indicated above, a full discussion of this field would exceed the space of a chapter. But if there is a core message to be distilled from this extensive and ever-growing corpus, it is that children's participation rights, essential as they may be, are unusually difficult to implement.[56] The scholarship acknowledges that successful implementation requires more than adequate legal and institutional reforms. Any earnest attempt at realizing children's participation rights must also involve efforts to transform prevailing "cultural attitudes" toward children, including entrenched fears that children might use their rights in ways that will jeopardize their own and society's well-being.[57] The literature also frequently returns to the problem of moving from "tokenistic" to "genuine" participation: from situations where children are present yet passive to situations where they can freely express their views and exert a certain degree of influence.[58]

Starting in the early 1990s, child rights scholars and experts have responded to these challenges by constructing increasingly sophisticated models to assess the quality of child participation in various settings and by assembling best practices and hands-on advice for practitioners. Interestingly, many of the more influential interventions in this field attempted to clar-

ify the scope and foundations of the UNCRC's provisions on civil and political rights, especially those contained in Article 12. More than simply offering advice on the path toward successful implementation, they also argue
from principle and try to make the case for why children's participation rights
should be accepted as high-priority norms. Frequently, such arguments boil
down to questions of what a child is and how his or her development as a subject would benefit from the practice of participation.

The conversation on the meaning of Article 12 is usually traced back to
1992, when UNICEF published Roger A. Hart's essay "Children's Participation: From Tokenism to Citizenship." In the best-known part of this study,
Hart—a professor of environmental psychology at New York University—
launched his "participation ladder," a model of eight different types of child-
adult interaction in decision-making processes, from varying degrees of symbolic involvement to more or less "child-initiated" activities with limited
adult direction.[59] Although Hart himself would later stress its limitations, the
model is still frequently invoked as a means of evaluating the quality of child
inclusion in different settings. It has also inspired the creation of alternative
models, which often utilize similar categories and ideas of what constitutes
qualitative participation.[60]

What is seldom noted is that Hart's study rested on a particular reading of
the UNCRC and the child as a subject of human rights. In fact, he expressed
strong reservations about the Convention. Most importantly, he was critical of the document's strong emphasis on child protection, something he regarded as a symptom of a wider tendency in industrialized countries to think
of childhood as an ideally "carefree" stage of life. His main point was that
children needed to become involved in community affairs to experience firsthand the features of democratic citizenship. As he wrote, "It is unrealistic to
expect them suddenly to become responsible, participating adult citizens at
the age of 16, 18, or 21 without prior exposure to the skills and responsibilities involved. An understanding of democratic participation and the confidence and competence to participate can only be acquired gradually through
practice; it cannot be taught as an abstraction."[61] From Hart's perspective, the
main purpose of children's rights was not to shield the child from the complexities of adult life but to enable children to evolve into reasonable citizens.

Hart was not making a case for complete child liberation. The point was
not to suggest that child-initiated processes are always preferable or that child-
adult interaction constitutes a zero-sum game, with authority as the bone of

contention. What he was calling for was an understanding of children's rights as a means of facilitating cooperative activities that included both children and adults. While stressing the significance of UNCRC and Article 12, Hart lamented that the Convention did not sufficiently highlight "the responsibilities which go along with rights," responsibilities children could learn to appreciate only if they were engaged in creative interaction "with competent, caring adults." In order to illustrate the perils of unrestricted freedom for children, he pointed to William Golding's 1954 classic *Lord of the Flies*, which revolves around a group of castaway boys whose alternative political order soon collapses into complete savagery, as well as to "current examples" like the "street gangs of Santiago in Chile or Medellin in Colombia."[62] On Hart's account, Article 12 did not grant children the right to self-rule. Rather, the article emphasized that children had to evolve into active and responsible citizens, which they could do only by participating in community-oriented projects with other children and supportive adults. His was a strongly relational conception of the child subject of human rights.[63]

In the early 2000s, UNICEF followed up Hart's pioneering work with equally seminal publications by British child rights consultant Gerison Lansdown on child participation in democratic decision-making. She also pointed to the restricted nature of children's civil and political rights under the UNCRC. Article 12 "does not give children the right to autonomy. It does not give children the right to control over all decisions irrespective of their implications either for themselves or others. It does not give children the right to ride roughshod over the rights of their parents."[64] Nevertheless, Lansdown claimed that the Convention was imbued with a clear "participatory thrust," requiring adults to make sure children could express their views freely and exert a certain degree of influence in all decisions that affect them. Article 12, she concluded, offers a "radical and profound challenge to traditional attitudes, which assume that children should be seen and not heard."[65]

The core of Lansdown's intervention was to justify why children's participation rights mattered. As is typical for the field, she highlighted how such rights would benefit both the child as a subject of evolving capacities and the different social settings in which he or she is situated. Child participation, Lansdown first of all claimed, leads to better decisions. She cited studies indicating that school environments with high levels of pupil involvement are "more harmonious, have better staff/pupil relationships and more effective learning environments."[66] But she also imagined participation as trans-

formative for children. Taking part in different forms of democratic deliberation would allow children to "experience the implications of democratic
decision-making" and come to grips with what it means to be part of a society
where you have "rights and duties" in relation to other human beings and to
public institutions. "One of the more effective ways of encouraging children
to accept responsibility," Lansdown argued, "is to first respect their rights."[67]
Lansdown further suggested that participation could effectively strengthen
children's ability to claim their rights as well: "Children who are encouraged
to talk are empowered to challenge abuses of their rights and are not simply
reliant on adults to protect them."[68] Only in the last instance did Lansdown
assert that children's participation rights were in fact human rights, thus
qualifying as high-priority norms regardless of what changes they brought
about in the subject and his or her surroundings.[69]

This way of thinking about children's participation rights as transformative for the child and his or her environment is not limited to a handful of ac-
ademics. It is widely reflected in the ways these rights are understood in international development and human rights circles. The 2003 edition of UNICEF's
annual report *The State of the World's Children* focused entirely on child participation and struck a similar chord as Hart and Lansdown. Children's participation rights were deemed essential because engaging children "in dialogue and exchange allows them to learn constructive ways of influencing the
world around them. The social give and take of participation encourages children to assume increasing responsibilities as active, tolerant and democratic
citizens in formation."[70] In 2006, the UN Committee on the Rights of the
Child likewise asserted that the child's freedom of expression and right to
participation are "beneficial for the child, for the family, for the community,
the school, the State, for democracy." The "deeper meaning" of Article 12, the
Committee continued, is that it calls for "a new social contract," a political order in which children are "fully recognised as rights-holders" and capable of
playing a "catalysing role" in efforts to safeguard internationally recognized
human rights.[71]

Recently, child rights scholars have started to push back against the tendency to interpret the Convention's provisions on civil and political rights as
means of stimulating children's development. In a series of balanced interventions, legal scholar Rebecca Thorburn Stern points out how this interpretation reflects an age-old and deeply problematic view of children as "human
becomings" rather than "competent human beings." She suggests that efforts

to implement the content of Article 12 should aim at improving the status and agency of children in the present, not just focus on "creating well-adjusted citizens for the future."[72] While she does not delve more deeply into the grounds for this view, she seems to draw on an idea, common in the philosophy of human rights, that in order to qualify as a rights bearer, you need only to belong to a species that has certain characteristic features and capacities and not necessarily to possess such capacities as an individual.[73]

Yet it is striking that even scholars who actively seek to avoid looking at children's rights as investments still tend to invoke future-oriented arguments when explaining why Article 12 should be taken seriously. In her dissertation, Thorburn Stern maintains that a central purpose underlying both this specific article in UNCRC and international human rights law more broadly is to "enlarge opportunities for popular participation" and "to level out inequalities between citizens." At the end of her account, she raises the question of why child participation is a good thing. Her answer suggests that improved child participation in democratic decision-making will likely lead to better outcomes, since it will mean that more perspectives are taken into account. She goes on to assert that child participation "can also make democracy more inclusive, which in turn can benefit other groups in society." In sum, she presents the promotion of Article 12 as part of a much wider project of enhancing democracy, of continuously pushing the boundaries of who gets to be part of the political community. The bottom line is that this article is of high priority not only because it covers certain rights of inherent value but also because the realization of these rights will benefit the workings of democratic society.[74]

To some extent, this preoccupation with the instrumental value of children's civil and political rights has to do with the situation—and, indeed, conceptual space—in which many child rights advocates find themselves. Many of the presumptions guiding more general human rights activists—including the established idea of rights-holders as autonomous human beings or of human rights as having intrinsic value—are problematic starting points in the field of children's civil and political rights. Childhood is, after all, intrinsically developmental, and some attitude of paternalism (in the sense of parenthood) is always necessary. But more pointedly, child rights scholars and activists have to grapple with dominant perceptions of children as irrational and of childhood as an experience that is ideally shielded from politics. They are constantly forced to answer questions of why children's civil and political rights matter, on what grounds they should be legitimated, and the social and political implications of efforts to implement them.

Concluding Reflections

Throughout this chapter, I have suggested that the UN Convention on the Rights of the Child (1989) inaugurated a novel and more agentic understanding of the child as a bearer of human rights. At the same time, I have argued that this was a limited breakthrough. For one, the Convention proposed that there was a distinction between having rights and having the right to exercise rights, with the latter being dependent on the subject's "age and maturity" or "evolving capacities." The subsequent commentary also re-described children's civil and political rights as rights of participation, a move which effectively freed those rights from associations with political protest and dissent. Instead, civil and political rights were repackaged as calls for increased child involvement in different processes on the assumption that such involvement would help children become mature and responsible future citizens. In linking civil and political rights to the subject's age and maturity, the UNCRC and later interpretations did more than simply expand the ambit of children's rights and offer a new vision of childhood. They also said in plain language what until then had been only implied in much of international human rights discourse: that the ideal human rights subject is not a child but a rational and autonomous adult. What this account further suggests is that children's human rights—in particular to participation—are frequently imagined as means of making the child become that very human rights subject.

CHAPTER 12

The Secular Subject of Human Rights

Jenna Reinbold

IN 1947, as the First Commission on Human Rights worked to create what would eventually become the Universal Declaration of Human Rights, the United Nations Educational, Scientific, and Cultural Organization (UNESCO) tasked itself with conducting an inquiry into "the theoretical problems raised by the elaboration of an International Declaration of the Rights of Man."[1] These theoretical problems were potentially numerous, ranging from the question of whether and how to prioritize matters of "political freedom" versus matters of "economic and social freedom"; whether to conceive of such rights as unchangeable or existing "only in relation to the conditions of time and place"; and whether human rights should be understood to pertain to humans as individuals or as members of communities.[2] Many of these theoretical problems would occupy human rights advocates well beyond the specific context of the drafting of the Declaration itself, and, indeed, many continue to surface today. One such enduring theoretical problem concerns the foundation of human rights—that is, the question of whether human rights require a global embrace of a particular set of "common speculative ideas [and] the affirmation of one and the same conception of the world, of man and of knowledge."[3] In an effort to come to a fuller understanding of this issue, UNESCO reached out to high-profile scholars and religious leaders worldwide and presented them with a set of questions that it hoped would facilitate the development of a universalizable formulation of human rights capable of "reconcil[ing] the various divergent or opposing formulations now in existence."[4]

UNESCO received input from dozens of people, and Jacques Maritain, a prominent Catholic philosopher and human rights advocate, penned an introduction to the consolidated responses designed to synopsize the various perspectives that had surfaced from the inquiry. While the dominant tone of Maritain's introduction was confident, even triumphalist, in its assurance that a type of "intellectual agreement" about the nature of human rights could be reached under the right circumstances, he also emphatically disclaimed the idea that a universal formulation of human rights would require a global commitment to any particular set of speculative ideas.[5] In the face of UNESCO's quest to discern key points of convergence among the world's diverse conceptions of human rights' foundations, Maritain painted a somewhat different picture of the world—a picture marked by constitutive and irreconcilable *difference* concerning human rights' foundations, and thus a world in need of a markedly different strategy for settling this difficult question:

> I am quite certain that my way of justifying belief in the rights of man is the only way with a firm foundation in truth. [. . .] If both believed in the democratic charter, a Christian and a rationalist would still give mutually incompatible justifications for their belief, if their hearts and minds and blood were involved, and they would fight each other for them. And God forbid that I should say it does not matter to know which of the two is right! It matters essentially.[6]

Notwithstanding such intractable and even inimical differences, Maritain expressed confidence in the possibility that the Commission could establish a universalizable foundation for human rights though the articulation of "a sort of common denominator, a sort of unwritten common law, at the point where in practice the most widely separated theoretical ideologies and mental traditions converge."[7] The key to uncovering and activating such a common denominator, according to Maritain, lay not in uncovering a substantive point of global convergence but rather in creating a mechanism whereby people would be encouraged to quell their tendencies toward religious and ideological dogmatism and, in place of such tendencies, to develop a disposition toward "co-operation in the comparison, recasting, and fixing of formulae, to make them acceptable to both parties as points of conversion in practice, however opposed in theoretic viewpoints."[8] The key, in other words, would be to create a document capable of engendering a particular *sensibility*—a specific "philosophy of life," as he called it—that would incline people across the globe to step back from their theological and ideological differences in the interest of cultivating accord within an increasingly pluralistic societies.[9] I will argue that although Maritain hardly articulated it as such, his proffered solution to the problem of human rights' foundations was to advocate for a secular subject of human rights.

Given the very common tendency to associate secularism either with legal mechanisms designed to separate religion from politics or with overtly anti-religious ethical and epistemological discourses, it is important to clarify that neither of these topics will be the focus of this inquiry. In the first place, though the legal-political dynamic of secularism is certainly implicated in the particular "philosophy of life" that I am highlighting, "the secular subject of human rights" as I will treat it refers to a broader and somewhat more nebulous phenomenon. "Secularism" here refers to a particular orientation that simultaneously presumes and promotes the notion that there are many reasonable ways for humans to be religious and that one of the fundamental tasks of a political system is to effectively mediate these various modes of religiosity. Secularism as I use the term refers to a twofold commitment to the preservation of religious pluralism and the peaceful negotiation of the differences that inevitably arise within and between religious communities. To be a secular subject is to have internalized these commitments to such a degree that one would be willing, when pressed, to prioritize the peaceful resolution of religious difference over one's own particular religious inclinations. Yet even this description does not fully capture the logic of secularism, for, as we shall see, the secular subject of human rights may also be a subject who, for various reasons, feels her deepest religious inclinations to sync so closely with the mandate to cultivate and mediate religious pluralism that she never finds herself called upon to prioritize one value over the other in the first place.

This brand of secularism also differs significantly from the straightforward anti-religiosity that many people (including particular members of the First Human Rights Commission)[10] commonly associate with the term. To claim that the subject of human rights is a fundamentally secular subject is not to propose that human rights are areligious or antireligious in nature. For one thing, Maritain's own words make clear that his solution to the problem of the contested foundations of human rights was not to efface or eliminate the various ideologies and traditions that give rise to these differing conceptions of human rights. It was, instead, to devise some way of placing these ideologies and traditions into cooperative interaction with each other in service of some higher sociopolitical goal. What is more, while this effort to secure a pragmatic common denominator for human rights was certainly calibrated to avoid favoring any specific theological formulation of human rights,

this project was also permeated with its own unique religious sensibility—
what UNESCO members described as a "faith in the inherent dignity of men
and women."[11] Notwithstanding the variety of ways in which different societies might be inclined to envision and protect it, Maritain and fellow ne-
gotiators of the Declaration posited human dignity as an item of such universal veneration—and yet, crucially, of such indeterminate substance—that
it could reconcile divergent viewpoints without appearing to people to be a
mere political contrivance. Far from a vehicle of atheism or even agnosticism,
this conception of human dignity surfaces within the UNESCO inquiry, and
indeed throughout the negotiation of the Declaration, as a locus of widely-
agreed-upon sacredness. Thus, in its very aspiration to mediate between potentially competing religious orientations, the Declaration is imbricated with
a particular logic that is no less religious for its apparent detachment from the
world's institutionalized religious traditions. This underlying religious logic
becomes apparent only when we shift our understanding of the secular from
particular church-state projects or particular anti-religious discourses to the
broad "context of understanding" that has given rise to the twofold presumption that religious pluralism is a fundamental feature of human life and that
the vicissitudes of this pluralism can be tempered through the enshrinement
of an item whose value is assumed by all people of all religious backgrounds
to be beyond question.[12] As these various points imply, to say that the Declaration endeavors to engender a secular subject of human rights is to assert
something not merely about human rights but about secularism itself.

The "Immanent Transcendence" of Human Dignity

The Declaration's very particular secular logic is the product of a unique set of
circumstances faced by human rights advocates at the time of its creation. In
the course of enumerating the various basic rights found in the Declaration's
thirty articles, the theorists and delegates who worked on this document
sought to give some convincing account of not just the rights themselves but,
in the words of Commission Chair Eleanor Roosevelt, "why we have rights to
begin with."[13] Aware that the document they were creating would not contain mechanisms of legal enforcement, Commission members endeavored to
put forth a formulation of human rights that would not merely list important rights but would also inspire people to embrace such rights from the inside out, so to speak—that is, to embrace human rights for reasons other than
the threat of legal or political sanction. Many members of the Commission

understood this task to entail a moral and perhaps even a metaphysical logic. In other words, rather than aspiring to create a strictly legal framework, they understood their task to be the creation of a document that would function as "a true spiritual guide for humanity."[14] Notwithstanding the evident religiosity of key figures such as Roosevelt, Maritain, and Charles Malik, Commission members were cognizant of their role as drafters of a universal document, and they were aware of the fact that to wield this brand of "spiritual" authority within the postwar world, the Declaration would have to offer a formulation of human rights capable of doing a variety of things at once. As the UNESCO inquiry put it, this formulation must be:

> Sufficiently definite to have real significance both as an inspiration and as a guide to practice, but also sufficiently general and flexible to apply to all men, and to be capable of modification to suit peoples at different stages of social and political development while yet retaining significance for them and their aspirations.[15]

Simultaneously "definite" and "general," resonant and yet also universally accessible, the Declaration's formulation of human rights needed to be able to hit a register that was deeply affective and, at the same time, essentially devoid of any content that would make it appear parochial.

Is it possible to envision such a delicately calibrated formulation of human rights? What would such a formulation look like? It was clear to members of the First Commission on Human Rights that this formulation could not overtly presume the supremacy of any particular theological framework. The Commission was somewhat less unanimous in its agreement that in addition to avoiding the language of particular institutionalized religions, the Declaration should also avoid even more general reference to God or to the "divine origin" of humankind in its articulation of why we have rights to begin with.[16] Despite some delegates' claims that a theistic language provided "the only possible ultimate argument" for humans' universal entitlement to the Declaration's rights, the majority of Commission members concluded that such language raised intractable questions that would serve to betray the universality of this document.[17] Ultimately, even an early reference to "nature"—that is, to the idea that human beings are endowed "by nature" with reason and conscience—was removed from the Declaration in the face of concerns that the term either provided a means for Christian theology to "trickle down" into the Declaration's political framework or, inversely, that it would infuse the

Declaration with a materialist logic that was essentially *anti*-religious.[18] The final result of these negotiations was a declaration that makes no reference whatsoever to the transcendent, whether in the form of a deity or some other transhuman phenomenon such as nature.

The systematic omission of these various transcendent points of reference gave rise to an unprecedented political document: a declaration that narrates its tenets into existence without the slightest recourse to the entities that have served to ground other history-making political declarations. Whether they take the form of "God" or the French "Être suprême," such transhuman entities have typically played a seminal role in establishing the legitimacy of documents that are designed, as are all declarations, to inaugurate novel political worlds.[19] The Declaration is no different from other declarations in its endeavor to reach beyond the specific political configurations of its time to lay an indisputable foundation for something new, but it differs markedly in the emphatically secular manner in which it attempts to do this.

That said, to describe the Declaration as emphatically secular is decidedly *not* to imply that this document offers up a purely positivist account of human rights' foundations, for this is also not the case. Even as Commission members harbored particular disagreements about the role and the trustworthiness of the state in securing basic human rights, they were in broad agreement that the Declaration should *not* establish the state as the ultimate arbiter or source of this document's enumerated rights.[20] Rather, the various legal and political apparatuses of the world should be understood to be responsive to—yet never the *source of*—the inherent rights and conception of the person specified by the Declaration. The atrocities of World War II and the Holocaust had served to cast profound suspicion upon the notion that rights exist only as products of government and drove Commission members to aim for a declaration in which, as Mary Ann Glendon puts it, "fundamental rights are recognized, rather than conferred."[21]

In their endeavor to chart a path between the "overt propositional religiosity" of previous declarations and a positivism that would derive human rights solely from the agency of particular political institutions, the First Commission on Human Rights aimed to imbue the Declaration with what Johannes Morsink has recently called "a kind of immanent transcendence."[22] The Declaration answers the foundational question of why we have rights to begin with by, in Morsink's words, "[p]iggybacking the rights in the Declaration on the birth of people into the human family."[23] This condition of possessing rights by virtue of our membership in the human family—a condition that is thoroughly immanent and yet also transcends local, national, and even international circumstances—is articulated in the Declaration's opening invocation of the "inherent dignity" of all humans.[24] As the Declaration puts it in its very first words, "recognition of the inherent dignity and of the equal and inalienable rights of all members of the human family is the foundation of freedom, justice, and peace in the world."[25] Though this invocation is unquestionably embedded in a consequentialist logic oriented toward the cultivation of such things as "friendly relations between nations" and the prevention of "rebellion," the Declaration's articulation of human dignity is hardly the product of a straightforwardly utilitarian logic. As words such as "recognition" and "inherent" imply, human dignity stands within the Declaration as a feature that is "always-already-given"—the product not of theological or consequentialist argumentation but, rather, a foundational referent to which all arguments about human rights values should be beholden.[26] In this sense, the Declaration simultaneously presumes and performs the existence of such inherent dignity.[27]

The Commission's efforts to imbue the Declaration with an immanent transcendence is not the product of aversion to religion; rather, it is the result of an endeavor to navigate what Charles Taylor has famously called "a secular age." In his expansive exploration of the topic, Taylor describes this age as one marked by a shift from an existence in which "it was virtually impossible not to believe in God, to one in which faith, even for the staunchest believer, is one human possibility among others."[28] This shift could be imagined to produce any number of possible human responses. One such response has been the emergence of subjects sufficiently comfortable within (or, perhaps in some cases, sufficiently resigned to) the metaphysical pluralism of the world to have committed themselves to the mind-set of cooperative "comparison" and "recasting" that Maritain prescribes in his description of the UNESCO inquiry. A commitment of this sort may very well require bracketing certain theological convictions in the interest of gaining consensus on points of tremendous practical importance. But this commitment is by no means incompatible with a capacity for deep-seated faith—whether it be a faith in the existence of a particular deity or a more "immanent" faith in the fundamental sacredness of human dignity. In fact, a conviction that human dignity is sacrosanct—a characteristic that humans possess prior to and independent of their membership within any social or political community—would, if one were to come from a position of faith, likely be a highly desirable quality for the human rights subject to have. In a world where metaphysical consensus is in limited supply, dignity appears to continue to enjoy something of a global status as a human quality that is—or, in a just world, should be—beyond question. In this respect, inherent human dignity would appear to present an ideal example of what Maritain calls a "practical point of conversion" among otherwise irreconcilable theological and ideological differences.

Bearing this in mind, it should come as no surprise that in the course of negotiating the Declaration, the First Human Rights Commission consistently singled out human dignity as an item of sufficiently universal "givenness," to be capable of doing the foundation building once reserved for (increasingly disputed) theological precepts, and yet also an item of sufficient generality, to avoid falling into conflict with any of the varied theologies that people hold dear. As Roosevelt describes of her own approach to human rights' foundations,

> I happen to believe that we are born free and equal in dignity and rights because there is a divine Creator, and there is a divine spark in men. But, there were other [Commission members] who wanted it expressed in such a way that they could think in their particular way about this question, and, finally, these words were agreed upon because they stated the fact that all men were born free and equal, but they left each of us to put it in our own reason, as we say, for that end.[29]

The sentiment embodied in the words of Roosevelt and Maritain (neither of whom are areligious by any stretch of the imagination) is very much secular in Taylor's paradigmatic sense of the term. The blossoming international landscape of the postwar era presented the Commission with a world no longer confident of the ability of any one transcendent point of reference to secure the foundations of human rights. Faced with such a situation, they appealed to the immanent transcendence of inherent dignity in an effort to formulate a ballast for human rights that they imagined would be both conceptually open and universally resonant.

Secular Subjects

The First Commission on Human Rights endeavored to create a declaration that would not merely enumerate discrete rights but would inspire individuals to act and live ethically within a religiously diverse world. I have argued that this endeavor is marked by a particular mythopoeic logic: that is, in the absence of recourse to mechanisms of legal enforcement, the Commission embedded human rights within an evocative narrative that they hoped would be deeply internalized by its global audience.[30] Rather than compelling people to respect such rights out of fear of punishment, the Declaration would ideally inspire people, in Roosevelt's words, to "progress inwardly."[31] This inward progress was envisioned by most Commission members to be the next best option to the coercive power of a fully fledged legal regime, the impossibility of which they had resigned themselves to early in their negotiations of this document. However, to inspire this brand of inward progress, and to make good on its claim to be a universalizable expression of human rights, the Declaration would clearly have to avoid the imputation of cultural or ideological bias. It was with this mandate in mind that Commission members aspired to create a document that would downplay its own constructedness and position itself instead as an instantiation of fundamental human realities underlying the predilections of any particular society. Such normative, naturalizing narratives are the hallmark of myth as understood by scholars of religion, very much in contrast to the conventional use of the term as a marker of fallaciousness or disingenuousness.

Notwithstanding the expansive scope of the category of myth as I use it here, however, the Declaration's brand of mythmaking is by no means "generic" or agnostic as to the particular type of inward progress it envisions for its audience. At a number of points, the Declaration gestures toward a set of quite specific sentiments undergirding its enumerated rights. The subject of human rights is, for example, expected to understand herself as a member of the "human family" and thus to be inclined to act toward others "in a spirit of brotherhood."[32] This subject is presumed to be predisposed toward the belief that humans inherently possess a dignity that transcends their particular social and political locations. Thus, though the Declaration pointedly refrains from prescribing or favoring a particular religious orientation, reading it through the lens of Taylor's formulation of secularism allows us to see the way in which this document nevertheless aspires to generate and propagate a particular secular sensibility. This secular sensibility consists of four interrelated characteristics: an inclination to see one's own deep convictions as one option among many reasonable possibilities; an eagerness to seek out—and, if necessary, to devise—points of confluence between one's worldview and others'; a willingness to prioritize certain fundamental democratic ideals over the truth claims of particular religions (including one's own); and, a faith in, perhaps even a veneration of, inherent human dignity.

To understand the secular subject of human rights in this way is to appreciate how such a subjectivity could be embraced by religiously committed advocates such as Roosevelt and Malik just as surely as by more areligious Commission members. On the other hand, an understanding of this subject also points to an underlying critique of human rights with which theorists and advocates have increasingly been forced to wrestle as scholarship on secularism has risen to prominence. To understand this critique, it is important to appreciate the manner in which Taylor's work has been groundbreaking, in large part because it has furnished a detailed view of the particular genealogy of our secular age and, in doing so, has revealed the historical contingency of the secular sensibility I have described above. The opening lines of *A Secular Age* give a clear sense of this contingency:

> What does it mean to say that we live in a secular age? Almost everyone would agree that in some sense we do; I mean the "we" who live in the West, or perhaps Northwest, or otherwise put, the North Atlantic world—though secularity extends also partially, and in different ways, beyond this world. And the judgment of secularity seems hard to resist when we compare these societies with anything else in human history: that is, with almost all other contemporary societies (e.g., Islamic countries, India, Africa), on the one hand; and with the rest of human history, Atlantic or otherwise, on the other.[33]

To understand the secular orientation described above as historically contingent is to begin to understand the ways in which the secular subject is intricately embedded in a matrix of very specific social, political, and religious dynamics. It is also to appreciate the ways in which the parochialism of these dynamics is often invisible to inheritors of this history. Recently, our growing understanding of the genealogy of the secular has converged with a multivalent cultural relativist critique to call attention to the possibility that human rights' particular brand of secularism might fall short of a universal orientation *not* because the secular is anti-religious in a straightforward sense but because this brand of secularism presumes certain habits of mind that are themselves far from universal. Taylor's genealogy, in other words, affords a striking glimpse into the cultural relativism of secularism itself.

The most prevalent form of the cultural relativist critique of human rights involves a censure of the individualism of such rights—that is, a concern that human rights' emphasis on the fundamental autonomy and well-being of the individual inevitably comes at the expense of the "agentive social ontology," which Mark Goodale describes in Chapter 2 of this volume. However, an exploration of the secular subject of human rights points toward a somewhat different facet of the cultural relativist critique: namely, the question of whether, as Michael Freeman puts it, "the priority that human rights discourse gives to human rights over other values is itself a universally valid value."[34] In other words, if there is a cultural and even a metaphysical specificity to the secular sensibility described above, isn't it likely to be the case that certain subjects will find the mandates and aspirations of the Declaration unproblematic and easy to embrace, while others might find these demands and aspirations considerably more counterintuitive? One way to come to terms with this question would perhaps be to avow without apology that universal human rights do indeed make an implicit demand that members of the human rights community not merely respect particular rights but also internalize a particular "philosophy of life." However, if this brand of secularism is indeed culturally specific in the way that Taylor has described—if it is the product of a particular genealogy within "Latin Christendom"—we must ask how such an implicit demand of secularism is distinguishable from other types of cultural and epistemological imperialism of which human rights have been accused. This critical imperative becomes even more pressing when we consider the burgeoning body of scholarship that has built upon Taylor's insights to highlight the heavy entanglement of this brand of secularism not merely with the history of Latin Christendom but also with the much more specific history of Protestantism.[35]

These questions bear in crucial ways upon our understanding of the foundations of universal human rights, but they also venture far beyond matters of foundations. As scholars such as Saba Mahmood and Elizabeth Shakman Hurd have pointed out, the deep-seated secular orientation embedded in the language of the Declaration has played out in crucial ways within the realm of rights-oriented policymaking on both the domestic and international levels—aided in no small part by the ascendency of contemporary human rights discourses.[36] Such theorists have pushed against the tendency, once almost unquestioned within international relations, to identify secularism as merely a straightforward political mechanism for separating religion from the public sphere, and they have worked to emphasize the subtle ways in which secular forms of governance often seek, in Mahmood's words, "not so much to banish religion from the public domain but to reshape the form it takes, the subjectivities it endorses, and the epistemological claims it can make."[37] Here, Mahmood draws attention to a disciplinary logic that subtly equates the cultivation of human rights with the cultivation of a very particular religious sensibility: a sensibility marked by a refusal to be overly "militant" in one's commitment to any particular religion.[38] What does it mean for one to be overly militant in one's commitment to religion? Mahmood describes the improperly militant subject as one who refuses to approach religion as "an abstracted category of beliefs and doctrines from which the individual believer stands apart to examine, compare, and evaluate its various manifestations."[39] This militant subject stands in contrast to the more desirable subject, who approaches religion as "an object of individual free choice whose abstract truths nonetheless have universal value—so long as they do not contradict the dictates of reason and science."[40]

Referencing Tony Blair, who has, in recent years, famously taken an interest in religion as a mechanism for rights building, Hurd illustrates this normative brand of secularism as resting on a perceived conflict between "two faces of faith," one "bad" and the other "good."[41]

> Bad religion is understood to slip easily into violence. Bad religion is sectarian. It is understood to be divisive and associated with the failure of the state to properly domesticate it—or, in some cases, with the failure of religion to properly domesticate itself. Contemporary notions of religious violence, Brian Goldstone argues, are anchored in the opposition between a terrifying figure of the premodern past, on the one hand, and an enlightened believer at home in the world on the other: "While the latter is rendered normative, the former has to be subject to correction or made extinct."[42]

This bisection of religion is not necessarily intentionally nefarious; indeed, this bifurcation performs at least two crucial functions within today's world of human rights advocacy. In the first place, it allows policymakers and religious actors to banish those who commit acts of violence or extremism in the name of religion beyond the realm of tolerance that might otherwise be afforded to the world's variety of religions. Moreover, it serves the additional important purpose of pushing against the tendency to associate *all* religion with violence and extremism (a tendency that has been the harbinger of a very different sort of secularism than the one discussed here). Yet, as Mahmood illustrates, this bisection of religion into "tolerant" and "intolerant" slips rather easily into the vilification of nonviolent religious groups who are perceived as evincing unacceptably "traditionalist" orientations toward their respective religions—that is, who refuse to understand their religion as one reasonable option among many and who instead see their religion as calling on them to engage in active efforts to "preserve orthodox norms and values and conservative behavior."[43] Ultimately, Mahmood expresses concern about the way in which this bifurcation of religion invites policymakers to view a range of religious sensibilities not merely as politically inconvenient but as anathema to the ethos of rights-building itself. In many cases, it is a small step from this understanding of religion to a realm of subtle and more overt efforts to actively shape "how individuals and groups live out and practice their religion."[44]

The possibility that the particular narrative of the Universal Declaration of Human Rights might furnish an invitation to favor particular religious sensibilities and delegitimize others is a disturbing charge to reckon with. Such a development appears to work in flagrant contradiction to the Human Rights Commission's concerted efforts to imbue the Declaration with a logic that would resonate universally among individuals and societies across the world while also transcending the fraught terrain of humankind's irreconcilable theological legacies. Far from an invitation to privilege particular religious orientations, the Declaration was crafted not merely to lay out particular rights but to serve, as Maritain put it, as a catalyst of "dynamic unification" that would simultaneously bring disparate rights *and* disparate theologies into productive conjunction with each other.[45] To draw upon the words of Talal Asad, the Declaration was envisioned by its creators to serve as a "medium" capable of redefining and transcending practices of the self that are articulated through religion.[46] However, to view the subject of human rights as a particular type of secular subject is to begin to see the way in which the Declaration's mediating capacity is deeply dependent upon its ability to generate a subject that takes for granted the value of religious pluralism, the interchangeability of core religious tenets, and the preeminence of human dignity. The fact that the historical and cultural contingency of such a sensibility appears to have escaped the notice of the framers of the Declaration—and, indeed, the fact that it continues to escape many human rights advocates today—may be less a testament to the universality of this sensibility than it is to the invisibility of its genealogy. While the framers of the Declaration, working as they were in the 1940s, may be forgiven for their inattentiveness to this genealogy and its implications, such inattentiveness becomes less excusable as scholarship on secularism flourishes.

Salvaging the Secular Subject of Human Rights?

In *Beyond Religious Freedom*, Hurd begins her critique of contemporary rights-oriented policymaking with an epigraph by Julian Rivers: "The reinvention of government as the benign promoter of a new syncretistic public orthodoxy is only one step from oppression."[47] One of the irksome characteristics of Hurd's subfield of secular studies is that it tends to be vehemently deconstructive, offering little in the way of a convincing alternative to the mythopoeic narrative of immanent transcendence created by the framers of the Universal Declaration of Human Rights. Then again, given the complex and often barely perceptible dynamics that have converged to give rise to the secular subject of human rights—dynamics that are simultaneously historical, epistemological, and religious—it is hardly surprising to witness a deep contradiction between the observations of theorists such as Asad, Mahmood, and Hurd and the work of the Declaration's framers. To perceive the secular subject of human rights through this complex genealogical lens is to understand how the mechanism that Commission members perceived as effecting a radical broadening of the human rights realm to encompass all possible religious orientations might also have served as a mechanism of limitation—a mechanism that inadvertently withdraws the mantle of legitimacy from particular religious sensibilities and, in so doing, invites political disciplining of these sensibilities in the name of furthering human rights. These surprising contradictions become apparent only when we recognize the ways in which the Universal Declaration of Human Rights aims not just to enumerate rights but to inspire particular affective orientations and thereby to actively constitute particular kinds of subjects. As the authors of the UNESCO inquiry put it in their own description of the Declaration, "an international declaration of human rights must be the expression of a faith to be maintained no less than a programme of actions to be carried out."[48] Such endeavors are never wholly agnostic; they are the product of "a far more porous relationship" between religion, politics, and history than conventional conceptions of the secular suggest.[49]

Irksome or not, then, this questioning of the nature and the possible implications of human rights' particular brand of secularism is deeply important. Not only does a critical appraisal of this sort present a valuable supplement

to recent explorations of the specifically Christian roots of contemporary human rights, but it furnishes a crucial vantage point from which to interrogate
a variety of "religious freedom" issues that have gained an increasingly high
profile in today's worlds of human rights advocacy.[50] Whatever approaches
advocates and policymakers ultimately opt for as they navigate today's inter-
penetrations of religion and human rights, a critical appraisal of the secular subject of human rights provides a fuller understanding of the tensions
that potentially lurk between these two important realms. This is far from a
purely deconstructive endeavor; an appraisal of this sort represents an important step not merely in the critique of such rights but also in the "perfect-
ibility" of such rights in the Derridean sense of the term.[51] Human rights,
Jacques Derrida reminds us, are not "natural" but decidedly historical; they
have been, and they must continue to be, "enriched, refined, clarified, and
defined."[52] Even as we recognize the Commission's own efforts to natural-
ize these rights by grounding them within the inherence of human dignity, a
critical appraisal of the deep-seated presumptions that undergird this project
represents an important step in the work of self-questioning that Derrida prescribes as an essential feature of human rights' continuing development. In a
world in which human rights are under attack from a growing variety of cultural relativist positions, this work of self-reflection will be crucial not merely
to the refinement of human rights but to their ongoing legitimacy.

CHAPTER 13

The Subject of Human Rights

An Interview with Samuel Moyn

Samuel Moyn and Alexandre Lefebvre

Alexandre Lefebvre (AL): Sam, you are one of the most important scholars and commentators working on human rights in the world today. Over the past ten years, you have written a trilogy of books that recast debates in several fields, including history, political science, law, anthropology, and philosophy. In *The Last Utopia: Human Rights in History* (2010) you provocatively claim that human rights as we know and practice them today are of relatively recent vintage—the 1970s—and arose in response to the collapse of prior universalistic schemes. In *Christian Human Rights* (2015) you again go against the grain of conventional thinking, this time by arguing that contrary to received wisdom that human rights are essentially progressivist and secular, they were almost exclusively championed in the first half of the twentieth century by Christian authorities, intellectuals, and politicians. Finally, in *Not Enough: Human Rights in an Unequal World* (2018) you attend to the at-first-glance surprising concurrence of the neoliberal and human rights revolutions in the 1970s and observe, if not a mutual complicity between the two, then at least a mutual tolerability.

In this interview, I'd like to hear your thoughts about the subject of human rights, both in terms of how human rights discourses envisage the subject they are meant to protect and how human rights shape the sense we have of ourselves and the wider world. To my mind, this theme lies at the heart of your work on human rights, right from *The Last Utopia*. One way to read this book is that human rights caught on because they were the right discourse at the right time: given widespread disenchantment with social and political utopias on offer in the early 1970s, the language of human rights suited a

North Atlantic public looking for a more minimal, as well as more moral and less political, alternative. But is a more robust interpretation of your argument also possible, one in which human rights do not just suit the temperament of the times but end up profoundly reshaping it? After all, as you say, more than anything, human rights have served to transform the terrain of moral and political idealism.[1] How do you think that human rights ideas and institutions inform how we conceive of ourselves as moral and political subjects today?

Samuel Moyn (SM): Every argument about historical change in effect presupposes some account of the subject through which it can work, even if it skirts the topic explicitly. As someone deeply interested in Continental philosophy and political theory, I have always thought that the horizon for all future social explanation was set in the middle of the twentieth century, when a number of thinkers converged on the premise that any social explanation had to work in and through an account of subject formation, and vice versa. The form that this project took then, because of the popularity of existentialism, Marxism, and psychoanalysis, led to a profusion of rival approaches that, in my opinion, still sets the bar of explanatory ambition—one which practically nobody matches today.[2] The "marriage of Marx and Freud" touted back then may not have worked perfectly, but at least it recognized the mutual necessity of social and subjective accounts.

According to that standard, I would respond that it would be putting things generously to say that there is even an implicit account of subject formation in my books. It seems closest to the surface in *The Last Utopia*, whereas *Not Enough* specifically disclaims intervention in the now-raging debates about the nature and origins of neoliberal subjectivity.[3] As you suggest, while I see profound social causes to the reorientation of subjectivity at the basis of the explosion of human rights activism, I also strongly imply that one of the limits of this explosion is how little, reciprocally, the new subjective formation changed the world in turn. Part of the reason, as you have set out in your own work, is that from their 1940s beginnings, various figures imagined human rights primarily as a form of self-help (and with social transformation following as an effect).[4] And along with others like Jan Eckel, I have stressed in *The Last Utopia* that in the 1960s and 1970s, what was at stake in the reorientation of emotional life and practical commitment was much more a kind of spiritual hygiene.[5] Easily the most striking piece of evidence I found in my time researching the book, as well as one I often report to audiences since it is such an amazing and important fact, is that Peter Benenson, the founder of Amnesty International, explained in private that he didn't care if human rights activism made a difference, so long as it gave young people something to believe in after the failure of socialism. "The real martyrs prefer to suffer," Benenson explained, and "the real saints are no worse off in prison than anywhere on this earth."[6]

The highly cognitive register of Benenson's suggestion—that human rights are about *belief* and its preservation first and foremost—betrays some of the barely post-Christian assumptions he brought to the invention of human rights activism, and we will get into that material, I'm sure. But it would trivialize Benenson's success, as well as the human rights activism that has burgeoned since, if one failed to note that the early human rights subject was also practically oriented and highly invested in a dense repertory of everyday practices, even if these did not lead to big and demonstrable advances in social justice. What seems to have been at stake, certainly before the bureaucratization and professionalization of the human rights movement set in from the 1980s onward, was a mode of personal orientation to uncontroversial morality or a mode of subjective response that promised to save the world in small steps —one prisoner at a time, you might say—while not risking the unintended consequences of past "utopias." In this vein, it would be rewarding to reinterpret early Amnesty activities like letter writing and lighting candles as modern spiritual exercises, more mute and practical, less cognitive and mentalistic, than some of the theoretical statements from the 1940s that you have so interestingly interpreted or than Benenson's own passing comment might suggest.

AL: Do you believe, then, that human rights can serve as the basis for one's own way of life? In *Christian Human Rights* you seem skeptical. "Unlike Christianity," you write, "human rights do not give much of a chance for spiritual transfiguration for the rare authentic seeker of transcendence."[7] Is the idea here that if one's vision of a spiritually fulfilling life requires a transcendent dimension (as in, for example, Christianity), then human rights can't do the job? Or are you saying something more strident: namely, that human rights lack a certain something—whether that be spiritual depth, practical and quotidian embodiment, artistic expression, or whatever else—to become a viable spiritual option?

SM: When I wrote in *Christian Human Rights* that whatever Benenson's aspirations, human rights had failed to offer the opportunity for spiritual transfiguration that Christianity long did, what I meant had less to do with the abstract possibilities of human rights than with its concrete history or histories.

In part for that reason, I think we have to disaggregate the human rights phenomenon to answer this question—both chronologically and geographically. It may be that for a few human rights ascetics now and again, there is a quasi-religious way of life available within the framework—and Stephen Hopgood's portrait of early Amnesty suggests that it is best to interpret what Benenson achieved in the short term in precisely this direction.[8] But nowadays, for the vast majority of participants in the human rights enterprise, there is a much more arm's-length relationship, not so much to the transcendent as to plausibly self-transformative practices of any kind. If human rights movements in their most common forms involve spiritual exercises in which the remaking of the self is at stake, then so does any activity which takes on the bureaucratic and corporatized existence of a compartmentalized job spent mostly sitting in front of a screen and engaging in the commonplace activities of the average cubicle dweller of late modernity, whether she sits in one in business or government. I wouldn't want to define the spiritual or the notion of self-making so broadly—or, if we did, we would have to specify that there is little unique in the most characteristic forms of human rights mobilization.

Benenson achieved a kind of participatory vision of human rights, but you might say the human rights movement became too bureaucratic—both in its governmentalized and nongovernmentalized forms—to capitalize on the care of the self that human rights might otherwise have offered. To extend the analogy, you might then contend that human rights requires a kind of Reformation to unlock the authentic spiritual possibilities some have seen in the movement and to oppose its calcification and institutionalization.

When writing *Christian Human Rights* I also meant that whether because of its bureaucratization or its substance, human rights practices have proven nowhere near as popular and widespread in their times as even the old philosophical schools that first attracted Pierre Hadot's revolutionary interpretation of philosophy as a way of life, to say nothing of the Christian religion.[9] The Catholic Church was huge and is today a global church for diverse kinds of people, no matter what valid critiques the Reformation may have made of it; but the human rights movement never got that far, offering a much less successful recipe for self-making than what we call "religions."

This wasn't a matter of destiny, perhaps, but our starting point has to be a fair appreciation of the limits of the human rights movement in any form close to its current one as a spiritual option—by contrast not merely to prior religious options but also to prior secular ones, such as socialism (which had its own cultures, including cultures of the self). In short, the issue is not "transcendence" but the failure of human rights to become a live spiritual option for a sufficient number of people. Probably this does have something to do with the normative content of human rights, but my suspicion is that it has far more to do precisely with the kinds of care and practices of the self that human rights have involved, whether in their early more participatory form or later more institutionalized form.

AL: How about we approach the question from the opposite direction? Today the idea of human rights appears to be instrumental in generating a particular nativist discourse, especially among political conservatives in the United States (but also in Europe, Canada, and Australia). This has less to do with the familiar worry that human rights might interfere with national sovereignty. Something more direct seems to be at play: human rights are portrayed as embodying an ethos that conflicts not merely with American power but with fundamental American values. I would love to hear your thoughts on this, especially since your work, along with that of other scholars such as Marco Duranti, has demonstrated that the most important champions of human rights in the early twentieth century came from the Christian right, not the secular left.

SM: The opposition to human rights has changed its nature over time. The European far right for more than a century treated the very idea of natural universal rights as a constituent feature of a much larger plot, associated with the French Revolution as well as Freemasonry and the Jewish people, to shake the old order to its foundations. Of course, the far right was, in a sense, entirely correct to treat the abstraction and universalism of the French Revolution as mortal threats. And great scholars have suggested that the era of fascism was something like the last gasp of the Old Regime in European history, when the principles of a nationalism that had once been strongly associated with liberalism transformed into the old right's new standard.[10] For the old right, there was lots of anti-Americanism, because the United States was correctly seen to be an entirely post-feudal and in some major respects post-national state, grounded on the assertion of the natural rights of equal individuals—whatever the country's own vast concessions to patriarchy and racism.

During and after World War II, everything changed. As Marco Duranti and I have shown, as the left moved toward socialism as a result of World War II, the right moved leftward too, brilliantly adopting the rhetoric of innate rights as a safeguard against "totalitarian" states not just under communism but under the ideology of planned welfare that so many embraced back then.[11] As I argued in *Christian Human Rights*, French Catholic Jacques Maritain and German Protestant Gerhard Ritter are excellent intellectual examples of this reorientation—though as I also observe, the votaries of new post-fascist conservative democracy were never entirely free of anxiety in its deployment of human rights, given the persisting risk of their confusion with revolutionary politics.

In retrospect, however, we can say that this moment—including the debate between progressives adhering to socialism more than before or since, as well as post-fascist conservatives sometimes invoking human rights—presupposed lots of ethnic and other homogeneity at the national level, where most political battles were being fought. We have to acknowledge that even though fascist nationalism was defeated, for conservatives and progressives alike in Europe after World War II lots of ethnic and other homogeneity went without saying. Indeed, the way World War II ended—what Mark Mazower calls the "brutal peace"[12]—accelerated this homogeneity, and the new states that began to form globally breathed the same spirit. The birth of Israel without Palestinians, and a "partition" that forced catastrophic migrations of Hindus and Muslims in the creation of new states in South Asia, are graphic examples from the same year in which the Universal Declaration was proclaimed.

What we see today is an identification of human rights not with more or less homogenous welfare states but with far more diverse (and more unequal) citizenship, both at home and abroad—or, more exactly, a new kind of citizenship focused far more on status equality and the value of recognition of "difference" and pluralism but much less on material equality and the redistribution of income and wealth than in the middle of the twentieth century. In this atmosphere, populists can mobilize around opposition to human rights in the name of the "real people"—in part by stigmatizing "strangers" old and new, in part through nostalgia for a lost welfare state once privileging white male workers. In the absence of the old presupposition of homogeneity, and with the rise of a left focused on status equality rather than material equality, human rights play very differently in domestic politics. And, of course, the rise of an international and transnational human rights movement abets the perception that the principles are "cosmopolitan."

AL: As presently constituted, then, would it be fair to say that at least with respect to identity and subject formation, human rights discourses and institutions are more likely to fuel rather than to check the rise of populist and nativist imaginaries?

SM: I think so. For all the talk of the grassroots uptake of human rights around the world—and there is some—in many places human rights have become strongly identified with cosmopolitanism and elitism. Especially in Europe, where the regional human rights project has been one of the most extraordinary achievements of the global movement, leaders have castigated the very idea of human rights as the globalizing creed of the rich and rootless. Whether we consider politicians who have succeeded in swinging their country away from liberal democracy (such as Hungarian Viktor Orbán, who warned that "nowhere do human rights prescribe national suicide") or else politicians in Western European countries where liberal democracy has not been frontally challenged to the same degree, both speak that way.[13]

I think there is considerable sentiment at the moment to push back against such characterizations. But in my view the road to redemption runs through acknowledgement that there is a kernel of truth to them. In its current form, human rights literacy, and more generally the normative values of human rights, tends to be associated with education and wealth, and the narrower elements of the movement—from college courses to internships to law school clinics to rich NGOs—tilt even more in this direction. Human rights have been successfully branded by their foes as minority principles that interfere with the perquisites of majorities, which has been disastrous for the movement and norms alike.[14]

There is no reason to believe, however, that this outcome is set in stone. Debate rages around whether the missed connection lies primarily at the level of what I called "branding"—more generously put, public relations—or at the level of substance. But the answer is clearly both. Philosophically, understood as normative principles, human rights are ultimately about setting priorities. Only very rarely are they a matter of nonnegotiable trumps. Once those priorities are clear to their defenders, they need to be linked to an overall policy package that serves and speaks to majorities in a democracy—and the package arguably ought to be reached more democratically. If human rights were joined normatively to a larger set of ends (such as distributive equality) that clearly do serve majority interests, and if the movement made democratic agitation more central to its mobilization (and elite actors like bureaucrats and judges less), it might experience more success. And with respect to your own historical work on human rights as a way of life, it might seem that human rights are today failing on this count because they do not offer something credible enough to a big enough group of people.

AL: Picking up from this last set of observations, let's talk about your most recent work. *Not Enough* belongs to and in some respects has given rise to what we might call a left critical body of scholarship that draws more or less direct associations between human rights and neoliberalism. One of the implications of this association relevant for this book (that is, *The Subject of Human Rights*) is that human rights engenders and fosters a particular type of subject, one largely disembedded from structures and also divorced from more radical political projects. Could you speak a little about the alternative forms of subject or subjectivities you might imagine or hope for given contemporary injustices, inequalities, and so on?

SM: I would not draw as direct a link between human rights and neoliberalism as some—especially some Foucauldians who are interested in the homology of human rights and neoliberalism as (allegedly) corresponding ways of life or some Marxists who consider human rights the superstructure of the neoliberalized capitalist base. But it is true that everyone interested in human rights needs to think hard about how the ascendancy of the principles—and the way of life associated with them, however increasingly bureaucratic and institutionalized—fits in our neoliberal age.

As you say, it is incumbent on such critics to imagine how to either fully displace human rights and neoliberal subject formation or, as I would prefer, save the former from the latter as part of a newly constelled arrangement for mobilization and subjectivity alike. As a historian, I look back to the vast literature on subject formation under socialism—including communism, on which there has been much better research on this score—for models.[15] What a new vision of human rights would look like is, of course, anyone's guess. But we can speculate that it would be more attentive to democratic action, majority politics, and equal outcomes, and thus a less professionalized self than one more familiar from histories of the modern age that emphasize the experience of collective solidarity locally or globally. Subjectivity has always been defined by its tools, as Martin Heidegger's *Being and Time* most classically showed. In the internet age, we simply don't know yet how the familiar uses of a new platform for old-school informational politics (such as "naming and shaming") will give way to other and more surprising forms.

AL: Can you elaborate on what you've found in the literature on socialism and subject formation—and, more generally, in the literature on social democracy (along with welfarism and distributive equality) and subject formation—that is more attentive to solidarity and equality than what we might find in human rights discourses? How do these models and experiences from the past refract through our own very different economic, political, and technological situation?

SM: Well, there is very little to go on when it comes to scholarship on social democracy so far. You observe that Foucauldian "asceticism" and ethics have rarely been pursued past the classical sources on which he focused and the early modern period, at the latest, in the hands of others.[16] Ironically, to the extent that (sometimes now former) Foucauldians such as Stephen Kotkin, along with others I mentioned a moment ago, have engaged state socialism, their work tends to be confined largely to one sole (if vast) place: the Soviet Union. In short, there is a lot more to be done. I can think of important French scholarship, above all by Marcel Gauchet (whose chair at l'École des hautes études en sciences sociales referred to the constitution of the subject), which does examine the fate of selfhood and practices of self-cultivation.[17]

On the basis of this kind of work, one might argue that mid-twentieth-century movements featured two big differences from later mainstream human rights movements. We can conveniently approach the implications of these differences for self-cultivation and subject formation by looking in turn at political parties and trade unions, which were the privileged mobilizational forms of the socialist and social democratic state, just as NGOs of a very different kind are a symbol of our own priorities.

The party has a very different relationship to politics than the contemporary NGO. Roughly, the goal of parties is to seek and exercise power, not to remain "outside" it. I would hypothesize that this feature had big ramifications for subject formation. The party member was partisan and open to exercising power. The human rights activist is "neutral," appealing to natural law or otherwise allegedly consensual norms, and goes so far as to criticize power but has no particular views about how to exercise it—only to rule out excess and wrongdoing. As a result, the relationship between subjectivity and power, that classic Foucauldian nexus, is worth further study.

Similarly, when it comes to trade unions, notwithstanding famous and obvious bureaucratization (of the kind that inspired our most classic stories of bureaucracy), the trade union was much less elitist than common human rights NGOs.[18] I don't want to exaggerate this feature, but there was clearly more room in this kind of politics for quotidian agitation that grew organically out of the activity that the activism criticized. That is, workers labored during the day and found time to engage in trade union politics on lunch hours or during evenings—unless, of course, strikes broke out. Now, for the trade union subject, as you might call it, the emotional and physical demands and scripts were just very different. They were more exhausting, as Oscar Wilde observed in his quip that the trouble with socialism is that it takes up too many evenings. But it may also have remained closer than the most bureaucratic forms of human rights activism to the community of "victims." Indeed, trade unions were essentially about inviting victims to take control of their own destiny, something human rights organizations have done far less well.

AL: Today, as you very well know (and contribute to, I should add), the cause of distributive equality is making a comeback. Witness the success of the Bernie Sanders campaign in 2016 and calls today, however passingly it may turn out to be, for democratic socialism in the United States. In light of what you said above, what hope do you hold out for the future of activism along these lines? Because, if I understand you correctly, there's a Tocquevillian insight going on. In *The Old Regime and the Revolution*, Alexis de Tocqueville observed that the French Revolution took the shape it did because it was carried out by subjects (that is, by revolutionaries) who had been raised within a culture that had been actively depoliticized and bureaucratized for over a century and a half. Like human rights activists of today, perhaps, condemnation of an existing state of affairs came readily enough, as did enthusiasm for new general principles to lead the way, but with very little experience and capacity in the actual exercise of political power.

SM: This is absolutely a valid concern, and certainly I could not exempt myself from my criticism of recent generations that have tended to favor armchair speculation over the sort of pragmatic knowledge rooted in everyday political work. Edmund Burke's and Alexis de Tocqueville's anxieties about the abstractions and speculation of activist intellectuals (especially when out of power) are certainly germane too, not just the critique you mention of the torpor that had descended on France because of the character of Old Regime rule. But intellectual critique is never out of place, even if it doesn't offer good alternatives, let alone prepare students (to say nothing of teachers) for rule. And what is the alternative to shouldering the burden of the risks of reactivation?

Fortunately, in any case, it seems as if people in search of viable alternatives are doing very well on their own, learning new modes of sociability, including ones that combine grassroots forces and intellectuals who might once have gone on to our own version of bureaucratic life—the university—but are not doing so because their path is blocked. And I believe Pankaj Mishra is accurate when he writes, "The days when young people transposed their political idealism into the vernacular of liberal internationalism seem to be behind us. Young men and women are more likely today to join domestic political upsurges against neoliberalism than to fall for a human rights anti-politics miraculously placed beyond political economy."[19] Of course, I would clarify this statement by saying, as we have covered, that not all forms of human rights have been anti-political, and current forms of political "upsurges" can and should incorporate the values once pursued anti-politically by human rights activists. Insofar as it is true that political idealism is returning people to mobilization, it is also exposing them to the sorts of lessons experience brings and to forms of subjectivity that are not so much oriented to critiquing power as to exercising it for the local, national, and global good.

AL: Could we be looking at a "best of both worlds"–type situation? Just now, you sounded hopeful that engaged activism against neoliberalism might learn and benefit from a human rights perspective. Does influence run in the other direction? I note, for example, that in his recent report on poverty and human rights in the United States, the UN Special Rapporteur on extreme poverty and human rights, Philip Alston, devoted significant attention not only to poverty but also to economic inequality.[20] How optimistic do you feel about such attempts to wield human rights law against economic inequality?

SM: I am worried that there is little directly egalitarian support in human rights law to do so, and even more that human rights organizations as we know them are the wrong kind of group to "wield" egalitarian norms even if they were there. But there is every reason to welcome it when people are trying either to read distributive egalitarianism into human rights late in the day or escalate their movements to challenge inequality from the ground up—especially in the absence of other movements engaged with the problem.

I could be wrong in my pessimism. For one thing, as Philip Alston's work shows, there is considerable mileage you can get out of human rights law when you can claim that inequality is having an indirect effect on norms it consecrates. You are correct: reporting on his time in Alabama and elsewhere, he certainly has talked a lot about inequality.

But I guess I don't see that the sorts of activism and mobilization that bureaucratic professionals in and around the United Nations or in nongovernmental groups can do will make tremendous change on its own. I was surprised, actually, by how successfully Alston not only garnered attention on that particular country visit but even antagonized some of America's politicians, such as Nikki Haley. It still seems to me, however, the sort of activism that is like lighting a match in a tempest.

For some time, it has seemed clear that the most successful movements are those that engage deeply with grassroots causes around the world. For example, in a recent essay, Mark Goodale has argued that one age of human rights is ending and the idea will survive, if at all, only when it is fully owned by ordinary people around the world.[21] But we are, I believe, only at the beginning of figuring out whether that can happen and what it would look like. As I observed earlier, compared to prior Western exports like Christianity, Marxism, and nationalism, human rights have fared poorly in garnering global popular appeal and especially in penetrating to grassroots. Perhaps our interest in the subject of human rights must return to the way that prior forms of spiritual practice associated with "religion" swept the world with ease and we should also attend to the obstacles that have blocked human rights from becoming a "way of life" for millions, no matter where they live, on the surface of the earth.

AL: How could human rights better resonate at the grassroots level? This is, of course, the problem that the human rights education movement comes up against: how to tailor the meaning and relevance of human rights for various audiences. For example, how should human rights education be designed for judges or teachers or teenagers or children? All of these require different models. Too often, however, as Danielle Celermajer and others have observed, human rights education is practiced with the belief (or, better, the wish or hope) that conveying information about human rights norms, ideas, and history will suffice for learners to commit to them. But, of course, more innovative and better adapted alternatives can be and are being imagined.[22] If you were to design human rights education, conceived in the broadest sense, how would you proceed?

SM: Perhaps they can't. Not all ideas are created equal in their ability to travel horizontally across space or, once there, penetrate vertically across all levels of society.[23] Professionals in the field, as Celermajer might suggest, first think of approaching and enlightening professionals in fields like the military and police that have historically been the source of the worst violations. If that project succeeds, the theory goes, it may not matter to reach ordinary people, who tend to be the victims of bureaucratically organized harm, including in many cases of atrocity. If this is true, it may be enough for human rights to remain professional ideals. But I would agree with you that the hope and significance people invest in human rights suggest that many would like to see these concepts not only penetrate much more deeply but become something like a way of life that inflects the spiritual history of humanity, much like processes of religious conversion or syncretism in the past.

As I suggest at the end of *Christian Human Rights*, it is possible that if this becomes the goal, the movement may have to learn more from prior religions than it has to teach—in the development not so much of moving stories (which the human rights movement has in volumes) but aesthetic cultures, corporal practices, participatory rituals, and so forth. What does seem clear is that human rights and most other ideas face serious limits when they are approached too cognitively, apart from their propagation as modes of being or ways of life. To extend Max Weber's famous contraposition, human rights, to the extent it has had these things, skipped the stage of prophets and went directly on to priests, who tend to present human rights in terms of rules and violations. Prophets spread visionary conceptions by opening up the promise of a new way of being human. I'm just not sure human rights have found their prophet—assuming they have a chance of spreading in the first place. There was a reason Christianity could become a way of life, while stamp-collecting, including stamps in honor of human rights, could never become more than a diversion for a few.[24]

AL: A final question to return us to the nexus between subjectivity and power that we opened with. Much contemporary critical literature on human rights continues to stress that the subject of human rights is constructed and that human rights are contingent political discourses, not metaphysical attributes of human nature. How much purchase do you think this denaturalizing form of critique has on the contemporary politics of human rights?

SM: A great deal, I'd say. There is, of course, the countertrend among analytic philosophers of human rights to insist that, instead of constructions of politics and law, human rights reflect the enduring interests of a more or less stable human nature.[25] Nobody can rule out such a proposition, but it seems to me that the critical energy put into demonstrating the intellectual and practical contingency of our commitments to and movements around human rights suggests it is likely to be one more passing fancy. Yet it is only fair to ask those, like me, who have argued that point to explain (as Foucault was often pushed to do) the ethical basis of their own critique and whether they are tacitly or otherwise relying on premises of a more or less naturalistic theory of human beings. Karl Marx criticized bourgeois rights, but—much more clearly than Foucault—in the name of an alternative theory of human nature or "species being." As Horace claimed long ago, "*Naturam expellas furca, tamen usque recurret et mala perrumpet furtim fastidia victrix*" ("You can try to expel nature with a pitchfork, but she will come right back, victorious over your arrogant and ignorant scorn").[26]

Notes

Introduction

1. See Cruft, Liao, and Renzo, eds., *Philosophical Foundations of Human Rights*, Etinson, ed., *Human Rights: Moral or Political?*, Shelton, ed., *The Oxford Handbook of International Human Rights Law*, Douzinas and Gearty, eds., *The Meanings of Rights*, and Gearty and Douzinas, eds., *The Cambridge Companion to Human Rights Law*.

2. On the Asian values debate, see Bauer and Bell, eds., *The East Asian Challenge for Human Rights*. On feminist critiques, see Peters and Wolper, eds., *Women's Rights, Human Rights*, and Charlesworth, Chinkin, and Wright, "Feminist Approaches to International Law."

3. See Ishay, *The History of Human Rights*, 108–116.

4. Hunt, *Inventing Human Rights*, 150.

5. See Dembour, "What Are Human Rights? Four Schools of Thought," and Stammers, "Social Movements and the Social Construction of Rights."

6. Hunt, *Inventing Human Rights*, Rorty, "Human Rights, Rationality, and Sentimentality," Sliwinski, *Human Rights in Camera*, and Lefebvre, *Human Rights As a Way of Life*.

7. See Chouliaraki, *The Spectatorship of Suffering*, and McLagan, "Introduction: Making Human Rights Claims Public."

8. See Griffin, *On Human Rights*, for the argument from normative agency. See Forst, *The Right to Justification*, with respect to the interest and right to justification.

9. See Joas, *The Sacredness of the Person*, and Reinbold, *Seeing the Myth in Human Rights*.

10. See, for example, Irigaray, *Speculum of the Other Woman*.

11. Charlesworth, Chinkin, and Wright, "Feminist Approaches to International Law."

12. Byrnes, "The Convention Against Torture."

13. Oliver, "The Social Model of Disability: Thirty Years On."

14. Kittay, "The Ethics of Care, Dependence, and Disability," and Davy, "Philosophical Inclusive Design: Intellectual Disability and the Limits of Individual Autonomy in Moral and Political Theory."

15. Nedelsky, *Law's Relations*, Fineman, "Cracking the Foundational Myths: Independence, Autonomy, and Self-Sufficiency," and Mackenzie, Catriona, and Stoljar, eds., *Relational Autonomy*.

16. See, for example, Dodson and Celermajer in the present volume, and Mutua, "Savages, Victims, and Saviors," 201.

17. Kapur, "Human Rights in the 21st Century." See also Anghie, Chimni, Mickelson, and Okafor, eds., *The Third World and International Order*.

18. Armitage, "John Locke, Carolina, and the 'Two Treatises of Government,'" 602.

19. Pitts, "Empire and Legal Universalisms in the Eighteenth Century." See also Mehta, *Liberalism and Empire*.

20. Pitts, "Empire and Legal Universalisms in the Eighteenth Century," 120.

21. Anaya, *Indigenous Peoples in International Law*, and Van Krieken, "The Barbarism of Civilization."

22. Singer, *Animal Liberation*. On animal rights, see Cavalieri, *The Animal Question*.

23. Derrida, *The Animal That Therefore I Am*.

24. Haraway, "A Cyborg Manifesto," and Plumwood, *Feminism and the Mastery of Nature*.

25. See Keck and Sikkink, "Transnational Advocacy Networks in International and Regional Politics."

26. See Moyn, *Not Enough*.

27. See Celermajer, *The Prevention of Torture*.

28. See Lacey, *State Punishment*.

29. See Lifton, *The Nazi Doctors*.

30. Marx, "On the Jewish Question."

31. Brown, "The Most We Can Hope For," Marks, "Four Human Rights Myths," Golder and McLoughlin, eds., *The Politics of Legality in a Neoliberal Age*.

32. For a recent volume, see Schippers, ed., *Critical Perspectives on Human Rights*.

33. See Foucault, *Discipline and Punish* (1975), and Foucault, *The History of Sexuality, Volume 1* (1976).

34. See Butler, *Gender Trouble*, and Butler, *The Psychic Life of Power*; Golder, *Foucault and the Politics of Rights*, 61–88.

35. See Felski, *The Limits of Critique*.

36. For a summary, see Lefebvre, *Human Rights and the Care of the Self*, 9–10, 195.

37. See Bajaj and Flowers, *Human Rights Education*.

Chapter 1

1. Bradley and Petro, eds., *Truth Claims*.

2. European Union, *European Convention for the Protection of Human Rights and Fundamental Freedoms*, and European Union, *Treaty on European Union*.

3. African Charter on Human and Peoples' Rights (www.achpr.org/instruments /achpr/) and American Convention on Human Rights (https://www.oas.org/dil/trea ties_b-32_american_convention_on_human_rights.htm).

4. Nedelsky, *Law's Relations*.

5. Civil Partnership Act, 2004, c. 33 (Eng.).

6. Marriage (Same Sex Couples) Act, 2013, c. 30 (Eng).

7. See Nedelsky, *Law's Relations*, Chapter 3, n.37 and n.38 for discussion of the U.S. case, *Lochner v. New York*, 198 U.S. 45 (1905), and the judicial era it ushered in.

8. Reich, *Aftershock*.

9. Moyn, "A Powerless Companion."

10. Markovits, *The Meritocracy Trap*.

11. Moyn, 149.

12. Douzinas, *Human Rights and Empire*.

13. See Marks, "Human Rights and Root Causes."

14. See Nedelsky, *Private Property and the Limits of American Constitutionalism*.

15. See Rosenberg, *The Hollow Hope*.

16. Williams, *The Alchemy of Race and Rights*.

17. See Nedelsky, "Reconceiving Rights and Constitutionalism."

Chapter 2

1. See Goodale, *A Revolution in Fragments*.

2. Postero, *The Indigenous State*.

3. Goodale, *Dilemmas of Modernity*.

4. Hardt and Negri, *Empire*.

5. Panikkar, "Is the Notion of Human Rights a Western Concept?"; see also Eberhard, "Au-delà de l'universalisme et du relativisme: L'horizon d'un pluralisme responsable," and Goodale, "Toward a Critical Anthropology of Human Rights."

6. Goodale and Merry, *The Practice of Human Rights*, 24.

7. Goodale and Merry, *The Practice of Human Rights*, 25.

8. Goodale, "The Myth of Universality," and Goodale, ed., *Letters to the Contrary*.

9. Keane, *Ethical Life*.

10. See Goodale, "The Myth of Universality."

11. See Holmes and Marcus, "Para-Ethnography," 595.

12. Holmes and Marcus, "Para-Ethnography," 595.

13. Lambek, ed., *Ordinary Ethics*.

14. Turner, "Human Rights, Human Difference."

15. See Goodale, *Surrendering to Utopia*.

16. See Wilson, ed., *Human Rights, Culture and Context*, Cowan, Dembour, and Wilson, eds., *Culture and Rights*, and Wilson and Mitchell, eds., *Human Rights in Global Perspective*.

17. See Dunkerley, "Evo Morales, the 'Two Bolivias' and the Third Bolivian Revolution."

18. Speed, *Rights in Rebellion*.

19. Speed, *Rights in Rebellion*, 47.

20. Speed, *Rights in Rebellion*, 169.

21. Speed, *Rights in Rebellion*, 165.

22. Robbins, "Recognition, Reciprocity, and Justice," 185, quoting from Strathern, *Kinship, Law and the Unexpected*, 114.

23. Robbins, "Recognition, Reciprocity, and Justice," 175.

24. Robbins, "Recognition, Reciprocity, and Justice," 175.

25. Mauss, *The Gift.*

26. Goodale, *A Revolution in Fragments.*

27. Salomon, "Review of *To Make the Earth Bear Fruit*," 654.

28. Descola, *Par-delà nature et culture.*

29. Besson, "International Human Rights Law and Mirrors," 8.

30. See, for example, Nedelsky, *Law's Relations.*

31. Escobar, "Latin America at a Crossroads."

32. Kohn, *How Forests Think.* See also de la Cadena, *Earth Beings.*

33. See also Gareau, "We Have Never Been Human," Haraway, *When Species Meet*, and Latour, *An Inquiry into Modes of Existence.*

34. Goodale, "The Myth of Universality."

35. Escobar, *Encountering Development.*

36. Davis and Mohamed, "Global Rights, Local Risk."

37. Mertus, *Human Rights Matters.*

38. Mertus, *Human Rights Matters*, 22.

39. See Reinbold, *Seeing the Myth in Human Rights.*

40. Goodale, "Human Values and Moral Exclusion."

41. See Piketty, *Capital in the Twenty-First Century*, Moyn, *Not Enough.*

Chapter 3

1. MacKinnon, *Are Women Human?*, 41 and 43.

2. MacKinnon, *Are Women Human?*, 43.

3. Charlesworth, "Human Rights As Men's Rights," 103–13, Bunch, "Transforming Human Rights," 11.

4. An Earnest Englishwoman, "Are Women Animals?," 11.

5. Derrida, "'Eating Well,'" 114.

6. Derrida, "On Reading Heidegger," 183.

7. Sellars, *The Rise and Rise of Human Rights*, 197.

8. Descartes, *Discourse on Method and Other Writings*, 73–76. For a brilliant exposition, see Shannon, *The Accommodated Animal.*

9. Cavendish, *Observations upon Experimental Philosophy*, 176.

10. Wollstonecraft, *A Vindication of the Rights of Woman*, 74.

11. Wollstonecraft, *A Vindication of the Rights of Woman*, 130.

12. Wollstonecraft, *A Vindication of the Rights of Woman*, 161.

13. Wollstonecraft, *A Vindication of the Rights of Woman*, 160–61.

14. Lawrence, *A Philosophical and Practical Treatise on Horses,* 118–19.

15. Lawrence, *A Philosophical and Practical Treatise on Horses,* 119–20.

16. Young, *An Essay on Humanity to Animals,* 8.

17. Bentham, *An Introduction to the Principles of Morals and Legislation,* ccix.

18. Bentham, "Anarchical Fallacies", 496–501, 505, 508, and 521.

19. See Douzinas, *The Radical Philosophy of Rights*, for a history of the concept of the "person."

20. An Earnest Englishwoman, "Are Women Animals?," 11.

21. I discuss the links between sexism and racism in Bourke, *What It Means to Be Human*.

22. "Cruelty to Animals: Also to Women and Children," 1.

23. Vanessa, "Vivisection," unpaginated.

24. "Suffragettes and Animals' Rights," 13. Also see "Women and Vivisection," 235, and "Suffragettes – Furs – Murderous Millinery – Vivisection," 34.

25. A rare exception is the Oldfield quotation, above.

26. Derrida, "On Reading Heidegger," 183.

27. *Opinions of Women on Women's Suffrage*, 20.

28. Oldfield, "The Scientific View," 60–61.

29. "Miss Müller and Woman Suffrage," 6.

30. J. Ellice Hopkins, *Is It Natural?*, 3–4.

31. Singer, "Severe Impairment and the Beginning of Life," 248.

32. Tooley, "Abortion and Infanticide," 57 and 84.

33. Wise, *Unlocking the Cage*, 35–38.

34. Cavalieri and Singer, "A Declaration on Great Apes," 4–6.

35. Cavalieri and Singer, "A Declaration on Great Apes," 4–6.

36. "The Woman About Town," 423.

37. De Cyon, "The Anti-Vivisectionist Agitation," 506–10.

38. Warbasse, *The Conquest of Disease Through Animal Experimentation*, 158.

39. Lubinski, "Screw the Whales, Save Me!," 401.

40. Bryant, "Sacrificing the Sacrifice of Animals."

41. Wise, "Animal Rights, One Step at a Time," 33.

42. Bryant, "Sacrificing the Sacrifice of Animals," 253.

43. Haraway, *The Haraway Reader*, 141.

44. Braidotti, *Transpositions*, 107.

45. Simone Weil, quoted in Diamond, "Injustice and Animals," 128.

46. Derrida, "Violence Against Animals," 64–65.

47. Derrida, "Violence Against Animals," 64–65.

48. Douzinas, *The End of Human Rights*.

49. Derrida, "The Animal That Therefore I Am (More to Follow)," 380.

50. Derrida, "The Animal That Therefore I Am (More to Follow)," 374 and 378–79.

51. An interesting example of this problem has been given by Haraway, *The Haraway Reader*, 58–9.

52. Clark, "'The Animal' and 'The Feminist,'" 518.

53. Donovan, "Feminism and the Treatment of Animals," 307.

Chapter 4

1. On definitions, see Dodson, "The End in the Beginning."

2. Simpson, "Subjects of Sovereignty," 200.

3. Simpson, "Subjects of Sovereignty," 215.

4. Deloria, *Indians in Unexpected Places*, 27.

5. See Anaya, *Indigenous Peoples in International Law*, and Cobo, *Discrimination Against Indigenous Populations*, especially Chapter 20.

6. See Pritchard, ed., *Indigenous Peoples, the United Nations and Human Rights*.

7. See Alfred and Corntassel, "Being Indigenous."

8. See Sanders, "The UN Working Group on Indigenous Populations."

9. See Carpenter and Riley, "Indigenous Peoples and the Jurisgenerative Moment," 173.

10. See Iorns, "Indigenous Peoples and Self Determination: Challenging State Sovereignty."

11. See Henry and Pene, "Kaupapa Maori."

12. See Kohn, *How Forests Think*.

13. Hendry and Tatum, "Human Rights, Indigenous Peoples, and the Pursuit of Justice," 354.

14. See also Deloria and Lytle, *American Indians, American Justice*, and Porter, "Strengthening Tribal Sovereignty Through Peacemaking: How the Anglo-American Legal Tradition Destroys Indigenous Societies."

15. See Anghie, *Imperialism, Sovereignty and the Making of International Law*, and Chimni, "The Past, Present and Future of International Law," 499.

16. Alfred and Corntassel, "Being Indigenous," 611–12.

17. See Green, "Decolonization and Recolonization," Slowey, *Navigating Neoliberalism*, and Coulthard, "From Wards of the State to Subjects of Recognition?"

18. Right into the 1960s, Aboriginal people lived under a different legal regime, mostly as wards of the state, and every aspect of their lives was controlled by the state. An exemption card allowed an individual Aboriginal person to live outside this regime amongst non-Indigenous Australians.

19. The Royal Commission into Aboriginal Deaths in Custody (RCIADIC), established in 1987, examined the full spectrum of structural factors underpinning the overrepresentation of Aboriginal people in the criminal justice system and their mistreatment in that system.

20. Pursuant to a recommendation of the RCIADIC, an Indigenous-specific commissioner was established within the Australian Human Rights Commission. Michael Dodson was the first commissioner to hold that office, from 1993 to 1998.

21. *Bringing Them Home* was the report of the Inquiry into the Forced Removal of Aboriginal and Torres Strait Islander Children from Their Families, which Dodson headed.

22. See also Dodson, "Land Rights and Social Justice."

23. The Uluru Statement from the Heart was the statement transmitted by Indigenous peoples who gathered for a constitutional convention in 2017 to develop a public proposal for large-scale reforms that would provide a framework for the appropriate recognition of Indigenous peoples. It can be found at https://www.referendumcouncil.org.au/sites/default/files/2017-05/Uluru_Statement_From_The_Heart_0.PDF.

Chapter 5

1. Salim fled Iraq with her family when she was a young child, grew up in northern Iran, and returned to Iraq in 2012.

2. See Phelps, "The Limits of Admittance and Diversity in Iraqi Kurdistan: Femininity and the Body of Du'a Khalil."

3. Report of the Secretary-General on Conflict-Related Sexual Violence: Report of the Secretary-General, S/2017/249.

4. Because Salim was able to track down only one white dress—most families lost all possessions when fleeing ISIS—she altered the style of the dress for each woman by using a scarf, belt, or different draping pattern.

5. Derived from personal correspondence with Salim, October 10, 2019.

6. Charland, "Constitutive Rhetoric," 140. Also see Hesford, *Spectacular Rhetorics*.

7. Stasiullis, quoted in Falcon, *Power Interrupted*, 19.

8. Butler, *Precarious Life*, 35.

9. Butler, *Precarious Life*, 35.

10. Sjoberg, cited in Pruitt, Berents, and Munro, "Gender and Age in the Constitution of Male Youth," 691.

11. See, for example, Abu-Lughod, *Do Muslim Women Need Saving?*; Kapur, *Erotic Justice*, and "Human Rights in the 21st Century"; Mohanty, "Under Western Eyes."

12. See Puar, "Precarity Talk: A Virtual Roundtable."

13. See Hesford and Shuman, "Precarious Narratives"; Turner, *Vulnerability and Human Rights*.

14. Jansson and Eduards, "The Politics of Gender in the UN Security Council Resolutions," 593.

15. See the UN Human Rights Commission, Report on the Protection of Civilians in Armed Conflict in Iraq.

16. Ryan, "Iraqi Kurds, Battling Islamic Threat, Press Washington for Arms."

17. Abu-Lughod, *Do Muslim Women Need Saving?*, 66.

18. See Lutz and Collins, *Reading National Geographic*.

19. MacDonald, "SUR/VEIL," 25–26.

20. See, for example, the Fox News story "ISIS Tightens Grip on Yazidi Captives Held as Sex Slaves" and the Conservative News Service article "ISIS Genocide of Yazidis: 'Girls As Young As 9 Were Raped, As Were Pregnant Women.'"

21. For example, President Trump's Executive Order 13769, "Protecting the Nation from Foreign Terrorist Entry into the United States."

22. Jaleel, "Weapons of Sex, Weapons of War," 116.

23. Jaleel, "Weapons of Sex, Weapons of War," 125.

24. Jansson and Eduards, "The Politics of Gender in the UN Security Council Resolutions," 600.

25. UN Human Rights Council, "They Came to Destroy," A/HRC/32/CRP.2.

26. Jansson and Eduards, "The Politics of Gender in the UN Security Council Resolutions," 592.

27. Pratt, "Reconceptualizing Gender," 776.

28. Herbert, "The Sexual Politics of U.S. Inter/National Security," 92.

29. Jansson and Eduards, "The Politics of Gender in the UN Security Council Resolutions," 595.

30. Report of the Secretary-General on Conflict-Related Sexual Violence, 3–6.

31. Report of the Secretary-General on Conflict-Related Sexual Violence, 3.

32. Giddings, quoted in Jansson and Eduards, "The Politics of Gender in the UN Security Council Resolutions," 596.

33. Giddings, quoted in Jansson and Eduards, "The Politics of Gender in the UN Security Council Resolutions," 595.

34. Pratt, "Reconceptualizing Gender," 775.

35. Human Rights Watch, "Iraq: ISIS Escapees Describe Systematic Rape." https://www.hrw.org/news/2015/04/14/iraq-isis-escapees-describe-systematic-rape.

36. George, "Yazidi Women Welcomed Back to the Faith." http://www.unhcr.org/en-us/news/stories/2015/6/56ec1e9611/yazidi-women-welcomed-back-to-the-faith.html.

37. George, "Yazidi Society Changes to Try and Rescue a Generation of Traumatized Women."

38. See Hesford and Shuman, "Precarious Narratives."

39. Derived from personal correspondence with Salim, October 10, 2019.

40. Pratt, "Reconceptualizing Gender," 775.

41. Kweskin, "Yezidi Vulnerability Before ISIS."

42. Bowring, "Minority Rights in Post-War Iraq," 323.

43. Westcott, "Iraq's Yazidis Return to a Healthcare Crisis."

44. UN Meetings Coverage and Press Release. Prevention, Protection, Prosecution Stressed, SC/12751.

45. UN Meetings Coverage and Press Release. Prevention, Protection, Prosecution Stressed, SC/12751.

46. Auchter, "Gendering Terror," 135.

Chapter 6

1. See, however, Hesford, *Spectacular Rhetorics*, and Cohen, *States of Denial*.

2. See Sunstein, "On the Expressive Function of Law."

3. On the distinction between "education" and "training," see Tight, *Key Concepts in Adult Education and Training*.

4. See Bullock and Johnson, "The Impact of the Human Rights Act."

5. On the situational hypothesis concerning institutional violence, see, for example, Crelinsten, "The World of Torture: A Constructed Reality," and Celermajer, *Issues Paper 2*.

6. See Nowak, *Report of the Special Rapporteur on Torture*, 94(x).

7. UN General Assembly, Resolution 49/184, United Nations Decade for Human Rights Education, A/RES/49/184 (December 23, 1994).

8. UN General Assembly, Resolution 59/113 A, World Programme for Human Rights Education A/RES/59/113 (adopted December 10, 2004).

9. UN General Assembly, Resolution 66/137, United Nations Declaration on Human Rights Education and Training, A/RES/66/137 (adopted December 19, 2011).

10. The United Nations Office of the High Commissioner for Human Rights keeps an updated database on Human Rights Education and Training, which includes lists of institutions that develop and deliver human rights education programs, including formal university and more informal short courses, and materials and resources. See http://hre.ohchr.org/hret/Intro.aspx?Lng=en, accessed October 6, 2017.

11. UN Office of the High Commissioner for Human Rights and UN Educational, Scientific, and Cultural Organization. *Plan of Action: World Programme for Human Rights Education.*

12. Previous to the study that formed the basis of this chapter, no comprehensive study or analysis of human rights education for law enforcement personnel had been undertaken. The data that forms the analysis for this chapter was collected by the author as part of a larger torture prevention project. For details on the process of collecting education and training resources, see Celermajer, *International Review.*

13. This project was undertaken as a partnership between the University of Sydney, the Centre for the Study of Human Rights at the University of Colombo, and the Kathmandu School of Law and work with police in Sri Lanka and Nepal. For an overview of the project, see Celermajer, *Project Overview,* and Celermajer, *The Prevention of Torture.* On the training research, see Celermajer, *International Review.*

14. On an alternative approach, teaching nonviolent interviewing techniques to law enforcement personnel, see Chen and Spronken, eds., *Three Approaches to Combating Torture in China.*

15. See Sydney Centre for International Law, *Human Rights in the Criminal Justice System in Nepal.*

16. See Marotta, "The Blue Flame and the Gold Shield."

17. See, for example, Commonwealth Secretariat, *Commonwealth Manual on Human Rights Training for Police,"*65–66.

18. United Nations, *Human Rights and Law Enforcement,* 10.

19. See Fishbein and Ajzen, *Belief, Attitude, Intention, and Behavior,* and Sallis, Owen, and Fisher, "Ecological Models of Health Behaviour."

20. O'Neill, *Police Reform and Human Rights,* 9.

21. See Kelman, "The Social Context of Torture," and Zimbardo, *The Lucifer Effect.*

22. See Northern Ireland Human Rights Commission, *Course for All,* 3.29.

23. See, for example, Organization for Security and Cooperation in Europe (OSCE), *Guidelines on Human Rights Education.*

24. For an example of the absence of guidance, see Sydney Centre for International Law, *Human Rights in the Criminal Justice System in Nepal,* 28. For an exam-

ple of an exception, see New Zealand Police and New Zealand Human Rights Commission, *Human Rights Training*, 9.

25. Confidential interview, April 14, 2012. See Allport, *The Nature of Prejudice*.

26. The phrase was coined by Robert Jay Lifton. See Lifton, "Conditions of Atrocity."

27. See Fishbein and Ajzen, *Belief, Attitude, Intention, and Behavior*.

28. Argyris and Schon, *Theory in Practice*, 6–7.

29. See, for example, Crelinsten, "The World of Torture," Milgram, *Obedience to Authority*, and Zimbardo, Maslach, and Haney, "Reflections on the Stanford Prison Experiment."

30. See Sallis, Owen, and Fisher, "Ecological Models of Health Behaviour."

31. See Donovan and Vlais, *VicHealth Review*; NIMH Collaborative HIV/STD Prevention Trial Group, "The Community Popular Opinion Leader HIV Prevention Programme."

32. See Kant, *Groundwork of the Metaphysics of Morals*, 400.

33. See Luban, "Liberalism and the Unpleasant Question of Torture."

34. See, for example, the *Political Treatise*, I, 4–7 (Spinoza, *Complete Works*, 681–82).

35. See Hunt, *Inventing Human Rights*.

36. See Wahl, *In the Eye of the Torturer*.

37. An important difference between the two thinkers is that for Spinoza, human beings will always act according to the natural law of seeking the greatest possible benefit for themselves. The question is whether they can develop active and adequate ideas that allow them to recognize what is truly in their interest, as distinct from being passively effected and thus in a reactive and partial mode.

38. See the *Ethics*, IV, appendix (Spinoza, *A Spinoza Reader: The Ethics and Other Works*, 239).

39. See Celermajer, *The Prevention of Torture*.

40. Spinoza, *Complete Works*, 682.

Chapter 7

1. Tibbitts, "Understanding What We Do."

2. See, for example, Celermajer and Grewal, "Preventing Human Rights Violations."

3. Freire, *Pedagogy of the Oppressed*.

4. Amnesty International, "Human Rights Friendly School Projects." *Available at* http://www.amnesty.org/en/human-rights-education/projects-initiatives/rfsp. Cited in Bajaj, "Human Rights Education."

5. Keet, "It Is Time," and Zembylas, "Toward a Critical-Sentimental Orientation."

6. Personal interviews with human rights educators with the Commonwealth Human Rights Network and the South Asian Human Rights Documentation Center 2012; Celermajer and Grewal, "Preventing Human Rights Violations."

7. For example, see Keohane, "Steven Krasner: Subversive Realist," and Herrmann and Shannon, "Defending International Norms."

8. For example, see Keohane, *After Hegemony*, and Hathaway, "Do Human Rights Treaties Make a Difference?"

9. Checkel, "Why Comply?", Checkel, "Norms, Institutions, and National Identity," and Klotz, "Transnational Activism and Global Transformations."

10. Risse, Ropp, and Sikkink, *The Power of Human Rights*, Keck and Sikkink, *Activists Beyond Borders*.

11. Simmons, *Mobilizing for Human Rights*.

12. Rorty, *Contingency, Irony, and Solidarity*.

13. Keck and Sikkink, *Activists Beyond Borders*.

14. Hawkins, "Explaining Costly International Institutions."

15. See Human Rights Watch, *Broken System*, available at https://www.hrw.org/sites/default/files/reports/india0809web.pdf.

16. Personal interviews with human rights professionals in New Delhi, 2012, and Human Rights Watch, *Broken System*.

17. Schimmelfennig, "Strategic Calculation and International Socialization," Risse, Ropp, and Sikkink, *The Power of Human Rights*.

18. The course in which officers are enrolled discusses classical liberal philosophers such as John Locke and explains social contract theory.

19. Hobbes, *Leviathan*, and Locke, *Two Treatises of Government*.

20. Katzenstein, *The Culture of National Security*.

21. Risse, Ropp, and Sikkink, *The Power of Human Rights*.

22. Simmons, *Mobilizing for Human Rights*.

23. Personal interviews with police reform experts and human rights activists in New Delhi; Asian Centre for Human Rights, *Torture in India*.

24. Dolan, "Unthinkable and Tragic."

25. Checkel, "Norms, Institutions, and National Identity."

26. Celermajer and Saul, "Preventing Torture in Nepal," and Celermajer, *The Prevention of Torture*.

Chapter 8

1. Felman and Laub, *Testimony*, 5.

2. Dwyer and Santikarma, "Posttraumatic Politics," 407.

3. Million, *Therapeutic Nations*, 2.

4. Avruch, "Truth and Reconciliation Commissions," 42.

5. Minow, *Between Vengeance and Forgiveness*, 270.

6. Regulation 2001/10 on the Establishment of a Commission for Reception, Truth and Reconciliation in East Timor, Section 2.2.

7. See Gone, "Redressing First Nations Historical Trauma," 691.

8. Shaw, "Memory Frictions," 184.

9. Coxshall, "From the Peruvian Reconciliation Commission," 213.

10. Gramsci, *Quaderni del carcere*, 2271.

11. Taylor, *The Anatomy of the Nuremberg Trials*, 4–5.

12. Arendt, *Eichmann in Jerusalem*.

13. The media coverage of the Eichmann trial is discussed by Lipstadt, *The Eichmann Trial*, Chapter 4, and Shandler, *While America Watches*.

14. Chakravarti, "More Than 'Cheap Sentimentality,'" 224.

15. Minow, *Between Vengeance and Forgiveness*, 127.

16. Lund, "'Healing the Nation,'" 103.

17. "Priests Stand Up for Victims during Colombia Peace Talks," *Catholic Herald*, June 22, 2016. Accessed April 14, 2017.

18. Young, *The Harmony of Illusions*, 121.

19. Young, *The Harmony of Illusions*, 121.

20. Fassin and Rechtman, *The Empire of Trauma*.

21. Leys, *Trauma*, 16.

22. Marshall and Pienaar, "'You Are Not Alone,'" 525.

23. Yalom and Leszcz, *The Theory and Practice of Group Psychotherapy*, 6.

24. Marshall and Pienaar, "'You Are Not Alone,'" 526.

25. Marshall and Pienaar, "'You Are Not Alone,'" 535.

26. With a team of research assistants, I took part in all seven of the Commission's National Events. I offer a more ethnographically complete discussion of Canada's truth commission in *Truth and Indignation*.

27. Phil Fontaine, the former Grand Chief of the Assembly of First Nations and a participant in the negotiations of the Settlement Agreement, as a representative of the survivors, expressed this view at the Faculty of Law at the University of Toronto, February 9, 2016.

28. See Nwogu, "When and Why It Started," and Robins, "Challenging the Therapeutic Ethic."

29. Truth and Reconciliation Commission, Canada, *Sharing Your Truth*, film screened at the TRC Atlantic National Event, October 27, 2011.

30. Murray Sinclair, "Commissioner's Welcome."

31. Auger, "How to Share Your Truth Information Session."

32. Niezen, *Truth and Indignation*.

33. Truth and Reconciliation Commission of Canada, *What We Have Learned*, 121.

34. Truth and Reconciliation Commission of Canada, *The Survivors Speak*, 24.

35. Truth and Reconciliation Commission of Canada, *The Survivors Speak*, 51.

36. Truth and Reconciliation Commission of Canada, *The Survivors Speak*, 157.

37. Marie-Pierre Gadoua, interview with Lucy Kuptana, Inuvik, October 14, 2011.

38. Lund, "'Healing the Nation,'" 106.

39. Leys, *Trauma*, 12.

40. Sarah Jerome, interview with Marie-Pierre Gadoua, Inuvik, October 14, 2011.

41. Tutu, "Foreword."

42. Wilson, "The Truth and Reconciliation Commission of Canada," 135.

43. Avruch, "Truth and Reconciliation Commissions," 46.

44. Federman, "The 'Ideal Perpetrator.'"

45. Celermajer, *The Prevention of Torture*, 189.

46. Celermajer, *The Prevention of Torture*, 190.

Chapter 9

1. See, for example, Rancière, "Who Is the Subject of the Rights of Man?," Rancière, *Aesthetics and Its Discontents*, Rancière, *Dissensus*, Richard, *Políticas y estéticas de la memoria*, Richard, *Fracturas de la memoria*, Hesford, *Spectacular Rhetorics*, Draper, *Afterlives of Confinement*, and Rosenberg, *After Human Rights*.

2. See, for example, Rajca, "Unraveling Normalized Rhetoric of Violence and Human Rights," Rajca, *Dissensual Subjects*, Rajca, "Urban Imaginaries, Spatial Practices, and Cinematic Aesthetics."

3. See Rancière, *Aesthetics and Its Discontents*, and *Dissensus*.

4. Rancière, *The Emancipated Spectator*, 74.

5. Rancière, *The Emancipated Spectator*, 74.

6. Hesford, *Spectacular Rhetorics*, 22.

7. Richard, *Fracturas de la memoria*, 92.

8. Rancière, *The Emancipated Spectator*, 72.

9. Rancière, *The Emancipated Spectator*, 72.

10. Rolnik, *Guerra dos lugares*, 12. All translations from Portuguese in this essay are my own.

11. Rolnik, *Guerra dos lugares*, 13.

12. Rolnik, *Guerra dos lugares*, 15.

13. Rolnik, *Guerra dos lugares*, 15.

14. See Moyn, *Not Enough*.

15. Rolnik, *Guerra dos lugares*, 16.

16. Pallamin, *Arte, cultura e cidade*, 78.

17. Pallamin, *Arte, cultura e cidade*, 78.

18. Rolnik, *Guerra dos lugares*, 376.

19. Rolnik, *Guerra dos lugares*, 376.

20. Pallamin, *Arte, cultura e cidade*, 73.

21. Pallamin, *Arte, cultura e cidade*, 117.

22. Pallamin, *Arte, cultura e cidade*, 123.

23. Stevens, "Occupied City," 25.

24. Stevens, "Occupied City," 28.

25. Stevens, "Occupied City," 36.

26. Rancière, *The Emancipated Spectator*, 77.

27. Carla Caffé has published a book detailing this experience: *Era o Hotel Cambridge*.

28. Rancière, *The Emancipated Spectator*, 81.

29. Rancière, *The Emancipated Spectator*, 124.

30. Rosenberg, *After Human Rights*, 155.

31. Hesford, *Spectacular Rhetorics*, 156.

32. Caldeira, *City of Walls*, 141–2.

Chapter 10

1. UN General Assembly, Resolution 49/184, United Nations Decade for Human Rights Education (December 23, 1994).

2. UN General Assembly, Resolution 62/171, International Year of Human Rights Learning (December 18, 2007).

3. UN Development Programme and Office of the High Commissioner for Human Rights, *Toolkit for Collaboration with National Human Rights Institutions*, xiv.

4. UN Educational, Scientific and Cultural Organization, 61st Annual DPI/NGO Conference, "Reaffirming Human Rights for All" (September 3–5, 2008).

5. Koenig, "Human Rights As a Way of Life."

6. Hadot, "Philosophy As a Way of Life."

7. Nickel, "Human Rights."

8. Amnesty International, "Who We Are."

9. Ivison, *Rights*, 21.

10. See Davidson and Worms, eds., *Pierre Hadot*, and Chase, Clark, and McGhee, eds., *Philosophy As a Way of Life*.

11. Hadot, *What Is Ancient Philosophy?*, 2.

12. Hadot, *What Is Ancient Philosophy?*, 179–80.

13. Hadot, "Spiritual Exercises," 102.

14. Marcus Aurelius, *The Meditations*, 2.1.

15. See Irvine, *A Guide to the Good Life*, 65–84.

16. Hadot, *What Is Ancient Philosophy?*, 22–38, 146–171.

17. Hadot, *The Inner Citadel*, 243–307.

18. See, for example, Foucault, *The Hermeneutics of the Self*.

19. UN General Assembly, Resolution 217 A (III), Universal Declaration of Human Rights, (December 10, 1948), emphasis added.

20. Glendon, *A World Made New*, 161. She cites Cassin, *La pensée et l'action*, 114.

21. See Hadot, *The Inner Citadel*, 31–33, 50, Foucault, "Self-Writing."

22. Cited in Hadot, "Spiritual Exercises," 84.

23. UN Economic and Social Council, Drafting Committee on an International Bill of Human Rights, 1st Session, 11th Meeting, E/CN.4/AC.1/SR.11 (June 19, 1947).

24. UN Economic and Social Council, Drafting Committee on an International Bill of Human Rights, 1st Session, 2nd Meeting, E/CN.4/AC.1/SR.2 (June 11, 1947).

25. Taylor, *Modern Social Imaginaries*, and Foucault, *The Order of Things*.

26. A fuller account of the authors I discuss below can be found in Lefebvre, *Human Rights and the Care of the Self*, and Lefebvre, *Human Rights As a Way of Life*.

27. Wollstonecraft, *A Vindication of the Rights of Woman*, 87, 105.

28. See Tomaselli, "Introduction," and Botting, *Wollstonecraft, Mill, and Women's Human Rights*.

29. Wollstonecraft, *A Vindication of the Rights of Woman*, 101.

30. Wollstonecraft, *A Vindication of the Rights of Woman*, 76–77.

31. Wollstonecraft, *A Vindication of the Rights of Woman*, 137, 144, 67.

32. Wollstonecraft, *A Vindication of the Rights of Woman*, 143.

33. See Wolin, *Tocqueville Between Two Worlds*, 304–65.

34. See Jaume, *Tocqueville*, 139–72.

35. Tocqueville, *Democracy in America*, 482–84, 511–14, 661–73.

36. Of course, at the time, these universal rights were far from universal. See Keyssar, *The Right to Vote*, 29.

37. Tocqueville, *Democracy in America*, 488.

38. Pascal, *Pensées*, 214.

39. Tocqueville, *Democracy in America*, 486.

40. Tocqueville, *Democracy in America*, 228.

41. See Lefebvre, *Human Rights and the Care of the Self*, 119–40.

42. Morsink, *The Universal Declaration of Human Rights*, 324, 378.

43. Malik, "The Challenge of Human Rights," 158–59.

44. See Lefebvre, *Human Rights and the Care of the Self*, 141–63, Mitoma, "Charles H. Malik and Human Rights," and Glendon, *The Forum and the Tower*, 199–220.

45. Malik, "An International Bill of Rights," 59

46. Foucault, *The Hermeneutics of the Self*, 252.

47. Celermajer, *The Prevention of Torture*, and Wahl, *Just Violence*.

Chapter 11

1. See Grant, *Child Health and Human Rights*.

2. Cowden, *Children's Rights*, 4.

3. Josefsson, "Children at the Borders," 23.

4. Lauren, *The Evolution of International Human Rights*.

5. Moody, "The United Nations Declaration of the Rights of the Child."

6. Van Bueren, *The International Law on the Rights of the Child*.

7. Reynaert and Roose, "Children's Rights and the Capability Approach," 178.

8. Wall, *Ethics in Light of Childhood*, 23.

9. See, for example, Adami, "A Narratable Self."

10. UN General Assembly, Resolution 44/25, Convention on the Rights of the Child, Article 12.

11. See, for example, Hammarberg, "The UN Convention on the Rights of the Child."

12. UN Committee on the Rights of the Child, 1st Session, 22nd meeting, CRC/C/5, para. 13.

13. Quennerstedt, "Children, But Not Really Humans?," 632.

14. Tisdall, "Children and Young People's Participation," 192.

15. A recording of de Cuéllar's speech is available at http://legal.un.org/avl/ha/crc/crc.html#, accessed February 20, 2018.

16. In the 1980s, UNICEF explicitly invoked a rhetoric of children as "zones of peace" in human relations. For more, see Black, *The Children and the Nations*, 375.

17. Cantwell, "The Origins, Development and Significance of the UN Convention on the Rights of the Child," 21.

18. Alston and Parker, "Introduction," vii.

19. See, for example, responses by Denmark and the Netherlands in UN Economic and Social Council, Commission on Human Rights, 35th Session, E/CN.4/1324.

20. For more on NGO involvement, see Longford, "NGOs and the Rights of the Child."

21. Veerman, *The Rights of the Child and the Changing Image of Childhood*, 183.

22. Holzscheiter, *Children's Rights in International Politics*, 160–63.

23. Holzscheiter, *Children's Rights in International Politics*, 168–73.

24. Holzscheiter, *Children's Rights in International Politics*, 174.

25. Korczak's most influential piece on the topic, *The Child's Right to Respect*, was published in Polish in 1929. For an English translation, see Korczak, *When I Am Little Again*.

26. Hammarberg, "Children Have the Right to Be Heard," 82.

27. Freeman, "Introduction," xv.

28. For more on child liberationism, see Cowden, *Children's Rights*, 6–8.

29. Cohen, "The Relevance of Theories of Natural Law and Legal Positivism," 59–60.

30. UN Economic and Social Council, Commission on Human Rights, 43rd Session, E/CN.4/1987/25, para. 12.

31. LeBlanc, *The Convention on the Rights of the Child*, 7–16.

32. UN Economic and Social Council, Commission on Human Rights, 35th Session, E/CN.4/1324, and above all reactions from Denmark, Federal Republic of Germany, the Netherlands, and Sweden.

33. UN Economic and Social Council, Commission on Human Rights, 36th Session, E/CN.4/1349.

34. UN Economic and Social Council, Commission on Human Rights, 36th Session, E/CN.4/1349.

35. For a summary of the discussions during the last round of revisions, see UN Economic and Social Council, Commission on Human Rights, 45th Session, E/CN.4/1989/48, paras. 234–67.

36. Cohen, "The Role of the United States," 191.

37. Cohen, "The Role of the United States," 188.

38. Keys, *Reclaiming American Virtue*, 273.

39. UN Economic and Social Council, Commission on Human Rights, 40th Session, E/CN.4/1984/71.

40. UN Economic and Social Council, Commission on Human Rights, 45th Session, E/CN.4/1989/48, paras. 234–67.

41. Miljeteig-Olsen, "Advocacy of Children's Rights," 149.

42. UN Economic and Social Council, Commission on Human Rights, 35th Session, E/CN.4/1324, jj.

43. Veerman, *The Rights of the Child and the Changing Image of Childhood*, 75–112.

44. The text of the 1924 Geneva Declaration is available at http://www.un-doc uments.net/gdrc1924.htm, accessed February 22, 2018.

45. Sellick, "Responding to Children Affected by Armed Conflict," 38.

46. UN Economic and Social Council, Commission on Human Rights, 43rd Session, 55th meeting, E/CN.4/1987/SR.55.

47. UN General Assembly, Resolution 44/25, Convention on the Rights of the Child, A/RES/44/25, Article 29.

48. UN Economic and Social Council, Commission on Human Rights UN Doc, 37th Session, E/CN.4/L.1575, 75.

49. Van Bueren, *The International Law on the Rights of the Child*, 3.

50. Laufer-Ukeles, "The Relational Rights of Children."

51. Quennerstedt, "Children, But Not Really Humans?," 632.

52. UN Committee on the Rights of the Child, 1st Session, 22nd meeting, CRC/C/5, para. 13.

53. Lücker-Babel, "The Right of the Child to Express Views and to Be Heard," 404.

54. Cornwall and Brock, "What Do Buzzwords Do for Development Policy?," 1046.

55. UN Committee on the Rights of the Child, 51st Session, CRC/C/GC/12, para. 3.

56. Tisdall, "Children and Young People's Participation," 186.

57. Lundy, "'Voice' Is Not Enough."

58. Woodhead, "Foreword," xxi.

59. Hart, *Children's Participation*, 8–14.

60. Malone and Hartung, "Challenges of Participatory Practice with Children," 27–30.

61. Hart, *Children's Participation*, 4.

62. Hart, *Children's Participation*, 5.

63. Hart, *Children's Participation*, 6–7.

64. Lansdown, *Promoting Children's Participation in Democratic Decision-Making*, 2.

65. Lansdown, *Promoting Children's Participation in Democratic Decision-Making*, 2.

66. Lansdown, *Promoting Children's Participation in Democratic Decision-Making*, 8.

67. Lansdown, *Promoting Children's Participation in Democratic Decision-Making*, 8.

68. Lansdown, *Promoting Children's Participation in Democratic Decision-Making*, 7.

69. Lansdown, *Promoting Children's Participation in Democratic Decision-Making*, 7.

70. United Nations Children's Fund, *The State of the World's Children 2003*, 4.

71. UN Committee on the Rights of the Child, Recommendations: Day of General Discussion on the Right of the Child to Be Heard.

72. Stern, "The Child's Right to Participation," 127, and Stern, *Implementing Article 12*, 170.

73. See, for example, Tasioulas, "On the Foundations of Human Rights," 55.

74. Stern, "The Child's Right to Participation," 174, 270–71.

Chapter 12

1. "Memorandum and Questionnaire Circulated by UNESCO on the Theoretical Bases of the Rights of Man," in Goodale, ed., *Letters to the Contrary*, 51. My use of the UNESCO Human Rights Survey is intended to illustrate a particular logic of secularism perceptible within the Universal Declaration of Human Rights, but it is not intended to imply that the First Human Rights Commission made direct use of the survey itself in their work.

2. "The Grounds of an International Declaration of Human Rights," in Goodale, ed., *Letters to the Contrary*, 56–8.

3. "Foreword and Introduction to Human Rights, Comments and Interpretations, UNESCO, 1949," in Goodale, ed., *Letters to the Contrary*, 68.

4. "Memorandum and Questionnaire Circulated by UNESCO on the Theoretical Bases of the Rights of Man," in Goodale, ed., *Letters to the Contrary*, 51.

5. "Foreword and Introduction to Human Rights, Comments and Interpretations, UNESCO, 1949," in Goodale, ed., *Letters to the Contrary*, 68.

6. "Foreword and Introduction to Human Rights, Comments and Interpretations, UNESCO, 1949," in Goodale, ed., *Letters to the Contrary*, 69.

7. "Foreword and Introduction to Human Rights, Comments and Interpretations, UNESCO, 1949," in Goodale, ed., *Letters to the Contrary*, 68.

8. "Foreword and Introduction to Human Rights, Comments and Interpretations, UNESCO, 1949," in Goodale, ed., *Letters to the Contrary*, 69.

9. "Foreword and Introduction to Human Rights, Comments and Interpretations, UNESCO, 1949," in Goodale, ed., *Letters to the Contrary*, 74.

10. With respect to Malik's understanding of secularism (and its discontents), see Lefebvre, *Human Rights and the Care of the Self*, 141–62.

11. "The Grounds of an International Declaration of Human Rights," in Goodale, ed., *Letters to the Contrary*, 55.

12. Taylor, *A Secular Age*, 3.

13. Roosevelt, quoted in Glendon, *A World Made New*, 146.

14. Hernán Santa Cruz, quoted in UN Economic and Social Council, Commission on Human Rights, Drafting Committee, 1st Session, 2nd Meeting, E/CN.4/AC.1/SR.2, 3.

15. "Memorandum and Questionnaire Circulated by UNESCO on the Theoretical Bases of the Rights of Man," in Goodale, ed., *Letters to the Contrary*, 51.

16. Morsink, *The Universal Declaration of Human Rights and the Challenge of Religion*, 6.

17. Morsink, *The Universal Declaration of Human Rights and the Challenge of Religion*, 7.

18. Morsink, *The Universal Declaration of Human Rights and the Challenge of Religion*, 5–6.

19. For a seminal exploration of this logic, see Derrida, "Declarations of Independence."

20. Reinbold, *Seeing the Myth in Human Rights*, 52–3.

21. Glendon, *A World Made New*, 176.

22. Morsink, *The Universal Declaration of Human Rights and the Challenge of Religion*, 7.

23. Morsink, *The Universal Declaration of Human Rights and the Challenge of Religion*, 7.

24. Morsink, *The Universal Declaration of Human Rights and the Challenge of Religion*, 7, and UN General Assembly, Resolution 217 A (III), Universal Declaration of Human Rights, A/RES/3/217 A, Preamble.

25. UN General Assembly, Resolution 217 A (III), Universal Declaration of Human Rights, A/RES/3/217 A, Preamble.

26. Reinbold, *Seeing the Myth in Human Rights*, 56.

27. See Derrida, "Declarations of Independence," 10.

28. Taylor, *A Secular Age*, 4.

29. Roosevelt, "Making Human Rights Come Alive," in Roosevelt, *What I Hope to Leave Behind*, 561.

30. Reinbold, *Seeing the Myth in Human Rights*.

31. Roosevelt, quoted in Glendon, *A World Made New*, 239.

32. UN General Assembly, Resolution 217 A (III), Universal Declaration of Human Rights, A/RES/3/217 A, Preamble and Article One.

33. Taylor, *A Secular Age*, 1.

34. Freeman, "The Problem of Secularism in Human Rights Theory," 376.

35. See Taylor, *A Secular Age*.

36. See Mahmood, "Secularism, Hermeneutics, and Empire," 323–47, Hurd, *Beyond Religious Freedom*, Asad, *Formations of the Secular*, and Sullivan, *The Impossibility of Religious Freedom*.

37. Mahmood, "Secularism, Hermeneutics, and Empire," 326.

38. Mahmood, "Secularism, Hermeneutics, and Empire," 334.

39. Mahmood, "Secularism, Hermeneutics, and Empire," 341.

40. Mahmood, "Secularism, Hermeneutics, and Empire," 341.

41. Hurd, *Beyond Religious Freedom*, 22.

42. Hurd, *Beyond Religious Freedom*, 23.

43. Cheryl Bernard, quoted in Mahmood, "Secularism, Hermeneutics, and Empire," 332.

44. Hurd, *Beyond Religious Freedom*, 2.

45. Maritain, "Introduction," in UN Educational, Scientific, and Cultural Organization, ed., *Human Rights, Comments and Interpretations*, 8.

46. Asad, *Formations of the Secular*, 5.

47. Hurd, *Beyond Religious Freedom*, xvi.

48. "The Grounds of an International Declaration of Human Rights," in Goodale, ed., *Letters to the Contrary*, 54.

49. Mahmood, "Secularism, Hermeneutics, and Empire," 3.

50. See Moyn, *Christian Human Rights*, and Duranti, *The Conservative Human Rights Revolution*.

51. Derrida, quoted in Reinbold, *Seeing the Myth in Human Rights*, 123.

52. Reinbold, *Seeing the Myth in Human Rights*, 123.

Chapter 13

1. Moyn, *The Last Utopia*, 8.

2. See Moyn, "Freud's Discontents," and "The Assumption by Man of His Original Fracturing."

3. See *Not Enough*, 256n3.

4. Lefebvre, *Human Rights and the Care of the Self*, 119–63.

5. Eckel, "The Rebirth of Politics from the Spirit of Morality."

6. Cited in *The Last Utopia*, 130.

7. Moyn, *Christian Human Rights*, 176.

8. Hopgood, *Keepers of the Flame*.

9. Hadot, "Spiritual Exercises."

10. See Mayer, *The Persistence of the Old Regime*.

11. Duranti, *The Conservative Human Rights Revolution*.

12. Mazower, *Dark Continent*, 212–49.

13. Orbán, "Prime Minister Viktor Orbán's Speech at the Ceremonial Swearing-in of New Border Guards."

14. Moyn, "How the Human Rights Movement Failed."

15. See Halfin, *Red Autobiographies*, and Hellbeck, *Revolution on My Mind*.

16. Lefebvre, *Human Rights and the Care of the Self*, 9–24.

17. See Gauchet, *L'avènement de la démocratie*.

18. See Michels, *Political Parties*.

19. Mishra, "The Mask It Wears."

20. Alston, "Statement on Visit to the USA."

21. Goodale, "What Are Human Rights Good For?"

22. Celermajer, *The Prevention of Torture*, Bajaj, *Schooling for Social Change*, and Tibbitts, "Evolution of Human Rights Education Models."

23. See Moyn and Sartori, eds., *Global Intellectual History*.

24. Burke, "Premature Memorials to the United Nations Human Rights Program."

25. Griffin, *On Human Rights*, Tasioulas, "Towards a Philosophy of Human Rights."

26. Horace, *Epistles*, I. X. 24.

Bibliography

Abu-Lughod, Lila. *Do Muslim Women Need Saving?* Cambridge: Harvard University Press, 2013.

Adami, Rebecca. "A Narratable Self as Addressed by Human Rights." *Policy Futures in Education* 15, no. 3 (2017): 252–61.

African Charter on Human and Peoples' Rights. *African Charter of Human and Peoples' Rights.* Nairobi, 1981. http://www.achpr.org/legalinstruments/detail?id=49.

Alfred, Taiaiake, and Jeff Corntassel. "Being Indigenous: Resurgences against Contemporary Colonialism." *Government and Opposition* 40, no. 4 (2005): 597–614.

Allport, Gordon W. *The Nature of Prejudice.* Reading: Addison-Wesley Publishing Company, 1954.

Alston, Philip. "Statement on Visit to the USA, by Professor Philip Alston, United Nations Special Rapporteur on Extreme Poverty and Human Rights." December 15, 2017, Office of the High Commissioner for Human Rights, https://www.ohchr.org/EN/NewsEvents/Pages/DisplayNews.aspx?NewsID=22533.

Alston, Philip, and Stephen Parker. "Introduction." In *Children, Rights, and the Law,* edited by Philip Alston, Stephen Parker, and John Seymour, vi–xiv. Oxford: Clarendon Press, 1992.

Amin-Khan, Tariq. "New Orientalism, Securitisation and the Western Media's Incendiary Racism." *Third World Quarterly* 33, no. 9 (2012): 1595–1610.

Amnesty International. "Human Rights Friendly School Projects." Accessed February 1, 2019. https://www.amnesty.org/en/human-rights-education/human-rights-friendly-schools/.

———. "Who We Are." Accessed April 5, 2018. https://www.amnesty.org/en/who-we-are/.

An Earnest Englishwoman. "[Letter to the Editor] Are Women Animals?" *The Times,* April 16, 1872.

Anaya, S. James. *Indigenous Peoples in International Law.* Oxford: Oxford University Press, 1996.

Anghie, Antony. *Imperialism, Sovereignty and the Making of International Law.* Cambridge: Cambridge University Press, 2005.

Anghie, Antony, Bhupinder Chimni, Karin Mickelson, and Obiora Okafor, eds. *The Third World and International Order: Law, Politics and Globalization.* Leiden: Brill-Nijhoff, 2003.

"Women and Vivisection." *The Animals' Guardian,* December 1911.

"Suffragettes and Animals' Rights." *The Animals' Guardian,* January 1912.

"Suffragettes – Furs – Murderous Millinery – Vivisection." *The Animals' Guardian,* February 1912.

Arendt, Hannah. *Eichmann in Jerusalem: A Report on the Banality of Evil.* New York: Penguin, 2006.

Argyris, Chris, and Donald A. Schon. *Theory in Practice: Increasing Professional Effectiveness.* San Francisco: Jossey-Bass, 1974.

Armitage, David. "John Locke, Carolina, and the 'Two Treatises of Government.'" *Political Theory* 32, no. 5 (2004): 602–27.

Asad, Talal. *Formations of the Secular: Christianity, Islam, Modernity.* Stanford: Stanford University Press, 2003.

Asian Centre for Human Rights. *Torture in India 2011.* New Delhi: Asian Centre for Human Rights, 2011.

Auchter, Jessica. "Gendering Terror." *International Feminist Journal of Politics* 14, no. 1 (2012): 121–39.

Auger, Darlene. "How to Share Your Truth Information Session." TRC Atlantic National Event, Halifax, October 27, 2011.

Avruch, Kevin. "Truth and Reconciliation Commissions: Problems in Transitional Justice and the Reconstruction of Identity." *Transcultural Psychiatry* 47, no. 1 (2010): 33–49.

Bajaj, Monisha. "Human Rights Education: Ideology, Location, and Approaches." *Human Rights Quarterly* 33, no. 2 (2011): 481–508.

———. *Schooling for Social Change: The Rise and Impact of Human Rights Education in India.* London: Bloomsbury, 2012.

Bajaj, Monisha, and Nancy Flowers. *Human Rights Education: Theory, Research, Praxis.* Philadelphia: University of Pennsylvania Press, 2017.Bauer, Joanne R., and Daniel A. Bell, eds. *The East Asian Challenge for Human Rights.* Cambridge: Cambridge University Press, 1999.

Bentham, Jeremy. "Anarchical Fallacies." In *Nonsense upon Stilts: Bentham, Burke, and Marx on the Rights of Man,* edited by Jeremy Waldron, 46–76. London: Routledge, 2014.

———. *An Introduction to the Principles of Morals and Legislation.* Edited by J. H. Burns and H. L. A. Hart. Oxford: Clarendon Press, 1970.

Besson, Samantha. "International Human Rights Law and Mirrors: A Tribute to Allen Buchanan." *ESIL Reflections* 7, no. 2 (2018): 1–11.

Bieling, Peter J., Randi E. McCabe, and Martin M. Antony. *Cognitive-Behavioral Therapy in Groups.* New York: Guilford Press, 2006.

Black, Maggie. *The Children and the Nations: The Story of UNICEF.* New York: UNICEF, 1986.

Borrows, John. "Living Law on a Living Earth: Aboriginal Religion, Law, and the Constitution." In *Law and Religious Pluralism in Canada*, edited by Richard Moon, 161–91. Toronto: UBC Press, 2008.

Botting, Eileen Hunt. *Wollstonecraft, Mill, and Women's Human Rights.* New Haven: Yale University Press, 2016.

Bourke, Joanna. *What It Means to Be Human: Reflections from 1791 to the Present.* London: Virago, 2011.

Bowring, Bill. "Minority Rights in Post-War Iraq: An Impending Catastrophe." *International Journal of Contemporary Iraqi Studies* 5, no. 3 (2011): 319–36.

Bradley, Mark Philip, and Patrice Petro, eds. *Truth Claims: Representation and Human Rights.* New Brunswick, NJ: Rutgers University Press, 2002.

Braidotti, Rosi. *Transpositions: On Nomadic Ethics.* Cambridge: Polity Press, 2006.

Brown, Wendy. "'The Most We Can Hope For...': Human Rights and the Politics of Fatalism." *The South Atlantic Quarterly* 103, nos. 2–3 (2004): 451–63.

Bryant, Taimie L. "Sacrificing the Sacrifice of Animals: Legal Personhood for Animals, the Status of Animals as Property, and the Presumed Primacy of Humans." *Rutgers Law Journal* 39, no. 2 (2008): 247–330.

Buffon, Veronica, and Christine Allison. "The Gendering of Victimhood: Western Media and the Sinjar Genocide." *Kurdish Studies* 4, no. 2 (2016): 176–95.

Bullock, Karen, and Paul Johnson. "The Impact of the Human Rights Act 1998 on Policing in England and Wales." *British Journal of Criminology* 52, no. 3 (2011): 630–50.

Bunch, Charlotte. "Transforming Human Rights from a Feminist Perspective." In *Women's Rights, Human Rights: International Feminist Perspectives*, edited by Julie Peters and Andrea Wolper, 11–17. New York: Routledge, 1995.

Burke, Roland. "Premature Memorials to the United Nations Human Rights Program: International Postage Stamps and the Commemoration of the 1948 Universal Declaration of Human Rights." *History & Memory* 28, no. 2 (2016): 152–81.

Butler, Judith. *Frames of War: When Is Life Grievable?* New York: Verso, 2010.

———. *Gender Trouble: Feminism and the Subversion of Identity.* New York: Routledge, 1990.

———. *Precarious Life: The Powers of Mourning and Violence.* New York: Verso, 2006.

———. "Precarious Life, Vulnerability, and the Ethics of Cohabitation." *Journal of Speculative Philosophy* 26, no. 2 (2012): 134–51.

———. *The Psychic Life of Power.* Stanford: Stanford University Press, 1997.

Byrnes, Andrew. "The Convention Against Torture." In *Women and International Human Rights Law*, edited by Kelly Dawn Askin and Dorean M. Koenig, 183–208. Ardsley: Transnational Publishers, 2000.

Cadena, Marisol de la. *Earth Beings: Ecologies of Practice Across Andean Worlds.* Durham: Duke University Press, 2015.

Caffé, Carla. *Era o Hotel Cambridge: Arquitetura, Cinema e Educação.* São Paulo: Edições Sesc, 2017.

Caldeira, Teresa Pires do Rio. *City of Walls: Crime, Segregation, and Citizenship in São Paulo*. Berkeley: University of California Press, 2000.

Callimachi, Rukmini. "ISIS Enshrines a Theology of Rape." *New York Times*, August 14, 2015. https://www.nytimes.com/2015/08/14/world/middleeast/isis-enshrines -a-theology-of-rape.html.

Cantwell, Nigel. "The Origins, Development and Significance of the UN Convention on the Rights of the Child." In *The UN Convention on the Rights of the Child: A Guide to the "Travaux Préparatoires,"* edited by Sharon Detrick, 19–30. Dordrecht: Martinus Nijhoff Publishers, 1992.

Carpenter, Kristen A., and Angela Riley. "Indigenous Peoples and the Jurisgenerative Moment in Human Rights." *California Law Review* 102, no. 1 (2014): 173–234.

Cassin, René. *La pensée et l'action*. Boulogne-sur-Seine: F. Lalou, 1972.

"Priests Stand Up for Victims during Colombia Peace Talks." *Catholic Herald*, June 22, 2016. http://www.catholicherald.co.uk/news/2016/06/22/priests-stand-up-for-vic tims-during-colombia-peace-talks.

Cavalieri, Paola. *The Animal Question: Why Nonhuman Animals Deserve Human Rights*. Translated by Catherine Woollard. Oxford: Oxford University Press, 2001.

Cavalieri, Paola, and Peter Singer. "A Declaration on Great Apes." In *The Great Ape Project: Equality Beyond Humanity*, edited by Paola Cavalieri and Peter Singer, 4–6. London: Fourth Estate, 1993.

Cavendish, Margaret. *Observations upon Experimental Philosophy*. Edited by Eileen O'Neill. Cambridge: Cambridge University Press, 2001.

Celermajer, Danielle. *International Review: Current Approaches to Human Rights Training in the Law Enforcement and Security Sectors*. Sydney: University of Sydney, 2015.

———. *Issues Paper 2: Exploring the Root Causes of Torture*. Sydney: University of Sydney, 2015.

———. *The Prevention of Torture: An Ecological Approach*. Cambridge: Cambridge University Press, 2018.

———. *Project Overview: Enhancing Human Rights Protections in the Security Sector in the Asia Pacific Project*. Sydney: University of Sydney, 2015.

Celermajer, Danielle, and Kiran Grewal. "Preventing Human Rights Violations 'from the Inside': Enhancing the Role of Human Rights Education in Security Sector Reform." *Journal of Human Rights Practice* 5, no. 2 (2013): 243–66.

Celermajer, Danielle, and Jack Saul. "Preventing Torture in Nepal: A Public Health and Human Rights Intervention." *Journal of Bioethical Inquiry* 13, no. 2 (2016): 223–37.

Chakravarti, Sonali. "More Than 'Cheap Sentimentality': Victim Testimony at Nuremberg, the Eichmann Trial and Truth Commissions." *Constellations* 15, no. 2 (2008): 223–35.

Chapman, Michael W. "ISIS Genocide of Yazidis: 'Girls As Young As 9 Were Raped, As Were Pregnant Women.'" *CNS News*, October 7, 2016. https://www.cnsnews .com/news/article/michael-w-chapman/isis-genocide-yazidis-girls-young-9 -were-raped-were-pregnant-women.

————. "Yazidi Children Screamed and Cried Outside the Door While ISIS Fighters Raped Their Mothers." *CNS News*, October 21, 2016. https://www.cnsnews.com
/news/article/michael-w-chapman/yazidi-children-screamed-and-cried-outside
-door-while-isis-fighters.

Charland, Maurice. "Constitutive Rhetoric: The Case of the Peuple Quebecois." *Quarterly Journal of Speech* 73, no. 2 (1987): 133–50.

Charlesworth, Hilary. "Human Rights As Men's Rights." In *Women's Rights, Human
Rights: International Feminist Perspectives*, edited by Julie Peters and Andrea Wolper, 103–13. New York: Routledge, 1995.

Charlesworth, Hilary, Christine Chinkin, and Shelley Wright. "Feminist Approaches
to International Law." *The American Journal of International Law* 85, no. 4 (1991):
613–45.

Chase, Michael, Stephen R. L. Clark, and Michael McGhee. *Philosophy As a Way of
Life: Ancients and Moderns – Essays in Honor of Pierre Hadot*. Malden: Wiley-
Blackwell, 2013.

Checkel, Jeffrey T. "Norms, Institutions, and National Identity in Contemporary Europe." *International Studies Quarterly* 43, no. 1 (1999): 83–114.

————. "Why Comply? Social Learning and European Identity Change." *International Organization* 55, no. 3 (2001): 553–88.

Chimni, Bhupinder S. "The Past, Present and Future of International Law: A Critical
Third World Approach." *Melbourne Journal of International Law* 8, no. 2 (2007):
499–515.

Chouliaraki, Lilie. *The Spectatorship of Suffering*. London: Sage Publications, 2006.

Clark, Emily. "'The Animal' and 'The Feminist.'" *Hypatia* 27, no. 3 (2012): 516–20.

Cobo, José Martínez. *Study of the Problem of Discrimination Against Indigenous Populations: Final Report Submitted by the Special Rapporteur, Mr. José Martínez
Cobo*. New York: United Nations, 1987.

Cohen, Cynthia Price. "The Relevance of Theories of Natural Law and Legal Positivism." In *The Ideologies of Children's Rights*, edited by Michael Freeman and Philip
Veerman, 53–70. Dordrect: Martinus Nijhoff Publishers, 1992.

————. "The Role of the United States in the Drafting of the Convention on the Rights
of the Child." *Emory International Law Review* 20, no. 1 (2006): 185–98.

Cohen, Stanley. *States of Denial: Knowing About Atrocities and Suffering*. Cambridge:
Polity Press, 2013.

Commonwealth Secretariat. *Commonwealth Manual on Human Rights Training for
Police*. London: Commonwealth Secretariat, 2006.

Cornwall, Andrea, and Karen Brock. "What Do Buzzwords Do for Development Policy? A Critical Look at 'Participation,' 'Empowerment' and 'Poverty Reduction.'"
Third World Quarterly 26, no. 7 (2005): 1043–60.

Coulthard, Glen. "The Dene Nation, Land Claims and the Politics of Recognition in
the North." In *Recognition Versus Self-Determination: Dilemmas of Emancipatory
Politics*, edited by Avigail Eisenberg, Jeremy Webber, Glen Coulthard, and Andrée
Boisselle, 147–73. Toronto: UBC Press, 2015.

————. "From Wards of the State to Subjects of Recognition? Marx, Indigenous Peoples, and the Politics of Dispossession in Denendeh." In *Theorizing Native Studies*, edited by Audra Simpson and Andrea Smith, 56–98. Durham: Duke University Press, 2014.

Cowan, Jane K., Marie-Bénédicte Dembour, and Richard A. Wilson, eds. *Culture and Rights: Anthropological Perspectives*. Cambridge: Cambridge University Press, 2001.

Cowden, Mhairi. *Children's Rights: From Philosophy to Public Policy*. New York: Palgrave Macmillan, 2016.

Coxshall, Wendy. "From the Peruvian Reconciliation Commission to Ethnography: Narratives, Relatedness, and Silence." *PoLAR: Political and Legal Anthropology Review* 28, no. 2 (2005), 203–23.

Crelinsten, Ronald D. "The World of Torture: A Constructed Reality." *Theoretical Criminology* 7, no. 3 (2003): 293–318.

Cruft, Rowan S., Matthew Liao, and Massimo Renzo, eds. *Philosophical Foundations of Human Rights*. Oxford: Oxford University Press, 2015.

de Cuéllar, Javier Pérez. "Statement by Secretary-General Mr. Javier Pérez de Cuéllar Emphasizing the Importance of Making the Rights of the Child a Reality for All Children in All Parts of the World." New York, November 20, 1989. http://legal.un.org/avl/ha/crc/crc.html.

Davidson, Arnold I., and Frédéric Worms, eds. *Pierre Hadot: L'enseignement des antiques, l'enseignement des modernes*. Paris: Éditions Rue d'Ulm, 2010.

Davis, Sara L. M., and Charmain Mohamed. "Global Rights, Local Risk: Community Advocacy on Right to Health in China." In *Human Rights Transformation in Practice*, edited by Tine Destrooper and Sally Engle Merry, 229–50. Philadelphia: University of Pennsylvania Press, 2018.

Davy, Laura. "Philosophical Inclusive Design: Intellectual Disability and the Limits of Individual Autonomy in Moral and Political Theory." *Hypatia* 30, no. 1 (2014): 132–48.

De Cyon, E. "The Anti-Vivisectionist Agitation." *The Contemporary Review* 43 (1883): 498–510.

Deloria, Philip J. *Indians in Unexpected Places*. Lawrence: University Press of Kansas, 2004.

Deloria, Vine Jr., and Clifford M. Lytle. *American Indians, American Justice*. Austin: University of Texas Press, 1983.

Dembour, Marie-Bénédicte. "What Are Human Rights? Four Schools of Thought." *Human Rights Quarterly* 32, no. 1 (2010): 1–20.

Derrida, Jacques. "The Animal That Therefore I Am (More to Follow)." Translated by David Wills. *Critical Inquiry* 28, no. 2 (2002): 369–418.

———. *The Animal That Therefore I Am*. Edited by Marie-Louis Mallet. Translated by David Wills. New York: Fordham University Press, 2008.

———. "Declarations of Independence." *New Political Science* 7, no. 1 (1986): 7–15.

———. "'Eating Well,' or the Calculation of the Subject: An Interview with Jacques Derrida." In *Who Comes After the Subject?*, edited by Eduardo Cadava, Peter Connor, and Jean-Luc Nancy, 96–119. New York: Routledge, 1991.

———. "On Reading Heidegger: An Outline of Remarks to the Essex Colloquium." *Research in Phenomenology* 17 (1987): 171–88.

———. "Violence Against Animals." In Jacques Derrida and Elisabeth Roudinesco, *For What Tomorrow . . .: A Dialogue*, 62–67. Translated by Jeff Fort. Stanford: Stanford University Press, 2004.

Descartes, René. *Discourse on Method and Other Writings*. Translated by F. E. Sutcliffe. London: Penguin, 1968.

Descola, Philippe. *Par-delà nature et culture*. Paris: Gallimard, 2005.

Diamond, Cora. "Injustice and Animals." In *Slow Cures and Bad Philosophers: Essays on Wittgenstein, Medicine, and Bioethics*, edited by Carl Elliott, 118–48. Durham: Duke University Press, 2001.

Dodson, Michael. "The End in the Beginning: Re(de)finding Aboriginality." In *Blacklines: Contemporary Critical Writing by Indigenous Australians*, edited by Michele Grossman, 25–42. Melbourne: Melbourne University Press, 2003.

———. "Land Rights and Social Justice." In *Our Land Is Our Life: Land Rights—Past, Present and Future*, edited by Galarrwuy Yunupingu, 39–51. Santa Lucia: University of Queensland Press, 1997.

Dolan, Thomas M. "Unthinkable and Tragic: The Psychology of Weapons Taboos in War." *International Organization* 67, no. 1 (2013): 37–63.

Donovan, Josephine. "Feminism and the Treatment of Animals: From Care to Dialogue." *Signs* 31, no. 2 (2006): 305–29.

Donovan, Robert J., and Rodney Vlais. *VicHealth Review of Communication Components of Social Marketing/Public Education Campaigns Focusing on Violence Against Women*. Melbourne: Victorian Health Promotion Foundation, 2005.

Douzinas, Costas. *The End of Human Rights*. London: Bloomsbury, 2000.

———. *Human Rights and Empire*. London: Routledge, 2007.

———. *The Radical Philosophy of Rights*. London: Routledge, 2019.

Douzinas, Costas, and Conor Gearty. *The Meanings of Rights: The Philosophy and Social Theory of Human Rights*. Cambridge: Cambridge University Press, 2014.

Draper, Susana. *Afterlives of Confinement: Spatial Transitions in Postdictatorship Latin America*. Pittsburgh: University of Pittsburgh Press, 2015.

Dunkerley, James. "Evo Morales, the 'Two Bolivias' and the Third Bolivian Revolution." *Journal of Latin American Studies* 39, no. 1 (2007): 133–66.

Duranti, Marco. *The Conservative Human Rights Revolution: European Identity, Transnational Politics, and the Origins of the European Convention*. Oxford: Oxford University Press, 2017.

Dwyer, Leslie, and Degung Santikarma. "Posttraumatic Politics: Violence, Memory, and Biomedical Discourse in Bali." In *Understanding Trauma: Integrating Biological, Clinical, and Cultural Perspectives*, edited by Laurence J. Kirmayer, Robert Lemelson, and Mark Barad, 403–22. Cambridge: Cambridge University Press, 2007.

Eberhard, Christoph. "Au-delà de l'universalisme et du relativisme: L'horizon d'un pluralisme responsable." *Anthropologie et Sociétés* 33, no. 3 (2009): 79–100.

Eckel, Jan. "The Rebirth of Politics from the Spirit of Morality: Explaining the Human

Rights Revolution of the 1970s." In *The Breakthrough: Human Rights in the 1970s*, edited by Jan Eckel and Samuel Moyn, 226–60. Philadelphia: University of Pennsylvania Press, 2013.

Escobar, Arturo. *Encountering Development: The Making and Unmaking of the Third World*. Princeton: Princeton University Press, 1995.

———. "Latin America at a Crossroads: Alternative Modernizations, Post-Liberalism, or Post-Development?" *Cultural Studies* 24, no. 1 (2010): 1–65.

Etinson, Adam, ed. *Human Rights: Moral or Political?* Oxford: Oxford University Press, 2018.

European Union. *European Convention for the Protection of Human Rights and Fundamental Freedoms*. Rome, 1950. https://www.echr.coe.int/Documents/Convention_ENG.pdf.

European Union. *Treaty on European Union*. Maastricht, 1992. https://eur-lex.europa.eu/legal-content/EN/TXT/?uri=celex%3A12012M%2FTXT.

Evans-Campbell, Teresa. "Historical Trauma in American Indian/Native Alaska Communities: A Multilevel Framework for Exploring Impacts on Individuals, Families, and Communities." *Journal of Interpersonal Violence* 23, no. 3 (2008): 316–38.

Exec. Order No. 13,769, 82 Fed. Reg. 8977. January 27, 2017. Protecting the Nation from Foreign Terrorist Entry into the United States.

Falcon, Sylvanna, M. *Power Interrupted: Antiracist and Feminist Activism Inside the United Nations*. Seattle: University of Washington Press, 2016.

Fassin, Didier, and Richard Rechtman. *The Empire of Trauma: An Inquiry into the Condition of Victimhood*. Princeton: Princeton University Press, 2009.

Federman, Sarah. "The 'Ideal Perpetrator': The French National Railways and the Social Construction of Accountability." *Security Dialogue* 49, no. 5 (2018): 327–44.

Felman, Shoshana, and Dori Laub. *Testimony: Crises of Witnessing in Literature, Psychoanalysis, and History*. New York: Routledge, 1991.

Felski, Rita. *The Limits of Critique*. Chicago: University of Chicago Press, 2015.

Fineman, Martha Albertson. "Cracking the Foundational Myths: Independence, Autonomy, and Self-Sufficiency." *Journal of Gender, Social Policy and the Law* 8, no. 1 (2000): 13–29.

———. "The Vulnerable Subject and the Responsive State." *Emory Law Review* 60, no. 2 (2010): 251–75.

Fishbein, Martin, and Icek Ajzen. *Belief, Attitude, Intention, and Behavior: An Introduction to Theory and Research*. Reading: Addison-Wesley Publishing Company, 1975.

Flanagan, Thomas, André Le Dressay, and Christopher Alcantara. *Beyond the Indian Act: Restoring Aboriginal Property Rights*. Montreal: McGill–Queen's University Press, 2010.

Focus on the Family. "Life Challenges." Accessed February 1, 2019. https://www.focusonthefamily.com/lifechallenges.

Foster, Johanna E., and Sherizaan Minwalla. "Voices of Yazidi Women: Perceptions of Journalistic Practices in the Reporting on ISIS Sexual Violence." *Women's Studies International Forum* 67 (2018): 53–64.

Foucault, Michel. *About the Beginning of the Hermeneutics of the Self: Lectures at Dartmouth College, 1980*. Translated by Graham Burchell. Chicago: University of Chicago Press, 2015.

———. *Discipline and Punish: The Birth of the Prison*. Translated by Alan Sheridan. New York: Vintage, 1995.

———. *The Hermeneutics of the Subject: Lectures at the Collège de France, 1981–1982*. Translated by Graham Burchell. New York: Palgrave Macmillan, 2005.

———. *The History of Sexuality, Volume 1: An Introduction*. Translated by Robert Hurley. New York: Vintage, 1990.

———. *The Order of Things: An Archaeology of the Human Sciences*. New York: Pantheon Books, 1971.

———. "Self-Writing." In *Ethics: Subjectivity and Truth*, edited by Paul Rabinow, 207–22. New York: New Press, 1997.

Forst, Rainer. *The Right to Justification: Elements of a Constructivist Theory of Justice*. Translated by Jeffrey Flynn. New York: Columbia University Press, 2014.

"ISIS Tightens Grip on Yazidi Captives Held As Sex Slaves." *Fox News World*, July 6, 2017. http://www.foxnews.com/world/2016/07/06/isis-tightens-grip-on-yazidi-captives-held-as-sex-slaves.html.

Freeman, Michael. "Introduction." In *Children's Rights: Volume I*, edited by Michael Freeman, xi–xlii. Aldershot: Ashgate, 2004.

———. "The Problem of Secularism in Human Rights Theory." *Human Rights Quarterly* 26, no. 2 (2004): 375–400.

Freire, Paulo. *Pedagogy of the Oppressed*. New York: Continuum, 2000.

Gareau, Brian J. "We Have Never Been Human: Agential Nature, ANT, and Marxist Political Ecology." *Capitalism, Nature, Socialism* 16, no. 4 (2005): 128–40.

Gauchet, Marcel. *L'avènement de la démocratie*. 4 Volumes. Paris: Gallimard, 2010.

Gearty, Conor, and Costas Douzinas. *The Cambridge Companion to Human Rights Law*. Cambridge: Cambridge University Press, 2012.

George, Susannah. "Yazidi Society Changes to Try and Rescue a Generation of Traumatized Women." PRI's *The World*. May 18, 2015. https://www.pri.org/stories/2015-05-18/yazidi-society-changes-try-and-rescue-generation-traumatized-women.

———. "Yazidi Women Welcomed Back to the Faith." *UNHCR USA News*, June 15, 2015. http://www.unhcr.org/en-us/news/stories/2015/6/56ec1e9611/yazidi-women-welcomed-back-to-the-faith.html.

Glendon, Mary Ann. *The Forum and the Tower: How Scholars and Politicians Have Imagined the World, from Plato to Eleanor Roosevelt*. Oxford: Oxford University Press, 2011.

———. *A World Made New: Eleanor Roosevelt and the Universal Declaration of Human Rights*. New York: Random House, 2001.

Golder, Ben. *Foucault and the Politics of Rights*. Stanford: Stanford University Press, 2015.

Golder, Ben, and Daniel McLoughlin, eds. *The Politics of Legality in a Neoliberal Age*. New York: Routledge, 2018.

Gone, Joseph P. "Redressing First Nations Historical Trauma: Theorizing Mechanisms for Indigenous Culture as Mental Health Treatment." *Transcultural Psychiatry* 50, no. 5 (2013): 683–706.

Goodale, Mark. *Dilemmas of Modernity: Bolivian Encounters with Law and Liberalism*. Stanford: Stanford University Press, 2008.

———. "Human Values and Moral Exclusion." *Ethics & Global Politics* 9, no. 1 (2016): 1–13.

———, ed. *Letters to the Contrary: A Curated History of the UNESCO Human Rights Survey*. Stanford: Stanford University Press, 2018.

———. "The Myth of Universality: The UNESCO 'Philosophers' Committee' and the Making of Human Rights." *Law & Social Inquiry* 43, no. 3 (2018): 596–617.

———. *A Revolution in Fragments: Traversing Scales of Justice, Ideology, and Practice in Bolivia*. Durham: Duke University Press, 2019.

———. *Surrendering to Utopia: An Anthropology of Human Rights*. Stanford: Stanford University Press, 2009.

———. "Toward a Critical Anthropology of Human Rights." *Current Anthropology* 47, no. 3 (2006): 485–511.

———. "What Are Human Rights Good For?" *Boston Review*, July 19, 2018. http://bostonreview.net/global-justice/mark-goodale-what-are-human-rights-good.

Goodale, Mark, and Sally Engle Merry. *The Practice of Human Rights: Tracking Law Between the Global and the Local*. Cambridge: Cambridge University Press, 2007.

Government of Canada. *Indian Residential Schools Settlement Agreement, Schedule "N," Mandate for the Truth and Reconciliation Commission*. Ottawa: Government of Canada, 2007. http://www.residentialschoolsettlement.ca/SCHEDULE_N.pdf.

Gramsci, Antonio. *Quaderni del carcere*. Edited by Valentino Gerratana. 4 Volumes. Torino: Giulio Einaudi, 1975.

Grant, Jim. *Child Health and Human Rights*. Washington DC: National Academy Press, 1994.

Green, Joyce. "Decolonization and Recolonization." In *Changing Canada: Political Economy as Transformation*, edited by Wallace Clement and Leah Vosko, 51–78. Montreal: McGill–Queen's University Press, 2003.

Griffin, James. *On Human Rights*. Oxford: Oxford University Press, 2008.

Hadot, Pierre. *The Inner Citadel: The Meditations of Marcus Aurelius*. Translated by Michael Chase. Cambridge: Harvard University Press, 1998.

———. "Philosophy as a Way of Life." In Pierre Hadot, *Philosophy As a Way of Life*, 264–76. Oxford: Blackwell, 1995.

———. "Spiritual Exercises." In Pierre Hadot, *Philosophy As a Way of Life*, 81–125. Oxford: Blackwell, 1995.

———. *What Is Ancient Philosophy?* Translated by Michael Chase. Cambridge: Harvard University Press, 2002.

Halfin, Igal. *Red Autobiographies: Initiating the Bolshevik Self.* Seattle: University of Washington Press, 2011.

Hammarberg, Thomas. "Children Have the Right to Be Heard and Adults Should Listen to Their Views." In *Janusz Korczak: The Child's Right to Respect*, edited by the Office of the Commissioner for Human Rights, 81–90. Strasbourg: Council of Europe Publishing, 2009.

———. "The UN Convention on the Rights of the Child—And How to Make It Work." *Human Rights Quarterly* 12, no. 1 (1990): 97–105.

Haraway, Donna J. "A Cyborg Manifesto: Science, Technology, and Socialist-Feminism in the Late Twentieth Century." In Donna J. Haraway, *Simians, Cyborgs and Women: The Reinvention of Nature*, 149–82. New York: Routledge, 1991.

———. *The Haraway Reader.* New York: Routledge, 2004.

———. *When Species Meet.* Minneapolis: University of Minnesota Press, 2008.

Hardt, Michael, and Antonio Negri. *Empire.* Cambridge: Harvard University Press, 2000.

Hart, Roger A. *Children's Participation: From Tokenism to Citizenship.* Florence: UNICEF, 1992.

Hathaway, Oona A. "Do Human Rights Treaties Make a Difference?" *Yale Law Journal* 111, no. 8 (2002): 1935–2042.

Hawkins, Darren. "Explaining Costly International Institutions: Persuasion and Enforceable Human Rights Norms." *International Studies Quarterly* 48, no. 4 (2004): 779–804.

Hawkins, Stephanie L. *American Iconographic: National Geographic, Global Culture, and the Visual Imagination.* Charlottesville: University of Virginia Press, 2010.

Hellbeck, Jochen. *Revolution on My Mind: Writing a Diary Under Stalin.* Cambridge: Harvard University Press, 2006.

Hendry, Jennifer, and Melissa L. Tatum. "Human Rights, Indigenous Peoples, and the Pursuit of Justice." *Yale Law & Policy Review* 34, no. 2 (2016): 351–86.

Henry, Ella, and Hone Pene. "*Kaupapa Maori*: Locating Indigenous Ontology, Epistemology and Methodology in the Academy." *Organization* 8, no. 2 (2001): 234–42.

Herbert, Laura. "The Sexual Politics of U.S. Inter/National Security." In *From Human Trafficking to Human Rights: Reframing Contemporary Slavery*, edited by Alison Brysk and Austin Choi-Fitzpatrick, 86–106. Philadelphia: University of Pennsylvania Press, 2018.

Herrmann, Richard K., and Vaughn P. Shannon. "Defending International Norms: The Role of Obligation, Material Interest, and Perception in Decision Making." *International Organization* 55, no. 3 (2001): 621–54.

Hesford, Wendy S. *Spectacular Rhetorics: Human Rights Visions, Recognitions, Feminisms.* Durham: Duke University Press, 2011.

———. "Trafficking American Exceptionality." *Women's Studies in Communication,* forthcoming.

Hesford, Wendy S., Adela C. Licona, and Christa Teston, eds. *Precarious Rhetorics.* Columbus: The Ohio State University Press, 2018.

Hesford, Wendy S., and Amy Shuman. "Precarious Narratives: Media Accounts of Islamic State Sexual Violence." In *Precarious Rhetorics*, edited by Wendy S. Hesford, Adela C. Licona, and Christa Teston, 41–61. Columbus: The Ohio State University Press, 2018.

Hobbes, Thomas. *Leviathan.* Edited by Edwin Curley. Indianapolis: Hackett, 1994.

Holmes, Douglas R., and George E. Marcus. "Collaboration Today and the Re-Imagination of the Classic Scene of Fieldwork Encounter." *Collaborative Anthropologies* 1, no. 1 (2008): 81–101.

———. "Cultures of Expertise and the Management of Globalization: Toward a Re-Functioning of Ethnography." In *Global Assemblages: Technology, Politics, and Ethics as Anthropological Problems*, edited by Aihwa Ong and Stephen J. Collier, 235–52. Oxford: Blackwell, 2005.

———. "Para-Ethnography." In *The Sage Encyclopedia of Qualitative Research Methods*, edited by Lisa M. Given, 596–97. London: Sage Publications, 2008.

Holzscheiter, Anna. *Children's Rights in International Politics: The Transformative Power of Discourse, Transformations of the State.* New York: Palgrave Macmillan, 2010.

Hopgood, Stephen. *Keepers of the Flame: Understanding Amnesty International.* Ithaca: Cornell University Press, 2006.

Hopkins, J. Ellice. *Is It Natural?* London: Hatchards, 1885.

Horace. *Satires and Epistles.* Translated by John Davie. Oxford: Oxford University Press, 2011.

Human Rights and Equal Opportunity Commission (Australia). *Bringing Them Home.* Sydney: Human Rights and Equal Opportunity Commission, 1997. https://www.humanrights.gov.au/publications/bringing-them-home-chapter-1.

Human Rights Watch. *Broken System: Dysfunction, Abuse, and Impunity in the Indian Police.* New York: Human Rights Watch, 2009.

———. "Iraq: ISIS Escapees Describe Systematic Rape." *Human Rights Watch News*, April 14, 2015.

Hunt, Lynn. *Inventing Human Rights: A History.* New York: W. W. Norton & Company, 2007.

Hurd, Elizabeth Shakman. *Beyond Religious Freedom: The New Global Politics of Religion.* Princeton: Princeton University Press, 2015.

Iorns, Catherine J. "Indigenous Peoples and Self Determination: Challenging State Sovereignty." *Case Western Reserve Journal of International Law* 24, no. 2 (1992): 199–348.

Irigaray, Luce. *Speculum of the Other Woman.* Translated by Gillian C. Gill. Ithaca: Cornell University Press, 1985.

Irvine, William B. *A Guide to the Good Life: The Ancient Art of Stoic Joy.* Oxford: Oxford University Press, 2009.

Ishay, Micheline. *The History of Human Rights: From Ancient Times to the Globaliza-tion Era*. Berkeley: University of California Press, 2004.

Ivison, Duncan. *Rights*. London: Routledge, 2014.

Jaleel, Rana. "Weapons of Sex, Weapons of War." *Cultural Studies* 27, no. 1 (2013): 115–35.

Jansson, Maria, and Maud Eduards. "The Politics of Gender in the UN Security Coun-cil Resolutions on Women, Peace and Security." *International Feminist Journal of Politics* 18, no. 4 (2016): 590–604.

Jaume, Lucien. *Tocqueville: The Aristocratic Sources of Liberty*. Translated by Arthur Goldhammer. Princeton: Princeton University Press, 2013.

Joas, Hans. *The Sacredness of the Person: A New Genealogy of Human Rights*. Wash-ington DC: Georgetown University Press, 2013.

Josefsson, Jonathan. "Children at the Borders." PhD diss., Linköping University, 2016.

Kant, Immanuel. *Groundwork of the Metaphysics of Morals*. Translated and edited by Mary J. Gregor. Cambridge: Cambridge University Press, 2012.

Kapur, Ratna. *Erotic Justice: Law and the New Politics of Postcolonialism*. London: Glass House, 2005.

———. "Human Rights in the 21st Century: Take a Walk on the Dark Side." *Sydney Law Review* 28, no. 4 (2016): 665–87.

Katzenstein, Peter J., ed. *The Culture of National Security: Norms and Identity in World Politics*. New York: Columbia University Press, 1996.

Keane, Webb. *Ethical Life: Its Natural and Social Histories*. Princeton: Princeton Uni-versity Press, 2016.

Keck, Margaret E., and Kathryn Sikkink. *Activists Beyond Borders: Advocacy Net-works in International Politics*. Ithaca: Cornell University Press, 1998.

———. "Transnational Advocacy Networks in International and Regional Politics." *International Social Science Journal* 51, no. 159 (2002): 89–101.

Keet, André. "It Is Time: Critical Human Rights Education in an Age of Counter-Hegemonic Distrust." *Education As Change* 19, no. 3 (2015): 46–64.

Kelman, Herbert C. "The Social Context of Torture: Policy Process and Authority Structure." In *The Politics of Pain: Torturers and Their Masters*, edited by Ron-ald D. Crelinsten and Alex P. Schmid, 19–34. Boulder: Westview Press, 1995.

Keohane, Robert O. *After Hegemony: Cooperation and Discord in the World Political Economy*. Princeton: Princeton University Press, 1984.

———. "Steven Krasner: Subversive Realist." In *Back to Basics: State Power in a Con-temporary World*, edited by Martha Finnemore and Judith Goldstein, 28–52. Ox-ford: Oxford University Press, 2013.

Kesselring, Rita. *Bodies of Truth: Law, Memory, and Emancipation in Post-Apartheid South Africa*. Stanford: Stanford University Press, 2017.

Keys, Barbara J. *Reclaiming American Virtue: The Human Rights Revolution of the 1970s*. Cambridge: Harvard University Press, 2014.

Keyssar, Alexander. *The Right to Vote: The Contested History of Democracy in the United States*. New York: Basic Books, 2009.

Kittay, Eva Feder. "The Ethics of Care, Dependence, and Disability." *Ratio Juris* 24, no. 1 (2011): 49–58.

Klotz, Audie. "Transnational Activism and Global Transformations: The Anti-Apartheid and Abolitionist Experiences." *European Journal of International Relations* 8, no. 1 (2002): 49–76.

Koenig, Shulamith. "Human Rights As a Way of Life." *UN Chronicle*, September 2012. http://unchronicle.un.org/article/human-rights-way-life/.

Kohn, Eduardo. *How Forests Think: Toward an Anthropology Beyond the Human*. Berkeley: University of California Press, 2013.

Korczak, Janusz, *When I Am Little Again and The Child's Right to Respect*. Translated by E. P. Kulawiec. Lanham: University Press of America, 1992.

Krystal, Henry, ed. *Massive Psychic Trauma*. New York: International Universities Press, 1969.

Kweskin, Benjamin. "Yezidi Vulnerability Before ISIS." *Kurdistan24*, January 4, 2016. http://www.kurdistan24.net/en/opinion/cd2dc087-9661-4817-aca5-0a340592e0be /Yezidi-vulnerability-before-ISIS-.

Lacey, Nicola. *State Punishment: Political Principles and Community Values*. London: Routledge, 1988.

Lambek, Michael, ed. *Ordinary Ethics: Anthropology, Language, and Action*. New York: Fordham University Press, 2010.

Lansdown, Gerison. *Promoting Children's Participation in Democratic Decision-Making*. Florence: UNICEF, 2001.

Latour, Bruno. *An Inquiry into Modes of Existence: An Anthropology of the Moderns*. Cambridge: Harvard University Press, 2013.

Laufer-Ukeles, Pamela. "The Relational Rights of Children." *Connecticut Law Review* 48, no. 3 (2016): 741–816.

Lauren, Paul Gordon. *The Evolution of International Human Rights: Visions Seen*. Philadelphia: University of Pennsylvania Press, 2011.

Lawrence, John. *A Philosophical and Practical Treatise on Horses and on the Moral Duties of Man Towards the Brute Creation*. London: T. Longman, 1796.

League of Nations. *Geneva Declaration of the Rights of the Child*. September 26, 1924. http://www.un-documents.net/gdrc1924.htm.

Leary, Mary Graw. "Modern Day Slavery: Implications of a Label." *St. Louis University Law Journal* 60, no. 1 (2015): 115–44.

LeBlanc, Lawrence J. *The Convention on the Rights of the Child: United Nations Lawmaking on Human Rights*. Lincoln: University of Nebraska Press, 1995.

Lefebvre, Alexandre. *Human Rights and the Care of the Self*. Durham: Duke University Press, 2018.

———. *Human Rights As a Way of Life: On Bergson's Political Philosophy*. Stanford: Stanford University Press, 2013.

Lekas, Annalise. "#ISIS: The Largest Threat to World Peace Trending Now." *Emory International Law Review* 30, no. 2 (2015): 313–51.

Leys, Ruth. *Trauma: A Genealogy*. Chicago: University of Chicago Press, 2000.

Lifton, Robert Jay. "Conditions of Atrocity." *The Nation*, May 31, 2004. https://www.thenation.com/article/conditions-atrocity/.

———. *The Nazi Doctors: Medical Killing and the Psychology of Genocide*. New York: Basic Books, 1988.

Lipstadt, Deborah E. *The Eichmann Trial*. New York: Schocken, 2011.

Locke, John. *Two Treatises of Government*. Edited by Peter Laslett. Cambridge: Cambridge University Press, 1988.

Longford, Michael. "NGOs and the Rights of the Child." In *The Conscience of the World: The Influence of Non-Governmental Organisations in the UN System*, edited by Peter Willetts, 214–40. London: C. Hurst & Co. Publishers, 1996.

Lorey, Isabell. *State of Insecurity: Government of the Precarious*. Translated by Aileen Derieg. New York: Verso, 2015.

Luban, David. "Liberalism and the Unpleasant Question of Torture." *Virginia Law Review* 91, no. 6 (2005): 1425–61.

Lubinski, Joseph. "Screw the Whales, Save Me! The Endangered Species Act, Animal Protection, and Civil Rights." *Journal of Law in Society* 4, no. 2 (2003): 377–412.

Lücker-Babel, Marie-Françoise. "The Right of the Child to Express Views and to Be Heard: An Attempt to Interpret Article 12 of the UN Convention on the Rights of the Child." *The International Journal of Children's Rights* 3, nos. 3–4 (1995): 391–404.

Lund, Giuliana. "'Healing the Nation': Medicolonial Discourse and the State of Emergency From Apartheid to Truth and Reconciliation." *Cultural Critique* 54 (2003): 88–119.

Lundy, Laura. "'Voice' Is Not Enough: Conceptualising Article 12 of the United Nations Convention on the Rights of the Child." *British Educational Research Journal* 33, no. 6 (2007): 927–42.

Lutz, Catherine A., and Jane L. Collins. *Reading National Geographic*. Chicago: University of Chicago Press, 1993.

MacDonald, Megan. "SUR/VEIL: The Veil as Blank(et) Signifier." In *Muslim Women, Transnational Feminism and the Ethics of Pedagogy*, edited by Lisa Taylor and Jasmin Zine, 25–58. New York: Routledge, 2014.

Mackenzie, Catriona, and Natalie Stoljar, eds. *Relational Autonomy: Feminist Perspectives on Autonomy, Agency and the Social Self*. Oxford: Oxford University Press, 2000.

MacKinnon, Catharine A. *Are Women Human? And Other International Dialogues*. Cambridge: Harvard University Press, 2006.

Mahdavi, Pardis. *From Trafficking to Terror: Constructing a Global Social Problem*. New York: Routledge, 2014.

Mahmood, Saba. "Secularism, Hermeneutics, and Empire: The Politics of Islamic Reformation." *Public Culture* 18, no. 2 (2006): 323–47.

Malik, Charles. "The Challenge of Human Rights." In *The Challenge of Human Rights: Charles Malik and the Universal Declaration*, edited by Habib C. Malik, 153–66. Oxford: Charles Malik Foundation, 2000.

———. "An International Bill of Rights." In *The Challenge of Human Rights: Charles Malik and the Universal Declaration*, edited by Habib C. Malik, 53–60. Oxford: Charles Malik Foundation, 2000.

Malone, Karen, and Catherine Hartung. "Challenges of Participatory Practice with Children." In *A Handbook of Children and Young People's Participation: Perspectives from Theory and Practice*, edited by Barry Percy-Smith and Nigel Thomas, 24–38. London: Routledge, 2010.

Marcus Aurelius. *The Meditations of Marcus Aurelius Antoninus*. Translated by A. S. L. Farquharson. Oxford: Oxford University Press, 1989.

Markovits, Daniel. *The Meritocracy Trap*. New York: Penguin, forthcoming.

Marks, Susan. "Four Human Rights Myths." In *Human Rights: Old Problems, New Possibilities*, edited by David Kinley, Wojciech Sadurski, and Kevin Walton, 217–35. Cheltenham: Edward Elgar Publishing, 2013.

———. "Human Rights and Root Causes." *Modern Law Review* 74, no. 1 (2011): 57–78.

Marotta, Francesca. "The Blue Flame and the Gold Shield: Methodology, Challenges and Lessons Learned on Human Rights Training for Police." *International Peacekeeping* 6, no. 4 (1999): 69–92.

Marshall, Christine, and Kiran Pienaar. "'You Are Not Alone': The Discursive Construction of the 'Suffering Victim' Identity on *The Oprah Winfrey Show*." *Southern African Linguistics and Applied Language Studies* 26, no. 4 (2008): 525–46.

Marx, Karl. "On the Jewish Question." In *Nonsense upon Stilts: Bentham, Burke, and Marx on the Rights of Man*, edited by Jeremy Waldron, 137–50. London: Routledge, 2014.

Mattingly, Cheryl, and Linda C. Garro, eds. *Narrative and the Cultural Construction of Illness and Healing*. Berkeley: University of California Press, 2000.

Mauss, Marcel. *The Gift: The Form and Reason for Exchange in Archaic Societies*. London: Routledge, 2006.

Mayer, Arno J. *The Persistence of the Old Regime: Europe to the Great War*. New York: Verso, 2010.

Mazower, Mark. *Dark Continent: Europe's Twentieth Century*. New York: Alfred A. Knopf, 1998.

McLagan, Meg. "Introduction: Making Human Rights Claims Public." *American Anthropologist* 108, no. 1 (2006): 191–95.

Mehta, Uday Singh. *Liberalism and Empire: A Study in Nineteenth-Century British Liberal Thought*. Chicago: University of Chicago Press, 1999.

Mertus, Julie. *Human Rights Matters: Local Politics and National Human Rights Institutions*. Stanford: Stanford University Press, 2009.

Michels, Robert. *Political Parties: A Sociological Study of the Oligarchical Tendencies of Modern Democracy.* Translated by Eden Paul and Cedar Paul. New York: The Free Press, 1962.

Milgram, Stanley. *Obedience to Authority: An Experimental View.* New York: Harper & Row, 1974.

Miljeteig-Olsen, Per. "Advocacy of Children's Rights—The Convention as More than a Legal Document." *Human Rights Quarterly* 12, no. 1 (1990): 148–55.

Million, Dian. *Therapeutic Nations: Healing in an Age of Indigenous Human Rights.* Tucson: University of Arizona Press, 2013.

Mills, Catherine. "Normative Violence, Vulnerability, and Responsibility." *Differences* 18, no. 2 (2007): 133–56.

Minow, Martha. *Between Vengeance and Forgiveness: Facing History After Genocide and Mass Violence.* Boston: Beacon Press, 1998.

———. "Institutions and Emotions: Redressing Mass Violence." In *The Passions of Law,* edited by Susan Bandes, 265–83. New York: New York University Press, 1999.

Mishra, Pankaj. "The Mask It Wears." *London Review of Books,* June 21, 2018. https://www.lrb.co.uk/v40/n12/pankaj-mishra/the-mask-it-wears.

Mitchell, Katharyne. "Geographies of Identity: The New Exceptionalism." *Progress in Human Geography* 30, no. 1 (2006): 95–106.

Mitoma, Glenn. "Charles H. Malik and Human Rights: Notes on a Biography." *Biography* 33, no. 1 (2010): 222–41.

Mohanty, Chandra Talpade. "Under Western Eyes: Feminist Scholarship and Colonial Discourses." In *Third World Women and the Politics of Feminism,* edited by Chandra Talpade Mohanty, Ann Russo, and Lourdes Torres, 51–80. Bloomington: Indiana University Press, 1991.

Moody, Zoe. "The United Nations Declaration of the Rights of the Child (1959): Genesis, Transformation and Dissemination of a Treaty (re)Constituting a Transnational Cause." *Prospects* 45, no. 1 (2015): 15–29.

Morsink, Johannes. *The Universal Declaration of Human Rights and the Challenge of Religion.* Columbia: University of Missouri Press, 2017.

———. *The Universal Declaration of Human Rights: Origins, Drafting, and Intent.* Philadelphia: University of Pennsylvania Press, 1999.

Moyn, Samuel. "The Assumption by Man of His Original Fracturing: Marcel Gauchet, Gladys Swain, and the History of the Self." *Modern Intellectual History* 6, no. 2 (2009): 315–41.

———. *Christian Human Rights.* Philadelphia: University of Pennsylvania Press, 2015.

———. "Freud's Discontents." *The Nation,* April 2, 2016. https://www.thenation.com/article/freuds-discontents/.

———. "How the Human Rights Movement Failed." *New York Times,* April 23, 2018. https://www.nytimes.com/2018/04/23/opinion/human-rights-movement-failed.html.

———. *The Last Utopia: Human Rights in History.* Cambridge: Harvard University Press, 2010.

———. *Not Enough: Human Rights in an Unequal World.* Cambridge: Harvard University Press, 2018.

———. "A Powerless Companion: Human Rights in the Age of Neoliberalism." *Law and Contemporary Problems* 77, no. 4 (2014): 147–69.

Moyn, Samuel, and Andrew Sartori, eds. *Global Intellectual History.* New York: Columbia University Press, 2013.

Müller, F. Henrietta. "Miss Müller and Woman Suffrage." *The Times,* July 5, 1884.

Murphy, Ann V. "Corporeal Vulnerability and the New Humanism." *Hypatia* 26, no. 3 (2011): 575–90.

Mutua, Makau. "Savages, Victims, and Saviors: The Metaphor of Human Rights." *Harvard International Law Journal* 42, no. 1 (2001): 201–45.

Nagy, Rosemary L. "The Scope and Bounds of Transitional Justice and the Canadian Truth and Reconciliation Commission." *International Journal of Transitional Justice* 7, no. 1 (2013): 52–73.

Napoleon, Val. "Aboriginal Self Determination: Individual Self and Collective Selves." *Atlantis* 29, no. 2 (2005): 31–46.

National Society for Women's Suffrage (Great Britain). *Opinions of Women on Women's Suffrage.* London: Central Committee of the National Society for Women's Suffrage, 1879.

Nedelsky, Jennifer. *Law's Relations: A Relational Theory of Self, Autonomy, and Law.* Oxford: Oxford University Press, 2011.

———. *Private Property and the Limits of American Constitutionalism: The Madisonian Framework and Its Legacy.* Chicago: University of Chicago Press, 1990.

———. "Reconceiving Rights and Constitutionalism." *Journal of Human Rights* 7, no. 2 (2008): 139–73.

"Cruelty to Animals: Also to Women and Children." *The New York Ledger.* August 3, 1867.

New Zealand Police and New Zealand Human Rights Commission. *Human Rights Training: Facilitators' Guide.* 2006.

Nickel, James. "Human Rights." In *The Stanford Encyclopedia of Philosophy* (Spring 2017 Edition), edited by Edward N. Zalta. https://plato.stanford.edu/archives/spr 2017/entries/rights-human/.

Niezen, Ronald. *Truth and Indignation: Canada's Truth and Reconciliation Commission on Indian Residential Schools.* Toronto: University of Toronto Press, 2013.

Niezen, Ronald, and Marie-Pierre Gadoua. "Témoignage et histoire dans la Commission de vérité et de réconciliation du Canada." *Canadian Journal of Law and Society* 29, no. 1 (2014): 21–42.

NIMH Collaborative HIV/STD Prevention Trial Group. "The Community Popular Opinion Leader HIV Prevention Programme: Conceptual Basis and Intervention Procedures." *AIDS* 21, no. 2 (2007): S59–S68.

Nordland, Rod. "Despite U.S. Claims, Yazidis Say Crisis Is Not Over." *New York Times.* August 14, 2014. https://www.nytimes.com/2014/08/15/world/middleeast /iraq-yazidis-obama-sinjar-crisis.html.

Northern Ireland Human Rights Commission. *Human Rights in Police Training; Report Four: Course for All*. Belfast: Northern Ireland Human Rights Commission, April 2004.

Nowak, Manfred. *Report of the Special Rapporteur on Torture and Other Cruel, Inhuman or Degrading Treatment or Punishment – Mission to Sri Lanka*. Geneva: United Nations, 2008.

Nwogu, Nneoma V. "When and Why It Started: Deconstructing Victim-Centered Truth Commissions in the Context of Ethnicity-Based Conflict." *International Journal of Transitional Justice* 4, no. 2 (2010): 275–89.

Oldfield, Josiah. "The Scientific View." In *The New Charter: A Discussion of the Rights of Man and the Rights of Animals*, edited by Henry Salt, London: Charles Bell and Sons, 1896.

Oliver, Mike. "The Social Model of Disability: Thirty Years On." *Disability & Society* 28, no. 7 (2013): 1024–26.

O'Neill, William G. *Police Reform and Human Rights*. New York: Hurist, 2004.

O'Neill, Daniel I. *The Burke-Wollstonecraft Debate: Savagery, Civilization, and Democracy*. University Park: Pennsylvania State University Press, 2007.

Orbán, Viktor. "Prime Minister Viktor Orbán's Speech at the Ceremonial Swearing-in of New Border Guards." January 12, 2017, Cabinet Office of The Prime Minister, Hungary. http://www.miniszterelnok.hu/prime-minister-viktor-orbans-speech-at-the-ceremonial-swearing-in-of-new-border-guards/.

Organization of American States. *American Convention on Human Rights*. San José, Costa Rica, 1969. https://www.cidh.oas.org/basicos/english/basic3.american%20convention.htm.

Organization for Security and Cooperation in Europe. *Guidelines on Human Rights Education for Law Enforcement Officials*. Warsaw: Office for Democratic Institutions and Human Rights, 2012.

Pallamin, Vera. *Arte, cultura e cidade: aspectos estético-políticos contemporâneos*. São Paulo: Annablume, 2015.

Panikkar, R. "Is the Notion of Human Rights a Western Concept?" *Diogenes* 30 (1982): 75–102.

Pascal, Blaise. *Pensées*. Translated by Roger Ariew. Indianapolis: Hackett, 2005.

Peters, Julie, and Andrea Wolper. *Women's Rights, Human Rights: International Feminist Perspectives*. New York: Routledge, 1995

Phelps, Sandra Marie. "The Limits of Admittance and Diversity in Iraqi Kurdistan: Femininity and the Body of Du'a Khalil." *Totalitarian Movements and Political Religions* 11, nos. 3–4 (2010): 457–72.

Piketty, Thomas. *Capital in the Twenty-First Century*. Cambridge, MA: Harvard University Press, 2013.

Pitts, Jennifer. "Empire and Legal Universalisms in the Eighteenth Century." *The American Historical Review* 117, no. 1 (2012): 92–121.

Plumwood, Val. *Feminism and the Mastery of Nature*. New York: Routledge, 1994.

Porter, Robert B. "Strengthening Tribal Sovereignty Through Peacemaking: How the

Anglo-American Legal Tradition Destroys Indigenous Societies." *Columbia Human Rights Law Review* 28, no. 2 (1997): 235–305.

Postero, Nancy Grey. *The Indigenous State: Race, Politics, and Performance in Plurinational Bolivia*. Berkeley, CA: University of California Press, 2017.

Pratt, Nicola. "Reconceptualizing Gender, Reinscribing Racial-Sexual Boundaries in International Security: The Case of UN Security Council Resolution 1325 on 'Women, Peace and Security.'" *International Studies Quarterly* 57, no. 4 (2013): 772–83.

Pritchard, Sarah, ed. *Indigenous Peoples, the United Nations and Human Rights*. London: Zed Books, 1998.

Pruitt, Lesley, Helen Berents, and Gayle Munro. "Gender and Age in the Constitution of Male Youth in the European Migration 'Crisis.'" *Signs* 43, no. 3 (2018): 688–709.

Puar, Jasbir. "Precarity Talk: A Virtual Roundtable with Lauren Berlant, Judith Butler, Bojana Cvejic, Isabell Lorey, Jasbir Puar, and Ana Vujanovic." *TDR: The Drama Review* 56, no. 4 (2012): 163–77.

Quennerstedt, Ann. "Children, But Not Really Humans? Critical Reflections on the Hampering Effect of the '3 p's.'" *International Journal of Children's Rights* 18, no. 4 (2010): 619–35.

Rajca, Andrew C. *Dissensual Subjects: Memory, Human Rights, and Postdictatorship in Argentina, Brazil, and Uruguay*. Evanston: Northwestern University Press, 2018.

———. "Unraveling Normalized Rhetoric of Violence and Human Rights: the Dissensual Intervention of Sergio Bianchi's *Quanto Vale Ou É Por Quilo?*" *Journal of Latin American Cultural Studies* 22, no. 3 (2013): 305–21.

———. "Urban Imaginaries, Spatial Practices, and Cinematic Aesthetics in Sérgio Bianchi's *Os inquilinos.*" *Arizona Journal of Hispanic Cultural Studies*, forthcoming.

Rancière, Jacques. *Aesthetics and Its Discontents*. Translated by Steven Corcoran. Cambridge: Polity Press, 2009.

———. "Who Is the Subject of the Rights of Man?" *South Atlantic Quarterly* 103, nos. 2–3 (2004): 297–310.

———. *The Emancipated Spectator*. London: Verso, 2009.

Rancière, Jacques, and Steve Corcoran. *Dissensus: On Politics and Aesthetics*. New York: Continuum, 2010.

Reich, Robert B. *Aftershock: The Next Economy and America's Future*. New York: Alfred A. Knopf, 2010.

Reinbold, Jenna. *Seeing the Myth in Human Rights*. Philadelphia: University of Pennsylvania Press, 2017.

Reynaert, Didier, and Rudi Roose. "Children's Rights and the Capability Approach: Discussing Children's Agency Against the Horizon of the Institutionalised Youth Land." In *Children's Rights and the Capability Approach: Challenges and Prospects*, edited by Daniel Stoecklin and Jean-Michel Bonvin, 175–93. Dordrecht: Springer, 2014.

Richard, Nelly. *Fracturas de la memoria: arte y pensamiento crítico*. Buenos Aires: Siglo Veintiuno Editores, 2007.

————, ed. *Políticas y estéticas de la memoria*. Santiago: Editorial Cuarto Propio, 2000.

Risse, Thomas, Stephen C. Ropp, and Kathryn Sikkink, eds. *The Power of Human Rights: International Norms and Domestic Change*. Cambridge: Cambridge University Press, 1999.

Robbins, Joel. "Recognition, Reciprocity, and Justice: Melanesian Reflections on the Rights of Relationships." In *Mirrors of Justice: Law and Power in the Post–Cold War Era*, edited by Kamari Maxine Clarke and Mark Goodale, 171–90. New York: Cambridge University Press, 2010.

Robins, Simon. "Challenging the Therapeutic Ethic: A Victim-Centred Evaluation of Transitional Justice Process in Timor-Leste." *International Journal of Transitional Justice* 6, no. 1 (2012): 83–105.

Robinson, Dylan. "Intergenerational Sense, Intergenerational Responsibility." In *Arts of Engagement: Taking Aesthetic Action In and Beyond Canada's Truth and Reconciliation Commission*, edited by Dylan Robinson and Keavy Martin, 43–65. Waterloo: Wilfred Laurier University Press, 2016.

Rolnik, Raquel. *Guerra dos Lugares: A colonização da terra e da moradia na era das finanças*. São Paulo: Boitempo, 2015.

Roosevelt, Eleanor. *What I Hope to Leave Behind: The Essential Essays of Eleanor Roosevelt*. Edited by Allida M. Black. New York: Carlson Pub, 1995.

Rorty, Richard. *Contingency, Irony, and Solidarity*. Cambridge: Cambridge University Press, 1989.

————. "Human Rights, Rationality, and Sentimentality." In Richard Rorty, *Truth and Progress: Philosophical Papers Volume 3*, 167–85. Cambridge: Cambridge University Press, 1998.

Rosenberg, Fernando J. *After Human Rights: Literature, Visual Arts, and Film in Latin America, 1990–2010*. Pittsburgh: University of Pittsburgh Press, 2016.

Rosenberg, Gerald N. *The Hollow Hope: Can Courts Bring About Social Change?* Chicago: University of Chicago Press, 1991.

Ross, Fiona. *Bearing Witness: Women and the Truth and Reconciliation Commission in South Africa*. London: Pluto, 2003

Ryan, Missy. "Iraqi Kurds, Battling Islamic Threat, Press Washington for Arms." *Reuters: World News*. July 31, 2014.

Sallis, James F., Neville Owen, and Edwin B. Fisher. "Ecological Models of Health Behavior." In *Health Behavior and Health Education: Theory, Research and Practice*, edited by Karen Glanz, Barbara K. Rimer, and K. Viswanath, 465–86. San Francisco: Jossey Bass, 2002.

Salomon, Frank. "Review of Olivia Harris, *To Make the Earth Bear Fruit: Ethnographic Essays on Fertility, Work and Gender in Highland Bolivia*." *Journal of Latin American Studies* 33, no. 3 (2001): 654–56.

Sanders, Douglas. "The UN Working Group on Indigenous Populations." *Human Rights Quarterly* 11, no. 3 (1989): 406–33.

Shelton, Dinah, ed. *The Oxford Handbook of International Human Rights Law*. Oxford: Oxford University Press, 2013.

Schimmelfennig, Frank. "Strategic Calculation and International Socialization: Membership Incentives, Party Constellations, and Sustained Compliance in Central and Eastern Europe." *International Organization* 59, no. 4 (2005): 827–60.

Schippers, Birgit, ed. *Critical Perspectives on Human Rights*. London: Rowman & Littlefield, 2019.

Sellars, Kirsten. *The Rise and Rise of Human Rights*. Stroud: Sutton, 2002.

Sellick, Patricia. "Responding to Children Affected by Armed Conflict: A Case Study of Save the Children Fund 1919–1999." PhD diss., University of Bradford, 2001.

Shandler, Jeffrey. *While America Watches: Televising the Holocaust*. Oxford: Oxford University Press, 1999.

Shannon, Laurie. *The Accommodated Animal: Cosmopolity in Shakespearean Locales*. Chicago: University of Chicago Press, 2013.

Shaw, Rosaline. "Memory Frictions: Localizing the Truth and Reconciliation Commission in Sierra Leone." *International Journal of Transitional Justice* 1, no. 2 (2007): 183–207.

Simmons, Beth A. *Mobilizing for Human Rights: International Law in Domestic Politics*. Cambridge: Cambridge University Press, 2009.

Simpson, Audra. "Subjects of Sovereignty: Indigeneity, the Revenue Rule, and Juridics of Failed Consent." *Law and Contemporary Problems* 71, no. 3 (2008): 191–215.

Sinclair, Murray. "Commissioner's Welcome." TRC Saskatoon National Event, Saskatoon, June 21, 2012.

Singer, Peter. *Animal Liberation: A New Ethics for Our Treatment of Animals*. New York: HarperCollins, 1975.

———. "Severe Impairment and the Beginning of Life." *The APA Newsletter on Philosophy and Medicine* 99, no. 2 (2000): 248.

Sliwinski, Sharon. *Human Rights in Camera*. Chicago: University of Chicago Press, 2011.

Slowey, Gabrielle A. *Navigating Neoliberalism: Self-Determination and the Mikisew Cree First Nation*. Vancouver: UBC Press, 2008.

Speed, Shannon. *Rights in Rebellion: Indigenous Struggle and Human Rights in Chiapas*. Stanford: Stanford University Press, 2008.

Spence, Donald P. *Narrative Truth and Historical Truth: Meaning and Interpretation in Psychoanalysis*. New York: W.W. Norton & Company, 1982.

Spinoza, Benedict de. *Complete Works*. Translated by Samuel Shirley. Edited by Michael L. Morgan. Indianapolis: Hackett, 2002.

———. *A Spinoza Reader: The Ethics and Other Works*. Translated and edited by Edwin Curley. Princeton: Princeton University Press, 1994.

———. *Theological-Political Treatise*. Translated by Michael Silverthorne and Jonathan Israel. Cambridge: Cambridge University Press, 2007.

Spivak, Gayatri. "Can the Subaltern Speak?" In *Colonial Discourse and Post-Colonial Theory: A Reader*, edited by Patrick Williams and Laura Chrisman, 90–105. New York: Columbia University Press, 1994.

The Sporting Times. "The Woman About Town." December 20, 1871.

Stammers, Neil. "Social Movements and the Social Construction of Rights." *Human Rights Quarterly* 21, no. 4 (1999): 980–1008.

Strathern, Marilyn. *Kinship, Law and the Unexpected: Relatives Are Always a Surprise.* Cambridge: Cambridge University Press, 2005.

Stern, Rebecca. "The Child's Right to Participation – Reality or Rhetoric?" PhD diss., Uppsala University, 2006.

———. *Implementing Article 12 of the UN Convention on the Rights of the Child: Participation, Power and Attitudes.* Leiden: Brill-Nijhoff, 2017.

Stevens, Jeroen. "Occupied City: Hotel Cambridge and Central São Paulo Between Urban Decay and Resurrection." In *From Conflict to Inclusion in Housing: Interactions of Communities, Residents, and Activists,* edited by Graham Cairns, Georgios Artopoulos, and Kirsten Day, 23–39. London: UCL Press, 2017.

Strasser, Fred. "ISIS Makes Sex Slavery Key Tactic of Terrorism Action Against Violent Extremism Must Address Abuse of Women, U.N. Official Says." *United States Institute of Peace,* October 6, 2016.

Sullivan, Winnifred F. *The Impossibility of Religious Freedom.* Princeton: Princeton University Press, 2005.

Sunstein, Cass R. "On the Expressive Function of Law." *University of Pennsylvania Law Review* 144, no. 5 (1996): 2021–53.

Sydney Centre for International Law. *Human Rights in the Criminal Justice System in Nepal: Law Enforcement Training Manual.* Kathmandu and Sydney: Kathmandu School of Law, 2009.

Szörényi, Anna. "Rethinking the Boundaries: Towards a Butlerian Ethics of Vulnerability in Sex Trafficking Debates." *Feminist Review* 107, no. 1 (2014): 20–36.

Tasioulas, John. "On the Foundations of Human Rights." In *Philosophical Foundations of Human Rights,* edited by Rowan Cruft, S. Matthew Liao, and Massimo Renzo, 45–70. Oxford: Oxford University Press, 2015.

———. "Towards a Philosophy of Human Rights." *Current Legal Problems* 65, no. 1 (2012): 1–30.

Taylor, Charles. *Modern Social Imaginaries.* Durham: Duke University Press, 2004.

———. *A Secular Age.* Cambridge: Harvard University Press, 2007.

Taylor, Telford. *The Anatomy of the Nuremberg Trials: A Personal Memoir.* New York: Alfred A. Knopf, 1992.

Teubner, Gunther. *Law As an Autopoietic System.* Translated by Anne Bankowska and Ruth Adler. Oxford: Blackwell, 1993.

Tibbitts, Felisa L. "Evolution of Human Rights Education Models." In *Human Rights Education: Theory, Research, Praxis,* edited by Monisha Bajaj, 69–95. Philadelphia: University of Pennsylvania Press, 2017.

———. "Understanding What We Do: Emerging Models for Human Rights Education." *International Review of Education* 48, no. 3 (2002): 159–71.

Tight, Malcolm. *Key Concepts in Adult Education and Training.* London: Routledge, 2002.

Tisdall, E. Kay M. "Children and Young People's Participation: A Critical Consideration of Article 12." In *The Routledge International Handbook of Children's Rights Studies*, edited by Wouter Vandenhole, Ellen Desmet, Didier Reyneart, and Sara Lambrechts, 185–200. New York: Routledge, 2015.

Tocqueville, Alexis de. *Democracy in America.* Translated by Harvey C. Mansfield and Dalba Winthrop. Chicago: Chicago University Press, 2000.

Tomaselli, Sylvana. "Introduction." In Mary Wollstonecraft, *A Vindication of the Rights of Men and a Vindication of the Rights of Woman*, edited by Sylvana Tomaselli, ix–xxix. Cambridge: Cambridge University Press, 1995.

Tooley, Michael. "Abortion and Infanticide." In *Applied Ethics*, edited by Peter Singer, 57–86. Oxford: Oxford University Press, 1986.

Truth and Reconciliation Commission of Canada. *Sharing Your Truth.* Film screened at the TRC Atlantic National Event, October 27, 2011.

———. *The Survivors Speak: A Report of the Truth and Reconciliation Commission of Canada.* Winnipeg: Truth and Reconciliation Commission of Canada, 2015.

———. *What We Have Learned: Principles of Truth and Reconciliation.* Winnipeg: Truth and Reconciliation Commission of Canada, 2015.

Turner, Bryan S. *Vulnerability and Human Rights.* University Park: Pennsylvania State University Press, 2006.

Turner, Terence. "Human Rights, Human Difference: Anthropology's Contribution to an Emancipatory Cultural Politics." *Journal of Anthropological Research* 53, no. 3 (1997): 273–91.

Tutu, Mpho. "Foreword." In *Bodies of Truth: Law, Memory, and Emancipation in Post-Apartheid South Africa*, edited by Rita Kesselring, vii–viii. Stanford: Stanford University Press, 2017.

Uluru Convention. Uluru Statement from the Heart. May 26, 2017. https://www.referendumcouncil.org.au/sites/default/files/2017-05/Uluru_Statement_From_The_Heart_0.PDF.

UN Committee on the Rights of the Child. 1st Session, 22nd meeting, CRC/C/5 (October 30, 1991).

———. Recommendations: Day of General Discussion on the Right of the Child to Be Heard, (September 29, 2006).

———. 51st Session, CRC/C/GC/12 (July 20, 2009).

UN Development Programme and Office of the High Commissioner for Human Rights. *Toolkit for Collaboration with National Human Rights Institutions.* New York: United Nations, 2010.

UN Economic and Social Council. Commission on Human Rights, 35th Session, E/CN.4/1324 (December 27, 1978).

———. Commission on Human Rights, 36th Session, E/CN.4/1349 (January 17, 1980).

———. Commission on Human Rights, 36th Session, E/CN.4/1349 (February 17, 1981).

———. Commission on Human Rights, 37th Session, E/CN.4/L.1575 (February 17, 1981).

————. Commission on Human Rights, 40th Session, E/CN.4/1984/71 (February 23, 1984).

————. Commission on Human Rights, 43rd Session, E/CN.4/1987/25 (March 9, 1987).

————. Commission on Human Rights, 43rd Session, 55th meeting, E/CN.4/1987/SR.55 (March 11, 1987).

————. Commission on Human Rights, 45th Session, E/CN.4/1989/48 (March 2, 1989).

————. Commission on Human Rights, Drafting Committee, 1st Session, 2nd Meeting, E/CN.4/AC.1/SR.2 (June 11, 1947).

————. Commission on Human Rights, Subcommission on Prevention of Discrimination and Protection of Minorities, Working Group on Indigenous Populations, 13th Session, E/CN.4/Sub.2/AC.4/1995/3 (June 21, 1995).

————. Drafting Committee on an International Bill of Human Rights, 1st Session, 11th Meeting, E/CN.4/AC.1/SR.11 (June 19, 1947).

————. Resolution 608 (XXI), Supplementary Convention on the Abolition of Slavery, the Slave Trade, and Institutions and Practices Similar to Slavery, E/CONF.24/23.

UN Educational, Scientific, and Cultural Organization, ed. *Human Rights, Comments and Interpretations*. New York: A. Wingate, 1949.

————. 61st Annual DPI/NGO Conference, "Reaffirming Human Rights for All" (September 3–5, 2008).

UN General Assembly. Resolution 39/46, Convention Against Torture and Other Cruel, Inhuman or Degrading Treatment or Punishment, A/RES/39/46 (December 10, 1984).

————. Resolution 317 (IV), Convention for the Suppression of the Traffic in Persons and of the Exploitation of the Prostitution of Others, A/RES/4/317 (December 2, 1949).

————. Resolution 34/180, Convention on the Elimination of All Forms of Discrimination Against Women, A/RES/34/180 (December 18, 1979).

————. Resolution 44/25, Convention on the Rights of the Child, A/RES/44/25 (November 20, 1989).

————. Resolution 61/106, Convention on the Rights of Persons with Disabilities, A/RES/61/106 (December 13, 2006).

————. Resolution 47/135, Declaration on the Rights of Persons Belonging to National or Ethnic, Religious and Linguistic Minorities, A/RES/47/135 (December 18, 1992).

————. Resolution 71/321, Enhancing the Participation of Indigenous Peoples' Representatives and Institutions in Meetings of Relevant United Nations Bodies on Issues Affecting Them, A/RES/71/321 (September 21, 2017).

————. Resolution 2106 (XX), International Convention on the Elimination of All Forms of Racial Discrimination, A/RES/20/2106 (December 21, 1965).

————. Resolution 45/158, International Convention on the Protection of the Rights of All Migrant Workers and Members of Their Families, A/RES/45/158 (December 18, 1990).

———. Resolution 2200 A (XXI), International Covenant on Economic, Social and Cultural Rights, International Covenant on Civil and Political Rights and Optional Protocol to the International Covenant on Civil and Political Rights, A/RES/21/2200 (December 16, 1966).

———. Resolution 62/171, International Year of Human Rights Learning, A/RES/62/171 (December 18, 2007).

———. Resolution 260 (III), Prevention and Punishment of the Crime of Genocide, A/RES/3/260 (December 9, 1948).

———. Resolution 49/184, United Nations Decade for Human Rights Education, A/RES/49/184 (December 23, 1994).

———. Resolution 66/137, United Nations Declaration on Human Rights Education and Training, A/RES/66/137 (February 16, 2012).

———. Resolution 62/295, United Nations Declaration on the Rights of Indigenous Peoples, A/RES/61/295 (December 13, 2007).

———. Resolution 217 A (III), Universal Declaration of Human Rights, A/RES/3/217 A (December 10, 1948).

———. Resolution 59/113 A, World Programme for Human Rights Education A/RES/59/113 (December 10, 2004).

UN Human Rights Council. "They came to destroy": ISIS Crimes Against the Yazidis, A/HRC/32/CRP.2 (June 15, 2016).

UN Meetings Coverage and Press Release. Prevention, Protection, Prosecution Stressed as Security Council Holds Open Debate on Human Trafficking, Modern Slavery, Forced Labour in Conflict Situations, SC/12751 (March 15, 2017).

———. Shame, Stigma Integral to Logic of Sexual Violence as War Tactic, Special Adviser Tells Security Council, as Speakers Demand Recognition for Survivors, SC/12819 (May 15, 2017).

UN Office of the High Commissioner for Human Rights and UN Assistance Mission for Iraq Human Rights Office. Report on the Protection of Civilians in Armed Conflict in Iraq: 6 July – 10 September 2014. New York: United Nations, 2014.

UN Security Council. Report of the Secretary-General on Conflict-Related Sexual Violence: Report of the Secretary-General, S/2017/249 (April 17, 2017).

———. Resolution 1325 [On Women and Peace and Security], S/RES/1325 (October 31, 2000).

———. Resolution 1820, S/RES/1820 (June 19, 2008).

———. Resolution 1888, S/RES/1888 (September 30, 2009).

———. Resolution 1889, S/RES/1880 (October 5, 2009).

———. Resolution 1960, S/RES/1960 (December 16, 2010).

———. Resolution 2106, S/RES/2106 (June 24, 2013).

———. Resolution 2112, S/RES/2122 (October 18, 2013).

"ISIL's 'Genocide' Against Yazidis is Ongoing, UN Rights Panel Says, Calling for International Action." UN News, August 3, 2017. https://news.un.org/en/story/2017/08/562772-isils-genocide-against-yazidis-ongoing-un-rights-panel-says-calling.

United Nations. *Human Rights and Law Enforcement: A Manual on Human Rights Training for the Police.* New York: Office of the High Commissioner for Human Rights, 1997.

———. *Report of the Special Rapporteur on Torture and Other Cruel, Inhuman or Degrading Treatment or Punishment.* New York: United Nations, 2016.

———. *World Program for Human Rights Education: Plan of Action.* New York: Office of the High Commissioner for Human Rights, 2012, HR/PUB/12/3, 28c(iv).

United Nations Children's Fund. *The State of the World's Children 2003: Child Participation.* New York: UNICEF, 2002.

United Nations Transitional Administration in East Timor (UNTAET). 2001. Regulation No 2001/10 on the Establishment of a Commission for Reception, Truth and Reconciliation in East Timor. Doc no. UNTAET/2001/10, 13 July, https://peace keeping.un.org/mission/past/etimor/untaetR/Reg10e.pdf.

Van Bueren, Geraldine. *The International Law on the Rights of the Child.* Dordrect: Martinus Nijhoff Publishers, 1995.

Van Krieken, Robert. "The Barbarism of Civilization: Cultural Genocide and the 'Stolen Generations.'" *The British Journal of Sociology* 50, no. 2 (2003): 297–315.

Van Maanen, G. E., Andries Johannes Van der Walt, Gregory S. Alexander, and Maastrichts Europees Instituut voor Transnationaal Rechtswetenschappelijk Onderzoek, eds. *Property Law on the Threshold of the 21st Century: Proceedings of an International Colloquium "Property Law on the Threshold of the 21st Century."* Antwerp: Maklu, 1996.

Vanessa. "Vivisection: Demoralising to Vivisectors and Spectators. Part III." *The Women's Penny Paper,* December 13, 1890.

Veerman, Philip E. *The Rights of the Child and the Changing Image of Childhood.* Dordrecht: Martinus Nijhoff Publishers, 1992.

Wahl, Rachel. *In the Eye of the Torturer.* Stanford: Stanford University Press, 2016.

———. *Just Violence: Torture and Human Rights in the Eyes of the Police.* Stanford: Stanford University Press, 2017.

Wall, John. *Ethics in Light of Childhood.* Washington, DC: Georgetown University Press, 2010.

Warbasse, James Peter. *The Conquest of Disease Through Animal Experimentation.* New York: D. Appleton and Company, 1910.

Weidong, Chen and Taru Spronken, eds. *Three Approaches to Combating Torture in China.* Antwerp: Intersentia, 2012.

Westcott, Tom. "Iraq's Yazidis return to a Healthcare Crisis." *IRIN News,* March 16, 2018. https://www.irinnews.org/feature/2018/03/16/iraq-s-yazidis-return-health care-crisis.

Whyte, Jessica. *The Morals of the Market: Human Rights and the Rise of Neoliberalism.* New York: Verso, forthcoming.

Williams, Patricia. *The Alchemy of Race and Rights.* Cambridge, MA: Harvard University Press, 1991.

Wilson, Marie. "The Truth and Reconciliation Commission of Canada." In *Indige-*

nous Peoples' Access to Justice, Including Truth and Reconciliation Process, edited by Wilton Littlechild and Elsa Stamatopoulou, 127–39. New York: Institute for the Study of Human Rights at Columbia University, 2014.

Wilson, Richard, ed. *Human Rights, Culture and Context: Anthropological Perspectives*. London: Pluto Press, 1997.

Wilson, Richard, and Jon P. Mitchell, eds. *Human Rights in Global Perspective: Anthropological Studies of Rights, Claims and Entitlements*. New York: Routledge, 2003.

Wise, Stephen M. "Animal Rights, One Step at a Time." In *Animal Rights: Current Debates and New Directions*, edited by Cass R. Sunstein and Martha C. Nussbaum, 19–50. Oxford: Oxford University Press, 2004.

———. *Rattling the Cage: Toward Legal Rights for Animals*. Cambridge: Perseus, 2000.

———. *Unlocking the Cage: Science and the Case for Animal Rights*. Oxford: Perseus, 2002.

Wolin, Sheldon S. *Tocqueville Between Two Worlds: The Making of a Political and Theoretical Life*. Princeton: Princeton University Press, 2001.

Wollstonecraft, Mary. *A Vindication of the Rights of Men and a Vindication of the Rights of Woman*. Edited by Sylvana Tomaselli. Cambridge: Cambridge University Press, 1995.

Woodhead, Martin. "Foreword." In *A Handbook of Children and Young People's Participation Perspectives from Theory and Practice*, edited by Barry Percy-Smith and Nigel Thomas, xix–xxii. London: Routledge, 2010.

Yalom, Irvin D., and Molyn Leszcz. *The Theory and Practice of Group Psychotherapy*. New York: Basic Books, 2005.

Young, Allan. *The Harmony of Illusions: Inventing Post-Traumatic Stress Disorder*. Princeton: Princeton University Press, 1995.

Young, Thomas. *An Essay on Humanity to Animals*. London: T. Cadell, jun., and W. Davies, 1798.

Zembylas, Michalinos. "Toward a Critical-Sentimental Orientation in Human Rights Education." *Educational Philosophy and Theory* 48, no. 11 (2016): 1151–67.

Zimbardo, Philip. *The Lucifer Effect: Understanding How Good People Turn Evil*. New York: Random House, 2007.

Zimbardo, Phillip, Christina Maslach, and Craig Haney. "Reflections on the Stanford Prison Experiment: Genesis, Transformations, Consequences." In *Obedience to Authority: Current Perspectives on the Milgram Paradigm*, edited by Thomas Blass, 193–237. London: Lawrence Erlbaum, 2000.

Contributors

Joanna Bourke is Professor of History at Birkbeck College, University of London.

Danielle Celermajer is Professor in the Department of Sociology and Social Policy at the University of Sydney.

Michael Dodson is the Northern Territory Aboriginal Treaty Commissioner in Australia and formerly Director of the Australian National University's National Centre for Indigenous Studies.

Mark Goodale is Professor of Cultural and Social Anthropology and Director of the Laboratory of Cultural and Social Anthropology (LACS) at the University of Lausanne.

Wendy S. Hesford is Ohio Eminent Scholar and Professor of English at The Ohio State University.

Alexandre Lefebvre is Associate Professor in the Department of Government and International Relations, and Philosophy, at the University of Sydney.

Linde Lindkvist is Senior Lecturer in Human Rights Studies at the School of Human Rights, University College Stockholm.

Samuel Moyn is Henry R. Luce Professor of Jurisprudence at Yale Law School and Professor of History at Yale University.

Jennifer Nedelsky is Professor of Law at Osgoode Hall Law School, York University.

Ronald Niezen is Katharine A. Pearson Chair in Civil Society and Public Policy in the Faculty of Law and Department of Anthropology at McGill University.

Andrew C. Rajca is Associate Professor of Portuguese, Spanish, and Latin American Cultural Studies at the University of South Carolina.

Jenna Reinbold is Associate Professor of Religion at Colgate University.

Rachel Wahl is Assistant Professor in the Social Foundations Program, Department of Leadership, Foundations, and Policy at the Curry School of Education and Human Development at the University of Virginia.

Index

Branding Humanity: Competing Narratives of Rights, Violence, and Global Citizenship
Amal Hassan Fadlalla
2018

Remote Freedoms: Politics, Personhood and Human Rights in Aboriginal Central Australia
Sarah E. Holcombe
2018

Letters to the Contrary: A Curated History of the UNESCO Human Rights Survey
Mark Goodale
2018

Just Violence: Torture and Human Rights in the Eyes of the Police
Rachel Wahl
2017

Bodies of Truth: Law, Memory, and Emancipation in Post-Apartheid South Africa
Rita Kesselring
2016

Rights After Wrongs: Local Knowledge and Human Rights in Zimbabwe
Shannon Morreira
2016

If God Were a Human Rights Activist
Boaventura de Sousa Santos
2015

Digging for the Disappeared: Forensic Science After Atrocity
Adam Rosenblatt
2015

The Rise and Fall of Human Rights: Cynicism and Politics in Occupied Palestine
Lori Allen
2013

Campaigning for Justice: Human Rights Advocacy in Practice
Jo Becker
2012

In the Wake of Neoliberalism: Citizenship and Human Rights in Argentina
Karen Ann Faulk
2012

Values in Translation: Human Rights and the Culture of the World Bank
Galit A. Sarfaty
2012

Disquieting Gifts: Humanitarianism in New Delhi
Erica Bornstein
2012

Stones of Hope: How African Activists Reclaim Human Rights to Challenge Global Poverty
Edited by Lucie E. White and Jeremy Perelman
2011

Judging War, Judging History: Behind Truth and Reconciliation
Pierre Hazan
2010

Localizing Transitional Justice: Interventions and Priorities After Mass Violence
Edited by Rosalind Shaw and Lars Waldorf, with Pierre Hazan
2010

Surrendering to Utopia: An Anthropology of Human Rights
Mark Goodale
2009

Human Rights for the 21st Century: Sovereignty, Civil Society, Culture
Helen M. Stacy
2009

Human Rights Matters: Local Politics and National Human Rights Institutions
Julie A. Mertus
2009

Lightning Source UK Ltd.
Milton Keynes UK
UKHW011016210121
377090UK00012B/336

9 781503 613713